T0258534

New Approaches in Fuzzy Logic

New Approaches in Fuzzy Logic

Edited by **Frank West**

New York

Published by NY Research Press,
23 West, 55th Street, Suite 816,
New York, NY 10019, USA
www.nyresearchpress.com

New Approaches in Fuzzy Logic
Edited by Frank West

International Standard Book Number: 978-1-63238-342-6 (Hardback)

Printed in the United States of America.

Contents

Preface   IX

Part 1   Human Health and Security   1

Chapter 1   **A Clinical Application of Fuzzy Logic**   3
Ahmad Esmaili Torshabi, Marco Riboldi,
Andera Pella, Ali Negarestani,
Mohamad Rahnema and Guido Baroni

Chapter 2   **Application of Fuzzy Logic in Diet Therapy –**
Advantages of Application   19
Jasenka Gajdoš Kljusurić,
Ivana Rumora and Želimir Kurtanjek

Chapter 3   **A Fuzzy Logic Approach for Remote**
Healthcare Monitoring by Learning
and Recognizing Human Activities of Daily Living   43
Hamid Medjahed, Dan Istrate, Jérôme Boudy,
Jean Louis Baldinger, Lamine Bougueroua,
Mohamed Achraf Dhouib and Bernadette Dorizzi

Chapter 4   **Fuzzy Logic and**
Neuro-Fuzzy Networks
for Environmental Hazard Assessment   65
Ignazio M. Mancini, Salvatore Masi,
Donatella Caniani and Donata S. Lioi

Chapter 5   **Adaptive Security Policy Using**
User Behavior Analysis and Human
Elements of Information Security   83
Ines Brosso and Alessandro La Neve

Chapter 6   **Fuzzy Clustering Approach**
for Accident Black Spot
Centers Determination   101
Yetis Sazi Murat

Part 2   Transportation and Communication   117

Chapter 7   Adaptive Fuzzy Wavelet NN Control
Strategy for Full Car Suspension System   119
Laiq Khan, Rabiah Badar and Shahid Qamar

Chapter 8   Fuzzy-Logic Analysis of the FDR Data
of a Transport Aircraft in Atmospheric Turbulence   147
C. Edward Lan and Ray C. Chang

Chapter 9   Fuzzy Logic for Multi-Hop
Broadcast in Vehicular Ad Hoc Networks   175
Celimuge Wu, Satoshi Ohzahata and Toshihiko Kato

Chapter 10   Condition Ranking and Rating
of Bridges Using Fuzzy Logic   193
Saptarshi Sasmal, K. Ramanjaneyulu
and Nagesh R. Iyer

Chapter 11   Fuzzy Logic Applied to Decision
Making in Wireless Sensor Networks   221
Antonio M. Ortiz and Teresa Olivares

Chapter 12   Fuzzy Logic on a Polygenic Multi-Agent
System for Steganalysis of Digital Images   241
Samuel Azevedo, Rummenigge Rudson
and Luiz Gonçalves

Part 3   Business, Environment and Energy   257

Chapter 13   Fuzzy Logic in Financial Management   259
Tomasz Korol

Chapter 14   Fuzzy Modeling of Geospatial Patterns   287
Alejandra A. López-Caloca and Carmen Reyes

Chapter 15   Generation Reliability Evaluation
in Deregulated Power Systems Using
Monte Carlo Simulation and Fuzzy Systems   309
H. Haroonabadi

Chapter 16   **Greenhouse Fuzzy and**
Neuro-Fuzzy Modeling Techniques   **323**
Gorrostieta-Hurtado Efren, Pedraza-Ortega Jesus Carlos,
Aceves-Fernández Marco Antonio, Ramos-Arreguín Juan Manuel,
Tovar-Arriaga Saúl and Sotomayor-Olmedo Artemio

Permissions

List of Contributors

Preface

This book has been an outcome of determined endeavour from a group of educationists in the field. The primary objective was to involve a broad spectrum of professionals from diverse cultural background involved in the field for developing new researches. The book not only targets students but also scholars pursuing higher research for further enhancement of the theoretical and practical applications of the subject.

Fuzzy logic has significant applications in numerous fields. The novel approaches in fuzzy logic have been described in this insightful book. The effectiveness of fuzzy logic in the advancement of rising technologies is elucidated in this book. It describes several applications in the field of health, communication, bioinformatics, transportations, financial management, security, energy and environment systems. This book will serve as a primary source of reference for all those interested in applied intelligent systems including researchers, medical practitioners, engineers and students.

It was an honour to edit such a profound book and also a challenging task to compile and examine all the relevant data for accuracy and originality. I wish to acknowledge the efforts of the contributors for submitting such brilliant and diverse chapters in the field and for endlessly working for the completion of the book. Last, but not the least; I thank my family for being a constant source of support in all my research endeavours.

Editor

Part 1

Human Health and Security

A Clinical Application of Fuzzy Logic

Ahmad Esmaili Torshabi[1], Marco Riboldi[2],
Andera Pella[2], Ali Negarestani[1],
Mohamad Rahnema[1] and Guido Baroni[2]
[1]*Department of Electrical & Computer,*
Kerman Graduate University of Technology, Kerman,
[2]*Bioengineering Unit, Centro Nazionale di Adroterapia Oncologica, Pavia,*
[1]*Iran*
[2]*Italy*

1. Introduction

In fuzzy logic, linguistic variables are used to represent operating parameters in order to apply a more human-like way of thinking [Zadeh, 1965, 1968, 1973, 1988, 1989]. Fuzzy logic incorporates a simple, *IF-THEN rule-based* approach to solve a problem rather than attempting to model a system mathematically and this property plays a central role in most of fuzzy logic applications [Kang et al., 2000; Lin & Wang, 1999; Shi et al., 1999]. Recently, the main features of fuzzy logic theory make it highly applicable in many systematic designs in order to obtain a better performance when data analysis is too complex or impractical for conventional mathematical models. This chapter represents how fuzzy logic, as explained theoretically in the previous chapters, can practically be applied on a real case. For this aim, a clinical application of fuzzy logic was taken into account for cancer treatment by developing a fuzzy correlation model.

Cancer is an inclusive phrase representing a large number of deseases in which unconrolled cells are divided and grown out of regular form and also are able to invade other healthy tissues. Cancer can usually be treated using surgery, chemotherapy or radiotherapy [Cassileth & Deng, 2004; Smith, 2006; Vickers, 2004]. In radiotherapy method the cancerious cells are bombarded by high energy ionizing radiation such as gamma ray or charge particle beams. The radiation ionizes the bonds of water molecoules located in cell environment and causes releasing of hydroxyl free radicals that have damaging effects for DNA. In external radiotherapy the first and most important step is tumor localization for obtaining maximum targeting accuracy. Tumor volume is visualized using 3D imaging systems [Balter & Kessler 2007; Evans, 2008] such as Computed Tomography (CT) or Magnetic Resonance Imaging (MRI) and then the contoured treatment region depicted by medical physicists is irradiated by means of an external beam extracted from the accelerator systems. In radiotherapy the correct and accurate information of tumor position during the treatment determine the degree of treatment success. Among different tumors, some typical tumors located in lung region of patient body move due to breathing cycle phenomena and this non-regular motion causes a constraint to achieve the accurate knowledge of tumor location during the treatment [Ramrath et al., 2007; Vedam et al., 2004]. In order to address this issue, one strategy is tracking the tumor motion by continuous monitoring systems such as fluoroscopy which is unsafe for patient due to its additional exposed dose [Dieterich et al., 2008; Keall etal., 2006]. Another alternative that is effective and acceptable, is finding real time tumor position information over time from external rib cage motion [Torshabi et al., 2010]. For this aim, the external breathing motion is synchronized and correlated with internal tumor motion by developing a correlation model in training step before the treatment. It should be mentioned that the external breathing motion is traced by means of specific external markers placed on thorax region (rib cage and abdomen) of patient and recorded by infrared tracking system. In contrast, the internal tumor motion is tracked using implanted internal clips inside or near the tumor volume and visualized using orthogonal X-ray imaging in snapshot mode. A correlation model based on fuzzy logic concept is proposed here to estimate the tumor motion from external markers data as input data when internal marker data is out of access. In order to investigate the clinical application of fuzzy logic, data from real patients were utilized for model testing and verification (Table 1). The end result is a nonlinear mapping from the motion data of external markers as input to an output which is the estimate of tumor motion. When tumor position was predicted by fuzzy model, the gated-respiratory radiotherapy can be applied to treat the tumor [Kubo & Hill 1996, Minohara et al. 2000, Ohara et al., 1989]. In this method the therapeutic beam is only ON in a pre-defined gating window in which tumor volume exists and otherwise, the beam is set to turn OFF for preventing healthy tissues against additional exposure. Therefore based on above description, the specific clinical application of fuzzy model in this chapter consists of all moving targets located in thorax region of patient body such as lung, chestwall and pancreas cancers.

Recently, several respiratory motion prediction models have been developed in different mathematical approaches [Kakar et al., 2005; Murphy et al., 2006; Ramarth et al., 2007; Riaz et al., 2009; Ruan et al., 2008; Vedam et al., 2004]. Since the breathing phenomenon has inherently high uncertainty and therefore causes a significant variability in input/output dataset, fuzzy logic seems to have suitable environment to correlate input data with tumor motion estimation with less error [Kakar et al., 2005; Torshabi et al., 2010].

Our patient database consists of a real database obtained from 130 patients, who received hypo-fractionated stereotactic body radiotherapy with CyberKnife® (Accuray Inc., Sunnyvale, CA) between 2005 and 2007, was analyzed [Brown et al., 2007; Hoogeman et al., 2009; Seppenwoolde et al., 2007]. The patient database is made available by the Georgetown University Medical Center (Washington, DC). Such database includes patients treated with real-time compensation of tumor motion by means of the Synchrony® respiratory tracking module, as available in the Cyberknife® system. This system provides tumor tracking relying on an external/internal correlation model between the motion of external infrared markers and of clips implanted near the tumor. The model is built at the beginning of each irradiation session and updated as needed over the course of treatment. Twenty patients were selected randomly among the population, as shown in table 1. The chosen patients were divided into control and worst groups and the 3D targeting error of each group were analyzed, separately. The worst group consists of tumor motions with large tracking error.

Case*	Site	Ext motion [mm]	Tumor motion [mm]			Synchrony® Error [mm]		Imaging intervals [s]		Treatment time [min]
			SI	LR	AP	Mean	STD	Mean	STD	
W	LLL	96.9	70.5	75.7	31.9	11.3	12.6	41.0	59.2	97.8
W	RLL	14.8	28.4	11.8	24.3	7.9	12.9	57.2	33.8	38.1
W	LLL	20.3	45.9	12.9	7.8	7.5	5.7	53.2	44.1	93.1
W	LLL	20.2	54.1	9.2	4.6	6.4	7.7	65.2	42.4	93.5
W	LEFT LUNG	95.9	23.4	24.5	37.2	6.2	10.5	67.5	29.6	27.0
W	LEFT LUNG ARTERY	8.6	9.1	33.5	20.1	5.9	11.7	63.7	62.1	87.1
W	LEFT LUNG	27.0	55.8	25.8	40.7	5.5	6.1	71.9	59.8	105.4
W	RIGHTLUNG	29.2	17.3	4.4	6.2	5.4	7.3	61.7	25.6	38.5
W	LLL	23.6	32.4	14.5	16.8	5.1	4.9	61.2	50.8	85.7
W	RUL	12.2	24.7	18.9	21.2	5.0	3.6	75.1	54.2	118.8
C	RLL	3.4	31.1	5.0	3.8	3.2	3.2	66.9	33.1	78.0
C	LLL	4.4	11.6	6.1	10.2	2.7	1.1	81.7	32.1	68.1
C	PANCREAS	3.3	15.8	15.9	12.0	2.2	2.3	55.8	33.0	90.1
C	RIGHT HILUM	1.4	18.2	12.4	7.7	1.8	1.9	73.7	38.2	61.4
C	LLL	2.7	23.8	3.1	1.8	1.7	1.2	65.1	32.0	68.3
C	CHESTWALL	1.9	2.6	3.2	7.7	1.4	0.9	63.6	31.7	59.4
C	LIVER	5.5	18.7	3.3	7.8	1.2	0.7	64.5	29.1	41.9
C	RUL	5.8	4.0	1.8	6.4	1.2	0.7	97.6	44.1	70.0
C	LEFT SPLENIC BED	6.0	2.0	3.5	4.3	0.9	0.4	81.7	32.8	61.3
C	LEFT FLANK	1.6	3.0	2.2	2.4	0.5	0.3	58.1	26.0	69.7

*W and C denote worst and control cases, respectively

** LLL, RLL and RUL indicate Left Lower Lung, Right Lower Lung and Right Upper Lung, correspondingly

Table 1. Features of the cases selected for this study.

One of the main factors affected on fuzzy model performance is data clustering for membership function generation [Jain et al., 1999]. Two most practical data clustering approaches considered in this chapter are Subtractive and Fuzzy C-Means (FCM) clustering [Bezdek, 1981; Chiu, 1994; Dunn, 1973; Jang et al., 1997].

In this chapter fuzzy model structure and different steps of model performance were explained graphically and finally we compared fuzzy model performance with two different correlation models based on Artificial Neural Network and State model [Procházka & Pavelka, 2007; Robert et al., 2002; Ruan et al., 2008; Seppenwoolde et al., 2007; Sharp et al., 2004; Su et al., 2005]. The state model was implemented as a linear/quadratic correlation between external marker motion and internal tumor motion. In this model The 3D movement of external markers was transformed into a mono-dimensional signal, by projecting the three-dimensional coordinates in the principal component space [Ruan et al., 2008]. Artificial Neural Networks (ANNs) are a mathematical method that simulates the behavior of a natural neural network, where several inputs are integrated to obtain outputs according to predefined rules. The nodes (synapses) are inter-connected with specific weight values, defined during the training phase and representing the significance of each connection. ANNs are widely used to predict signals that may be difficult to model.

The analyzed results of 3D targeting error assessment onto two control and worst groups represent that the implemented fuzzy logic-based correlation model represents the best performance rather than two alternative modelers. In general, fuzzy logic theory appears very useful when the process to be modeled is too complex for conventional techniques, or when the available dataset can be interpreted either qualitatively or with a large degree of uncertainty. Final verifications represent that this model can be potentially applicable for moving tumor located in lung and abdominal region of patient body as some typical cases depicted in table 1.

2. Development of fuzzy correlation model

In fuzzy logic-based systems, membership functions represent the magnitude of participation of each input, graphically. The proposed fuzzy correlation model involves data clustering [Jain et al., 1999] for membership function generation, as inputs for fuzzy inference system section (Figure 1, upper solid rectangle). Data clustering is an approach for finding similar data in a big dataset and puting them into a group. In the other word, data clustering analysis is the organization of a collection of dataset into clusters based on similarity. Therefore, clustering divides a dataset into several groups such that each group consists of a set of data points with same nature. the main purpose of data clustering is breaking a huge dataset into some small groups in order to make a further simplification for data analysis. Clustering algorithms are utilized not only to categorize the data but are also helpful for data compression and model construction. In some cases data clustering can discover a relevance knowledge among datapoints with same nature [Azuaje et al., 2000]. In the implemented fuzzy logic algorithm, data from all three external markers arranged in an input matrix with 9 columns and data from internal marker set in an output matrix with 1 column are clustered initially. Sugeno and Mamdani types of Fuzzy Inference Systems configured by 1) data fuzzification, 2) *if-then* rules induction, 3) application of implication method, 4) output aggregation and 5) defuzzification steps, utilized due to its specific effects on model performance (Figure 1, upper solid rectangles).

Fuzzy correlation model was developed in MatLab (The MathWorks Inc., Natick, MA, USA) using fuzzy logic toolbox. The model is built before the treatment using training data. Training data is 3D external markers motion as model input and internal implanted marker as model output. When the model is developed, it can be applied to estimate tumor motion as a function of time during the treatment (figure 2, solid blocks). The model can also be updated and re-built as needed during the treatment with X-ray imaging representing the internal marker location. Figure 2 shows a block diagram of model operation. The dashed rectangles (right side) in this figure represent the training and updating steps.

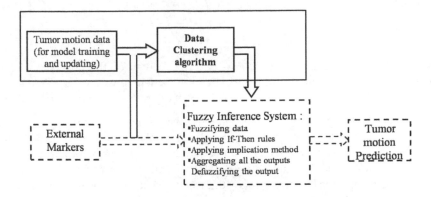

Fig. 1. Block diagram of fuzzy inference system (lower part) and data clustering algorithm (upper part)

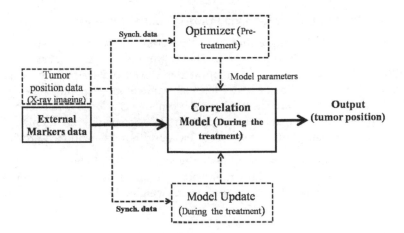

Fig. 2. Flowchart of correlation model performance

Between several techniques for data clustering, two of most representative techniques utilized in our model are: 1) Subtractive clustering, 2) Fuzzy C-Means clustering. In the training step, two fuzzy inference systems based on above clustering approaches are configured for motion prediction during the treatment. The properties and implementations of these inference systems are in the following paragraphs.

2.1 Membership function generation via subtractive clustering

The first clustering algorithm employed for data grouping in this work is on the basis of subtractive technique. In this algorithm, each data point of the dataset is assumed as potential cluster center and therefore a *density measure* at data point a_i is calculated as the following equation:

$$DM_j = \sum_{i=1}^{m} \exp\left(-\frac{\|a_i - c_j\|^2}{(r/2)^2}\right)$$

Where a_i is the ith measured data point, c_j is the center of the cluster, and r is the neighborhood radius or influence range. By this way, when density value of a data point is high, that data point is surrounded by a huge amount of other neighboring data points.

Subtractive clustering algorithm firstly nominates a datapoint as first cluster center such that its density value calculated by above formula is the largest. As the second step, the algorithm removes all data points belonging to the first cluster, configured with a pre-defined neighboring radius for determining the next data cluster and its center location. In the third and last step, this clustering algorithm continues density measurements on the rest of data points until all the data points are covered by the sufficient clusters. By ending these steps and when all of data were categorized, a set of fuzzy rules and membership functions are resulted.

2.2 Membership function generation via Fuzzy C-Means clustering

In Fuzzy C-Means clustering algorithm each data point in the dataset belongs to every cluster with a specific membership degree. The magnitude of this membership degree is determined by finding the distance of data point from cluster center. In the other word, each data point that is close to the cluster center has high value of membership degree, otherwise if a data point that lies far away from the cluster center has a low membership degree. It should be noted that in this way, before applying FCM technique our training dataset is clustered into n groups using subtractive clustering algorithm, as mentioned previously.

From mathematical point of view, membership functions in FCM clustering algorithm are obtained by minimization of the following objective function. This equation represents the distance from any given data point to a cluster center weighted by its membership degree:

$$J_m = \sum_{i=1}^{N} \sum_{j=1}^{C} u_{ij}^m |x_i - c_j|^2$$

where m is any real number greater than 1, u_{ij} is the degree of membership of x_i in cluster j, x_i is the ith measured data point, and c_j is the center of the cluster. The value of m was set to 2 in our objective function [Bedzek & Pal 1998; Yu 2004]. At first, FCM assumes the cluster centers in the mean location of each cluster. Next, the FCM algorithm sets a membership degree for each data point at each cluster, and then iteratively moves the cluster centers c_j and updates the membership degrees u_{ij}:

$$u_{ij} = \frac{1}{\sum_{k=1}^{C}\left(\frac{|x_i - c_j|}{|x_i - c_k|}\right)^{\frac{2}{m-1}}}$$

$$c_j = \frac{\sum_{i=1}^{N} u_{ij}^m \cdot x_i}{\sum_{i=1}^{N} u_{ij}^m}$$

This iteration process will continue till $|U^{(k+1)}-U^{(k)}| < \varepsilon$, where ε is a termination criterion between 0 and 1, U is $[u_{ij}]$ matrix and k is the number of iterations.

In should be noted that the structure of fuzzy inference systems is based on Sugeno (or Takagi-Sugeno-Kang) model [Sugeno & Takagi, 1985]. This model is computationally more efficient and thus gives a faster response, where quick decisions should be taken.

For better description, a typical fuzzy inference system on the basis of FCM clustering algorithm was built as example using the data of one chosen patient from table one with Right Lower Lung (RLL) cancer. Figure 3-a shows a set of Gaussian membership functions generated by this fuzzy inference system on input data given by three external markers that move on three X, Y and Z directions (totally 9 inputs) and figure 3-b illustrates the same membership functions using the same algorithm on output data given by implanted internal marker only on X direction. In this inference system three clusters and hence three *if-then* rules connected with AND operator, have been utilized.

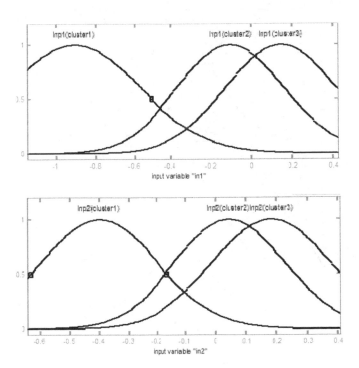

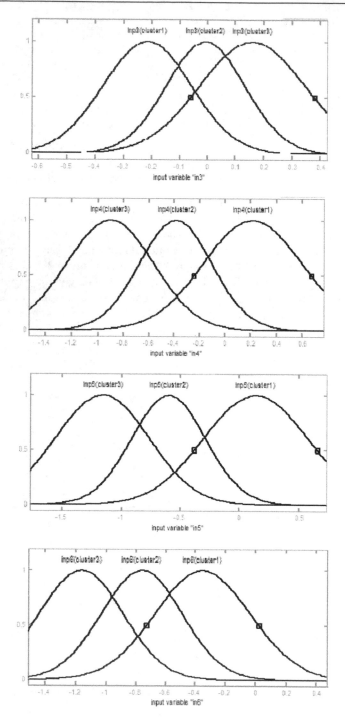

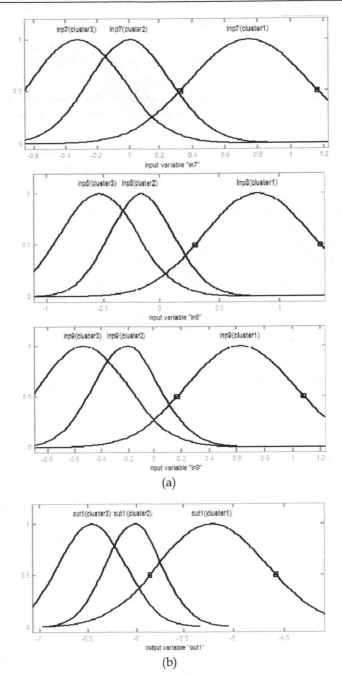

(a)

(b)

Fig. 3. Gaussian Membership functions generated by fuzzy inference system on the basis of FCM clustering algorithm using total 9 inputs dataset (panels a) and one output dataset (panel b)

3. Operation of fuzzy correlation model

When a fuzzy model was built by training dataset, each external marker data is applied as input and the following steps are accomplished by fuzzy model to estimate the tumor motion as output.

Fuzzification: This step takes the inputs and determine their participate degrees at each cluster via generated membership functions (similar to membership function visualized in the previous section).

Applying AND/OR operator: When the inputs were fuzzified, if the antecedent of a given rule has more than one part, the fuzzy operator is applied to obtain one number that represents the result of antecedent for that rule. In our typical example, three rules were used connected with AND operator. Figure 4 represents the contribution of each input membership function (filled by yellow) and one output membership functions (filled by blue) associated with applied input value.

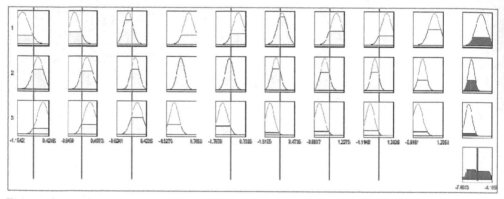

Fig. 4. Three rules connected with AND operator in antecedent (yellow) and consequent (blue) parts of FIS

Applying implication: Implication step in consequent part of FIS uses a single number given by the antecedent part, and the output is a truncated fuzzy set. In the other word, the consequent is reshaped using a function associated with antecedent. The implication step should be applied for each rule. In figure 5, the truncated output fuzzy set was shown by blue color for second rule of our FIS example. As shown in this example, the build-in function of implication step is on the basis of AND (*minimum selection criteria*) operation.

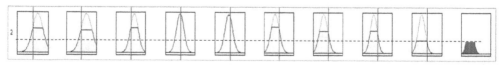

Fig. 5. Truncated output fuzzy set visualized by blue as result of implication step based on AND operation

Applying aggregation: This step receives all the truncated output fuzzy set of each rule and cumulate them as one fuzzy set. Figure 6 shows the aggregation step applied of our example. As shown, the lowest square represents the accumulation of all available truncated fuzzy sets.

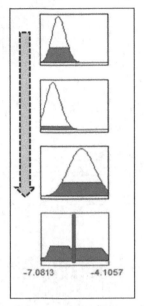

Fig. 6. Accumulation of all truncated fuzzy sets in aggregation step

Defuzzification: This step acts as final step and the input is aggregated fuzzy set where the output is a single number that returns the center of the cumulated area under the curve. Defuzzification is performed using five built-in methods. In our example the single output was obtained by Centroid Calculation method.

For real-time tumor tracking the correlation models should be executed without a significant delay such that on-time compensation strategy can be applied against tumor motion. Therefore, the execute time of each correlation model that strongly depends on the utilized mathematical procedures, should be taken into account for clinical application. The features of fuzzy model make it very quick in execution, such that the tumor position can be estimated in real-time condition.

As final part of this chapter, in order to visualize the performance of fuzzy model in tumor motion tracking, one patient database was selected for model configuration and operation. The chosen patient has Right Lower Lung (RLL) cancer belonging to control group. The number of training dataset used for model configuration in pre-treatment step for this case is 11. Figure 7 shows the tumor motion tracking of this case (red line) versus Cyberknife modeler (blue line) over 5 minutes of treatment time on X, Y and Z directions. The imaging points indicated by green squares in these figures were taken by stereoscopic X-ray imaging system and represent the exact position of tumor motion at that time. As mentioned in this chapter, these points are used for model performance assessment and also model updating during the treatment. As shown, there are five green square points on each panel that indicates the updating process has been done every one minute for this case.

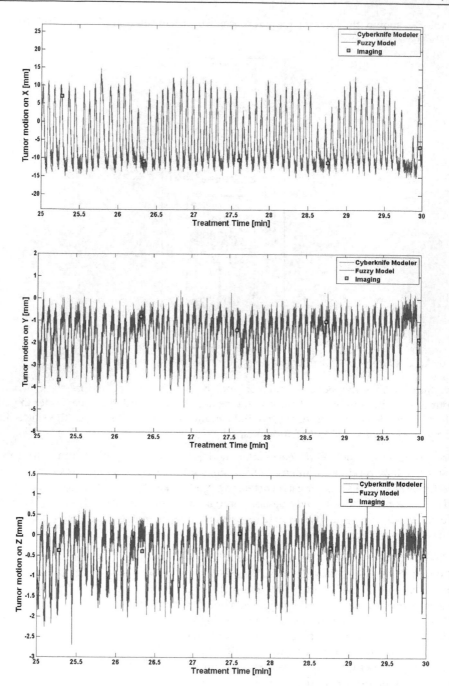

Fig. 7. Tumor motion tracking over time on X (upper panel), Y (middle panel) and Z (lower panel) directions in fuzzy model versus Cyberknife modeler

As depicted in figure 7, the performance of fuzzy correlation model in tumor tracking is comparable with Cyberknife modeler, although a negligible local noise is observed around the inhalation/exhalation peaks. In some peaks there are also some over estimation with respect to Cyberknife modeler performance that is highly visible in the last peak shown in middle panel of this figure.

Moreover, two alternative correlation models were taken into account based on artificial neural network and State model, as mentioned in Introduction section.

3D targeting error was calculated for control and worst cases applying fuzzy, ANNs and state models, by means of all imaging points in a same condition [Torshabi et al., 2010]. In this calculation imaging points were utilized as reference points in order to investigate the model performance accuracy. For this aim, the distance between predicted point as given output of three correlation models and corresponding imaging point is measured as model accuracy criteria .Where the assumed predicted point was close to the corresponding imaging point, that model acts reasonably. In contrast, when the predicted point is far away from the corresponding imaging point the accuracy of model performance is missing.

As resulted from this comparative assessment, it can be noted that for control cases where the tracking errors are in a normal interval, there is a good agreement between the performance of three modelers versus Cyberknife. In contrast, for worst cases the fuzzy model has the best performance even better than Cyberknife modeler. In this comparison state model acts as worst prediction model. In worst cases an error reduction improvement was resulted from fuzzy model with respect to Cyberknife that is 10.8% at the 95% confidence level. More detailed information concerning the structure and operation of state model and ANNs with respect to fuzzy model was given by Torshabi et al.

4. Conclusion

In this chapter a clinical application of fuzzy logic was taken into account for cancer treatment by developing a fuzzy correlation model. This model act as prediction model and track the moving targets, placed in lung and abdomen regions of patient body. For this aim the internal-external markers data were utilized for fuzzy model generation (pre-treatment), operation & updating (during the treatment). Fuzzy model structure and different steps of model performance were explained graphically for a real case. Finally a comparative investigation was preformed between fuzzy model performance and two different correlation models based on Artificial Neural Network and State model. The analyzed results represents that the fuzzy model performance is the best with less error and negligible executive time among the modelers. In general, fuzzy model features make it robust for modeling some systems that are too complex to be modeled by means of conventional mathematical techniques. The application of the fuzzy logic is also highly recommended whenever the available dataset is not qualitatively perfect or has a large degree of variability. As drawback point, it should be considered that the fuzzy model has some local small noises near the inhalation/exhalation peaks as depicted in figure 7, such that two artificial neural network and state models can track the motion more smoothly with less local ripples.

In current fuzzy model descibed above, a single output that is tumor motion is properly estimated by means of multi-inputs that is three external markers data. This motion prediction is suitable for treating the tumors by resiratory-gated radiotherapy approach which in the beam is irradiating only in a pre-defined gating window. As future work, the prediction of volumetric information of tumor motion will be invstigated that is needed for tumor treatment by Real-Time Tumor Tracking Radiotherapy. In this alternative method of radiotherapy that is still in reasearch step, 2D information of tumor contour motion at each moment of treatment time is required. Therefore, The prediction model must work as multi-input/multi-output model such that the multi-output is some finite pionts located on tumor contour at each tumor slice. By this way 3D information of tumor motion and also its deformation can be estimated during the breathing cycle. But the main open isuues that must be addressed in this proposal are restriction in extracting minimum required points of tumor contours at different tumor slices as multi-input data for model configuration and also low quality of Orthogonal X-ray images for model updating.

5. Acknowledgment

The authors acknowledge Sonja Dieterich for providing access to the clinical database. The research leading to these results has received funding from the European Community's Seventh Framework Programme ([FP7/2007-2013] under grant agreement n° 215840-2).

6. References

Azuaje, F.; Dubitzky, W.; Black, N. & Adamson, K. (2000) "Discovering Relevance Knowledge in Data: A Growing Cell Structures Approach," *IEEE Trans. Systs. Man. Cybern. B Cybern.*, Vol. 30, pp. 448-460

Balter, J.M. and Kessler, M.L. (2007). Imaging and alignment for image-guided radiation therapy. *J. Clin. Oncol.*, Vol. 25, pp. 931-937

Bezdek, J.C. (1981). Pattern Recognition with Fuzzy Objective Function Algoritms. Plenum Press, New York, USA

Bezdek, J.C.; Pal, N.R. (1998). Some new indexes of cluster validity. *IEEE Trans. Syst. Man. Cybern.*, Vol. 23, pp. 301-315

Brown, W.T.; Wu, X.; Fayad, F., Fowler, J.F., Amendola, B.E.; García, S., Han, H.; de la Zerda, A.; Bossart, E.; Huang, Z. & Schwade, J.G. (2007). CyberKnife radiosurgery for stage I lung cancer: results at 36 months, *Clin. Lung Cancer.* Vol. 8, pp. 488-492

Cassileth, B.R. and Deng G. (2004). Complementary and alternative therapies for cancer. *Oncologist.* Vol. 9, pp. 80-89

Chiu, S. (1994). Fuzzy Model Identification Based on Cluster Estimation. *J. Intell. Fuzzy. Syst.* Vol. 2, pp. 267-278

Dieterich, S.; Cleary, K.; D'Souza, W.; Murphy, M.; Wong, K.H. & Keall, P. (2008). Locating and targeting moving tumors with radiation beams. *Med. Phys.*, Vol. 35, pp. 5684-5694

Dunn, J.C. (1973). A Fuzzy Relative of the ISODATA Process and Its Use in Detecting Compact Well-Separated Clusters. *Journal of Cybernetics*, Vol. 3, pp. 32-57

Evans P.M. (2008). Anatomical imaging for radiotherapy. *Phys. Med. Biol.*, Vol. 53, pp. 151-191

Hoogeman, M.; Prevost, J.B.; Nuyttens, J.; Poll, J.; Levendag, P. & Heumen, B. (2009). Clinical accuracy of the respiratory tumor tracking system of the cyberknife: assessment by analysis of log files. *Radiation Oncology*, Vol. 74, pp. 297-303

Jain, A.K.; Murty, M.N. & Flynn, P.J. (1999). Data clustering: a review. *ACM Computing Surveys (CSUR).*, Vol. 31, pp. 264-323

Jang, J.; Chuen-Tsai, S. & Mizutani, E. (1997). Neuro fuzzy modeling and soft computing. Prentice-Hall, Englewood Cliffs

Kakar, M.; Nyström, H.; Aarup, L.R; Nøttrup, T.J. & Olsen, D.R. (2005). Respiratory motion prediction by using the adaptive neuro fuzzy inference system (ANFIS) *Phys. Med. Biol.*, Vol. 50, pp. 4721-4728

Kang, S.J.; Woo, C.H.; Hwang, H.S. & Woo, K.B. (2000). Evolutionary design of fuzzy rule base for nonlinear system modeling and control. *IEEE Trans. Fuzzy Syst.*, Vol. 8, pp. 37-45

Keall, P.J.; Mageras, G.S.; Balter, J.M.; Emery, R.S.; Forster, K.M.; Jiang, S.B.; Kapatoes, J.M.; Low, D.A.; Murphy, M.J.; Murray, B.R.; Ramsey, C.R.; van Herk, M.B.; Vedam, S.S.; Wong, J.W. & Yorke, E. (2006). The Management of Respiratory Motion in Radiation Oncology report of AAPM task group 76. *Med. Phys.*, Vol. 33, pp. 3874-3900

Kubo, H.D. & Hill, B.C. (1996). Respiration gated radiotherapy treatment: A technical study. *Phys. Med. Biol.* Vol. 41, pp. 83-91

Lin, C.K. & Wang, S.D. (1999). Fuzzy system identification using an adaptive learning rule with terminal attractors *J. Fuzzy Sets Syst.*, Vol. 101, pp. 343-352

Minohara, S.; Kanai, T.; Endo, M.; Noda, K. & Kanazawa, M. (2000). Respiratory gated irradiation system for heavy-ion radiotherapy. *Int. J. Radiat. Oncol., Biol., Phys.* Vol. 47, pp. 1097-1103

Murphy, M.J. & Dieterich, S. (2006). Comparative performance of linear and nonlinear neural networks to predict irregular breathing. *Phys. Med. Biol.*, Vol. 51, pp. 5903-5914

Ohara, K.; Okumura, T.; Akisada, M.; Inada, T.; Mori, T.; Yokota, H. & Calaguas, M.J. (1989). Irradiation synchronized with respiration gate. *Int. J. Radiat. Oncol., Biol., Phys.* Vol. 17, pp. 853-857

Procházka, A.; Pavelka, A. (2007). Feed-Foward and Recurrent Neural Networks in Signal Prediction. *Proceedings the 5th IEEE Int. Conference on Computational Cybernetics*, Gammarth, Tunisia, 2007

Ramrath, L.; Schlaefer, A.; Ernst, F.; Dieterich, S. & Schweikard, A. (2007). Prediction of respiratory motion with a multi-frequency based Extended Kalman Filter. *Proceedings of the 21st International Conference and Exhibition on Computer Assisted Radiology and Surgery (CARS'07)*, Vol. 21, Berlin, Germany, 2007

Riaz, N.; Shanker, P.; Gudmundsson, O.; Wiersrma, R.; Mao, W.; Widrow, B. & Xing, L. (2009). Predicting respiratory tumor motion with Multi-dimensional Adaptive Filters and Support Vector Regression. *Phys. Med. Biol.*, Vol. 54, pp. 5735-5718

Robert, C.; Gaudy, J.F. & Limoge, A. (2002). Electroencephalogram processing using neural networks. *Clinical Neurophysiology*, Vol. 113, pp. 694-701

Ruan, D.; Fessler, J.A; Balter, J.M; Berbeco, R.I.; Nishioka, S. & Shirato, H. (2008). Inference of hysteretic respiratory tumor motion from external surrogates: a state augmentation approach. *Phys. Med. Biol.*, Vol. 53, pp. 2923-2936

Seppenwoolde, Y.; Berbeco, R.I.; Nishioka, S.; Shirato, H. & Heijmen, B. (2007). Accuracy of tumor motion compensation algorithm from a robotic respiratory tracking system: a simulation study. *Med. Phys.*, Vol. 34, pp. 2774-2784

Sharp, G.C.; Jiang, S.B.; Shimizu, S. & Shirato, H. (2004). Prediction of respiratory tumour motion for real-time image-guided radiotherapy. *Phys. Med. Biol.*, Vol. 49, pp. 425-440

Shi, Y.; Eberhart, R. & Chen, Y. (1999). Implementation of evolutionary fuzzy systems. *IEEE Trans. Fuzzy Syst.*, Vol. 7, pp. 109-119

Smith, A. (2006). Proton therapy. Phys. Med. Biol., Vol. 51, pp. 491-504

Su, M.; Miften, M.; Whiddon, C.; Sun, X.; Light, K. & Marks, L. (2005). An artificial neural network for predicting the incidence of radiation pneumonitis. *Med. Phys.*, Vol. 32, pp. 318-325

Takagi, T. & Sugeno, M. (1985). Fuzzy identification of systems and its application to modeling and control. *IEEE Trans. Syst. Man. Cybern.*, Vol. 15, pp. 116-132

Torshabi, A.E.; Pella, A.; Riboldi, M. & Baroni, G. (2010). Targeting accuracy in real time tumor tracking via external sorrugates; a comparative study. *Tech. Canc. Res. Treat.*, Vol. 9, pp. 551-562

Vedam, S.S.; Keall, P.J.; Docef, A.; Todor, D.A.; Kini, V.R. & Mohan, R. (2004). Predicting respiratory motion for four-dimensional radiotherapy. *Med. Phys.*, Vol. 31, pp. 2274-2283

Vickers, A. (2004). Alternative cancer cures: 'unproven' or ,disproven'? *CA. Cancer J. Clin.* Vol. 54, pp. 110-118

Yu, J.; Cheng. Q.; Huang, H. (2004). Analysis of the weighting exponent in the FCM. *IEEE Trans. Syst. Man. Cybern.* Vol. 34, pp. 634-639

Zadeh, L.A. (1965). Fuzzy Sets. *Information and Control*, Vol. 8, pp. 338-353

Zadeh, L.A. (1968). Fuzzy algorithms. *Information and Control*, Vol. 12, pp. 94-102

Zadeh, L.A. (1973). Outline of a New Approach to the Analysis of Complex Systems and Decision Processes. *IEEE Trans. Systems, Man and Cybernetics.*, Vol. 3, pp. 28-44

Zadeh, L.A. (1988). Fuzzy Logic. *Computer*, Vol. 1, pp. 83-93

Zadeh, L.A. (1989). Knowledge representation in fuzzy logic. *IEEE Trans. Knowl. Data Eng.*,Vol. 1, pp. 89-100.

2

Application of Fuzzy Logic in Diet Therapy – Advantages of Application

Jasenka Gajdoš Kljusurić, Ivana Rumora and Želimir Kurtanjek
University of Zagreb,
Faculty of Food Technology and Biotechnology,
Croatia

1. Introduction

Computing, in its usual sense, is centred on manipulation of numbers and symbols. In contrasts, computing with linguistic variables is a methodology in which the object of computation are words and propositions drawn from a natural language, e.g., significant increase in price, small, large, far from recommendations, etc.

Computing with words is inspired by the remarkable human capability to perform a wide variety of physical and mental tasks without any measurements and any computation. A basic difference between perception and measurements is that, in general, the measurements are crisp whereas perceptions are fuzzy (Zadech, 1965, 1994, 1997, 2001; Wirsam et al., 1997; Hahn et al., 1995, 1995a; Darmon et al., 2002). Most of traditional tools for formal modelling, reasoning, and computing are crisp, deterministic, and precise in character. This methodology is a part of mathematical theories of artificial intelligence (Lehmann et al., 1992; Klir et al. 1997; Ray et al., 2002). Instead of Boolean logic, fuzzy logic uses a collection of fuzzy variables defined by membership functions and inference rules (Čerić & Dalbelo-Bašić, 2004; Gajdoš et al., 2001; Rumora et al., 2009).

Human nutrition, considering the daily intake of energy and nutrients, is often explained by computing with words (Brown et al., 1990; Bingham, 1987; Zadech, 1996; Wirsam & Hahn, 1999; Teodorescu et al., 1999), for instance the final conclusion regarding an analysed diet plan can result with phrases as: "the intake of Na should be considerably reduced" or "the consumption of fruits and vegetables must be increased". An important nutritionist's task is to improve the dietary habits of the whole population, on the long term, which would help to decrease the frequency of cardio-vascular disease and the morbidity of many chronic diseases such as diabetes (Katamay et al., 2007; Mahan & Escot-Stump, 2007). Hypertension, or high blood pressure, is one of the major diseases of the modern society. Hypertension has no initial symptoms but can lead to long-term diseases and complications. If it's uncontrolled can cause arteriosclerosis, cerebrovascular accidents, myocardial infarction, and end-stage renal disease (Alderman, 1999) and because physivally devastating is called the "silent killer". It is well known that there is a direct and positive relationship between age and gender with increased prevalence and severity of hypertension. Burt et al. (1995) have published that hypertension is a huge problem for people aged 60–74 years, 72.6% of the African American population and

50.6% of the Caucasian population had hypertension during 1988–1991 (Burt et al., 1995). Also African Americans, women older than 59 years, and older people have a higher prevalence and, even when treated, a greater severity of hypertension than Caucasians, men, and younger people (Hajjar & Kotchen, 2003 Appel, et al, 1997).

Nonpharmacological approach to treatment of the hypertension is currently in focus because of the higher awareness of the growing risk for the possible, future heart problems (MacMahon & Rogers, 1993; Appel, et al, 1997). For this reason, numerous researchers are focused on the clinically efficacious and cost effective interventions of dietary change (McCarron, 1998, Little et al., 2004).

Cook et al. (1995) presented that sustained reduction of 2 mmHg in diastolic blood pressure throughout lifestyle modifications, would result in (i) a 17% decrease in the prevalence of hypertension, (ii) as well as a 6% reduction in the risk of coronary heart disease, in elderly population. Alarming is the forecasting mentioned in Little et al. (2004) that the life expectation is decreasing by increment of blood pressure. Nutrition-based approaches are recommended as a first-line therapy for the prevention of the hypertension. Most recommendations for lifestyle modifications are focused on reducing salt intake, weight loss, and moderation of alcohol consumption. Other dietary interventions, particularly modifying whole dietary patterns, might also effectively reduce blood pressure and thereby control hypertension (Siri-Tarino et al., 2010).

Food guidelines and nutrient intake recommendations are usually expressed as specific quantities (crisp values). In meal planning, crisp values are to rigorous limitations, such as restrictions on nutrient intake, like for instance, the limits for sodium in the DASH diet – 2300 mg/day. Crisp values define the exclusive affiliation in the set, yes or not (Boolean logic). If the daily sodium recommendations are defined as 2300 mg, the daily offer that contains for example, 2350 mg, is according to crisp logic decision completely unacceptable. The overload of 50 mg of sodium per day could be an acceptable overload, but this offer with 2.2% more sodium than recommended will be excluded if the crisp value is overdrawn (Rumora et al., 2009). Fuzzy logic is used to describe unreliable (imprecise) data and knowledge, using linguistic variables, such as slightly deficiency or surplus, much more or less of some nutrient, etc. (Gajdoš et al., 2001; Čerić & Dalbelo-Bašić 2007).

The theory of fuzzy logic in this chapter was used in the planning and management of expenses in social nourishment concerning also the nutritive structure of meals. Modelling and planning of nourishment include a number of unspecified characteristics, which are depended on nutrient offer and also on age, gender and profession of a person (concerning the physical activity level) or population group. Some recommended nutrient and energy intakes are given as single numbers (crisp values). But for most nutrients are also given the average requirements (AR), the lowest threshold intake (LTI) and the calculated population reference intake, PRI (DRI, 1999, 2001, 2001a, 2001b). These intervals and the values of LTI, AR and PRI do not represent the full reality, which is a continuous transition from critical low intake to adequate intake to excess or even toxic amounts. In this work the daily recommendations as crisp numbers are modelled as fuzzy sets (Wirsam et al., 1997, 1997a). The daily recommended intake (DRI) for each observed nutrient and energy intake is "softened" by introduction of membership function of fuzzy sets defined for each individual nutrient.

This chapter follows the basics of use of fuzzy logic as:

a. fuzzification process – development of membership functions of fuzzy sets for input information's as nutrient and energy intake;
b. Optimisation in the Pareto sense that implies that all observed variables (energy and all nutrients) and their compliance with recommendations for the observed variables have equal importance
c. defuzzification process (Rödder & Zimmermann, 1977; Wirsam et al., 1997) - presenting results as a crisp values and compared to standard linear programming (LP) methodology.

Basic of the fuzzy logic use will be used in (a) menu offer analysis and (b) menu planning.

In the analysis and planning the main idea was to balance the daily energy and nutrient needs (Wirsam & Hahn, 1999; Wirsam et al., 1997) especially significant in the DASH diet (Gajdoš et al., 2001; Novák et al., 1999; Rumora et al, 2009). The algorithm used in the analysis and optimization is written in the programming system *W.R. Mathematica v.6.* (Stachowicz & Beall, 1995).

2. Diet therapy

Word "diet" implies the habitually amount and kind of food and drink taken by a person each day, so everyone is always on diet. From the medical point of view, diet means a prescribed selection of food. When this prescribed diet is related with therapy (what implies treatment) or a treatment of a disease – we are talking about diet therapy.

Diet therapy is concentrated on a diet planned to meet specific requirements of the individual, including or excluding certain foods.

2.1 DASH diet

Diet for hypertension is in the literature known as "DASH diet" (Dietary Approaches to Stop Hypertension). Basic DASH diet principle is a diversified diet. Studies have shown the Dietary Approaches to Stop Hypertension (DASH) is as effective for lowering blood pressure (BP) levels as the daily consumption of one prescription medication (Appel et al., 1997; Cook et al., 1995; Litle et al., 2004). Uncontrolled hypertension can cause arteriosclerosis, cerebrovascular accidents, myocardial infarction, and end-stage renal disease (Alderman, 1999) and because physically devastating is called the "silent killer" (Burt et al., 1995; Hajjar & Kotchen, 2003; Kumanyika, 1997). For a person with hypertension new eating style is a shock, and the following shock is a radical change in the costume eating habits (Cook et al., 1995). Effective DASH diet is abundant in dairy products (fat-free or low-fat), fruits and vegetables with a reduction in saturated fat, cholesterol, and total fat.

However, long-term adherence to dietary modification is difficult for most people (Little et al., 2004) and, there is a need for interventions that help people adhere to dietary modifications. The DASH diet leads to an establishment of these goals. DASH diet that emphasizes consumption of fruits, vegetables, and low-fat dairy products, includes whole grains, poultry, fish, and nuts, and is reduced in fat, red meat, sweets, and sugar-containing beverages with restriction of sodium intake.

Guidelines given by the DASH diet are valuable for those who know their daily intake, but the less troublesome step from the guidelines could be the reduction of sodium intake as well increase of fruit and vegetable consumption. Sometimes the first step is searching of readymade recipes based on the DASH diet guidelines (AHA, 2004). This is the reason way we have analysed such offers (recipes available from internet resources: AHA, 2004), what was the first goal in this work. The second goal was to propose – computer based menus that will help in the further menu planning. Having crisp values for daily needs it is possible to use them in computer-based planning of optimal menus with respect to agreed evidence-based dietary recommendations and guidelines.

Despite a reputation for genesis of cardiac disease, there is strong evidence for the cardiovascular benefits of saturated fats (McCarron, 1998) In 2010, a meta-analysis of prospective cohort studies including 348,000 subjects found no statistically significant relationship between cardiovascular disease and dietary saturated fat (Siri-Tarino et al, 2010) However, the authors noted that randomized controlled clinical trials in which saturated fat was replaced with polyunsaturated fat showed a reduction in heart disease, and that the ratio between polyunsaturated fat and saturated fat may be a key factor. In 2009, a systematic review of prospective cohort studies or randomized trials concluded that there was "insufficient evidence of association" between intake of saturated fatty acids and coronary heart disease, and pointed to strong evidence for protective factors such as vegetables and a Mediterranean diet and harmful factors such as trans fats and foods with a high glycemic index (Siri-Tarino et al., 2010). Pacific island populations who obtain 30-60% of their total caloric intake from fully saturated coconut fat have low rates of cardiovascular disease (McCarron, 1998).

3. Fuzzy sets

The foundation for the development of the fields of artificial intelligence and expert systems has become fuzzy set theory, especially in the applications of knowledge-based systems.

Fuzzy logic deals with reasoning that is approximate instead of fixed and exact. In contrast with Boolean logic theory, where binary sets have two-valued logic: true or false, fuzzy logic variables may have a truth value that ranges in degree between 0 and 1. Fuzzy logic has been extended to handle the concept of partial truth, where the truth value may range between completely true and completely false (Novák et al., 1999). Implying, when linguistic variables are used, these degrees may be managed by specific functions (Leventhal, et al, 1992).

While variables in mathematics usually take numerical values, in fuzzy logic applications, the non-numeric linguistic variables are often used to facilitate the expression of rules and facts (Zadech, 1996).

A linguistic variable such as *quality* may have a value such as *good* or its antonym *bad*. However, the great utility of linguistic variables is that they can be modified via linguistic hedges applied to primary terms. The linguistic hedges can be associated with certain functions. Linguistic variables are very often used in nutrition, ie. in analysis of nutrient intake, where an nutrient amount can be, sufficient, optimal or insufficiency. The application of fuzzy sets in nutrition will be explained in the following text.

3.1 Crisp and fuzzy interpretation of DRIs

Hahn and his co-workers (1995 & 1995a) have been the first that have applied fuzzy logic in defining nutrient intakes using membership functions. For each nutrient was determined a fuzzy set, μ (x_i). The tendency is to achieve maximal value (value 1) of the membership function μ, for each observed nutrient, which would mean that the input of the nutrient is optimal (Hahn et al., 1995). In Croatia are accepted the recommended dietary intakes (DRIs) for nutrients given as a range of allowances described by crisp numbers, DRIs, or an interval of estimated safe and adequate daily dietary intake (ESADDI). As crisp values (Wirsam et al., 1997a; Gajdoš et al., 2001; Rumora et al., 2009; Teodorescu et al., 1999), these numbers describe a range of allowed intake, x_a, of a nutrient a as followed:

$$x_{a,min} \leq x_a \leq x_{a,max} \tag{1}$$

This is the crisp formulation of allowances and can be used, for example, as restrictions in linear optimisation. The corresponding fuzzy set *allowed intake* can be defined by a characteristic membership function μ (x_a):

$$\mu(x_a) = \begin{cases} 1, \text{ for } x_{a,min} \leq x_a \leq x_{a,max} \\ 0, \text{ for } unaceptable\ intake \end{cases} \tag{2}$$

Fuzzy sets are used to represent the inherent imprecision and fuzziness of food quantities and nutrient values as well as to model the gradual boundaries of the daily recommended values associated with each nutrient. Knowing that cardiovascular diseases are considered as one of the leading causes of today mortality, especially for men aged 31-50 years, who conducted low active way of life with a diet that is mainly consumption of ready to eat or fast food, and that small interventions in the nourishment can achieve significant positive impact, fuzzy approach was used to plan daily menus.

3.2 Fuzzification

The process of transforming crisp values into grades of membership for linguistic terms of fuzzy sets comprises fuzzification. The membership function is used to associate a grade to each linguistic term. The fuzzification process is a modelling process where the membership functions of fuzzy sets for input information's as nutrient and energy intake are development.

Fuzzy membership functions are constructed to describe the range of nutrients intake from deficient to excess amounts. For optimisation three goal functions are considered: price, organic-chemical structure and meal preferences. Observing of two or more goal functions at the same time allows optimising in the Pareto sense. With the help of these sets, an evaluation as well as optimisation in the Pareto sense (considering the price, preferences and nutrient intake) is possible.

This study shows that the use of the fuzzy sets can be utilised for Pareto optimisation by which multiple object optimisation is achieved. The fuzzy model represents recommended energy and nutrient intake more adequately then the Dietary Recommended Intake, DRI, intake presented as crisp values, as well as to obtain acceptable price and preferences of menu selection for a population group.

Objective of the research is to propose a method of modelling and optimization that will consider the daily expenses, meal preferences in different regions and the energy and nutrient requirements of some gender and age group.

In the fuzzy set modelling of nutrients is important to construct the function following the basic properties of a fuzzy set (Dalbelo-Bašić, 2002; Buisson, 2008). Each membership function is defined by its core, height and support (Figure 1).

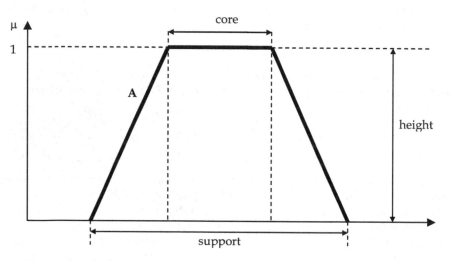

Fig. 1. Properties of a fuzzy set A.

In the construction of nutrient membership function of the following properties for fuzzy sets were used:

The core of fuzzy set A, *core(A)*, is a subset universal set X with the property μ_A (x) = 1, ie

$$core\ (A) = \{(x\ \in X \mid \mu_A\ (x=1)\} \tag{3}$$

The support of the fuzzy set A, *supp (A)*, is a subset of the universal set X with nonzero membership grades (μ_A(x)> 0), ie

$$supp\ (A) = \{(x\ \in X \mid \mu_A\ (x > 1)\} \tag{4}$$

The height of a fuzzy set, hgt(A), is the supremum (maximum) of the membership grades of A. So,

$$hgt\ (A) = max_{x \in X}\mu_A(X) \tag{5}$$

A fuzzy set A is normal if the height equal to 1, hgt(A) = 1. Any set that is not normal is called subnormal.

Core and support of a fuzzy set are ordinary subsets of X, while the height is a real number from the interval [0, 1].

The shape of the fuzzy set presented on figure 1 is the so called "bell-shape". Beside the bell-shape, commonly used shapes in nutrition evaluation and/or planning are: S and Z shape. Those two shapes depend on the preferred amounts of nutrient intakes (presented on Fig. 2).

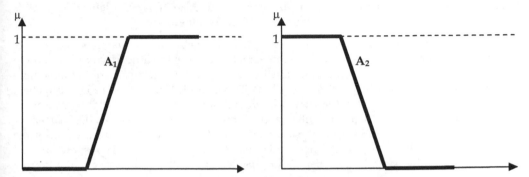

Fig. 2. Shape of a fuzzy set when the intake of the observed nutrient is preferred not be low $\mu(A_1)$ or, to be as lower as possible $\mu(A_2)$.

Example of the nutrient intake where low amounts are not preferred is the daily intake of dietary fibres. Nutrients that are not welcome in high amounts per day are alcohol and cholesterol.

3.3 Defuzzification

Fuzzy approach in nutrition planning is based on the use of the linguistic approach and its application to solve decision problems with linguistic information (Buisson, 2008). Computing with Words (CW) is defined as use of linguistic computational techniques to process linguistic information. An example can be given if one considers an ordinal scale with seven linguistic terms (T):

$$T=\{T_0=\text{"none"}, T_1=\text{"Very Low"}, T_2=\text{"Low"}, T_3=\text{"Medium"},$$
$$T_4=\text{"High"}, T_5=\text{"Very High"}, T_6=\text{"Perfect"}\} \tag{6}$$

Reproducing the mentioned linguistic terms (eq. 6) on the daily intake of alcohol and connecting it with the Z shape of its fuzzy set, the terms used would be connected as follows:

$$T=\{T_0=\text{"Preferred"}, T_1=\text{"Medium"}, T_2=\text{"Unacceptable"}\} \tag{7}$$

The approximate computational model processes the membership functions of the fuzzy terms and results in an aggregated fuzzy number. These aggregated fuzzy numbers do not necessarily belong to the initial set of linguistic terms. The ordering of the aggregated fuzzy values can be achieved by using a fuzzy ranking method to compare them. However, this comparison process can be quite complex and produce unreliable results, as it may: (i) involve considerable computations, (ii) produce inconsistency via respective fuzzy ranking methods, and (iii) generate counter-intuitive ranking outcomes for similar fuzzy numbers.

The process of producing a quantifiable result in fuzzy logic, given fuzzy sets and corresponding membership degrees is defuzzification. This means that for every possible value μ, should be given a result with a grade of membership that describes to what extent this value μ is reasonable to use. Defuzzification is a process of transformation of this fuzzy information into a single value μ' that will actually be applied in the decision making process. This transformation from a fuzzy set to a crisp number (defuzzification) is necessary because humans are more familiar with crisp values.

The goal, of using the fuzzy sets in nutrition is to optimize the diet so that the requirements for all observed nutrients are achieved. For example if there is too little dietary fibre and too much energy in the diet, adding wholemeal bread gives more dietary fibre but also more energy – so there is a conflict (Wirsam et al., 1997; Wirsam & Hahn, 1999; Teodorescu et al., 1999; McBride, 1997). To solve this conflict and to represent the logical "and" (because it is desirable to optimize both dietary fibre and energy), compromises are made (Wirsam & Hahn, 1999; Wirsam et al., 1999). Wirsam suggested the application of the product of the minimal membership vale and the harmonic mean to the fuzzy sets of the rest of observed nutrients, gives the name to the crisp value that defuzzifies the optimisation – the Prerow value (PV):

$$PV = \min[\mu(x_i)] \cdot (n-1) / \left(\sum_{i \neq i_{min}}^{n} \frac{1}{\mu(x_i)} \right) \tag{8}$$

$\mu(x_i)$ are the fuzzy sets for i nutrients that are observed. So defined Prerow value is now a measure for how close on average one comes to the recommendations - or how healthy our food is. With the Prerow value one can decide whether a certain nutrition situation is better or worse than the other. Wirsam has graded the PV values (between 0 and 1) of a nutritive offer concerning their impact on health (Wirsam & Hahn, 1999; Wirsam et al., 1999). In accordance with the health impact, the preferred PV values are PV>07, and an acceptable meal or menu offer with balanced energy and nutrient offers. Those offers that result with PV > 0.9 would be considered as optimal offers with highly appreciated energy and content of nutrients. Prerow value, so defined, is a measure of closeness of analysed or planned meal (menu) to the recommendations; in other words it means an index of measure how healthy is a given meal or a menu.

Its value can be between 0 and 1, the acceptable value is PV >0.7, what is according to Wirsam and co-workers (1997) a nutritionally acceptable offer. Combinations with PV<0.7 are nutritionally unacceptable because they can have a number of adverse effects on human health, especially over a longer period of time (Wirsam & Hahn, 1999).

4. Fuzzy logic based menu planning – Case study: DASH diet

The DASH diet is considered as a case study for fuzzy logic modelling and optimisation in nutrition, considered is the DASH diet. This diet is proven as a good treatment in the prevention of height blood pressure for the high-risk population, correcting inadequate nutrition. The principles of fuzzy logic were used in the analysis and optimization process, based on developed membership functions for nutrients and food groups, for the target population of men aged 31-50 years, according to guidelines that are outlined in the treatment of hypertension (DASH guidelines: AHA, 2004).

Basic emphasis was on nutrients whose intake, in the DASH diet, is generally important in the treatment. Emphasis was on the control of the daily intake of energy, intake of fats, saturated fats, cholesterol, magnesium, potassium, calcium, sodium, dietary fibre, proteins and carbohydrates.

Observed nutrients in DASH diet	DASH recommendations based on a daily eating plan of 2100 kcal (8790 kJ)
Total fat	27% of daily energy intake
Saturated fat	6% of daily energy intake
Protein	18% of daily energy intake
Carbohydrate	55% of daily energy intake
Cholesterol	150 mg
Sodium	2300* mg
Potassium	4700 mg
Calcium	1250 mg
Magnesium	500 mg
Dietary Fibre	30 g

* 1,500 mg sodium was a lower goal tested and found to be even better for lowering blood pressure. It was particularly effective for middle-aged and older individuals, African Americans, and those who already had high blood pressure. g = grams; mg = milligrams

Table 1. DASH diet guideline for a 2 100 kcal Eating Plan

Fuzzy logic modelling is applied for modelling and optimisation of nutritional requirements given by DASH diet guidelines that present crisp values, as presented in table 1 where are given crisp values that should be achieved for a daily intake based on 2,100 kcal (8790 kJ) eating plan (AHA, 2004).

4.1 Membership functions modelled according DASH guidelines

In order to visualize fuzzy concept, intake of a nutrient will be estimated with a value between 0 (not belonging to the set) and 1 (completely belongs). This value of belonging to a set is defining the acceptability or unacceptability grade regarding the DASH diet.

The modelling of a fuzzy set followed the instruction of Wirsam and co-workers (1997) where 5 points are crucial in the fuzzy set construction. Those five points will be explained on the presented example for sodium intake (Figure 3). The value y is the value of the fuzzy value μ.

Five points used in the construction of the fuzzy set:

- Fuzzy value for zero intake of a nutrient (y=0)
- Safe minimum limit of intake of a nutrient (y=0.9)
- Optimal intake of a nutrient (y=1)
- Safe upper limit of intake of a nutrient (y=0.9)
- The toxic perilous area (y=0)

This approach in modelling of fuzzy set membership functions for the daily input was presented in some other studies what indicates the successful applicability (Wirsam & Hahn, 1999; Wirsam et al., 1997; Gajdoš et al., 2001; Rumora et al.,, 2009).

As Wirsam and co-workers (1997) have pointed out, the 5th point is "approximately 3 times the recommended intake for the nutrient". They have also advised to smooth the parabolas, what has been done in presentation of membership function presented for sodium.

Daily intake of Na concerning the crisp values that define the daily recommended intake is very simple based on equation 1: $x_{Na,min} \leq x_{Na} \leq x_{Na,max}$, where the $x_{Na,min}$= 500 mg, and the $x_{Na,max}$ = 2300 mg.

Fuzzy membership functions are modelled to describe the range of nutrient intakes in the range from deficient to excess amounts.

The data used in construction of fuzzy sets, as well as for the presentation of sodium intake based on crisp values are given in table 2.

point	y = μ value	Intake of Na for normal diet (mg)	Intake of Na according DASH diet guidelines (mg)
1	0	0	0
2	0,9	500	500
3	1	1500	1000
4	0,9	2300	2000
5	0	6000	3000*

(*) Although the previous studies (Wirsam et al., 1997) have advised to use as a value for the 5th point – approximately 3 times the recommended intake for the nutrient – this was not applied, because the basic idea of the DASH diet is to reduce the intake of sodium.

Table 2. Values used in construction of membership functions (a) for normal daily intake of Na, (b) daily intake of Na based on DASH diet guidelines.

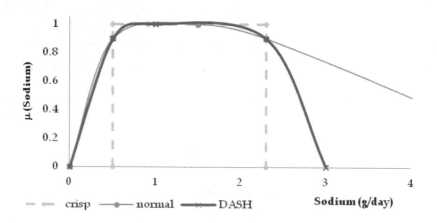

Fig. 3. Membership function, of (i) sodium as recommended by DRI and (ii) sodium according DASH guidelines and definition of the sodium daily intake based on crisp values

The aim of the study was to use fuzzy logic in planning of the diet guidelines for people suffering from hypertension based on membership functions, for energy and nutrients of significance in the DASH diet with a balanced level of foods from different food groups. Regarding the issue of hypertension, the most vulnerable group in the population is the male population aged 31-50 years. The membership functions for energy and nutrients according to guidelines of DASH diet were developed. In the target population there are many individuals who have an inactive sedentary lifestyle, so the energy level was created according the males with low physical activity.

Concerning the basic aim of the DASH diet approach, the end point (5th point) of a membership function could be approximately 3 times the recommended intake for the nutrient (Wirsam et al., 1997) but this was not applied for most of the nutrients due to the success of a DASH diet which occurs if the recommendations are respected.

The 11 fuzzy sets for amounts of energy and nutrients most that are the most important in the DASH guidelines are constructed based on the daily energy intake of 2100 kcal and according the DASH recommendations (Figure 4).

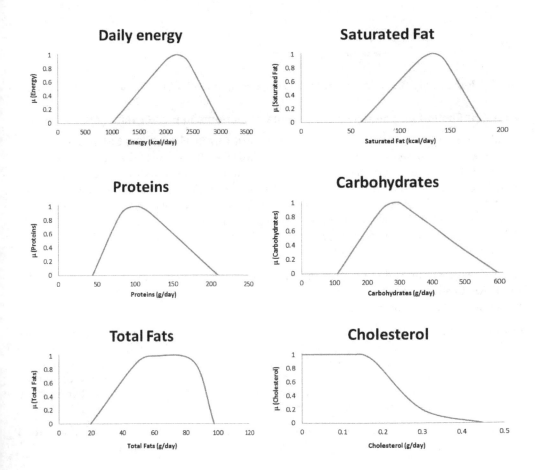

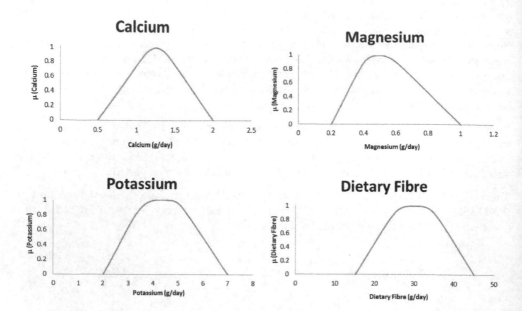

Fig. 4. Membership functions for nutrients important in the DASH diet (according table 1)

4.1.1 Application of membership functions of nutrients in menu evaluation

Database of meals with nutritional content is created in Excel using the USDA database rel. 22 (USDA, 2009) based on 7 days menus taken from the official site of the American Institute of Heart, Lung and Blood (NHLBI, 2010). It is assumed that seven-day menu suggested by NHLBI according guidelines of DASH diet (Table 3) is properly conceived and would be acceptable also for pregnant women regarding the average daily energy offers ranged from 8785 – 10344 kJ. Each day offers consisted of breakfast (B), lunch (L), snack (S) and dinner (D). So, the data basis of meals was built up of 28 dishes (7 B x 7 L x 7 S x 7 D) and an ideal case result would be 2401 daily offers.

Upon creation of an eating plan for individual or group, including the person that provides the DASH eating plan, it is necessary to determine its energy and nutritional needs what is presented in table 4, for the meals given by AHA (2004).

On-line found daily offers for a weak were (i) analysed in order to evaluate the eligibility with DASH diet guidelines, and using the optimisation tool, (ii) the dish offers were combined in daily menus and (iii) new menu offers were evaluated with the corresponding PV value. In the fuzzy logic analysis, the goal is to determine the adequacy of mutual combining the individual dishes of daily meals, and to determine the number of daily combinations that are nutritionally acceptable (PV > 0.7).

The aim was to (a) analyse the daily offers and to identify the critical variables (individual nutrients), (b) optimise a set of applicable menus that are nutritive balanced.

	Breakfast	Lunch	Dinner	Snack
Day 1	Bran flakes cereal with banana, low-fat milk, whole wheat bread with margarine & orange juice	Chicken salad with Italian dressing & fruit cocktail	Beef, eye of the round	Unsalted almonds, raisins & fruit yogurt
Day 2	Instant oatmeal, whole wheat bagel with peanut butter, banana & low-fat milk	Chicken breast sandwich & apple juice	Vegetarian spaghetti & canned pears	Unsalted almonds, dried apricots & fruit yogurt
Day 3	Bran flakes cereal with banana, low-fat milk whole wheat bread with margarine & orange juice	Beef barbeque sandwich with new potato salad & orange	Salad from different vegetables & cornbread muffin	Fruit yogurt, graham cracker rectangles & peanut butter
Day 4	Whole wheat bread with margarine, fruit yogurt, peach & grape juice	Ham and cheese sandwich &carrot sticks	Chicken with Spanish rice & low-fat milk	Unsalted almonds, apple juice, apricots & low-fat milk
Day 5	Whole grain oat rings cereal, banana, low-fat milk, raisin bagel with peanut butter & orange juice	Tuna salad plate, canned pineapple & unsalted almonds	Turkey meatloaf, whole wheat roll & peach	Fruit yogurt & unsalted sunflower seeds
Day 6	Low-fat granola bar, banana, fruit yogurt, orange juice & low-fat milk	Turkey breast sandwich with broccoli & orange	Baked fish (spicy) with cooked carrots, whole wheat roll & cookie	Unsalted peanuts, low-fat milk & dried apricots
Day 7	whole grain oat rings with banana, low-fat milk & fruit yogurt	Tuna salad sandwich, apple & low-fat milk	Zucchini lasagne salad, whole wheat roll with margarine & grape juice	Unsalted almonds, apple juice, dry apricots & whole wheat crackers

Table 3. Daily offers given by AHA (2004), based on DASH diet guideline

Observed	DASH Recommendations	Different daily offers						
		Day 1	Day 2	Day 3	Day 4	Day 5	Day 6	Day 7
Ed, kJ	8800	9063	8805	9844	9362	10344	9086	8785
Total fat , % Ed	27	21.2	23.9	25.3	23.5	22.3	32.4	24.2
Saturated fat , % Ed	6	6.5	6.6	6.3	6.0	5.0	6.1	6.6
Cholesterol , mg	150	143.4	124.3	131.9	162.1	166.4	115.4	83.0
Magnesium, mg	500	529.3	428.0	609.7	535.5	558.9	579.9	545.5
Potassium, mg	4700	4359.5	4445.6	6124.3	4782.2	4984.9	4484.7	4147.3
Calcium, mg	1250	1885.3	1533.3	1487.5	1602.7	1244.1	1294.8	1443.7
Sodium, mg	2300	2292.3	1891.8	2115.6	2190.3	2101.5	1619.6	1714.0
Dietary fiber, g	30	32.0	24.7	31.1	32.6	32.3	38.0	37.7
Protein, % Ed	18	19.1	18.8	20.4	20.8	20.3	17.8	18.1
Carbohydrate, % Ed	55	59.4	57.2	54.3	55.8	57.5	49.8	57.7

Table 4. Energy and nutrient content of daily offers given by AHA (2004), based on DASH diet guideline

To get an acceptable range of macro and individual entries micronutrients from existing recommendations (which represents an expression value), modelled are membership function.

Membership functions were modelled for the male population group aged 31-50, with low physical activity (PA=1), and potentially suffering from hypertension. Basic emphasis was on nutrients whose intake in the diet is general important in the treatment measures: energy, fat, saturated fat, cholesterol, magnesium, potassium, calcium, sodium, dietary fibre, proteins and carbohydrates. DASH diet guidelines emphasize the quality of fat, or fat consisting mostly n-3 and n-6 unsaturated fatty acids. Their membership functions were modelled according to their share in the total daily fat share. In addition, membership functions for individual nutrients were developed according the DASH diet guidelines.

Additionally, reviews by the American Heart Association led the Association to recommend reducing saturated fat intake to less than 7% of total calories according to its 2006 recommendations (Little et al., 2004).

The nutrient composition of the daily intake was analysed and planed following the flow chart presented on Fig. 5.

Basic guidelines for balanced energy and nutrient intake are the daily recommendations (DRI, 1990 & 2005) that define recommended daily needs of energy as well as macro and micronutrients (table 1).

5. Results

Our developed algorithm used in the daily menu analysis and optimization is written in the programming system *W.R. Mathematica v.6.*The algorithm included a feature that the solution may re-marked character (specific number) that allows decoding fuzziness, and also allows a man to understand and compare the results. Fuzziness was decoded with the assistance of Prerow features (PV value), which assesses the acceptability or unacceptability of a menu offer (a combination for a day). The combinations that resulted with a crisp value (PV value) within 0.7 to 1, was considered as acceptable daily offer, what is according to Wirsam et al. (1997) a nutritionally acceptable offer. What is the PV value closer to the value 1, the menu combination consists of nutrient amounts whose daily intake is optimal (0.9<PV<1).

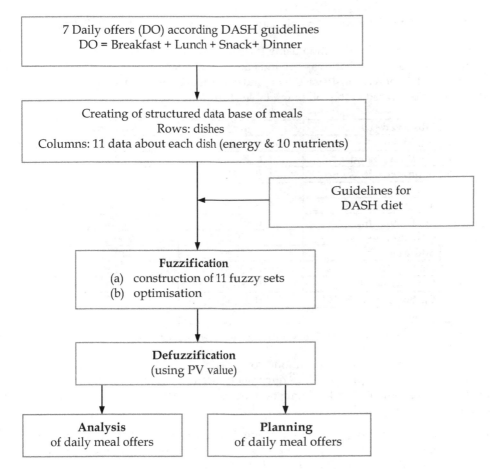

Fig. 5. Flow chart of the methodology used in evaluation and optimisation of meal offers

5.1 Results of the menu analysis

During the analysis the goal was to determine the adequacy of mutual combining of individual dishes of daily meals, and to determine the number of daily combinations that are nutritionally acceptable (PV > 0.7 connotes energy and nutrient intake of all observed nutrients in the acceptable range). Results of it are presented in table 5.

Daily combination		Prerow value (PV)
Day 1	B_1, L_1, S_1, D_1	0.533
Day 2	B_2, L_2, S_2, D_2	0.765
Day 3	B_3, L_3, S_3, D_3	0.831
Day 4	B_4, L_4, S_4, D_4	**0.433**
Day 5	B_5, L_5, S_5, D_5	0.761
Day 6	B_6, L_6, S_6, D_6	0.818
Day 7	B_7, L_7, S_7, D_7	0.841

Table 5. Evaluation of daily meal combinations based on one weak DASH diet plans

As the results of the defuzzification using PV value show, not all combinations have reached the limit value of 0.7, what was an indicator of acceptance of a daily offer. Using of membership functions constructed for nutrient intake allow also identifying critical nutrient(s), as presented in the following table (Table 6).

Observed (x_i)	$\mu(x_i)$	Amount
Ed, kJ	0.818636	9362
Total fat , % Ed	0.477551	23,5
Saturated fat , % Ed	0.905263	6,0
Cholesterol , mg	0.976364	162,1
Magnesium, mg	0.994118	535,5
Potassium, mg	0.900000	4782,2
Calcium, mg	0.909500	1602,7
Sodium, mg	0.837000	2190,3
Dietary fiber, g	0.800000	32,6
Protein, % Ed	0.986239	20,8
Carbohydrate, % Ed	0.990323	55,8
Total PV	0.433	

Table 6. Analysis of the offer of day 4 with aim to detect the critical point

Experimentally determined deviations of energy and nutrients intakes from the recommendations are presented. Adjustments needed for improvement of nutrition requirements corresponding to linguistic variable were determined by use of fuzzy sets without major change of the menus.

The intake of total fats $(\mu(x_i) = 0.477551)$ is identified as a critical nutrient. As can be seen, all other 10 observed variables (x_i) have acceptable amounts. But because of that one critical nutrient – this daily meal combination will not be preferred.

5.2 Results of the menu optimisation

Membership functions were also used for planning new daily menu offers, based on a weekly offer that is recommended as appropriate menus for people who conducted the program according to the DASH diet principles, for 7-days (tables 3 & 4). According to the principle of modelling and optimisation (Fig. 5), the input variables (menu for 7 were evaluated using membership functions, $\mu(x_i)$, and estimated after the defuzzification with the crisp value PV.

As it was mentioned, possible number of combinations is 2041, but how many of them are acceptable (PV>0.7) based on their nutrient and energy content will show on the defuzzification (Table 7).

Daily combination		Prerow value (PV)
1	B_4, L_4, S_4, D_4	0.433
2	B_4, L_4, S_5, D_4	0.477
3	B_1, L_1, S_1, D_1	0.533
.	.	.
.	.	.
.	.	.
2398	B_3, L_2, S_5, D_1	0.892
2399	B_1, L_3, S_5, D_2	0.893
2400	B_1, L_3, S_1, D_3	0.893
2401	B_1, L_2, S_5, D_3	0.894

Table 7. Daily offer combinations sorted according PV value (3 worst & 3 best)

A measurement of appropriate energy and nutrient intake with a respect to the recommendations, or optimal intake, is evaluated by Prerow value. PV value was used to evaluate the efficiency of meal combinations concerning the daily amount of energy and nutrients. The goal functions are optimised using originally developed program in W.R. *Mathematica* for modelling and optimisation in the Pareto sense. Sorted results, from those which are less appreciated to those that are highly recommended, have shown that 65 % are acceptable (PV>0.7), but the 35% of combinations should be avoided in the consummation (Table 7).

Buisson (2008) has in his study stressed out that use of fuzzy logic in meal planning results with applicable meal offers that are balanced regarding the energy and nutritive contents. Optimisation solutions provide assistance in the selection of foods and meals, and their combination with each other.

From the results of optimization using fuzzy logic, the proposed food guide, the DASH diet principles, can be used either for health reasons (decrease hypertension) or simply for a healthier diet. Developed software evaluates the optimal solutions considering the criterion of Prerow value, which presents the modified harmonic mean and defines a rigorous criterion in the defuzzification process.

Is there possibility that another computing approach could be more effective, can be answered only then if the same problem is solved with another tool. Fuzzy approach is placed in the nonlinear approach, so the alternative could be the linear approach, such as linear programming used in DASH diet planning.

5.3 Linear programming in DASH menu planning

The same goal (optimal daily meal offer) but solved by another tool is used in order to compare the final results and to extract advantages or disadvantages of menu planning based on fuzzy logic.

Linear programming is designed to address the problem by choosing between several possible or available variables in order to achieve the most suitable combination of the selected (optimal) result (Kalpić and Mornar, 1996; Deb, 2001, Darmon et al, 2002). Applying these premises (goal and constrains), models were constructed in order to find the so called – optimal solution. Models containing such target function and a set of admissible constrains are called linear models (Eckstein, 1967; Martić, 1996; Kalpić and Mornar, 1996) and are often used in menu planning (Gajdoš et al., 2001; Koroušić Seljak, 2009). Using linear optimisation in menu planning, it is very important to indicate the upper and lower limits, i.e. minimum and/or maximum value that is needed to satisfy the daily nutrition needs (Bhatti, 2000):

Minimum ≤ acceptable nutrient amounts ≤ Maximum (9)

Nutrient needs are often defined in ranges as mentioned in eq. 1) what will be in detail explained in materials and methods (especially in table 2 and figure 1).

According to the target group, males aged 30-51, it was important, from a set of data, choose those items that are crucial for the DASH diet (Table 8).

Observed	DASH Recommendations	Daily recommendations* used for LP	
		Minimum	Minimum
Ed, kJ	8800	8000	9600
Total fat , % Ed	27	24.3	29.7
Saturated fat , % Ed	6	5.4	6.6
Cholesterol , mg	150	135	165
Magnesium, mg	500	450	550
Potassium, mg	4700	4230	5170
Calcium, mg	1250	1125	1375
Sodium, mg	2300	2070	2530
Dietary fiber, g	30	27	33
Protein, % Ed	18	16.2	19.8
Carbohydrate, % Ed	55	50	60

*the range of the minimum and maximal value is ± 10% of the recommended value

Table 8. Recommended intake of energy and macronutrients according DAH guidelines and their limitations used in meal planning using linear programming

The aim is to reach a result that presents a daily energy and nutritive balanced offer with minimal cost. Price was placed in the aim function of the linear model where energy and 10 nutrients (total Proteins, Fats, Carbohydrates, Saturated Fats Dietary Fibres, Cholesterol, Calcium, Magnesium, Sodium and Potassium) were included in the constrains subjected to the goal function, as follows in the basic linear model.

Basic structure of the linear model:

Goal function:

$$\min F = p_1 \cdot B_1 + \ldots + p_7 \cdot B_7 + p_8 \cdot L_1 + \ldots + p_{14} \cdot L_7 + p_{15} \cdot S_1 + \ldots + p_{21} \cdot S_7 + p_{22} \cdot D_1 + \ldots + p_{28} \cdot D_7 \quad (10)$$

Constrains that will restrict energy and nutrient content of daily offers:

$$a_{ij} \cdot B_j + a_{ij} \cdot L_j + a_{ij} \cdot S_j + a_{ij} \cdot D_j \geq b_{i,\,min} \tag{11}$$

$$a_{ij} \cdot B_j + a_{ij} \cdot L_j + a_{ij} \cdot S_j + a_{ij} \cdot D_j \leq b_{i,\,max} \tag{12}$$

Where:

p_j -   Meal price

x_j -   Meals, number of the meals (j), j=1, ... , 7

a_{ij}-   Content of energy, water or nutrients, i, i=1, 2, . . ., 20, for observed meals, j

b_i -   Recommended intakes of energy, water or nutrients

In order to construct a linear models as similar as possible to the fuzzy model, the price of all offers was set equal to one, what would allow to optimise without of price influence (because the price was not included in the meal planning based on fuzzy logic). Program LINDO was used as linear optimisation program.

Each daily offer included the same offer as in the previous example: one breakfast (B), lunch (L), snack (S) and dinner (D). Again, the data basis of meals was built up of 28 dishes (7 B x 7 L x 7 S x 7 D) and an ideal case result would be 2401 daily offers. But using the optimisation tools, it will be cleared if all combinations (daily offers) are well balanced concerning the required energy and nutrient content. The aim was also to examine whether the target group will satisfy all energy and nutrient needs, without additional changes of the offers, through menu offers.

Daily meal offer, LP	
No. 1	B_1, L_2, S_5, D_1
No. 2	B_2, L_2, S_1, D_2
No. 3	B_1, L_2, S_1, D_7
No. 4	B_7, L_3, S_2, D_1
No. 5	B_1, L_1, S_2, D_5

Table 9. First five daily offers as a result of using linear optimisation tools

The nutrient compositions of daily intakes were based on restrictions selected with respect to the target group of men aged 31-50 with the emphasis to sedentary job. Based on the composition, weekly plan have been proposed that consisted of 7meals distributed during the day as breakfast, lunch, snack and dinner (Table 9). The average values of energy and nutrients of the offers can, without problems, composed menu offers for almost 2 months (even 63 daily offers satisfied all demands on energy and nutrients).The present study combines the limitations of menu offers (NHLBI, 2010) and of modelling approaches. In particular, the validity of results obtained with diet modelling analysis is dependent on how well the models simulate reality and on the quality of input data.

In order to identify the critical variables (individual meals) or constrains (nutrient requirements), the sensitivity test was used (Gajdoš et al., 2001). But collection of those result are much more demanding because each new solution requires repetition performance of the optimisation process. Until now, it has been used to design either individual diets (Soden and Fletcher, 1992; Colavita and D'Orsi, 1990) or population diets (Maes et al., 2008; Carlson et al., 2007; Cleveland et al., 1993; Darmon et al., 2002) and their implications in terms of food choices (Ferguson et al., 2006).

As some studies show (Carlson et al., 2007; Murphy and Britten, 2006; Katamay et al., 2007; Cleveland et al., 1993; Soden and Fletcher, 1992) the main goal of linear programming used in meal planning is to reach the nutrient-based recommendations and also translation of the set of nutrient-based recommendations into foods (not food composites) for each individual or group that is a representative sample of the target population (Maillot et al., 2010), that are in accordance with set limits and the goal function.

6. Conclusion

The menu planning based on fuzzy logic considered and including: i) recommendations as crisp values, ii) modelling of membership functions for daily energy and nutrient intake as well as for preferences and price (Pareto optimisation), iii) defuzzification and iv) identification of deviations in order to improve the daily intake.

The final result of the optimisation process was a set of daily menus, 65% of which are nutritional acceptable. The acceptable daily combinations can be used in healthy meal planning and in prevention and treatment of hypertension, changing nutritional habits according DASH guidelines. This would also help to avoid consumption of unacceptable daily offers (almost 35%) from the set.

The use of fuzzy logic has also highlighted the possibility of insufficient energy and nutrient intake when dishes from different daily offers are combined in an inadequate way.

Using optimisation in meal planning showed that the energy amount in the optimised meals is in proportion with DASH recommendations with no fear of the influence on health, as Wirsam and Hahn (1999) pointed out.

The results indicated that use of fuzzy logic is well suited to deal with the inherent imprecision of data associated with food quantities and their nutrient values, and to propagate it through computations in a mathematical way with a great applicability in diet planning as well as in the demanding cases as DASH diet planning.

From one weekly offer undertaken from NHLBI (2010) that is consisted from 7 daily offers based on 4 dishes (breakfast, lunch, snacks, and dinner) was possible to gain 2401 daily offers but using the optimisation approach it was shown that it is not possible to combine all dishes in new a daily offers because the nutrient composition will not satisfy needs of the target group, man aged 30-51 with the emphasis to hypertension.

From possible 2401 daily offers (new daily menus) the final menu set was reduced on 63 daily offers, almost 2 months. Each weekly plan that has been proposed consisted of 4 meals distributed during the day as breakfast, lunch, snack and dinner. This indicates the limitation of the optimisation approach regarding the input data set, the weekly offer undertaken from NHLBI (2010). This example has shown that when the importance of the objective function is reduced (equal for all offers), this is a deficiency of the LP in meal planning and is no competition at all to the application of fuzzy logic in meal planning.

But the great advantage of using fuzzy arithmetic in menu planning is the suitability to deal with the inherent imprecision of data associated with nutrient values. The fuzzification and defuzzification process are a great help in achievement of analysis or balanced menu offers.

In the future research, new variables will be added to the set of membership functions of energy and nutrients. Those two variables are (i) preferences of the consumer and (ii) the price of a daily menu combination. The following aim is to balance the menu offers globally, including all mentioned membership functions (11 presented in this chapter + 2 new: preference and price).

Before the construction of the membership function for the consumer preference, it is necessary to carry out the evaluation of the offers, i.e. of each meal (Breakfast, Lunch, Dinner and Snack). The evaluative scale can be arbitrary, for example, if the Likert-type scale from 1 to 5 is used, the values used in the construction of the curve should be as following: 1 - "totally unacceptable", 2 - "not acceptable" 3 - "moderately acceptable" , 4 - "acceptable", 5 - "very acceptable". Membership function that describes the preference of the consumer will have the shape "S" (Fig. 2, $\mu(A_1)$), because for the consumer is not acceptable to consume something that is not preferable. The membership function of acceptability (consumers preference) can also be used to exclude any food ingredient that is a potential allergen (a meal that contains any allergen is "totally unacceptable"). Allergens that could be removed in such menu planning are milk, eggs, nuts, grains, etc. Each offer that contain allergens would be unacceptable ($\mu(x)$ <0.5) and according the equation 8., the final PV value would not be acceptable.

Membership function for the price (daily price acceptance) of the daily menu offer should have the form "Z" (Fig. 2, $\mu(A_2)$), because user-friendly is the lower price ($\mu(x)$ > 0.7), although daily offers that are expensive should not be excluded because such offer can be nutritionally very acceptable.

This software should be also used in education of users (either healthy or sick) to enlarge their knowledge regarding food combining and menu planning. Efficient education based on the software that is based on using fuzzy logic, intended for nutrient intake analysis and/or planning, would be a powerful tool in the fight with the growing world problem – obesity.

7. References

Alderman, M. H. (1999). Barriers to blood pressure control. *American Journal of Hypertension*, Vol.12, (December, 1999) pp. 1268-1269, ISSN 0895-7061

American Heart Association (AHA) (2004). Heart disease and stroke statistics—2004 update. Dallas, TX7 American Heart

Association Available: http://www.americanheart.org/presenter.jhtml?identifier= 1928. Accessed December 6, 2004.

Appel, L. J.; Moore, T. J.; Obarzanek, E.; Vollmer, W. M.; Svetkey, L. P. & Sacks, F. M. (1997). A clinical trial of the effects of dietary patterns on blood pressure. *The New England Journal of Medicine*, 336, 1117–1124.

Bingham, S.A. (1987). The dietary assessment of individuals; methods, accuracy, new techniques and recommendations. *Nutrition Abstracts and Reviews*, Vol. 57, No. 9, pp. 705-742, ISSN 0029-6019

Brown, M.L.; Filer, L.J.; Guthrie, H.A.; Levander, O.A.; McComick, D.B.; Olson, R.E. & Steele, R.D. (1990). *Present Knowledge in Nutrition*, ISBN 1578811074, International Life Science Institute Nutrition Foundation Washington D.C.

Buisson, J-C. (2008). Nutri-Educ, a nutrition software application for balancing meals, using fuzzy arithmetic and heuristic search algorithms, *Artificial Intelligence in Medicine*, Vol.42, pp. 213-227, ISSN 0933-3657.

Burt, V. L.; Whelton, P.; Roccella, E. J.; Brown, C.; Cutler, J. A. & Higgins, M. (1995). Prevalence of hypertension in the US adult population: Results from the Third National Health and Nutrition Examination Survey, 1988–1991. *Hypertension*, Vol.25, No.3, (March, 1995), pp. 305–313, ISSN 1524-4563

Carlson, A.; Lino M. & Fungwe T. (2007). The low-cost, moderate-cost, and liberal food plans. Washington, DC: US Department of Agriculture, Center for Nutrition Policy and Promotion (CNPP-20.)

Cook, N. R.; Cohen, J.; Hebert, P. R.; Taylor, J. O. & Hennekens, C. H. (1995). Implications of small reductions in diastolic blood pressure for primary prevention. *Archives of Internal Medicine*, Vo.155. No.7, (November, 1995), pp. 701–709.

Čerić, V. & Dalbelo-Bašić, B. (2004). *Informacijska tehnologija u poslovanju*, ISBN: 953-197-640-6, Element, Zagreb.

Dantzig G.B. (1990). The diet problem, *Interfaces*, Vol.20, No.4, (July/August 1990), pp. 43–47, ISSN 0092-2102

Darmon N.; Ferguson E. & Briend A. (2002). Linear and nonlinear programming to optimize the nutrient density of a population's diet: an example based on diets of preschool children in rural Malawi, *American Journal of Clinical Nutrition*, Vol.75, No.2, (February, 2002) pp. 245–253, ISSN 0002-9165

Deb K. (2001). *Multi-Objective Optimization Using Evolutionary Algorithms*, ISBN 0471 87339 X, John Wiley & Sons, Ltd.

Dietary Reference Intakes (1999). A Risk Assessment Model for Establishing Upper Intake Levels for Nutrients, Institute of Medicine. ISBN 0-309-07520-3

Dietary Reference Intakes (2001). Intake of Calcium, Phosphorus, Magnesium, Vitamin D and Fluoride. National Academy Press, Washington, D.C., ISBN 0-309-06403-1

Dietary Reference Intakes (2001a) Intakes for Vitamin A, Vitamin K, Arsenic, Boron, Chromium, Copper, Iodine, Iron, Manganese, Molybdenum, Nickel, Silicon, Vanadium, and Zinc, Food and Nutrition Board, Institute of Medicine, ISBN 0-309-07279-4

Dietary Reference Intakes(2001b) Applications in Dietary Assessment: A Report of the Subcommittees on Interpretation and Uses of Dietary Reference Intakes and Upper Reference Levels of Nutrients, and the Standing Committee on the Scientific Evaluation of Dietary Reference Intakes, Food and Nutrition Board, Institute of Medicine. ISBN 0-309-07183-6

Ferguson E.L.; Darmon N.; Fahmida U.; Fitriyanti S.; Harper T.B. & Premachandra I.M. (2006). Design of optimal food-based complementary feeding recommendations and identification of key "problem nutrients" using goal programming, *Journal of Nutrition*, Vol.136, No.9, (September, 2006), pp. 2399–2404, ISSN 0022-3166

Gajdoš J.; Vidaček S. & Kurtanjek Ž. (2001). Meal planning in boarding schools in Croatia using optimisation of food components. *Current Studies of Biotechnology – Environment*, 2, (February, 2001), pp. 217-222.

Hahn, A.; Pfeifenberger, P. & Wirsam, B. (1995). Evaluation and optimisation of nutrient supply by fuzzy-logic. *Ernahrungs-Umschau*, Vol.42, pp. 367, ISSN 0174-0008

Hahn, P.; Pfeiffenberger, P.; Wirsam, B. & Leitzmann, C. (1995a). Bewertung und Optimierung der Nährstoffzufuhr mit Hilfe der Fuzzy-Logik. *Ernährungs-Umschau,* Vol.42, pp. 367-371, ISSN 0174-0008

Hajjar, I. & Kotchen, T. A. (2003). Trends in prevalence, awareness, treatment, and control of hypertension in the United States, 1988–2000. *Journal of the American Medical Association,* Vol.290, No.2, (July, 2003), 199– 206, ISSN: 0025-6196

Kalpić D. & Mornar V. (1996). *Operacijska istraživanja,* ISBN 9536363070, DRIP, Zagreb.

Katamay S.W.; Esslinger K.A.; Vigneault M.; Johnston J.L.; Junkins B.A.; Robbins L.G.; Sirois I.V.; Jones-McLean E.M.; Kennedy A.F.; Bush M.A.A.; Brulé D. & Martineau C. (2007). Eating well with Canada's Food Guide (2007): development of the food intake pattern, *Nutrition Reviews,* Vol.65, No4, pp. 155–166, ISSN 1753-4887

Klir, G.J.; Clair, U.S. & Yuan, B. (1997). *Fuzzy set theory – foundations and applications.* Prentice-Hall, Inc., London.

Koroušić Seljak B. (2009): Computer-based dietary menu planning, *Journal of Food Composition and Analysis,* Vol.22, No5, pp. 414-420, ISSN 0889-1575

Kumanyika, S. K. (1997). Can hypertension be prevented? Applications of risk modifications in Black populations: U.S. populations. *Proceedings of the Eleventh International Interdisciplinary Conference on Hypertension in Blacks.* (p. 72–77). New Orleans, LA: New York, Springer.

Lehmann, I.; Weber, R. & Zimmermann, H.J. (1992) Fuzzy Set Theory. *OR Spektrum* Vol.14, No.1, pp. 1-9, ISSN 0171-6468

Maes, L.; Vereecken, C.A.; Gedrich, K..; Rieken, K.; Sichert-Hellert, W.; De Bourdeaudhuij, I.; Kersting, M.; Manios, Y.; Plada, M.; Hagströmer, M.; Dietrich, S. & Matthys. C. on behalf of the HELENA Study Group (2008). A feasibility study of using a diet optimization approach in a web-based computer-tailoring intervention for adolescents, *International Journal of Obesity,* Vol.32, No.S5, (May, 2008), pp.S76–S81, ISSN 0307-0565

Leventhal, H.; Diefenbach, M., & Leventhal, E. A. (1992). Illness cognition: Using common sense to understand treatment adherence and affect cognition interactions. *Cognitive Therapy and Research,* Vol.16, No.2, (March, 1992) pp. 143–163, ISSN: 143-163

Little, P.; Kelly, J.; Barnett J.; Dorward, M.; Margetts, B., & Warm, D. (2004). Randomised controlled factorial trial of dietary advice for patients with a single high blood pressure reading in primary care. *British Medical Journal,* Vol.328, No.7447, (May, 2004), pp.1054.

MacMahon, S. & Rogers, A. (1993). The effects of blood pressure reduction in older patients: An overview of five randomized controlled trials in elderly hypertensives. *Clinical and Experimental Hypertension,* Vol.15, No.6, (November, 1993), pp. 967–968, ISSN: 1554-2815

McCarron, D. A. (1998). Diet and blood pressure – The paradigm shift. *Science,* Vol.281, No.5379, (August, 1998), pp. 933–934, ISSN: 1095-9203

Mahan K. L. & Escott-Stump S. (2007). *Krause's Food and Nutrition Therapy,* 12ed, ISBN 978-1-4160-3401-8, Saundres, Elsevier, Philadelphia,

Maillot M.; Vieux F.; Amiot M.J. & Darmon N. (2010). Individual diet modelling translates nutrient recommendations into realistic and individual-specific food choices, *American Journal of Clinical Nutrition,* Vol.91, No.2, (November, 2009) pp. 421-430, ISSN 0002-9165

Martić Lj. (1996) *Matematičke metode za ekonomske analize,* ISBN 067614-787-X, Školska knjiga, Zagreb.

NHLBI (2010). National Hart Lung and Blood Institute <http://www.n
    hlbi.nih.gov/health/public/ heart/hbp/dash/week_dash.html>. Accessed 25th
    March 2010.
Novák, V. (2005). Are fuzzy sets a reasonable tool for modeling vague phenomena?, *Fuzzy
    Sets and Systems* Vol.156, No.3, (January 2005), pp.341 – 348, ISSN 0165-0114
Novák, V.; Perfilieva, I. & Močkoř, J. (1999). *Mathematical principles of fuzzy logic* ISBN 0-7923-
    8595-0, Dodrecht: Kluwer Academic.
Ray, T.; Liew, K. M. & Saini, P. (2002). An intelligent information sharing strategy within a
    swarm for unconstrained and constrained optimisation problems. *Soft Computing*
    Vol.6, No.1, pp. 38-34, ISSN 1432-7643
Rödder, W. & Zimmermann, H.J. (1977). Analyse, Beschreibung und Optimirung von
    unscarf formulierten Problemen. *Zeitschrift für Operations Research*, Vol.21, pp. 1-18,
    ISSN 0340-9422
Rumora, I.; Gajdoš Kljusurić, J. & Bosanac, V. (2009). Analysis and optimisation of calcium
    content in menus and dairy offer in Croatian kindergartens. *Mljekarstvo*, Vol.59,
    No.3, (November, 2009), pp. 201-208, ISSN 0026-704X
Soden P.M. & Fletcher L.R. (1992). Modifying diets to satisfy nutritional requirements using
    linear programming, *British Journal of Nutrition*, Vol.68, No.3, (December, 1991), pp.
    565-572, ISSN 0007-1145
Siri-Tarino PW, Sun Q, Hu FB, Krauss RM (2010). "Saturated fat, carbohydrate, and
    cardiovascular disease". The American Journal of Clinical Nutrition, Vol.91, No.3,
    (March, 2010), pp. 502–509, ISSN 1938-3207
Stachowicz, M.S. and Beall, L. (1995). *Manual for Software Mathematica-Notebook*, Wolfram
    Research, Champaign, Illinois.
Teodorescu, H-N., Kandel, A., Jain, L.C. (1999). Soft *Computing in Human-Related Sciences*,
    ISBN 0849316359, CRC Press. New York,
Wirsam, B., Hahn, A. (1999). Fuzzy methods in nutrition planning and education and
    clinical nutrition, in Soft Computing in human-related sciences, ISBN 0849316359,
    CRC Press, Florida.
USDA, US Department of Agriculture (2009) USDA National Nutrient Database for
    Standard Reference, Release 22.
Wirsam, B., Hahn, A., Uthus, E.O., Leitzmann, C. (1997). Aplication of fuzzy methods for
    setting RDA's. Poster at the 16th International Congress of Nutrition by the
    International Union of Nutrition Sciences, Montreal, July/August 1997
Wirsam, B.; Hahn, A.; Uthus, E.O. & Leitzmann, C. (1997a). Fuzzy sets and fuzzy decision
    making in nutrition. European Journal of Clinical Nutrition, Vol.51, No.5, (May,
    1997), pp. 286-296, ISSN: 0954-3007
Zadech, L.A. (1965). Fuzzy Sets. *Information and Control* Vol.8, pp. 338-353, ISSN 1349-4198
Zadech, L. A. (1996). *Fuzzy Sets, Fuzzy Logic, Fuzzy Systems*, ISBN 9810224214, World
    Scientific Press.
Zadech, L.A. (1994). The role of fuzzy logic in modelling, identification and control.
    Modelling Identification & Control. Vol.15, No.3, pp. 191-203, ISSB 1890-1328.
Zadech, L.A. (1997). Toward a theory of fuzzy information granulation and its centrality in
    Human Reasoning and Fuzzy logic. *Fuzzy Sets & Systems*, Vol.90, No.2, pp. 111-127,
    ISSN: 0165-0114
Zadech, L.A. (2001) A new direction in AI- Toward a computational theory of perceptions.
    AI Magazine, Vol.22, No.19, pp. 73-84, ISSN 0738-4602

3

A Fuzzy Logic Approach for Remote Healthcare Monitoring by Learning and Recognizing Human Activities of Daily Living

Hamid Medjahed[1], Dan Istrate[1], Jérôme Boudy[2],
Jean Louis Baldinger[2], Lamine Bougueroua[1],
Mohamed Achraf Dhouib[1] and Bernadette Dorizzi[2]

[1]ESIGETEL-LRIT, Avon,
[2]Telecom SudParis, Evry,
France

1. Introduction

Improvement of life quality in the developed nations has systematically generated an increase in the life expectancy. A statistic studies curried out by the French national institute of statistic and economic studies (INSEE) shows a new distribution of age classes in France. In fact, almost one in three people will be over 60 years in 2050, against one in five in 2005, and France will have over 10 million of people over 75 years and over 4 million of people over 85 years. Nevertheless, the increasing number of elderly person implies more resources for aftercare, paramedical care and natural assistance in their habitats. The current healthcare infrastructure in those countries is widely considered to be inadequate to meet the needs of this increasingly older population. In this case a permanent assistance is necessary wherever they are, healthcare monitoring is a solution to deal with this problem and ensure the elderly to live safely and independently in their own home for as long as possible.

In order to improve the quality of life of elderly, researchers are developing technologies to enhance a resident's safety and monitor health conditions using sensors and other devices. Numerous projects are carried out in the world especially in Europe, Asia and North America on the home healthcare telemonitoring topic. They aim for example to define a generic architecture for such telemonitoring systems (Doermann et al., 1998), to conduct experiment of a remote monitoring system on a specific category of patients, like people with insufficient cardiac heart, asthma, diabets, patients with Alzheimer's disease, or cognitive impairments (Noury et al., 2003)., or to build smart apartments (Elger et al., 1998), sensors and alarm systems adapted to the healthcare telemonitoring requirements (West et al., 2005). The project CompanionAble is an Integration Project founded by European commission (FP7). In this project we propose a multimodal platform for recognizing human activities of daily living (ADLs) in the home environment, by using a set of sensors in order to provide proactive healthcare telemonitoring for elderly people at home. This platform uses a fuzzy logic approach to fuse three main subsystems, which have been technically validated from end to end, through their hardware and software. The first subsystem is Anason (Rougui et al., 2009) with its set of microphones that allow sound remote monitoring of the acoustical environment of the elderly. The second subsystem is RFpat (Medjahed et al., 2008), a wearable device fixed on the elderly person, which can measure physiological data (cardiac frequency, activity or agitation, posture and fall detection sensor). The last subsystem is a set of infrared sensors and domotic sensors like contact sensors, temperature sensors, smoke sensors and several other domotic sensors for environment conditions monitoring (Medjahed et al., 2008). This fuzzy logic approach allowed us to recognize several activities of daily living (ADLs) for ubiquitous healthcare. The decision of this multimodal data fusion platform is sent to a remote monitoring center to take action in the case of distress situation.

2. CompanionAble project

The CompanionAble project aim to provide the synergy of Robotics and Ambient Intelligence technologies and their semantic integration to provide for a care-giver's assistive environment. This will support the cognitive stimulation and therapy management of the care-recipient. This is mediated by a robotic companion (mobile facilitation) working collaboratively with a smart home environment (stationary facilitation).

There are widely acknowledged imperatives for helping the elderly live at home (semi)-independently for as long as possible. Without cognitive stimulation support the elderly dementia and depression sufferers can deteriorate rapidly and the carers will face a more demanding task. Both groups are increasingly at the risk of social exclusion.

The distinguishing advantages of the CompanionAble Framework Architecture arise from the objective of graceful, scalable and cost-effective integration. Thus CompanionAble addresses the issues of social inclusion and homecare of persons suffering from chronic cognitive disabilities prevalent among the increasing European older population. A participative and inclusive co-design and scenario validation approach will drive the RTD efforts in CompanionAble; involving care recipients and their close carers as well as the wider stakeholders. This is to ensure end-to-end systemic viability, flexibility, modularity and affordability as well as a focus on overall care support governance and integration with quality of experience issues such as dignity-privacy-security preserving responsibilities fully considered.

CompanionAble will be evaluated at a number of testbeds representing a diverse European user-base as the proving ground for its socio-technical-ethical validation. The collaboration of leading gerontologists, specialist elderly care institutions, industrial and academic RTD partners, including a strong cognitive robotics and smart-house capability makes for an excellent confluence of expertise for this innovative project.3. State of the art

Everyday life activities in the home split into two categories. Some activities show the motion of the human body and its structure. Examples are walking, running, standing up, setting down, laying and exercising. These activities may be mostly recognized by using sensors that are placed on the body (Lee et al., 2002). A second class of activities is recognized by identifying or looking for patterns in how people move things. In this work we focus on some activities identification belong to these both categories.

3.1 Data fusion

In order to maximize a correct recognition of the various ADLs like sleeping, cleaning, bathing etc..., data fusion over the different sensors types is studied. The area of data fusion has generated great interest among researchers in several science disciplines and engineering domains. We have identified two major classes of fusion techniques:

- Those that are based on probabilistic models such as Bayesian reasoning (Cowell et al., 1999) and the geometric decision reasoning like Mahalanobis distance, but their performances are limited when the data are heterogeneous and insufficient for a correct statistical modeling of classes.
- Those based on connectionist models such as neural networks MLP (Dreyfus et al., 2002) and SVM (Burges et al., 1998) which are very powerful because they can model the strong nonlinearity of data but with complex architecture.

Based on those facts the use of fuzzy logic in our platform is motivated by two main raisons from a global point of view:

- Firstly the characteristic of data to merge which are measurements obtained from different sensors, thus they could be imprecise and imperfect. Plus the lack of training sets that reflect activities of daily living.
- Secondly, Fuzzy logic can gather performance and intelligibility and it deals with imprecision and uncertainty. Its history proves that it is used in many cases which are necessary for pattern recognition applications. It has a background application history to clinical problems including use in automated diagnosis (Adlassnig et al., 1986), control systems (Mason et al., 1997), image processing (Lalande et al., 1997) and pattern recognition (Zahlmann et al., 1997). For medical experts it is easier to map their knowledge onto fuzzy relationships than to manipulate complex probabilistic tools.

3.2 Fuzzy logic and patterns recognition systems

Fuzzy logic is a fuzzy set theory, introduced by Lotfi A. Zadeh (Zadeh, 1978) in 1965; it is an extension of classical set theory. Historically, this was closely related to the concept of fuzzy measure, proposed just after by Sugeno (Sugeno, 1974). Similar attempts at proposing fuzzy concept were also made at the same time by Shafer (evidence theory (Shafer, 1974)) and Shackle (surprise theory (Shackle, 1961)). Since that time, fuzzy logic has been more studied, and several applications were developed, essentially in Japan. The use of fuzzy sets can be done mainly at two levels:

- **Attributes representation:** It may happen that data are uncompleted or noisy, unreliable, or some attributes are difficult to measure accurately or difficult to quantify numerically. At that time, it is natural to use fuzzy sets to describe the value of these parameters. The attributes are linguistic variables, whose values are built with adjectives and adverbs of language: large, small, medium etc...and as an illustrating example, we found the recognition system proposed by Mandal et al. (Mandal et al.,1992). Some methods are based on a discretization of the attributes space defined as language. Thus a numerical scale of length will be replaced by a set of fuzzy labels, for example (very small, small, medium, large, extra large), and any measure of length, even numerical is converted on this scale. The underlying idea is to work with the maximal granularity, i.e. the minimal accuracy.

- **Class representation:** Groups do not create a clear partition of the data space, but a fuzzy partition where recovery is allowed will be better adapted. A significant number of fuzzy patterns recognition methods, are just an extension of traditional methods based on the idea of fuzzy partition for example the fuzzy c-means algorithm (Pedrycz, 1990). Historically, the idea of fuzzy partition was first proposed by Ruspini in 1969 (Ruspini, 1969).

Rather than creating new methods of fusion and patterns recognition based on entirely different approaches, fuzzy logic fits naturally in the expression of the problem of classification, and tend to make a generalization of the classification methods that already exist. Taking into account the four steps of a recognition system proposed by Bezdek et Pal (Bezdek et al., 1992), fuzzy logic is very useful for these steps.

- **Data description:** Fuzzy logic is used to describe syntactic data (Mizumoto et al., 1972), numerical and contextual data, conceptual or rules based data (Pao et al., 1989) which is the most significant contribution for the data description.
- **Analysis of discriminate parameters:** In image processing, there are many techniques based on fuzzy logic for segmentation, detection, contrast enhancement (Keller et al 1992) and extraction (Pal et al., 1986).
- **Clustering algorithms:** The aim of these algorithms is to label a set of data into C groups, so that obtained groups contain the most possible similar individuals. Fuzzy c-mean algorithm and fuzzy ISODATA (Dunn, 1973) algorithm are the better known in this category.
- **Design of the discriminator:** The discriminator is designed to produce a fuzzy partition or a clear one, describing the data. This partition corresponds to a set of classes. Indeed the fuzzy ISODATA algorithm is adapted for this step.

3.3 Fuzzy logic steps

We concentrate our efforts in emphasizing the fuzzy logic concept in order to integrate this fundamental approach within the telemonitoring platform. The main concept of fuzzy logic is that many problems in the real world are imprecise rather than exact (Buckley et al., 2002). It is believed that the effectiveness of the human brain is not only from precise cognition, but also from fuzzy concepts, fuzzy judgment, and fuzzy reasoning. An advantage of fuzzy classification techniques lies in the fact that they provide a soft decision, a value that describes the degree to which a pattern fits within a class, rather than only a hard decision, i.e., a pattern matches a class or not. Fuzzy logic is based on natural language which makes it quite attracting field in artificial intelligence. It allows the natural description of problem domains, in linguistic terms, rather than in terms of relationships between precise numerical values.

A fuzzy set, as the foundation of fuzzy logic, is a set without a hard, clearly sharp defined boundary. A fuzzy set extends a standard set by allowing degrees of membership of an element to this set, measured by real numbers in the $[0;1]$ interval. If X is the universe of discourse (the input space variable) and its elements are denoted by x, then a fuzzy set A on X is defined as a set of ordered pairs $(x, \mu_A(x))$ such that:

$$A = \{x, \mu_A(x) \, / \, x, 0 \le \mu_A(x) \le 1 \ \}$$

(1)

Where $\mu_A(x)$ in equation (1), is the membership function (MF) of each x in A. In contrast to classical logic where the membership function _A(x) of an element x belonging to a set A could take only two values: $\mu_A(x) = 1$ if $x \in A$ or $\mu_A(x) = 0$ if $x \notin A$, fuzzy logic introduces the concept of membership degree of an element x to a set A and $\mu_A(x) \in [0;1]$, here we speak about the truth value.

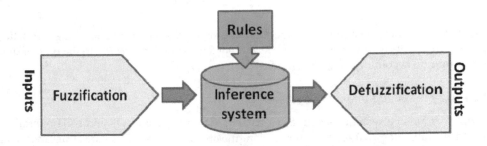

Fig. 1. Fuzzy inference system steps.

A typical fuzzy logic inference system has four components: the fuzzification, the fuzzy rule base plus the inference engine, and the defuzzification. Figure 1 shows those main fuzzy inference system steps.

3.3.1 Fuzzification

First step in fuzzy logic is to convert the measured data into a set of fuzzy variables. It is done by giving value (these will be our variables) to each of a membership functions set. Membership functions take different shape. A Triangular membership function with straight lines can formally be defined as follows:

$$\Lambda(x,a,b,c) = \begin{cases} 0, x \leq a \\ (x-a)/(b-a), a \leq x \leq b \\ (c-x)/(c-b), b \leq x \leq c \\ 0, x \geq c \end{cases}$$

(2)

Trapezoidal function furnished in the equation (3).

$$f(x,a,b,c,d) = \begin{cases} 0, x \leq a \\ (x-a)/(b-a), a \leq x \leq b \\ 1, b \leq x \leq c \\ (d-x)/(d-c), c \leq x \leq d \\ 0, x \geq d \end{cases}$$

(3)

A Gaussian membership function with the parameters m and σ to control the center and width of the function is defined by:

$$G(x,m,\sigma) = e^{\frac{-(x-m)^2}{2\sigma^2}}$$

(4)

The generalized Bell function depends on three parameters a, b, and c is given by:

$$f(x,a,b,c) = \frac{1}{1 + \left\| (x-c)/a \right\|^{2b}}$$

(5)

There are also other memberships functions like sigmoid shaped function, single function etc... The choice of the function shape is iteratively determined, according to the type of data and taking into account the experimental results.

3.3.2 Fuzzy rules and inference system

The fuzzy inference system uses fuzzy equivalents of logical AND, OR and NOT operations to build up fuzzy logic rules. An inference engine operates on rules that are structured in an IF-THEN format. The IF part of the rule is called the antecedent, while the THEN part of the rule is called the consequent. Rules are constructed from linguistic variables. These variables take on the fuzzy values or fuzzy terms that are represented as words and modeled as fuzzy subsets of an appropriate domain. There are several types of fuzzy rules, we only mention the two mains used in our system:

- **Mamdani rules** (Jang et al., 1997) : which are on the form: *If x_1 is A_1 and x_2 is A_2 and...and x_p is A_p Then y_1 is C_1 and y_2 is C_2 and...and y_p is C_p* Where A_i and C_i are fuzzy sets that define the partition space. The conclusion of a Mamdani rule is a fuzzy set. It uses the algebraic product and the maximum as T-norm and S-norm respectively, but there are many variations by using other operators.
- **Takagi/Sugeno rules** (Jang et al., 1997): those rules are on the form : *If x_1 is A_1 and x_2 is A_2 and...and x_p is A_p Then $y = b_0 + b_1 x_1 + b_2 x_2 + ... + b_p x_p$.* In the Sugeno model the conclusion is numerical. The rules aggregation is in fact the weighted sum of rules outputs.

3.3.3 Defuzzification

The last step of a fuzzy logic system consists in turning the fuzzy variables generated by the fuzzy logic rules into real values again which can then be used to perform some action. There are different defuzzification methods; in our platform decision module we could use Centroid Of Area (COA), Bisector Of Area (BOA), Mean Of Maximum (MOM), Smallest Of Maximum (SOM) and Largest Of Maximum (LOM). Equations 6, 7, 8 and 9 illustrate them.

$$Z_{COA} = \frac{\sum_{i=1}^{n} \mu_A(x_i) x_i}{\sum_{i=1}^{n} \mu_A(x_i)}$$

(6)

$$Z_{BOA} = x_M ; \sum_{i=1}^{M} \mu_A(x_i) = \sum_{j=M+1}^{n} \mu_A(x_j)$$

(7)

$$Z_{MOM} = \frac{\sum_{i=1}^{N} x_i^*}{N}$$ (8)

$$Z_{SOM} = \min(x_i^*) \ and \ Z_{LOM} = \max(x_i^*)$$ (9)

Where $x_i^* (i = 1,2,....,N)$ reach the maximal values of $\mu_A(x)$

4. The multimodal telemonitoring platform

We define a smart environment as one with the ability to adapt the environment to the inhabitants and meet the goals of comfort and efficiency. In order to achieve these goals, our first aim is focused on providing such as environment. We consider our system as an intelligent agent, which perceives the state of the environment using sensors and acts consequently using device controllers.

4.1 Sound environment analysis (Anason)

In-home healthcare devices face a real problem of acceptance by end users and also caregivers. Sound sensors are easily accepted by care receivers and their family, they are considered are less intrusive then cameras, smart T-shirts, etc In order to preserve the care-receiver privacy while ensuring his protection and safety, we propose to equip his house with some microphones. In this context, the sound signal flow is continuously analyzed but not continuously recorded. Among different everyday life sounds, only some of them are considered alarming sounds: glass breaking, screams, etc. In order to have a reliable sound telemonitoring system, every sound event is detected (a sudden change in the environmental noise), extracted, and used as input for the classification stage. The sound analysis system has been divided in three modules as shown in Figure 2.

The first module (M.1) is applied to each channel or microphone in order to detect sound events and to extract them from the signal flow. This module use an algorithm based on energy of discrete wavelet transform (DWT) coefficients was proposed and evaluated in (Rougui et al., 2009). This algorithm detects precisely the signal beginning and its end, using properties of wavelet transform.

The second module (M.2) is a low-stage classification one. It processes the sound received from the first module (M.1) in order to separate the speech signals from the sound ones. The method used by this module is based on Gaussian Mixture Model (GMM) [14] (K-means followed by Expectation Maximization in 20 steps). There are other possibilities for signal classification: Hidden Markov Model (HMM), Bayesian method, etc. Even if similar results have been obtained with other methods, their high complexity and high time consumption prevent from real-time implementation. A preliminary step before signal classification is the extraction of acoustic parameters: LFCC (Linear Frequency Cepstral Coefficients) 24 filters. The choice of this type of parameters relies on their properties: bank of filters with constant bandwidth, which leads to equal resolution at high frequencies often encountered in life sounds. The best performances have been obtained with 24 Gaussians.

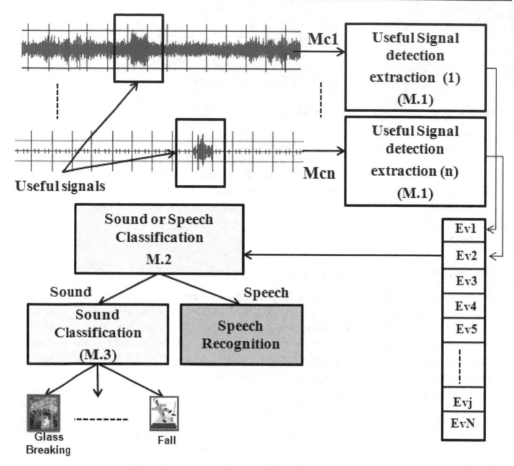

Fig. 2. Anason software architecture

The sound classification module (M.3) classifies the detected sound between predefined sound classes. This module is based, also, on a GMM algorithm. The LFCC acoustical parameters have been used for the same reasons than for sound/speech module and with the same composition: 24 filters. A loglikelihood is computed for the unknown signal according to each predefined sound classes; the sound class with the biggest log likelihood is the output of this module.

4.2 Vital signals wearable device (RFpat)

The wearable device named RFpat (Hoppenot et al., 2009), designed by Telecom SudParis and integrated by ASICA, is devoted to the surveillance of the vital status of the care receiver, transmitting a fall index after validation by an embedded algorithm. Further functionalities of the wearable device include the eventual use of the emergency call button, the determination of the heart pulse rate (beat/minute) and of a posture index, a movement frequency index and a technical status of the device.

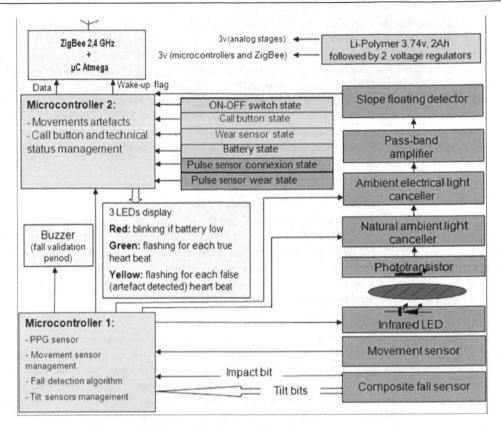

Fig. 3. Internal structure of the wearable device (RFpat)

In a case of emergency situation, for example if the care receiver has fallen down without standing up, with an eventual short delay, afterwards or has pushed the call button, the wearable device will transmit via ZigBee communication the corresponding alarm index to an in-home base station, which is connected to the multimodal platform. If no emergency event occurs, data are transmitted to this receiver every 30 seconds. In case of wireless link interruption, the data will be stored into an internal flash memory of the ZigBee transceiver and pushed through this ZigBee link when recovered.

The device use two microcontrollers (Figure 3), the first is processing "actimetric" sensors i.e. fall, movement and tilt sensor and driving analog switches used for the sampling process of the PPG signal pre-conditioner, the second being devoted to the processing of the pulse sensor. The ZigBee transceiver is also driven by the second microcontroller. All the circuits are supplied by a Lithium-Polymer battery element of 3.7 volts followed by 2 voltage regulators providing a voltage of 3 volts, one for the digital circuits and the ZigBee module, the second being used to supply the analog circuits.

The vital signals terminal is planned as a mobile device worn by the person of care in the smart home environment as well as in the short range outside environment (garden etc.).

The mobile device is connected to the base station with a ZigBee network. The simple version of the network is working with two nodes. One node is defined as the coordinator, which is the base station on the central smart home control PC. The other node is defined as one end device, which is normally the wearable device. In poor RF conditions another node defined as a routing device that can extend the range between the base station and the wearable device. We have chosen the ZigBee IEEE 802.15.4 protocol because it is a secure and common protocol in the smart home environment. The most important advantages are the good power management and a good indoor wireless range with added routers if needed, which was preferred to a high bandwidth (WiFi for instance). We normally transmit 3 bytes every 30 seconds.

4.3 Home automation sensors

The in-home healthcare monitoring systems have to solve an important issue of privacy. When developing our multi-modal platform, we chose the monitoring modules such that they have the less intrusive incidence on the monitored elderly person. We equipped our test apartment with wireless infrared sensors connected to a remote computer. The computer automatically receives and saves data obtained from the different sensors. Data corresponding to movements are collected twice per second, and stored with the event time in a specific file.

The sensors are activated by the person's passage underneath, and remained activated as long as there is movement under that sensor and for an additional time period of ½ seconds after the movement end. The results from the automatic processing of this data are displayed in the form of list with all movements noted together with the time and each movement's duration. This subsystem called Gardien is also able to display the data either in the form of graph (activity duration versus days) or as three-dimensional histograms (each sensor activation versus time).

A set of wireless ambient sensors is added to this subsystem, they are designated for telemonitoring the environment of the patient and his surroundings. It includes state change sensors for active devices detection, contact sensors which are responsible for door and windows opening /closing detection, temperature sensors, fire sensors, flood sensors and light sensors.

5. Fuzzy logic activities recognition approach

5.1 Parameter and method elaboration

The main advantages of using fuzzy logic system are the simplicity of the approach and the capacity of dealing with the complex data acquired from the different sensors. Fuzzy set theory offers a convenient way to do all possible combinations with these sensors. Fuzzy set theory is used in this system to monitor and to recognize the activities of people within the environment in order to timely provide support for safety, comfort, and convenience. Automatic health monitoring is predominantly composed of location and activity information. Abnormality also could be indicated by the lack of an activity or an abnormal activity detection which will cause or raise the home anxiety. Table 1 lists what we wish to automatically recognize.

ADLs of using devices	ADLs of Human body motion
getting up, toilet, bathing, going out of home, enter home, washing dishes, doing laundry, washing hands, watching TV, listening radio, cleaning talking on telephone, cooking	sleeping, walking, standing up setting down, laying exercising

Table 1. Fuzzy List ADLS to be recognized by the telemonitoring platform

The first step for developing this approach is the Fuzzification of system outputs and inputs obtained from each sensor and subsystem.

From Anason subsystem three inputs are built. The first one is the sound environment classification, all detected sound class and expressions are labeled on a numerical scale according to their source. Nine membership functions are set up in this numerical scale according to sound sources as it is in table 2.

Membership Function	Composition
Human Sound	snoring, yawn, sneezing, cough, cry, scream, laugh
Speech	key words and expressions
Multimedia Sounds	TV, radio, computer, music
Door sounds	door clapping, door knob, key ring
Water sounds	water flushing, water in washbasin, coffee filter
Ring tone	telephone ring, bell door, alarm, alarm clock
Object sound	chair, table, tear-turn paper, step foot
Machine sounds	coffee machine, dishwasher, electrical shaver, microwave, vacuum cleaner, washing machine, air conditioner
Dishwasher	glass vs glass, glass wood, plastic vs plastic, plastic vs wood, spoon vs table

Table 2. Fuzzy sets defined for the ANASON classification input

Two other inputs are associated to each SNR calculated on each microphone (two microphones are used in the current application), and these inputs are split into three fuzzy levels: low, medium and high.

The wearable terminal RFpat produce five inputs; Heart rate for which three fuzzy levels are specified normal, low and high; Activity which has four fuzzy sets: immobile, rest, normal and agitation; Posture is represented by two membership functions standing up / sitting down and lying; Fall and call have also two fuzzy levels: Fall/Call and No Fall/Call.

The defined area of each membership function associated to heart rate or activity is adapted to each monitored elderly person. In our application we use only posture, and activity inputs.

For each infrared sensor C_i a counter of motion detection with three fuzzy levels (low, medium, high) is associated, and a global one for all infrared sensors.

The time input has five membership functions morning, noon, afternoon, evening and night which are also adapted to patient habits.

For each main machine in the house a change state sensor S device,s name is associated. It has two membership functions turn on and turn off. One debit sensor for water is included in our application. Three membership functions characterize this sensor, low, medium and high. The output of our fuzzy logic ADL recognition contains some activities which are selected from the table I. They are Sleeping (S), Getting up (GU), Toileting (T), Bathing (B), Washing hands (WH), Washing dishes (WD), Doing laundry (DL), Cleaning (CL), Going out of home (GO), Enter home (EH), Walking (W), Standing up (SU), Setting down (SD),Laying (L), Resting (R), Watching TV (WT) and Talking on telephone (TT). These membership functions are ordered, firstly according to the area where they maybe occur and secondly according to the degree of similarity between them.

The next step of our fuzzy logic approach is the fuzzy inference engine which is formulated by a set of fuzzy IF-THEN rules. This second stage uses domain expert knowledge regarding activities to produce a confidence in the occurrence of an activity. Rules allow the recognition of common performances of an activity, as well as the ability to model special cases. An example fuzzy rule for alarm detection is:

If (Anason is Machine sound) and (Activity is motion) and ($C_{Overall}$ is high) and (C_B is high) and (C_5 is high) and (S_{vacuum} is turn on) Then (ADLs is Cleaning).

A confidence factor is accorded to each rule and in order to aggregate these rules we have the choice between Mamdani or Sugeno approaches available under our fuzzy logic component. After rules aggregation the Defuzzification is performed by the centroid of area for the ADLs output.

5.2 Software implementation

Figure 4 provides a synoptic block-diagram scheme of the software architecture of the ADL recognition platform; it is implemented under LabwindowsCVI and C++ software. It is developed in a form of design component. We can distinguish three main components, the acquisition module, the synchronization module and the fuzzy inference component.

It can run off-line by reading data from a data base or online by processing in real time data acquired via the acquisition module. To avoid the loss of data, a real time module with two multithreading tasks is integrated in the synchronization component. The platform is now synchronized on Gardien subsystem because of his smallest sampling rate (2 Hz) and periodicity. Indeed in some situations the RFpat system may be not used by the elderly person, namely if no recommendations relative to its cardiac watch or a particular risk of fall are given by the Doctor.

The telemonitoring system with its Fuzzy tools allows the easy configuration of input intervals of fuzzification, the writing of fuzzy rules and the configuration of the defuzzification method. The general interface of the system allows to build up membership functions of inputs and outputs and displaying them. We could also write rules on text file

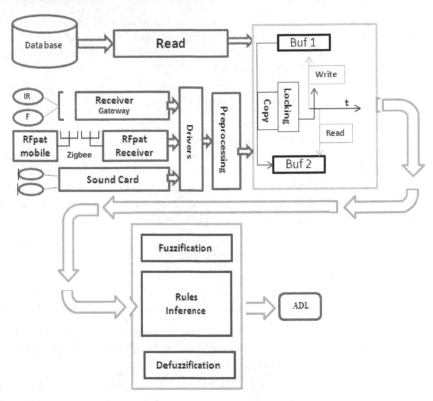

Fig. 4. software implementation design

by using a specific language, understandable by the telemonitoring system. This framework also allows for rules to be added, deleted, or modified to fit each particular resident based on knowledge about their typical daily activities, physical status, cognitive status, and age. The software implementation is validated with many experimental tests. The results and the rules which produced them are displayed on the main panel.

6. DSS integration system

The decision of this multimodal data fusion platform is sent to a real time decision integration system. This integration is performed by a multi-agent system (MAS) in which each agent coordinates separately with a decision support systems (DSS). The pertinence of each DSS is determined by the occurrence of false and undetected alarms.

The agent delegates the decisional task to its corresponding DSS. The out coming decisions' data are then formatted by the agent in an abstract decision report. This report format is recognized in the whole system and enables a central agent to make the final decision. A real-time negotiation of the decisions is able to improve the usage of appropriate resources within an acceptable response time. Thus, this multi-agent system architecture enables these DSS to have uniform view of the decision concept and to exchanges both knowledge and intelligence, even if they implement several decisional techniques (Neural networks, fuzzy logic). In a remote healthcare monitoring system, we need such a solution in order to understand the behavior of the patient and the state of its domicile. Then, we can make the system evolve according to the analyzed behavior.

6.1 Decision abstraction and priority assignation

In intelligent remote healthcare monitoring, a decision support system uses the data flow of several modalities to generate decisions about the patient's situation. To standardize the decision concept, we classify the generated decisions by the modalities used. The considered modalities in our system are: sound, speech, physiological data (e.g. activeness and pulse rate), actimetric data (localization, falls), video, sensor states and alarm calls. Generally, every decision is based on global pertinence calculated by combining the pertinence affected to each decision modality. For a d decision, the global pertinence is:

$$Gp(d) = \sum_{m_i} p_i(d) \cdot c_i \tag{10}$$

Where: m_i is the modalities used for the decision d, p_i is the pertinence of the decision d according to the modality m_i, c_i is the coefficient of the modality m_i accorded by the DSS.

When a DSS generates a decision, it sends the data concerning this decision to its encapsulating agent. The agent reorganizes these data in a decision report (type, pertinence, arrival date ...), which it then sends to the central agent.

The collective decision is made in two phases:

- Phase 1: the central agent starts the wait window of phase-1. The duration of the wait window depends on the trigger decision data (agent affinity, modalities used ...). In this paper, we do not detail the computing algorithm of the waiting duration. The decision messages received in phase-1 are called SEND decisions. A SEND decision is a spontaneous decision. It is not a response to a previous request. In the case of a trigger decision, we also define the pertinence threshold. The arriving decision reports during this first wait window are fused with the trigger decision. If the final decision's pertinence surpasses the threshold, the decision is confirmed as an alert. If the wait window is terminated without attaining the pertinence threshold, the central agent starts the second phase of decision.
- Phase 2: the central agent starts a new wait window. During this wait window, a real-time consensus is launched among the agents concerned by the trigger decision modalities. For this purpose, the central agent assigns to each concerned agent a consensus priority. This is computed as follows:

$$p_i(d) = \sum_{m_j \in d} A_{ij} \cdot c_j \tag{11}$$

Where m_j is the modalities used in the trigger decision d, c_j is the corresponding coefficient for each modality, A_{ij} is the affinity of the agent i for the modality m_j.

During this second wait window, the received message may be SEND decisions. As they do
not concern the launched consensus, they are placed in the wait queue. The response
messages are called CALL BACK decisions. At the end of the second wait window, the
central agent computes the global pertinence of the received CALL BACK decisions. If the
pertinence threshold is reached, the trigger decision is confirmed otherwise it is rejected and
a learning procedure is sent to the responsible agent. In this article, we do not detail the
inner learning procedure of such an agent.

6.2 Real-time scheduling of the collective decision process

One of the major problems in the field of multi-agent systems is the need for methods and
tools that facilitate the development of systems of this kind. In fact, the acceptance of multi-
agent system development methods in industry depends on the existence of the necessary
tools to support the analysis, design and implementation of agent-based software. The
emergence of useful real-time artificial intelligence systems makes the multi-agent system
especially appropriate for development in a real-time environment (Julian and Botti, 2004).
Furthermore, the response time of the DSS in a remote healthcare monitoring system is a
central issue. Unfortunately the DSS studied in this context does not give a real-time
response. For this reason we aim to control, as much as possible, the response time of their
encapsulating Agents. The Gaia role model we presented in section 3 guaranties that the
agent encapsulation of a DSS makes its response time transparent to the other agents.

6.2.1 General operating principle

This work has focused on a time-critical environment in which the acting systems can be
monitored by intelligent agents which require real-time communication in order to better
achieve the system's goal, which is detecting, as fast as possible, the distress situation of the
patient. The works of (Julian and Botti, 2004) define a real-time agent as an agent with
temporal restrictions in some of its responsibilities or tasks. According to this same work, a
real-time multi-agent system is one where at least one of its agents is a real-time agent. The
central agent is the unique decision output of our system. We will apply these definitions by
focusing on the real-time scheduling of the central agent tasks. Firstly the different tasks of
this agent must be defined. Subsequently, diverse scenarios and the priority assignation
rules may be defined.

As explained previously, the central agent receives all the decision reports in the system.
The first main issue is thus the scheduling of the treatment of these messages. For each
decision received the central agent chooses the concerned agents and assigns a response
deadline to each one, based on the degree of expertise of the concerned agent in the
modalities used. We propose a scheduling model that enables the reaching of a consensus
between the different concerned agents while respecting the defined response deadlines.

6.2.2 Definition of the central agent tasks

As described in figure 6, an agent has two main functions: conative and cognitive. In the
case of the central agent, the cognitive function consists of communicating with the other
agents. The conative function consists of making final decisions.

This classification leads us to this list of tasks assigned to the central agent:

- Cognitive tasks:
- Message reception: connection establishing and stream reading.
- Message classification: according to the type of the request, this task classifies each message in the appropriate wait queue.
- Entities representation: this task comes into play at each collective decision cycle. Its role is to keep the state of the other agents in the central agent memory, as well as that of the central agent itself.
- Message send : connection establishing and stream writing
- Conative tasks:
- Request analysis and execution: this task executes the selected message requests. Generally it triggers another task of the central agent (representation, message send, decision)
- Decision: this task maintains a fusion buffer in which the message execution task puts the decision message. When this task is activated, it adds all the un-executed messages in the highest priority wait queue to the fusion buffer.
- Deadline assignation: this task assigns an absolute deadline to each message before classification
- Message selection: this task selects the message to be executed from the message buffer.
- Phase manager: this task is responsible for the transition between the collective decision phases. It comes into operation when a wait window is closed or when a collective decision is made. Its main role is changing the priority of central agent tasks.

Each task is executed according to the automaton described in figure 6.

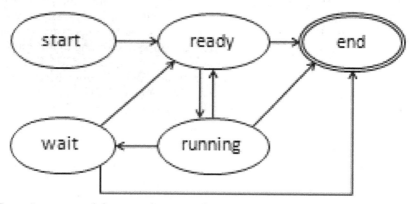

Fig. 6. Execution states of the central agent tasks.

6.2.3 Message classification

The central agent message buffer consists of 3 different wait queues (WQ): the CALL BACK queue, for the CALL BACK decision messages, the SEND queue, for the SEND decision message and the Best Effort queue, for the other communication messages (decisions, service requests …)

The BE queue is FIFO scheduled (First In First Out). There is no deadline or priority consideration in this queue. The CALL BACK and the SEND queue are EDF scheduled (George et al., 1996). EDF is the preemptive version of Earliest Deadline First non idling scheduling. EDF schedules the tasks according to their absolute deadlines: the task with the shortest absolute deadline has the highest priority.

Each message deadline must be determined before being classified in a wait queue. For this reason the Deadline assignation task, the message classification task and the message reception task must be fused. In fact, when a message arrives, the message reception task is activated. It cannot then be preempted before assigning the message to its corresponding wait queue.

6.2.4 Queue priority and message selection

The message queues have dynamic priorities. This priority is assigned by a phase manager task. In phase-1, the SEND queue has the highest priority. In phase-2, the CALL BACK queue has the highest priority. While the message buffer is not empty, the message execution task's state is *Ready*. When it passes to execution, it selects the shortest deadline message from the highest priority queue. During the wait window of phase-1, the received SEND must be executed first. Thus we assign the highest priority to the SEND queue. When this wait window is closed, the decision task gets the highest priority. The CALL BACK queue has the highest priority in phase-2. Thus a phase cannot be terminated until the corresponding wait queue is empty and all the received decisions fused.

6.2.5 Global scheduling of the central agent

The main scheduling algorithm of the central agent is FP/HPF. FP/HPF denotes the preemptive Fixed Priority Highest Priority First algorithm with an arbitrary priority assignment (Lehoczky, 1990).

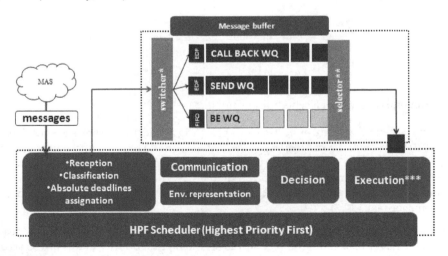

Fig. 7. Real-time scheduling of the central agent.

In table 2, we present the priority evolution of each task during the different steps of the 2-phase collective decision (the higher the number, the higher the priority). The phase manager task always has the highest priority. In fact, it is responsible for changing the system phase and the priority assignation.

6.2.6 Scheduling sample

In figure 8, we present a scheduling sample in a system composed of a central agent (CA) and five other agents (A1, A2, A3, A4, A5). The red arrows represent the movement of the task to the ready state. Here we present the priority assigned to each task at the beginning of each phase. We suppose that the message wait queues are initially empty.

Task	Wait For trigger	Phase-1		Phase-2	
		wait	Decision	wait	Decision
reception	4	4	2	3	1
Send	1	1	3	4	3
decision	2	2	4	1	4
execution	3	3	1	2	2
phase manager	5	5	5	5	5

Table 3. Priority variation of the central agent tasks

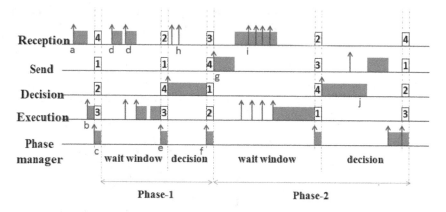

Fig. 8. Temporal diagram of a scheduling sample

Our sample scenario goes through these stages: a trigger decision from A3 is received. The execution task treats the received trigger and then requests that the phase manager start a new collective decision process. The phase manager starts the first phase. It opens a new wait window and changes the priority of the CA tasks. During phase-1, two SEND decisions are received (from A1 and A4). The first wait window is terminated by the phase manager task.

The highest priority is assigned to the decision task. The pertinence threshold is not reached. The phase manager task starts the second phase. The highest priority in this task is accorded to the send task in order to allow the CA to activate the consensus.

During the phase-1 decision process, the CA receives two SEND messages. The reception task is preempted because it has a lower priority. In phase-2, A1, A2, A4 and A5 are involved in the consensus (a choice based on the trigger decision modalities). A SEND and 3 CALL BACK decisions are received (positive: A1 and A5, negative: A4). The final fusion reaches the pertinence threshold. Two learning procedures are sent to A4 and A2. We suppose that the message buffer is initially empty.

The phase manager task is responsible for changing the priority of the central Agent tasks. We can observe on figure 8 the priority assigned to each task at the start of each new phase. The task manager is activated at the end of the wait windows to hand over to the decision task. At the end of its treatment, the decision task hands back to the phase manager task which starts a new phase by changing the priority of the other tasks.

7. Experimentation and results

The proposed method was experimentally achieved on a simulated data in order to demonstrate its effectiveness. This simulation gives very promising results for the ADLs recognition. Figure 9 shows results for a stream of a data. This fist study was devoted to the evaluation of the system by taking into account rules used in this fuzzy inference system.

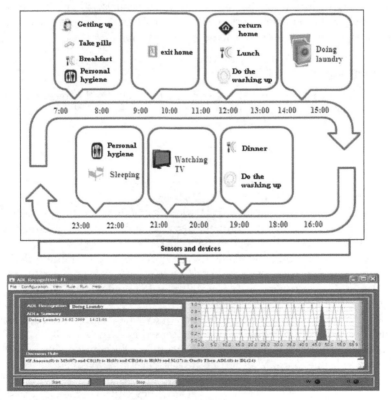

Fig. 9. ADLs recognition experiment for a stream data.

The used strategy consisted in realizing several tests with different combination rules, and based on obtained results one rule is added to the selected set of rules in order to get the missed detection. With this strategy good results are reached for the ADL output (about 97% of good ADL detection).

The experimentation described here is preliminary but demonstrates that ubiquitous, simple sensor devices can be used to recognize activities of daily living from real homes. The system can be easily retrofitted in existing home environments with no major modifications or damage.

8. Conclusion

In this chapter we have explore the cutting-edge research and technologies in monitoring daily activities using a set of sensors deployed in the house. The objective of the research is to provide a feasible solution for improving care for elderly people, while significantly reducing the healthcare cost. Focusing on the open problem of multiple persons monitoring, we have used an optimal set of sensors, design an algorithm for ADL recognition based on fuzzy logic, and implement a prototype. This approach provides robust and high accuracy recognition rate. Assisting elderly persons in place will benefit from the results of this research. The next objective of this research is to use these identification activities for building a model for measuring the home anxiety, that increases or decreases according to the detection activity and the state of each device in the home.

9. Acknowledgments

This work is supported by the European Commission in the frame of the Seventh Framework Program (FP7/2007-2011) within the CompanionAble Project (grant agreement n. 216487).

10. References

Adlassnig K. P., Fuzzy set theory in medical diagnosis, IEEE Tr. On Syst.,Man, and Cybernetics, March/April 1986,pp. 260–265.

Bezdek J. C. & Pal S. K., "Fuzzy Models for Pattern Recognition," IEEE Press, 1992.

Buckley,J.J , Eslami E, An introduction to fuzzy logic and fuzzy sets. Advances in Soft Computing. Physica-Verlag, Germany, 2002.

Burges C. J. C., A tutorial on SVM for Pattern Recognition. Data Mining and Knowledge Discovery, volume 2, 1998, pp. 121–167.

Cowell R., Dawid A., Lauritzen S. & Spiegelhalter D., Probabilistic Networks and Expert Systems, 1999, ISBN : 0-387-98767-3.

Doermann D. and Mihalcik D., A system approach to achieving carernet, an integrated and intelligent telecare system, IEEE Trans Biomed Eng, 2:1-9, 1998.

Dreyfus G., Martinez J.M, Samuelides M., Gordon M., Badran F., Thiria S. & Hrault L., R´eseaux de neurones. M´ethodologie et applications, Eyrolles, 2002.

Dunn J.C., A fuzzy relative of the isodata process and its use in detecting compact well-seperated clusters. IEEE Tran. on Systems, Man, and Cybernetics, pp. 32–57, 1973.

Elger G. & Furugren B., "smartbo",an ict an computer-based demonstration home for disabled people, in Proc. of the 3rd TIDE Congress : Technology for Inclusive Design and Equality Improving the Quality of Life for the European Citizen, Helsinki, Finland, 1998.

George, L., Rivierre, N., Spuri, M.: Preemptive and non-preemptive real-time uniprocessor scheduling". INRIA, research Report 2966, Sept. 1996.

Hoppenot P., Boudy J., Delarue S., Baldinger J.-L. , Colle E., "Assistance to the maintenance in residence of handicapped or old people JESA – Volume 43 – N° 3/2009 pp. 315 – 335.

Jang J.S.R., Sun C. T. & Mizutani E., Neuro-Fuzzy and Soft Computing :A Computational Approach to Learning and Machine Intelligence. Prentice Hall Upper Saddle River, NJ 1997.

Julian V., Botti V., Developing real-time multi-agent systems. Integr. Comput.-Aided Eng. vol. 11,n° 2, p. 135-149, Amsterdam, April 2004.

Keller J.M. & Krishnapuram R., "Fuzzy set methods in computer vision," In R.R. Yager and L.A. Zadeh, editors, An Introduction to Fuzzy logic Applications in Intelligent Systems Kluwer Academic, pp. 121–145, 1992.

Lalande A., Legrand L., Walker P. M., Jaulent M. C., Guy F., Cottin Y. & Brunotte F., Automatic detection of cardiac contours on MR images using fuzzy logic and dynamic programming, Proc. AMIA Ann. Fall Symp. 1997, pp. 474–478.

Lee S.W & Mase K., "Activity and location recognition using wearable sensors," IEEE Pervasive Computing, 1(3):2432, 2002.

Lehoczky J.P., Fixed priority scheduling of periodic task sets with arbitrary deadlines. Proc. 11th IEEE Real-Time Systems Symposium, FL, USA, pp. 201-209, 5-7 Dec. 1990.

Mandal D.P., Murthy C. A. & Pal S. K., "Formulation of a multivalued recognition system," IEEE Transactions on Systems, Man, and Cybernetics, 22:607–620 1992.

Mason D., Linkens D. & Edwards N., Self-learning fuzzy logic control in medicine, Proc. AIME'97, (E. Keravnou et al., eds.), Lecture Notes in Artificial Intelligence 1211, Springer-Verlag, Berlin 1997, pp. 300–303.

Medjahed H., Istrate D., Boudy J., Steenkeste F., Baldinger J.L., Belfeki I., Martins V. & Dorizzi B. , A Multimodal Platform for Database Recording and Elderly People Monitoring, BIOSIGNALS 2008, Jan 2008, Funchal-Madeira, Portugal, pp.385-392.

Mizumoto M., Toyoda J. & Tanaka K., "General formulation of formal grammars," Info Sci., 4:87-100, 1972.

Noury N., Barralon P., Virone G., Boissy P., Hamel M. & Rumeau P.,A smart sensor based on rules and its evaluation in daily routines, in Proc of the IEEE-EMBC, pages 3286-3289, Cancun, Mexico, September 2003.

Pal S.K. & Chakraborty B., "Fuzzy set theoretic measure for automatic feature evaluation," IEEE Transactions on Systems, Man, and Cybernetics, 16:754-760, 1986.

Pao Y. H., "Adaptive Pattern Recognition and Neural Networks," Addison-Wesley, 1989.

Pedrycz W., "Fuzzy sets in pattern recognition: methodology and methods," Pattern Recognition, 23(1/2):121-146, 1990.

Rougui J.E., Istrate D. & Souidene W., Audio Sound Event Identification for distress situations and context awareness, EMBC2009, September 2-6, Minneapolis, USA, 2009, pp. 3501-3504.

Ruspini E. H., "A new approach to clustering," Inform, Control, 15(1):22-32, 1969.

Shackle G.L., "Decision, Order and Time in Human Affairs," Cambridge Univ. Press

Shafer G., "A Mathematical Theory of Evidence," Princeton Univ. Press 1979.

Sugeno M., Theory of fuzzy integrals and its applications. Doct. Thesis, Tokyo IT 1974.

West G.A.W., Greenhill S. & Venkatesh S., A probabilistic approach to the anxious home for activity monitoring. in Proc. 29th Annual International Computer Software and Applications Conference: COMPSAC, pages 335-340, Edinburgh, Scotland 2005.

Zadeh L.A., Fuzzy sets as a basis for theory of possibility, Fuzzy Set Systems. pp. 3–28, 1978.

Zahlmann G., Scherf M. & Wegner A., A neurofuzzy classifier for a knowledge-based glaucoma monitor, Proc. AIME'97, (E. Keravnou et al., eds.), Lecture Notes in Artificial Intelligence 1211, Springer-Verlag, Berlin 1997, pp. 273–284.

4

Fuzzy Logic and Neuro-Fuzzy Networks for Environmental Hazard Assessment

Ignazio M. Mancini, Salvatore Masi,
Donatella Caniani and Donata S. Lioi
Department of Engineering and Physics of the Environment,
University of Basilicata,
Italy

1. Introduction

Pollution and management of the environment are serious problems which concern the entire planet; the main responsibility should be attributed to human activities that contribute significantly to damage the environment, leading to an imbalance of natural ecosystems. In recent years, numerous studies focused on the three environmental compartments: soil, water and air. The pollution of groundwater is a widespread problem. The causes of pollution are often linked to human activities, including waste disposal.

Solid waste management has become an important environmental issue in industrialized countries. The most serious problems are related to solid waste disposal. Landfill is still the most used disposal technique but not the safest. In fact, a breakdown of containment elements could easily occur even in controlled landfills. This breakdown could cause contamination of aquifer that is environmental pollution. Such contamination can be mitigated by performing remediation and environmental restoration. The assessment of environmental pollution risk can be performed with different degrees of detail and precision.

Various statistical and mathematical models can be used for a qualitative risk assessment. The planning of a program for environmental remediation and restoration can be supported by expeditious methodologies that allow us to obtain a hierarchical classification of contaminated sites. The literature offers some expeditious and qualitative methods including fuzzy logic (Zadeh, 1965), neural networks and neuro-fuzzy networks, which are more objective methods. The three artificial intelligence systems differ among themselves in some respects: fuzzy inference system learns knowledge of data only through the fuzzy rules; neural network is able to learn knowledge of data using the weights of synaptic connections; neuro-fuzzy systems are able to learn knowledge of neural data with neural paradigm and represent it in the form of fuzzy rules.

Fuzzy logic was founded in 1965 by Zadeh. The first applications date back to the nineties. They were mainly used to control industrial processes, household electrical appliances and means of transport. Later, this approach was used in several fields including the environment. In fact, it could be used for assessing environmental risk related to contamination of groundwater. The fuzzy approach is advantageous because it allows us a quick assessment of the risk, but is disadvantageous because of the increasing complexity in the definition of fuzzy rules along with the increasing of the number of parameters. In many situations, when the number of parameters are considered high in the analysis, application of these techniques is cumbersome and complex and could be used for neuro-fuzzy models. These models reduce the complexity because they use training data. The neuro-fuzzy model was supported by a sensitivity analysis in order to address the problem of subjectivity and uncertainty of model input data.

1.1 Fuzzy logic

Fuzzy logic is a binary logic, which is inspired by Buddhist philosophy, which considers the world as something continuous. The fuzzy logic theory derives from the Persian-American engineer, Lotfi Zadeh, who theorized it in 1965 in an article entitled "Information and Control". In traditional logic, Aristotelian principles of non-contradiction and the excluded middle are valid. The principle of non-contradiction states that if X is a generic set and x a generic element, then x may belong to the whole X or not. The fuzzy systems deal with data and their manipulation with greater flexibility than traditional systems. The binary logic (or classical) is only concerned with what is completely true and, as a result, with what is completely false. Fuzzy logic instead extends its interest even to what is not completely true, what is probable or uncertain. The fuzzy logic is based on a linguistic approach, in which words or phrases of natural language are used instead of numbers. This approach simplifies complex situations and concepts which may use the traditional logic. In particular, the fuzzy logic operates on mathematical entities that are fuzzy sets. Fuzzy sets obey rules, structures and axioms which are very similar to those of classical sets; the difference is that an object can simultaneously belong to several subsets, in contrast to the classical theory. In the fuzzy world, membership to a subset is associated to a degree of membership. The set of deduction rules to be applied to a given system to achieve results through the use of fuzzy logic is defined the fuzzy inference process. Main phases of the fuzzy approach (Fig. 1) are the following: definition of membership functions, fuzzification, inference and fuzzy output.

Definition of membership functions is the main step on which all the other subsequent operations are based. Such functions, representing the fuzzy sets, can take different shapes (trapezoidal, triangular, Gaussian, etc.) according to the situations, and by convention can take values included between 0 and 1.

The fuzzification is the process by which input variables are converted to fuzzy measures belonging to certain classes such as Very Low, Low, Medium, High, Very High. This operation normalizes all the data in the interval [0-1]. In this way, comparisons between different amounts, measured in different scales are also possible.

The inference is the phase in which rules of combination of fuzzy sets are applied and it is possible to deduce a result. The rules are linguistic expressions that are translated into a mathematical formalism with the exspression "if ... then" of the logic itself.

The output is a fuzzy membership value that can be used "pure" as a qualitative property or "defuzzificated", as a real number compatible with non-fuzzy approaches (Silvert, 2000).

"Defuzzification" can be done using different methods, the most widely used one is the center of gravity, which calculates the center of gravity of the final fuzzy set and returns the value of abscissa.

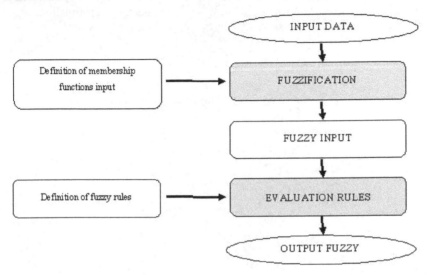

Fig. 1. Flow chart of the developed Fuzzy Inference System.

1.1.1 Fuzzification

Fuzzification is a procedure through which the input variables are turned into fuzzy measures of their membership to given classes. Such a conversion from deterministic sizes to fuzzy sizes is performed through the membership functions pre-set for those classes. A membership function (Fig.2) is a function which associates a value (usually numerical) with the level of membership to the set. By convention, the real number which represents the level of membership [μ (x)] takes a 0 value when the element does not belong to the set, and 1 when it belongs to it completely.

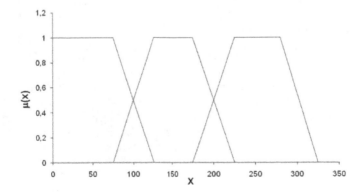

Fig. 2. Membership function.

Membership functions can be of several types: the simplest are made up of straight lines, while the most used are the triangular (Fig. 3) and trapezoidal (Fig. 4) functions; the former are characterized by a triangular trend while the latter by a trapezoidal one. The advantage of these functions is in their simplicity. The triangular membership function depends on three scalar parameters a, b and c and is given by the following expression:

$$f(x;a,b,c) = \max\left(\min\left(\frac{x-a}{b-a}, \frac{c-x}{c-b}\right), 0 \right) \qquad (1)$$

while the trapezoidal one depends on four scalar parameters (a, b, c and d), as shown in the following formula:

$$f(x;a,b,c,d) = \max\left(\min\left(\frac{x-a}{b-a}, 1, \frac{d-x}{d-c}\right), 0 \right) \qquad (2)$$

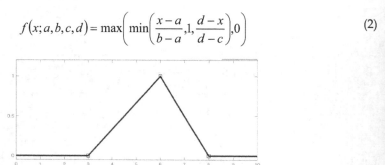

Fig. 3. Triangular membership function.

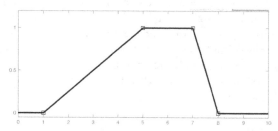

Fig. 4. Trapezoidal membership function.

There are other more complex functions, i.e. the Gauss function made up of a simple Gaussian curve (Fig. 5) which depends on parameters r and c (Eq. (3)); and the Gauss2 function (Fig. 6) given by the fusion of two different Gaussian functions and depending on four parameters: r_1 and c_1, which define the shape of the function in the left part, and r_2 e c_2, which define the shape of the function in the right part. Moreover, between these types of functions, there is the bell membership function (Gbell) (Fig. 7) which is a hybrid of the Gaussian function; it is mainly used to manage non-fuzzy sets and depends on three parameters: a, b and c (Eq. (4))

$$f(x;\sigma,c) = e^{\frac{-(x-c)^2}{2\sigma^2}} \qquad (3)$$

$$f(x;a,b,c) = \frac{1}{1 + \left| \frac{x-c}{a} \right|^{2b}}$$

(4)

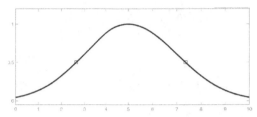

Fig. 5. Gauss membership function.

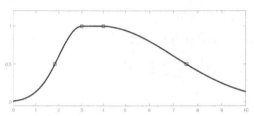

Fig. 6. Gauss2 membership function.

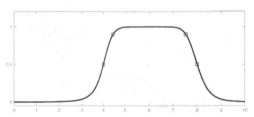

Fig. 7. Generalized bell (Gbell) membership function.

Despite their simplicity, such functions cannot be used to represent asymmetry, which is important in some applications.

In order to face a possible asymmetry, we can use another type of function, such as the sigmoid function (Fig. 8), which may have left or right asymmetry and a horizontal asymptote. This function is ruled by parameters a and c (Eq. (5))

$$f(x;a,c) = \frac{1}{1 + e^{-a(x-c)}}$$

(5)

In addition to this function, we have further asymmetric functions, the Dsigm and Psigm membership functions represented in Fig. 9 and10 and described by Eq. (6), depending on four parameters a_1, c_1, a_2 and c_2.

$$f(x;a,c) = \frac{1}{1 + e^{-a(x-c)}}$$

(6)

$$\begin{cases} 1, \ x \le a \\ 1 - 2\left(\dfrac{x-a}{b-a}\right)^2, \ a \le x \le \dfrac{a+b}{2} \\ 2\left(\dfrac{b-x}{b-a}\right), \ \dfrac{a+b}{2} \le x \le b \\ 0, \ x \ge b \end{cases} \tag{7}$$

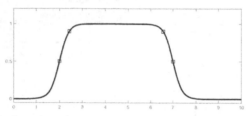

Fig. 8. Sigmoidale (Sig) membership function.

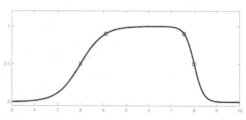

Fig. 9. Dsig membership function.

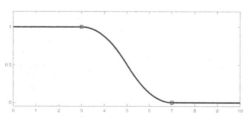

Fig. 10. Psig membership function.

Three more membership functions correlated with them are functions Z (Eq. (7)), S and Pi. The first one is an asymmetric function open to the left, the second is open to the right, while the third one is asymmetric but closed at both ends (Fig. 11-13).

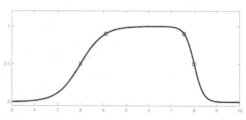

Fig. 11. Z membership function.

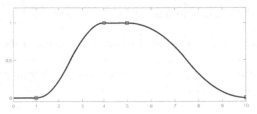

Fig. 12. Pi membership function.

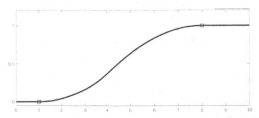

Fig. 13. S membership function.

1.1.2 Fuzzy inference

After the definition of the fuzzy data which comes from the fuzzification process, it is necessary to insert in the decisional engine the rules which supply the fuzzy output. The rules are usually made up of an if–then–else structure, which in its turn is made up of an antecedent which defines the conditions, and a consequent which defines the action. For each input variable of the model, in the antecedent we have a clause of the type (x is L) where L is a linguistic label revealing a fuzzy set. In this way, the antecedent supplies a characterization of the condition of the system we want to model, namely its description in quantitative terms. Usually the antecedent includes a conjunction of clauses, one for each observed variable, while the condition of the consequent determines the condition of outputs.

In conclusion, a fuzzy system can be considered as a non-linear function which transforms a certain number of input variables into output ones through a set of fuzzy rules. In the application of rules, some of them often lead to the same consequence with different levels of strength: in these cases the common custom is choosing the highest value. Following this phase, which is defined fuzzy inference, it is necessary to turn the data coming from the evaluation of rules into real numerical data: this process is the opposite of input fuzzification, in fact it is called either output fuzzification or defuzzification.

1.1.3 Defuzzification

Defuzzification consists in drawing the output deterministic value from the fuzzy model. A careful analysis of the problem is at the basis of a correct defuzzification: it can be linguistic, when the output is a predicate to which a level of membership is associated, or numerical, of "crisp" type (non-fuzzy) (used in fuzzy control). Many criteria of defuzzification exist: often in engineering the choice depends on computational simplicity. The most used defuzzification methods are the following:

- Centroid method: the chosen numerical value for the output is calculated as the centre of mass of the fuzzy set.
- Bisector method: the output is the abscissa of the bisector of the area subtended to the fuzzy data set.
- Middle of maximum method: the output value is determined as the average of maximum values (Mom: middle of maximum).
- Largest of maximum method: the output numerical value is calculated as the maximum of the maximum (Lom: Largest of maximum).
- Smallest of maximum method: the output value is represented by the output minimum value (Som: Smallest of maximum).

Among the methods found in literature, the most common are the centroid and maximum methods.

In the middle of the maximum method, output is obtained as the arithmetic mean of the values of "y" where fuzzy set height is maximum.

B' is the fuzzy set inferred by rules and

$$hgt(B') = \left\{ y \middle| \mu_{B'}(y) = \underset{y \in B'}{Sup}\, \mu_{B'}(y) \right\} \tag{8}$$

is the set value of "y" for which height "μB'(y)" is maximum.

Therefore, it has

$$y_{out} = \frac{\int_{hgt(B')} y\,dy}{\int_{hgt(B')} dy} \tag{9}$$

whose geometric significance is shown in Figure 14:

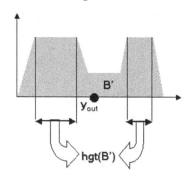

Fig. 14. Geometric significance of the Middle of maximum defuzzification method.

The output of the *Centroid method* is obtained as the abscissa of the center of gravity inferred from the rules in the space of fuzzy sets of algorithm output. The formula in the case of continuous function is:

$$y_{out} = \frac{\int y\mu(y)dy}{\int \mu(y)dy} \tag{10}$$

Whereas, the formula for discrete function is:

$$y_{out} = \frac{\sum_i y_i\mu(y_i)}{\sum_i \mu(y_i)} \tag{11}$$

In *Largest of maximum,* the precise value of the variable output is one of which the fuzzy subset has the maximum truth value. The main disadvantage of this method is that it does not consider the distribution of membership function.

However, the *smallest of maximum method* obtained the minimum value in fuzzy set as output.

2. Fuzzy neural network

The fuzzy neural network essentially fills the gaps in the fuzzy systems as well as other neurals. The fuzzy inference requires heuristics and does not acquire knowledge from input-output relationships as do neural networks. The advantage of a fuzzy neural network compared to a neural structure is that it can be represented by "linguistic rules". The nodes that form a neuro-fuzzy network have weights which do not commonly occur in a system based on a neural network. The network training is done using back-propagation algorithms. The Anfis models (Zimmermann 1991) acquire knowledge from data using algorithms typical of neural networks. This is represented using fuzzy rules. Substantially, neural networks are structured on different levels, starting from the input and output related systems which generate fuzzy rules that guide the process of construction output. As in fuzzy logic, the end result is linked to the fuzzy rules and membership functions. The membership functions can be of various types. The simplest consists of straight lines, while the most used functions are triangular and trapezoidal. There are more complex functions such as the Gauss function which consists of a simple Gaussian curve and function Gauss2 formed by the merger of two different Gaussian functions. In addition, among the functions of this kind, there is a bell membership function (Gbell) which is a hybrid of Gaussian function, and is used primarily to manage non-fuzzy sets. In order to meet any asymmetry, other functions can be used, such as Dsigm, Psigm and Pi.

The scientific literature has various applications of fuzzy neural network from the classical management of Humanoid Robots that will replace humans in dangerous jobs in the medical field or in the field of services (Dusko Katic et al., 2003). The fuzzy neural network was also used in the study of time series of solar activity (Abdel-Fattah Attia et al., 2005), in the assessment of noise in the workplace (Zaheeruddin Garima, 2006) and many others.

2.1 Architecture of a neuro-fuzzy network

The proposed forecasting model for assessing the environmental risk of contamination of aquifers is based on an Adaptive Neural Network Fuzzy Inference System (ANFIS)

(Zimmermann 1991; Jang. 1993). ANFIS algorithm allowed us to calibrate membership functions of the fuzzy inference training the Artificial Neural Network. In order to perform the training, the definition of a matrix of input parameters, a single output value and the number of times (numbers interpolating the training matrix) was necessary.

However, ANFIS models acquire knowledge from data using the typical neural networks algorithms but represent it using fuzzy rules.

TThese kind of neural networks are basically structured on five different levels which autonomously generate systems of fuzzy rules that guide the process of construction of the outputs, starting from related inputs and outputs.

Each node of the first level integrates the membership function associated with the represented fuzzy term. Variables X_i are the linguistic variables that are associated with terms placed in the nodes (A_{11} = Low, A_{21} = High etc.).

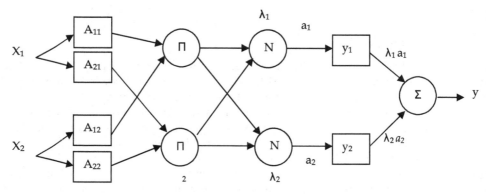

Fig. 15. Architecture of a neuro-fuzzy network.

Nodes of the second level incorporate the antecedents of fuzzy rules. Within these nodes, only an AND logical operation between the active inputs is performed.

In the third level, each node calculates the degree of fulfillment of each rule and returns a weighted term which enters as input in the corresponding node of the next level.

The nodes of this layer incorporate the resulting rules instead. Each node accepts the corresponding weight that comes from the previous level in input, in addition to all the input variables to the first level.

The fifth and last node simply performs the sum of all inputs and returns the final output of the system.

3 Case study

3.1 Fuzzy and neuro-fuzzy models for groundwater pollution risk assessment

This study proposes two methods for environmental risk assessment: fuzzy logic and fuzzy-neural networks. Fuzzy and neuro-fuzzy models have been used to assess environmental risk in landfills, by using groundwater intrinsic vulnerability of landfill hazard (Fig. 17).

Groundwater intrinsic vulnerability has been assessed by a method of zoning for homogeneous areas: the GNDCI-CNR method (M. Civita, 1990). However, landfills hazard has been determined through the use of fuzzy logic and neuro-fuzzy parameters (input data) by considering morphological, hydrological and environmental parameters for each site, such as: water table depth, leachate production, volume and type of waste, landfill coverage, landfill activity and proximity to river. Some of these were obtained using GIS applications.

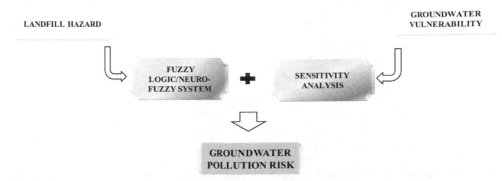

Fig. 16. Fuzzy and neuro-fuzzy models for the groundwater pollution risk.

For the simple management algorithm, the parameters previously indicated were used to define three different fuzzy inferences, as shown in the conceptual scheme in Figure 17. The results obtained through the first two fuzzy inferences, defined as *site vulnerability* and *landfill potentiality* respectively, were then aggregated to the crisp parameter called *landfill conditions*, by obtaining the hazard index of each landfill.

As shown in Figure 17, *site vulnerability*, defined through acclivity, depth to water table and watercourse proximity, allowed us to obtain the site's predisposition to suffer from contamination, namely the site's propensity to be contaminated because of a possible leachate seepage. The increase in vulnerability is favoured by low slopes, proximity to surface watercourses (meant as index, so the higher the index the higher the site vulnerability) and reduced depth of the water table. Thus, the values of the three parameters are low when the trend to undergo contamination is high. On the contrary, the *landfill potential* evaluates the potential of a landfill to release contaminants by virtue of the waste volume and the leachate production. Therefore, with the increase of these two factors such potential will increase. The procedure to determine the *landfill hazard index* combines the results obtained by the two previous fuzzy diagrams with the addition of the *landfill conditions*. The array of required training algorithm has been constructed, considering that the increase in values of the three parameters in the subset result in an increase in the hazard of landfills. The end result of the neuro-fuzzy process has been achieved through the training data which provided a numerical value between 0 and 1 representing the hazard index. In addition to training data that facilitates the definition of fuzzy rules, it is necessary to determine for each of the three fuzzy inferences the following: the type of membership function and the classes (very high, high, medium, low, very low). In conclusion, the results relating to site vulnerability, the landfill potential and the landfill hazard have been obtained.

Among the three output values for each landfill, our attention was mostly focused on the landfill hazard.

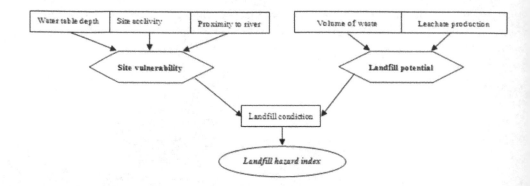

Fig. 17. Conceptual diagram of the implemented fuzzy model.

In addition, to address the risk of subjectivity and to overcome the problem of uncertainty, linked to input data and to the developed models, sensitivity analysis has been used, through which different fuzzy and neuro -fuzzy schemes have been compared. The various fuzzy schemes differ in the type of membership functions and defuzzification methods. Then, each fuzzy scheme is characterized by "if-then" fuzzy rules, membership functions and defuzzification method. The fuzzy rules have been defined considering that groundwater pollution risk rises with the increase of groundwater intrinsic vulnerability and landfill hazard.

However, the neuro-fuzzy schemes differ only in the type of membership functions, while the fuzzy rules are automatically generated by the algorithm using the assigned training matrix. The results obtained from the simulations of both models were compared with input data to identify the best fuzzy and neuro-fuzzy scheme.

The proposed algorithms have been applied to some uncontrolled landfills present in the Basilicata Region, detected through the 2002 census ("Corpo Forestale dello Stato [Forest Rangers]" and "Regional Reclamation Plan"), which identified 469 areas needing reclamation actions, environmental recovery and/or safety measures: 315 in the province of Potenza and 204 in the province of Matera. Among these areas, 290 are illegal landfills (Fig. 18): 122 in the province of Matera and 168 in the province of Potenza.

The comparison of each fuzzy and neuro-fuzzy scheme has been performed by applying statistical tests to the distributions of output data (environmental risk index). The results show that the best scheme for the fuzzy model is characterized by Gauss2 membership functions and Centroid defuzzification method, and the best scheme of neuro-fuzzy model is marked by Gauss membership function. The final results show the environmental risk index and have been recalculated for a classification of groundwater pollution risk in linguistic terms by using a cumulative frequency distribution curve (Fig. 19 and 20).

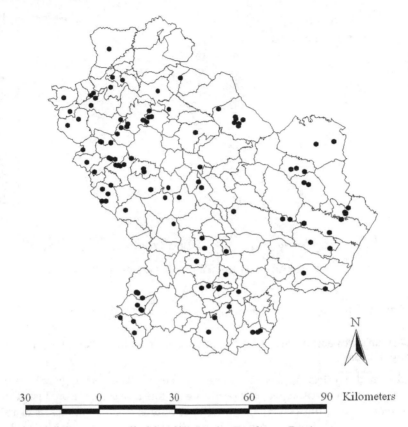

Fig. 18. Location of the uncontrolled landfills in the Basilicata Region.

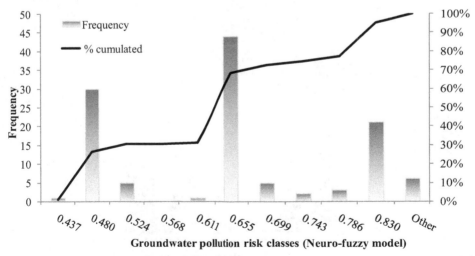

Fig. 19. Cumulated frequency curve of groundwater pollution risk for neuro-fuzzy model.

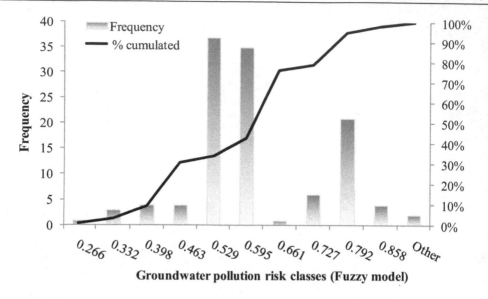

Groundwater pollution risk classes (Fuzzy model)

Fig. 20. Cumulated frequency curve of groundwater pollution risk for fuzzy model.

3.2 Comparison between environmental risk results obtained from the fuzzy and neuro-fuzzy models

The two designed models applied to some aquifers in Basilicata region have provided different results. For this reason, we next performed a statistical comparison. Visual analysis of histograms representing the percentage of aquifers falling in different classes of risk (fuzzy and neuro-fuzzy models) shows that distributions give different classes of risk (Fig. 21).

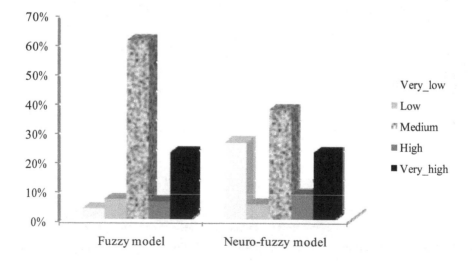

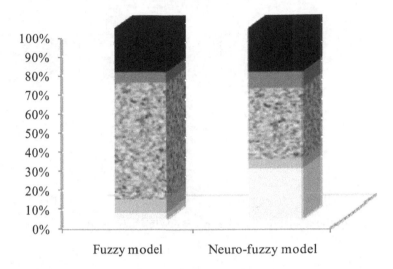

Fig. 21. Distributions of aquifers in classes of risk for fuzzy and neuro-fuzzy models.

We have evaluated the risk indices obtained from the two models for a more appropriate comparison. The assessment of the risk index without the subdivision into classes has demonstrated that the performance of the two distributions is very similar (Fig. 22) as confirmed by the box-plots (Fig. 23).

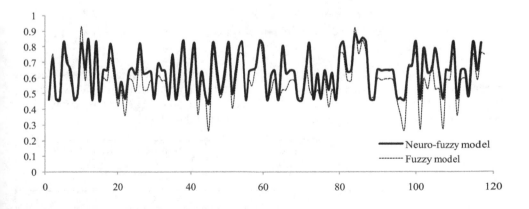

Fig. 22. Variation of the environmental risk index for each site.

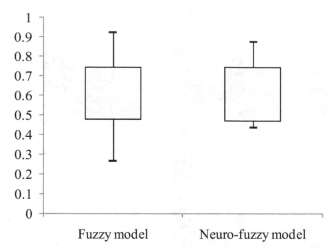

Fig. 23. Box-plots of the distributions of output data for fuzzy and neuro-fuzzy models.

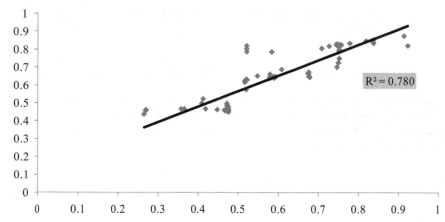

Fig. 24. Scatter plot between the environmental risk index obtained from the fuzzy and neuro-fuzzy models.

In fact, even the scatter plot (Fig. 24) shows a good correlation as evaluated by the coefficient of determination R^2, which is the square of the correlation coefficient $R = 0.8832$. Moreover, similarity between results of the two models can also be inferred from the comparison between variances and standard distributions and F test (Table 1).

	Environmental risk index (Fuzzy model)	Environmental risk index (Neuro-fuzzy model)
Standard deviation	0.136	0.133
Variance	0.018	0.018
F test	0.870	

Table 1. Statistical indices and test F results.

4. Conclusion

The fuzzy and neuro-fuzzy approaches used for the realization of models of environmental risk assessment have been fast, effective and affordable methods and at the same time useful support for decisions. The neuro-fuzzy model is faster in the application because by using training data, it is able to generate the fuzzy rules, which are particularly complex and increases along with the number of parameters assigned to the model.

In addition, integration of sensitivity analysis in the two models is a positive element because it is able to mitigate the problems of subjectivity and arbitrariness of the evaluation based on fuzzy approaches commonly found in literature, in particular with regards to the choice of membership functions. The case study proposed, in fact, shows that by varying the choice of the membership functions very different results if not contradictory can be obtained.

In conclusion, a model can be substituted with the exception of the neuro-fuzzy model that is rapidly applicable in case you have data available for training a neuro-fuzzy network.

The fuzzy method is advantageous because it allows a rapid and efficient risk assessment and is an inexpensive and expeditious planning tool for a program of remediation. However, it is disadvantageous due to the complexity in the definition of fuzzy rules especially when the number of parameters is high. In fact, in many situations when the number of parameters of the analysis is high, the application of these techniques is cumbersome and complex; in these cases, neuro-fuzzy models, that reduce the complexity of the models thanks to the training data, could be used. Using the adaptive methods of fuzzy inference neural networks, you can easily manage fuzzy rules of the analysis and reduce the artifices of fuzzy and neural models (Iyatomi et al., 2004).

The use of this kind of analysis with respect to neural models does not provide very different results, as assessed and analyzed even by Vieira et al. in 2004, but only a different training time influenced by the order of the model.

5. References

Abdel-Fattah, Attia, Rabab, Abdel-Hamid, & Maha, Quassim (2005). Prediction of solar activity based on neuro-fuzzy modeling, *Solar Physics* 227: 177–191.

Caniani, D., Lioi, D.S., Mancini, I.M., & Masi, S. (2011). Application of fuzzy logic and sensitivity analysis for soil contamination hazard classification. *Waste Management* 31 583–594.

Civita, M.; (1990) Legenda unicata per le Carte della vulnerabilità dei corpi idrici sotterranei/ Unified legend for the groundwater pollution vulnerability Maps. *Studi sulla Vulnerabilità degli Acquiferi*, 1 Pitagora, Bologna

Skarlatos, Dimitris, Karakasis, Kleomenis, & Trochidis, Athanassios, (2004)Railway wheel fault diagnosis using a fuzzy-logic method. *Applied Acoustics*, 65 (2004) 951–966.

Duško, Katic, & Miomir, Vukobratovic (2003). Survey of Intelligent Control Techniques for Humanoid Robots. *Journal of Intelligent and Robotic Systems*, 37-117-141.

Hitoshi, Iyatomi, & Masafumi, Hagiwara (2004). Adaptive fuzzy inference neural network. *Pattern Recognition* 37 2049-2057.

Mei-qin, LIU, Sen-lin, Zhang, & Gang-feng, YAN, (2008). A new neural network model for the feedback stabilization of nonlinear systems, Liu et al. / J Zhejiang Univ Sci A 9(8):1015-1023.

Miha, Mraz, (2001) The design of intelligent control of a kitchen refrigerator. *Mathematics and Computers in Simulation*, 56 259–267

Saad, R., & Halgamuge, S. K., (2004). Stability of hierarchical fuzzy systems generated by Neuro-Fuzzy, *Soft Computing* 8 409–416.

Saltelli, A., Chan, K., & Scott, E.M., (2000) Sensitivity analysis, Wiley & Sons

Silvert, William, (2000) Fuzzy indices of environmental conditions. *Ecological Modelling* 130, 111-119.

Van der Wal, A.J., (1995), Application of fuzzy logic control in industry. *Fuzzy Sets and Systems*, 74 33-41(1995).

Vieira, Josè, Fernando, Morgado Dias, & Alexandre, Mota (2004). Artificial neural networks and neuro-fuzzy systems for modelling and controlling real systems: a comparative study, *Engineering Applications of Artificial Intelligence*, 17 265–273.

Zadeh, L.A.; (1965) Information and control; *Fuzzy sets* 338-353 (1965).

Zaheeruddi, Garima(2006). A neuro-fuzzy approach for prediction of human work efficiency in noisy environment. *Applied Soft Computing* 6 283-294.

Zimmermann, H.-J. (1991). Fuzzy set theory and its applications, Dordrecht: Kluwer, second edition.

5

Adaptive Security Policy Using User Behavior Analysis and Human Elements of Information Security

Ines Brosso[1] and Alessandro La Neve[2]
[1]Faculty of Computing and Informatics,
Mackenzie Presbyterian University, Sao Paulo,
[2]Department of Electrical Engineering,
Centro Universitário da FEI, SP,
Brazil

1. Introduction

At present, security policy, to be effective, is primarily focused on people, being very rigid at this, and only later it cares about security attack attempts.

The security policy does not need to be rigid: rather it should be adaptable to the user behavior.

Analysis of human behavior, therefore, is the basis for an adaptive security policy. The behavior analysis of a person can be verified by a set of rules, which consider the variables that can influence human behavior, based on the information acquired about the environment, space, time, equipment, hardware and software. This information is used to analyze behavioral evidences about people, and establishes if it is possible to believe or not in the user. Therefore, according to the user behavior, levels of trust are released, which are based on the rules that were previously established for the parameters that are necessary to establish the evidences of behavioral trust, in its different degrees.

The adaptive security policy based on user behavior analysis is the basis for the information security management, when it comes to understanding the needs of users.

However, to achieve the whole security target in computing, and related technologies, it is necessary not only to have the most updated core technologies or security policies, but also to have the capacity to perform the analyses of the user behavior and the security environment. This work, in the context of computer security, uses the operant and conditioning behavior defined by Skinner (1991), which rewards a response of an individual until he is conditioned to associate the need for action.

The Skinner Theory may be very interesting to be used in Information Security Management Systems. In operant behavior, the environment is modified and produces consequences that are working on it again, changing the likelihood of a future similar occurrence. Operant conditioning is a mechanism for learning a new behavior.

When the organism answers an environmental stimulation, and the consequences of its reply are rewarded, the probability of similar answers increases; when the consequences are punitive, such probability diminishes. People associate experiences they have gone through to similar ones they may find in life: in this case they adopt the same behavior and repeat their actions.

The methodology for the preparation of this book chapter consisted of literature review, research on historical, social and psychological aspects of the Behavioral Theory, and the development of an Intelligent Security System. Studies and research on mathematical methods for handling trust information, fuzzy-logic, Information security management, context-aware computing and adaptive security policies, were also necessary.

In order to integrate information security management, based on adaptive security policy, with user behavior analysis, a deep understanding of Behavioral Theory, with historical, social and psychological aspects are necessary. At the same time, it also important to have full expertise in mathematical methods for handling information about people behavior, context-aware computing and self-aware computing systems, which can be the basis for an adaptive security policy based on user behavioral analysis.

This work was based on a doctoral thesis (Brosso, 2006) and research in the area.

2. Adaptive security policy

One of the more challenging questions in security is how to specify an adaptive security policy. The security policy does not need to be rigid, but it should be adaptable to the user behavior. In this context, this work exploits security aspects, user behavior analysis, trust in behavior, and biometric technologies to be the base of an adaptive security policy. The goal for specifying adaptive security is twofold:

- to provide an umbrella guide to decide which future events, actions, or responses are permitted in the current policy; and
- to allow new security goals to be stated, in order to initiate system responses to enforce that policy, if necessary.

The security policies for computing resources must match the security policies of the organizations that use them; therefore, computer security policies must be adaptable to meet the changing security environment of their user-base. The term "adaptive security" is intended to indicate that security policies and mechanisms can change in some automated or semi-automated way in response to events.

3. USER behavior analysis

The user behavior analysis helps to define an adaptive security policy to the information security management. Human behavior is based on contextual information, which is retrieved by behavioral history, history of behavior reinforcement and conduct of the person to interact with the environment immediately (Witter, 2005).The scientific analysis of human behavior starts with the knowledge of the environment and isolation of the parts of an event to determine the characteristics and the dimensions of the occasion where the behavior occurs, and to define the changes that were produced in response to the environment, space, time and opportunities.

The user behavior is a combination of n dimensions. The user behavior analysis uses the context variables of the environment and the trust, the concept that we human beings have regarding a person, and it is based on the behavior and reputation of a person. In this way, the environmental variables model of the user's behavior, in a conditioning process, uses the concepts of user, context, environment, time interval, behavior and trust, as follows:

- **User** - User is a person who has been approved in an authentication process to have access to software applications in a specific area of computer networks and wireless.
- **Context** - Any information that can be used to characterize the situation of the environment and the user.
- **Environment** – *Environmental technology*: the infrastructure needed in a specific area of computer networks, wired and wireless. *Technological environment:* local capture information, from behavior of users that interact with software and hardware applications.
- **Time interval** - The interval of time that elapses from the initial instant the user makes his identification on a software application access to the moment he exits the application, often called the session.
- **Behavior** - The behavior is the set of actions and responses that enable the intent of a person and the technological environment; or actions that a user performs when interacting with the software applications and the technological environment.
- **Trust** - Concept assigned to the user, which may vary according to the behavioral analysis of it. Based on the evidence of user behavior it is possible to determine the level of trust to give him. Trust is an abstract concept that expresses the belief that one has in the sincerity or authenticity of another person. The trust level of the person user is according to the analysis of his behavior. The concept of trust is a characteristic common to human beings, and is directly related to the perception, knowledge and reputation of a person about another. *Trust Restriction* -It refers to the behavior of the user that runs off the expected normality. A restriction may be due to a sequence of not recommended transactions, values or places different from usual, or others. The restriction of trust can be used in user adaptive security policy.

The focus of Behavior Analysis, as proposed by Skinner (1991), is currently applied in this work, for effective analysis of user behavior, to fulfill the requirements of user behavior analysis, according to the following steps:

Behavioral analysis is based on evidence of user behavior and comparison with information stored in databases of the same behavioral history. The behavioral analysis is carried out in two phases:

- The first is to compare the information obtained at the time the user interacts with the historical behavioral information.
- The second phase is to verify the existence, or absence, of behavioral constraints that can collaborate with the analysis, to convey or not to the user authentication.

The capture of user behavioral information in the environment is done analyzing some human elements of information security. It is closely associated with such characteristically human activities as philosophy, science, language, mathematics and art, and is normally considered to be a definitive characteristic of human nature. Human nature refers to the distinguishing characteristics, including ways of thinking, feeling and acting, that humans tend to have naturally.

Steps of analysis of user behavior	Description
Step 1: Target of the Behavior	Define the target of the behavior to be analyzed, to measure the frequency with which it occurs, or capture the variable and compare it with the restrictions and historical behavior in databases.
Step 2: Observe the behavior	Observe the behavior, the response and what will happen, or wait for the action of the user interaction in a given period of time, capturing the information received and waiting for the application to send a stimulus to the user to develop his behavior.
Step 3: Observe the behavior in terms of triple contingency	Observe the behavior in terms of triple contingency, which is the expression used to say that it will see the context, the response and what will happen; or wait for the action of the user interaction with the application software in a given period of time, capture the information received and wait for the application to send the user a stimulus to provoke a certain behavior.
Step 4: Behavior frequency	Record the rate of occurrence of the behavior, (frequency), in order to measure the behavior occurred throughout the process, and stores it in the user behavior database.
Step 5: Introduce the experimental variable	Where appropriate, introduce the experimental variable. It is applied to introduce a new tool for the user, such as a new code of access or a new field of application.
Step 6: Compare the frequency of behavior	Compare the frequency of behavior before and after the experimental variable or the occurrence of response. Currently, restrictions are compared to the user's past behavior. Thus, it can be said that the environment and both the virtual and physical space establish the conditions for a certain behavior.

Table 1. Steps of analysis of user behavior

The questions concerning these characteristics, what causes them and how this causation works, and how fixed human nature is, are amongst the oldest and most important questions in western philosophy. These questions have important implications particularly in ethics, politics and theology.

The user behavior analysis will also be concentrated on understanding how we can trust in the user.

In this work, relevant human elements like reason, logic and trust, are used in this study.

4. Human elements

Some Human Elements like reason, logic and trust help to analyze both the user behavior and to study a source of norms of conduct or ways of life to produce an adaptive security policy.

5. Reason

Beer (1994) explains that reason is a term that refers to the capacity that human beings have to make sense of things, to establish and verify facts, and to change or justify practices, institutions and beliefs. The concept of reason is sometimes referred to as rationality and was considered to be of higher stature than other characteristics of human nature. Reason is associated with thinking, by which it flows from one idea to a related one. It is the means by which rational beings understand themselves thinking about truth and falsehood, and what is good or bad. Reason relies on mental processes, related to the primary perceptive ability of humans, which gathers the perceptions of different senses and defines the order of the things that are perceived. Reasoning, in an argument, is valid if the argument's conclusion comes to be true when the premises, or the reasons given to support that conclusion, are true. If such reasoned conclusions are originally built only upon a foundation of sense perceptions, on the other hand, conclusions reached in this way are considered more certain than sense perceptions on their own.

Gilovich (1991) explains that psychologists and cognitive scientists have attempted to study and explain how people reason, what cognitive and neural processes are engaged, and how cultural factors affect the inferences that people draw to determine whether or not people are capable of rational thoughts in various different circumstances.

Experiments investigate how people make inferences about factual situations, hypothetical possibilities, probabilities, and counterfactual situations, and how it influences the human behavior. Humans have certain invariant structures, such as coherence and ability to establish relationships that give rise to the categories of reason that are structured in touch with reality, so that reason becomes a result of the action of biological maturation and the environment. Reason is a consideration that explains or justifies some behavior of humans in the field of logic.

6. Logic

Gottwald and Hajek (2005) wrote that, in contrast with traditional logic theory, where binary sets have two-valued logic, true or false, fuzzy logic variables may have a truth value, that ranges in degree from 0 to 1. In logic, a many-valued logic or multi-valued logic is a propositional calculus in which there are more than two truth values.

Fuzzy logic is a form of many-valued logic; it deals with reasoning that is approximate rather than fixed and exact and it has been extended to handle the concept of partial truth, where the truth value may range from completely true to completely false. While variables in mathematics usually take numerical values, in fuzzy logic applications, the non-numeric linguistic variables are often used to facilitate the expression of rules and facts.

Logical systems in general are based on some formalized language which includes a notion of well-formed formula, and then they are determined either semantically or syntactically. A logical system that is semantically determined means that one has a notion of interpretation or model, each such interpretation every well-formed formula has some (truth) value or represents a function into the set of (truth) values. It means, furthermore, that one has a notion of validity for well formed formulas and, based upon it, also a natural entailment relation between sets of well formed formulas and single formulas (or sometimes also whole sets of formulas).

That a logical system is syntactically determined means that one has a notion of proof and of provable formula, i.e. of (formal) theorem, as well as a notion of derivation from a set of premises. From a philosophical, especially epistemological point of view, the semantic aspect of (classical) logic is more basic than the syntactic one, because semantic ideas mainly determine what are suitable syntactic versions of the corresponding (system of) logic.

Fuzzy set theory defines fuzzy operators on fuzzy sets. The problem in applying this is that the appropriate fuzzy operator may not be known. For this reason, fuzzy logic usually uses IF-THEN rules, or constructs the equivalent ones, such as fuzzy associative matrices. There are also other operators, more linguistic in nature, called hedges that can be applied. These are generally adverbs such as "very", or "somewhat", which modify the meaning of a set using a mathematical formula.

Zadeh (1968) proposed that in mathematical logics, there are several formal systems of "fuzzy logic"; most of them belong to the so-called t-norm fuzzy logics. The notions of a "decidable subset" and "recursively enumerable subset" are basic ones for classical mathematics and classical logic. Ω denotes the set of rational numbers in [0,1]. A fuzzy subset $s : S \to [0,1]$ of a set S is recursively enumerable, if a recursive map $h : S \times N \to \Omega$ exists such that, for every x in S, the function $h(x,n)$ is increasing with respect to n and $s(x) = \lim h(x,n)$; s is decidable if both s and its complement $-s$ are recursively enumerable. An extension of such a theory to the general case of the L-subsets is proposed in Gerla (2006).

One of the main interests of the fuzzy logic theory is that many parameters can be taken into account since no mathematical modeling is required. This applies to the plant control area, but also to forecasting, decision support and risk scoring. On the other hand, Ang (2003) refers to neuro-fuzzy as combinations of artificial neural networks and fuzzy logic, the Neuro-Fuzzy Logic Rules and fuzzy sets are optimized by training strategies originated from neural network theory. In logic, trust is a dimensional, or multidimensional, variable, because it is possible to trust, not trust or have no evidence to attribute trust over an interval of time.

7. Trust

Trust is an abstract concept, and it reveals a belief in the sincerity or authenticity of one person in relation to another. Trust, a concept that we human beings have regarding a person, is based on the behavior and reputation of a person. This concept is not a unique and indivisible attribute that can be given to someone, and it is not the dichotomy of trust or not trust: on the contrary, it can be graded, and therefore it is dimensional and measurable. Trust levels may be stipulated based on the user behavioral analysis and on trust restrictions generated by the user. Trust level of the user is given according to the analysis of his behavior.

According to the user behavior, trust levels are released, to let the user have access to the application software. These levels, however, are not determined by clear and cut rules, that reflect a classification that can easily and universally be applied to human actions, but rather they must reflect the shady, undefined, and yet evident, characteristics of human behavior. With the increase of behavior information, a more efficient support for behavior evidences analysis is generated, and the system continues performing the evidences analysis of the behavior and adjusting the trust in the user.

Trust can change depending on the user, the localization, the time and the trust restrictions. With trust based on behavioral information and in the environment context information, it is possible to infer a minimum value for the initial trust, and, along the time, based on the behavior analysis and in the trust restrictions, the system will change the levels of trust.

The heuristics adopted to define the initial trust can be defined according to the user activity at a particular moment, its location, the time that the behavior currently occurs, and his historical behavior.

The attribution of the subsequent levels of trust is processed in two stages:

- 1st stage – Since there is not enough behavior information, it is attributed a minimum level of trust and, at the end, it accounts and stores the captured information.
- 2nd stage - In the subsequent accesses, when the user interaction increases, a verification is done, at first, in the trust restrictions database: if there are no restrictions, it compares the current behavior with the behavior information database, but if there are any changes in behavior, the alarm is triggered, the new behavior is stored, trust is re-calculated and security mechanisms are trigged.

According to the user behavior, levels of trust are released, based on the rules that were previously established for the parameters which help to establish the evidences of behavioral trust, in its different degrees.

Thus, it can be said that the environment and both the virtual and physical space establish the conditions for a certain behavior. It is necessary, therefore, to define some entities, used in behavior analysis, a set of context variables {who, where, when, what, why, how, rest}, that is, the evidence of the user behavior, as in table 2.

The set of context variables {who, where, when, what, why, how, rest} helps to decide what information is relevant to a system. However it is necessary to analyze the requirements and model the necessary information that each dimension can provide, since, in general, there is a tendency to develop a context model in which the user overrides associated problems, and this is a generalization to classify the context in temporal aspects, both static and dynamic.

To capture the behavior means to store the information of the behavioral variables {who, where, when, what, why, how and rest}, in a data structure represented by the matrix of user behavior. Given the uncertainty and doubt, it is often necessary to take decisions based on evidences, which are not always accurate. In these cases, trust should be used, which is a staff metric criterion adopted to evaluate evidence.

Variables	Description
Who	Identification. It identifies the user in an application software session. It helps User-behavior analysis, in classifying users according to their access patterns. This is useful for personalization, targeted advertising, priority, and capacity planning.
Where	Space Locality: It identifies either the location where the user is, or the device address that the user is accessing. It is of user interest, determining whether users in the same geographical region tend to receive or request similar notification and browsing content. For analysis, it should be defined a notification message to be locally shared, if at least two users in the same cluster receive the notification.
When	Time. It identifies the current time that the user is in a software application session.
What	Qualification. It identifies what the user is doing in a software application session.
Why	Intention. It means the action of the user to the stimulus received.
How	Method. It justifies the user repetitive activities in a software application session.
Rest	Restrictions. It identifies either the user behavior or the software application restrictions.

Table 2. Variables of the evidence of the user

The concept of trust is a characteristic common to humans, and is directly related to perception, knowledge and reputation that a person has about the other. According to Dempster (1967) and Shaffer (1976), a measure of confidence, in a universe set X that represents the total amount of confidence in the evidence of a particular set of circumstances, which varies between 0 and 1, is given by the function: Cf (x): P (X) ← [0, 1].

Based on the evidences of the behavior, the application software establishes if it trusts the user with values in the interval (mC, mD), where mC is the initial minimum trust and mD is the initial minimum diffidence.

The confidence (Cf), the diffidence (Df) and the uncertainty (If) express all the possibilities of trust attribution to a user, in this form:Cf + Df + If = 1. The uncertainty If is defined as: (If) = 1- (Cf + Df).

If Bj is a user behavior, the System, based on the evidences of the behavior, establishes if it trusts the user with values in the interval (mC, mD), where mC is the initial minimum trust and mD is the initial minimum diffidence. The system checks the uncertainty of confidence, which is given by: If (Bj) = 1 - (mC + mD). If the behavior Bj is considered normal, confidence is assigned to the user, linearly and slowly.

If there is uncertainty, safety mechanisms, like sensors that capture the user information, can be triggered and compare it with the existing one in databases. If there is an unusual behavior, behavioral constraints are generated, decreasing the confidence and increasing distrust. If there are any differences, confidence in the user will be decreased, and even access and continuity of operation are liable to be blocked. In case of indications of changes, in the user's behavior, if there are uncertainties and divergences, security mechanisms and alert signals are triggered.

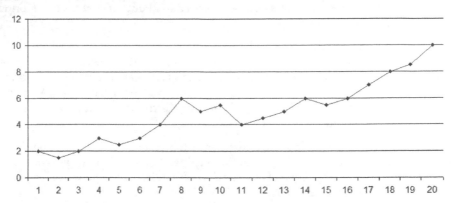

Fig. 1. The increase of trust

The loss of confidence grows fast, as it can be seen in figure 2.

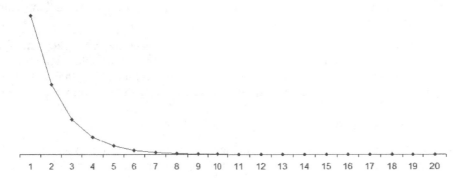

Fig. 2. The loss of trust

There is an uncertainty in the allocation of trust, however, because not always the complement of the expressed trust is distrust. Along the time, and in accordance with the behavior analysis, the user trust level can be subject to variations, and thus, it is necessary to interact with the user, to determine evidences so as to increase or to decrease trust in the user. Considering the definitions of reason, logic and trust, we can see that people use logic, deduction, and inductions, to reach conclusions that they think are true.

8. The information security

Information security means protecting information and information systems from unauthorized access, use, disclosure, disruption, modification, perusal, inspection, recording or destruction. The terms information security, computer security and information assurance are often interrelated and share the common goals for protecting the confidentiality, integrity and availability of data regardless of the form the data may take electronic, print, mobile or other forms. Computer security can focus on ensuring the availability and correct operation of a computer system without concern for the information stored or processed by the computer.

For the individual, information security has a significant effect on privacy, which is viewed very differently in different cultures. Governments, military corporations, financial institutions, hospitals, and private businesses amass a great deal of confidential information about their employees, customers, products, research, and financial status. Most of this information is now collected, processed and stored on electronic computers and transmitted to other computers across networks.

Should confidential information about a business customer, or a new product line, fall in the hands of a competitor, such breach in security could lead to losses in business, law suits or even bankruptcy of companies. Protecting confidential information is a business requirement, and in many cases also an ethical and legal requirement.

Information Security is composed of three main parts, namely hardware, software and communications, to identify and apply information security industry standards, as mechanisms of protection and prevention, at three levels or layers: physical, personal and organizational. Procedures or policies are essentially implemented to tell people (administrators, users and operators) how to use products to ensure information security within the organizations.

The field of information security has many areas including: securing network(s) and allied infrastructure, securing applications and databases, security testing, information systems auditing, business continuity planning, digital forensics science, security systems, etc. In this work we study an intelligent security system in collaboration with the information security.

9. An intelligent security system

It is here presented a study about an intelligent security system that uses an adaptive security policy using User Behavior Analysis and Human Elements of Information Security.

Figure 3 shows the mechanism that is used when the user accesses the computer: the intelligent security system verifies and analyzes the user behavior. This system is based on the fuzzy logic theory and must be able to acquire information about the environment, space, time, equipment, hardware, software and user behavior analysis, established for the variables {who, where, when, what, why, how, rest}. Fuzzy logic considers truth values, that are a value indicating the relation of a proposition to truth, ranging from 0 to 1 – but conceptually distinct, due to different interpretations.

The intelligent system proposes that, based on the evidences of the user behavior, it is possible to trust or not trust the user. Levels of trust are released, according to the user behavior and the rules that were previously established for the parameters which help to establish the evidences of behavioral trust, interacting with the environment information, so as to keep trust levels updated.

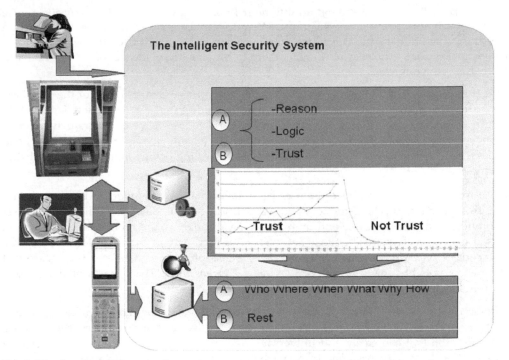

Fig. 3. The Intelligent Security System

The intelligent security system should be prepared not to anticipate every possible action that may be taken in the future, but to be flexible enough to adapt itself more easily to the changes that will certainly come, identifying technological trends and knowing more about human behavior, which will always be the crucial aspect of security.

Neural networks are systems that try to make use of some of the known or expected organizing principles of the human brain. Neural networks can be used if training data is available. It is not necessary to have a mathematical model of the problem of interest, and there is no need to provide any form of prior knowledge.

The neural function system has to learn what the behavioral changes of the user are, and incorporates them in the system, for a future fuzzy treatment. The fuzzy system evaluates, within an historical and behavioral perspective, human behavior, reflecting the perception or feeling that man or society have in relation to behavioral attitudes. Based on these attitudes weights are qualified and assigned.

On the other hand the solution obtained from the learning process usually cannot be interpreted. Neural networks and fuzzy systems have certain advantages over classical methods, especially when vague data or prior knowledge are involved. However, their applicability suffered from several weaknesses of the individual models. Therefore, combinations of neural networks with fuzzy systems have been proposed, where both models complement each other.

The proposed intelligent system adopts neuro-fuzzy logic because of its capacity to use past experiences and learn new ones. Weights can be attributed in the fuzzyfication process, according to the rules that were previously established for the variables {*who*, *where, when, what, why, how, rest*}, which help to establish the evidences of behavioral trust, in its different degrees.

The fuzzyfication of qualifiers should consider the intrinsic characteristics of the variables, according to specific application in which they are used. A financial institution, for instance, might consider the depositor of a bank for the variable *who*. Some qualifiers that could be associated to this variable might be: new or ancient (client), young or aged (person) , and others that the financial institution might find interesting or important in order to better define their clients.

A neuro-fuzzy system can feed the user behavioral database continuously, interacting with the fuzzyfication mechanism, so as to keep trust levels updated according to the user behavior, in a more accurate and faithful way, and to give more robustness to the system based on user behavior. The fuzzy set theory, as used here ,is based on if-then rules. The antecedent of a rule consists of fuzzy descriptions of input values, and the consequent defines a possibly fuzzy output value for the given input. The benefits of these fuzzy systems lie in the suitable knowledge representation.

According to the user behavior, levels of trust are released, to have access to the application software. These levels, however, are not determined by clear and cut rules, that reflect a classification that can easily and universally be applied to human actions, but rather they must reflect the shady, undefined, and yet evident, characteristics of human behavior.

In fact a major difficulty arises when actual values must be attributed to the parameter "m"(minimum), which is used in the $Cf(x)$ and $Df(x)$ functions, because of the subjectivity involved. Since there are no behavioral rules that can strictly be applied to people, no matter what their personal characteristics are, a more suitable mathematical tool, like soft-computing, should be used. The adoption of fuzzy logic, as a way of thinking, and then subsequently neuro-fuzzy systems, with learning possibilities, turned out to be a very interesting and effective solution.

Fuzzy logic allows that weights be attributed, based both on the designer's system needs and the experience drawn from historical events. With this in mind, and at hand, fuzzyfication rules, which are necessary to quantify vague and undefined qualifications, can be implemented resorting to the user behavior database, so as to find the optimal solution in each case, or set of cases.

The dynamism with which users access the system, constantly requires that the authentication system, as mentioned before, continuously revise, and possibly recalculate, trust levels to be released to the user, based on the behavioral history that the user himself continuously builds.

Neural networks are systems that try to make use of some of the known or expected organizing principles of the human brain. They consist of a number of independent, simple processors: the neurons. These neurons communicate with each other via weighted connections.

The modeling of single neurons and the called "learning rules" for modifying synaptic weights can be used in neural networks if training data are available. It is not necessary to have a mathematical model of the problem of interest, and there is no need to provide any form of prior knowledge. On the other hand the solution obtained from the learning process cannot usually be interpreted.

Although there are some approaches to extract rules from neural networks, most neural network architectures are black boxes. The fuzzy set theory makes possible that an object or a case belong to a set only to a certain degree that includes similarity, preference, and uncertainty.

The idea of combining fuzzy systems and neural networks is to design an architecture that uses a fuzzy system to represent knowledge in an interpretable manner and the learning ability of a neural network to optimize its parameters.

A combination can constitute an interpretable model that is capable of learning and can use problem-specific prior knowledge. Neural networks and fuzzy systems have established their reputation as alternative approaches to information processing.

Neuro-fuzzy models are neural networks with intrinsic fuzzy logic abilities, where the weights of the neurons in the network define the premise and consequent parameters of a fuzzy inference system. Premise parameters determine the shape and size of the input membership functions, whilst consequent parameters determine the characteristics of the output, exemplified in Figure 4.

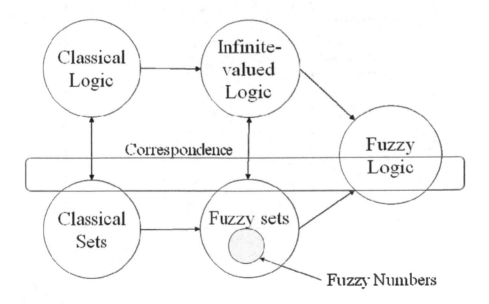

Fig. 4. The structure of Fuzzy Logic

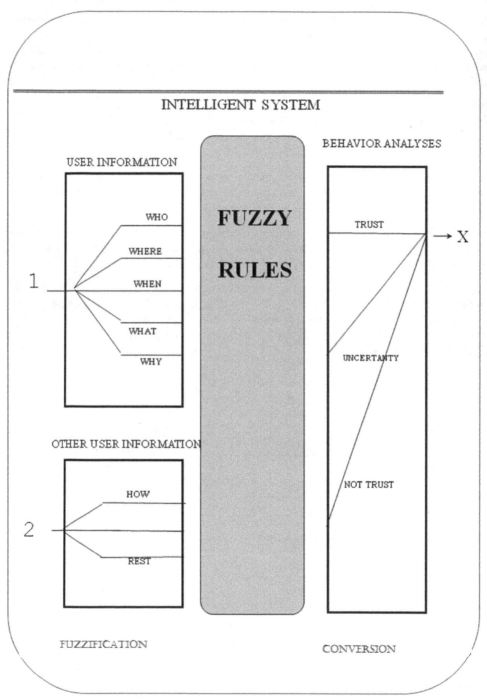

Fig. 5. The architectural of the Intelligent Security System with variables

It is therefore necessary to count on a mechanism with learning ability, such as a neuro system, that is able to give support to the fuzzyfication rules, according to the user behavioral changes. This will, not only update the user behavioral database, but it will interact with the fuzzyfication mechanism, so as to keep trust levels updated ,according to the user behavior, in a more accurate and faithful way.

With the increase of behavior information, a more efficient support for behavior evidences analysis is generated, and the system continues performing the evidences analysis of the behavior and adjusting the trust in the user. The trust can change depending on the user, the localization, the time and the trust restrictions.

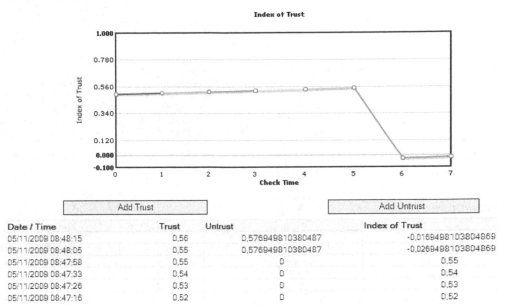

Index of Trust

Date / Time	Trust	Untrust	Index of Trust
05/11/2009 08:48:15	0,56	0,576949810380487	-0,0169498103804869
05/11/2009 08:48:05	0,55	0,576949810380487	-0,0269498103804869
05/11/2009 08:47:58	0,55	0	0,55
05/11/2009 08:47:33	0,54	0	0,54
05/11/2009 08:47:26	0,53	0	0,53
05/11/2009 08:47:16	0,52	0	0,52

Fig. 6. Trust variation.

The system attributes trust based on behavioral information and in the context information from the environment, and so, it is possible to infer a   minimum value for the initial trust, and along the time the system will change the trust, based on the behavior analysis and in the trust restrictions.

For the Intelligent System, "behavior" is the action of the user to the stimulus received, and "to capture the behavior" means to store the information of behavioral variables (*who, where, when, what, why and rest*) in a data structure represented by the matrix of user behavior.

The human behavior is uncertain and unpredictable. It is not algorithmic. It is based on the individual history of the person and groups. Therefore, the individual experience of the person should be considered in this analysis. The greater the amount of captured information, the better the analysis behavior will be. The user behavior is a combination of n dimensions. The focus of Behavior Analysis proposed by Skinner (2003) is currently applied to the system for effective analysis of user behavior according to the steps that were defined in table 1.

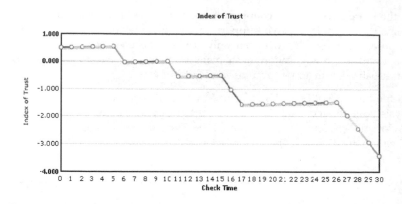

Fig. 7. Trust variation with trust restrictions.

Date / Time	Trust	Untrust	Index of Trust
05/11/2009 08:50:08	0.72	4.14346972096867	-3.42346972096867
05/11/2009 08:50:06	0.72	3.6567174650087	-2.9367174650087
05/11/2009 08:50:03	0.72	3.16996520904873	-2.44996520904873
05/11/2009 08:49:56	0.72	2.68321295308876	-1.96321295308876
05/11/2009 08:49:48	0.72	2.19646069712879	-1.47646069712879
05/11/2009 08:49:45	0.71	2.19646069712879	-1.48646069712879

10. Conclusion

To establish the policy and mechanisms for an adaptive security system, which is intended to protect society and its institutions, it is fundamental to know and analyze more deeply, besides the different technical and organizational aspects of the system, human behavior, which is often neglected.

Human behavioral characteristics, in fact, are some very important components that have to be considered, since they are partly subjective , but they are also strongly influenced by the social group the individuals belongs to: they may be predictable, to a certain extent, but they are certainly not ascertainable algorithmically.

Therefore, the need of mathematical support, in the design of an adaptive security system, conveys to the adoption of a neuro-fuzzy system. Neuro-fuzzy systems have the necessary flexibility to use past experiences, which are not algorithmic, and learn new ones. The neuro-fuzzy system allows that the user behavioral database be continuously updated, interacting with the fuzzyfication mechanism, so as to keep trust levels updated ,according to the user behavior, in a more accurate and faithful way.

The implemented Intelligent System was validated with tests and simulations to authenticate a person's identity using behavior analysis and trust restrictions, which are the basis for an adaptive security system. It acquired information in the context that was submitted, and they were used as a basis for user behavior. The System, based on the evidences of the user behavior, established if the user could be trusted or not, and to what extent.

So, according to the user behavior, levels of trust were released, to access the application software. Weights were attributed in the fuzzyfication process, according to the rules that were previously established for the parameters *(who, where, when, what, why, rest)*, which help to establish the evidences of behavioral trust, in its different degrees.

Therefore, with this approach, it was possible to define an adaptive security policy, based on the behavioral analysis of computer network users.

In future developments, the intelligent system for information security should be prepared, not to anticipate every possible action that may be taken, but to be adaptable enough to respond more rapidly to the changes that will certainly come. It should also be capable of identifying new technological trends and know more about human behavior, which will always be the crucial aspect of a security system.

Besides this, considering the steady and fast evolution of Information Technology and Communications in its manifold aspects, which are becoming more complex and sophisticated, it is necessary to think of a larger System, a Security Management System, that is not only robust enough to correspond to the current needs, but it may also be intelligent and prepared for the future, so as to guarantee to society the real benefits that Information Technology has to offer.

11. References

Ang, K. K., Quek, C., & Pasquier, M. (2003). "POPFNN-CRI(S): pseudo outer product based fuzzy neural network using the compositional rule of inference and singleton fuzzyfier." IEEE Transactions on Systems, Man and Cybernetics, Part B, 33(6), 838-849.

Azzini, A.; Marrara, S.; Sassi, R.; Scotti, F. (2007) A fuzzy approach to multimodal biometric authentication. In *Proceedings of the 11th International Conference on Knowledge-Based and Intelligent Information & Engineering Systems, KES'07*, Vietri sul Mare (SA), Italy, September.

Beer, Francis A., "Words of Reason", Political Communication 11 (Summer, 1994): 185-201.

Brosso, I. (2006) *Users continuous authentication in computers networks* – Doctoral Thesis in Digital Systems at Polytechnic School of Sao Paulo University, Brazil, from http://www.teses.usp.br/teses/disponiveis/3/3141/tde-08122006-170242/en.php

Brosso, I,; La Neve, A.; Bressan, G.; Ruggiero, W.V. (2010) A Continuous Authentication System Based on User Behavior Analysis, *International Conference on Availability, Reliability and Security, International Conference* , pp. 380-385, Krakow, Poland, February 15-February 18, ISBN: 978-0-7695-3965-2, retrieved December 2010 from http://doi.ieeecomputersociety.org/10.1109/ARES.2010.63

Dempster, A. P. (1967) Upper and Lower Probabilities Induced by a Multi-valued Mapping, *Annals of Mathematical Statistics*, Vol.38, pp.325-339.

Gerla, Giangiacomo (2006). "Effectiveness and Multivalued Logics". Journal of Symbolic Logic 71 (1): 137–162. doi:10.2178/jsl/1140641166. ISSN 0022-4812.

Gilovich, Thomas (1991), How We Know What Isn't So: The Fallibility of Human Reason in Everyday Life, New York: The Free Press, ISBN 0-02-911705-4

Gottwald, S., and Hajek, P. (2005). T-norm based mathematical fuzzy logics. In: Logical, Algebraic, Analytic, and Probabilistic Aspects of Triangular Norms (E.P. Klement and R. Mesiar, eds.), Elsevier, Dordrecht, 275-299

Hájek, Petr (1998). Metamathematics of fuzzy logic. Dordrecht: Kluwer. ISBN 0792352386.

Nauck, D.; Klawonn, F.; and Kruse, R. ; (1997) Foundations of Neuro-Fuzzy Systems, Wiley, Chichester.

Nurnberger, A. (2001) A Hierarchical Recurrent Neuro-Fuzzy System, In Proc. of Joint 9th IFSA World Congress and 20th NAFIPS International Conference, pp. 1407-1412, IEEE.

Platzaer, C (2004) Trust-based Security in Web Services. Master's Thesis – Technical University of Vienna, May.

Shaffer, G. (1976) A Mathemathical Theory of Evidence. Princeton, Princeton University Press.

Skinner, B.F. (1991). The Behavior of Organisms. p. 473. ISBN 0-87411-487-X. Copley Pub Group.

Truong, K.N.; Abowd, G.D.; Brotherton J.A. (2001) Who, What, When, Where, How: Design Issues of Capture & Access Applications. Georgia Institute of Technology

Technical Report GIT-GVU-01-02. January. York, J.; Pendharkar, P.C.(2004) Human–computer interaction issues for mobile computing in a variable work context, Int. J. Human-Computer Studies 60 ,771–797.

Weiser; M.; Gold, R.; & Brown, J. S. (1999) Ubiquitous computing - Retrieved 9 December 2010 from http://www.research.ibm.com/journal/sj/384/weiser.html.

Witter, G.P. (2005) Metaciência e Psicologia, (Portuguese language) ISBN: 8575161075 , São Paulo, Brazil. Editora: ALINEA

Zadeh, L.A. (1965). "Fuzzy sets". Information and Control 8 (3): 338–353. doi:10.1016/S0019-9958(65)90241-X. ISSN 0019-9958.

Zadeh, L.A. (1968). "Fuzzy algorithms". Information and Control 12 (2): 94–102. doi:10.1016/S0019-9958(68)90211-8. ISSN 0019-9958.

Zemankova-Leech, M. (1983). Fuzzy Relational Data Bases. Ph. D. Dissertation. Florida State University.

Zimmermann, H. (2001). Fuzzy set theory and its applications. Boston: Kluwer Academic Publishers. ISBN 0-7923-7435-5.

6

Fuzzy Clustering Approach for Accident Black Spot Centers Determination

Yetis Sazi Murat
Pamukkale University, Faculty of Engineering,
Civil Engineering Department,
Transportation Division, Denizli,
Turkey

1. Introduction

Traffic accident rates of Turkey are higher than most of the European Union countries and other countries in the world (Table 1). Every year, almost more than 8000 people die by traffic accidents in Turkey. This figure is very high comparing to many countries at same size. There have been many projects conducted by national or international organizations for decreasing these rates. In order to develop sustainable prevention models, accidents should be analyzed in detail considering primary and secondary reasons.

Traffic accident data can be analyzed in different ways, based on amount and types of data. The analysis is not complicated if the data are smooth and not dispersed. But it is not an easy task if the data are scattered. Although there is not a general definition for black spots, locations where at least more than one accident occured are treated as black spots. Based on this definition, the number of black spots can be increased and analysis of them is getting more difficult.

Country	Number of İnjured people (per 100 million veh-km)	Number of Dead people (per 100 million veh-km)
USA	58	0.3
England	60	1
Germany	351	1
Japan	111	1.4
France	27	1.9
Türkiye	108	7.5

Table 1. Traffic Accident rates (Murat and Sekerler, 2009)

Several methods can be used for determination of black spots and centers. It can be determined by eye using simple observations. But this simple approach can include subjective perceptions and also results obtained can not be sensitive and scientific. Besides to locations, other specifications of black spots should be taken into consideration for a scientific analysis. Developing countermeasures and classifying by characteristics for black spots that are intensified and covered whole area on the map is not an easy task. Although some black spots can have common characteristics, they can be located far away from each other. On the other hand, characteristics of black spots that are closely located to each other can be different. Therefore definition and analysis of black spots include uncertainties and conventional approaches can not be used for this purpose. In this study, cluster analysis approach is used for determination of black spots center and definition of the centers. Two types of analysis as k-means and fuzzy c-means are used. The (hard) k-means clustering approach is used as conventional method. In k-means clustering, the boundaries of clusters are determined as crisp. Thus some black spots that belong to a cluster based on their characteristics can be defined in different cluster by k-means clustering approach. But it can be defined in both clusters. To remove this deficiency, fuzzy c-means clustering approach is used. Fuzzy c-means are used for representing uncertainties in belonging to clusters. Thus some black spots are treated as members of two centers with two membership (belonging) values. In addition to determination of black spots centers, associative factors about the black spots are analyzed and discussed in the research.

In this study, first the black spots are determined using the data provided from Local Police Department, after that, the centers where black spots are intensified are revealed. These centers and the black spots around are considered in detail, the reasons of common results and findings are searched.

2. Literature review

There have been numerous studies about traffic safety. In this study, only GIS based studies and some important researches that include cluster analysis are taken into account and summarized.

Cluster analysis has been used in modeling traffic accident data by many researchers. Wong et al.(2004) used cluster analysis to develop a qualitative assessment methodology. Yannis et al. (2007) proposed a multilevel negative binomial modeling approach for the regional effect of enforcement on road accidents at Greece using cluster analysis. They made geographical and mathematical cluster analysis and reported that alcohol enforcement is the most significant one among the various types of enforcement.

Abdel-Aty and Radwan (2000), used Negative Binomial Distribution for modeling traffic accident occurrence and involvement. The models indicated that young and older drivers experience more accidents than middle aged drivers in heavy traffic volume, and reduced shoulder and median widths. They also obtained that heavy traffic volume, speeding, narrow lane width, larger number of lanes, urban roadway sections, narrow shoulder width and reduced median width increase the likelihood for accident involvement. Ng et al. (2002) aimed at developing an algorithm to estimate the number of traffic accidents and assess the risk of traffic accidents in Hong Kong. They presented an algorithm that involves a combination of mapping technique (Geographical Information System (GIS) techniques) and statistical methods. The results showed that the algorithm improves accident risk estimation when comparing to the estimated risk based on only the historical accident records. Abdel-Aty (2003) analyzed driver injury severity using ordered probit modeling approach. The models consider showed the significance of driver's age, gender, and seat belt use, point of impact, speed, and vehicle type on the injury severity level. An estimation model for collision risks of motor vehicles and bicycles is developed by Wang and Nihan (2004). They classified the accidents considering movements of traffic flows such as through, right turning, and left turning. A probability based method is used in the research. Three negative binomial regression models are improved in the study. The study showed that Negative Binomial regression approach can be used instead of Poisson regression approach. Abdel-Aty and Pange (2007) investigated crash data in two levels (i.e.collective and individual level). They focused real time estimation of crash likelihood and discussed advantages and disadvantages of the analysis in two levels. Saplıoğlu and Karaşahin (2006) examined traffic accidents of Isparta, Turkey using Geographical Information Systems. They determined black spots and found that there is an increase in number of black spots by the years. They also emphasized that most of the accidents are occurred in junctions. Another remarkable study has been accomplished in Singapore. Kamalasudhan et al. (2000) obtained accident density map using digital accident data. They searched black spots or hot spots using the accident density map. The types of accidents by the days, hours, pavement conditions and vehicle types are analyzed in the study.

Individual analysis of traffic accidents has been taken into consideration in most of the studies given in literature. Besides, analysis of density (i.e. densely recorded area) and determination of black spots are also very important for traffic safety researches. On the other hand, determination of black spots and their center is not an easy task and need to be made many trials. To handle this problem, cluster analysis approach is used in the research. The main objectives of this paper are determination of black spots' center by k-means and fuzzy clustering approaches and analysis of these points to reveal main reasons.

3. Cluster analysis approaches

In recent years, cluster analysis has been widely used in the engineering application such as civil engineering, target recognition, medical diagnosis etc. Cluster analysis is an unsupervised method for classifying data, i.e. to divide a given data into a set of classes or clusters.

3.1 Conventional (K-Means) clustering

K-means clustering approach is one of the popular methods used in industrial and scientific areas. Euclidian distance is used in k-means clustering algorithm. In this analysis, the desired number of clusters should be determined in the beginning. The following objective function is tried to be minimized in this approach.

$$J = \sum_{j=1}^{k}\sum_{i=1}^{n}\left\|x_i^{(j)} - c_j\right\|^2 \tag{1}$$

where, $\left\|x_i^{(j)} - c_j\right\|^2$ is the distance between the data $x_i^{(j)}$ and the corresponding center (c_j).

J is total distance.

The following steps are used in k-means clustering approach.

- Select the number of cluster centers (k)
- Assign each object to the nearest cluster center group
- After assigning all objects, recalculate locations of cluster center
- Repeat 2nd and 3rd steps till the cluster centers are fixed

One of the main disadvantages of this approach is determination of number of clusters in the beginning. Another disadvantage is sensitivity of the algorithm to the outliers.

3.2 Fuzzy C-Means clustering

Fuzzy C-Means (FCM) clustering algorithm has been widely used and applied in different areas. The description of the original fuzzy clustering algorithm based on objective function dates back to 1973 (Bezdek, 1973; Dunn, 1974). This algorithm was conceived in 1973 by Dunn (1974) and further generalized by Bezdek (1973). Among the existing fuzzy clustering methods, the Fuzzy c-means (FCM) algorithm proposed by Bezdek (1981) is the simplest and is the most popular technique of clustering. It is an extension of the hard K-means algorithm to fuzzy framework. Grubesic (2006) explored the use of a generalized partitioning method known as fuzzy clustering for crime hot-spot detection.

FCM algorithm is extension of Hard K-means with advantage of fuzzy set theory and contrary to the K-means method the FCM is more flexible because it shows those objects that have some interface with more than one cluster in the partition. In traditional clustering algorithms such as Hard K-Means, an element belongs fully to a cluster or not (i.e. 0 or 1). On the other hand, in Fuzzy clustering, each element can belongs to several clusters with different membership degrees. The main goal of any clustering algorithm is to determine appropriate the partition matrix $U(X)$ of a given data set X consisting of patterns ($X = \{x_1, x_2 \ldots \ldots x_N\}$) and to find the appropriate number of clusters. The objective function and constraints can be defined as;

Objective function

$$J(X;U,V) = \sum_{i=1}^{c} \sum_{k=1}^{N} (\mu_{ik})^m d^2(x_k, v_i) \tag{2}$$

$$V = [v_1, v_2, \ldots v_c], \ v_i \in R^n \tag{3}$$

Constraints

$$\sum_{i=1}^{c} u_{ik} = 1 \quad \forall k \in \{1, \ldots \ldots N\} \tag{4}$$

$$0 \prec \sum_{i=1}^{c} u_{ik} \prec N \quad \forall i \in \{1, \ldots \ldots c\} \tag{5}$$

Where, c is the number of cluster, v_i is the centroid, d is the Euclidian distance between rescaled feature vector and centroid of cluster, u_{ik} [0,1] denotes the degree of membership function of feature vector, $m[1\ \infty]$ is weight exponent for each fuzzy membership and it determines the fuzziness of the clusters and controls the extent of membership shared among the fuzzy clusters. U, which is given in equation (7), is the fuzzy partition matrix which contains the membership of each feature vector in each fuzzy cluster. It should be noted that, sum of membership values for a cluster must be equal to 1.

$$d^2(x_k, v_i) = (x_k, v_i)^T A_i (x_k, v_i) \tag{6}$$

$$U = \begin{bmatrix} u_{11} & u_{1k} & \cdots & u_{1N} \\ & \cdot & & \\ u_{i1} & u_{ik} & \cdots & u_{iN} \\ & \cdot\cdot & & \\ u_{c1} & u_{ck} & \cdots & u_{cN} \end{bmatrix}_{cxN} \tag{7}$$

The procedure of FCM based on iterative optimization (Bezdek, 1981) can be given as;

i.   Initialize fuzzy partition matrix U or Fuzzy cluster centroid matrix V using a random number generator.

ii. If the FCM algorithm is initialized with fuzzy partition matrix, the initial memberships belonging to cluster is adjusted using equation (8).

$$u_{ik} = \frac{u_{ik}^{initial}}{\sum_{i=1}^{c} u_{ik}^{initial}} \qquad for\ 1 \le i \le c,\ 1 \le k \le N \tag{8}$$

iii. If the FCM algorithm is initialized with fuzzy cluster centroid matrix containing the fuzzy cluster centroid, memberships belonging to cluster is determined using equation (9).

iv. v_i fuzzy centroid is computed by equation (9),

$$v_i = \frac{\sum_{k=1}^{N} (u_{ik})^m x_k}{\sum_{k=1}^{N} (u_{ik})^m} \tag{9}$$

v.   The fuzzy membership (u_{ik}) is updated by equation (10),

$$u_{ik} = \frac{(\frac{1}{d^2(x_k, v_i)})^{1/(m-1)}}{\sum_{i=1}^{c} (\frac{1}{d^2(x_k, v_i)})^{1/(m-1)}} \qquad for\ 1 \le i \le c,\ 1 \le k \le N \tag{10}$$

The steps (iii) and (iv) are repeated until the change in the value of memberships between two iterations is sufficiently small level.

3.1 Validation

The main problem in fuzzy clustering is that the number of clusters (c) must be specified beforehand. Selections of a different number of initial clusters result in different clustering partitions. Therefore, it is necessary to validate each of fuzzy partitions after the cluster analysis. Cluster validity refers to the problem whether a given fuzzy partition fits to the data all. The clustering algorithm always tries to find the best fit for a fixed number of clusters and the parameterized cluster shapes. However this does not mean that even the best fit is meaningful at all. Either the number of clusters might be wrong or the cluster shapes might not correspond to the groups in the data, if the data can be grouped in a meaningful way at all. In this study, several clustering indexes were used and tested for different values of both cluster number (c) and to examine their adequacy in analyzing of traffic accidents. These indexes are *Partition Coefficient (PC), Classification Entropy (CE), Partition Index (SC), Separation Index (S), Xie and Beni's Index (XB) and Dunn's Index (DI)*.

Partition Coefficient (PC) measures the amount of "overlapping" between two Fuzzy clusters (Bezdek, 1981). The disadvantage of this index is lack of direct connection to properties of the data. The optimal number of cluster is at the maximum value and the range of this index is [1/c, 1].

$$PC(c) = \frac{1}{N} \sum_{i=1}^{c} \sum_{k=1}^{N} (u_{ik})^2 \tag{11}$$

Classification Entropy (CE) measures the fuzziness of the cluster partition. The range of CE is $[0, \log a(c)]$ and optimal number of cluster is at minimum value.

$$CE(c) = -\frac{1}{N} \sum_{i=1}^{c} \sum_{k=1}^{N} u_{ik} \log_a a u_{ik} \tag{12}$$

Partition Index (SC) is the ratio of the sum compactness and separation of the clusters. It is a sum of individual cluster validity measures normalized through division by the fuzzy cardinality of each cluster. Comparing different partitions having equal of clusters, SC is useful index and a lower value of this index demonstrates a better partition.

$$SC(c) = \sum_{i=1}^{c} \frac{\sum_{k=1}^{N} (u_{ik})^m \|x_k - v_i\|^2}{N_i \sum_{k=1}^{c} (u_{ik})^m \|v_k - v_i\|^2} \tag{13}$$

Separation Index (S) uses a minimum distance separation for partition validity.

$$SC(c) = \frac{\sum_{i=1}^{c} \sum_{k=1}^{N} (u_{ik})^2 \|x_k - v_i\|^2}{N \min_{i,k} \|v_k - v_i\|^2} \tag{14}$$

Xie and Beni's Index (XB) aims to quantify the ratio of the total variation within clusters and separation of clusters. The optimal value of cluster is at minimum value of this index.

$$SC(c) = \frac{\sum_{i=1}^{c} \sum_{k=1}^{N} (u_{ik})^m \|x_k - v_i\|^2}{N \min_{i,k} \|x_k - v_i\|^2} \tag{15}$$

Dunn's Index (DI) is proposed to use the identification of compactness and separated cluster.

$$DI(c) = \min_{i \in c} \left\{ \min_{k \in c}, i \neq k \left\{ \frac{\min_{x \in C_i, y \in Ck} d(x,y)}{\max_{k \in C} \left\{ \max_{x,y \in C} d(x,y) \right\}} \right\} \right\} \tag{16}$$

4. Study area and available data

In this study, Denizli that is a medium sized city (current population is about 700000) of Turkey is considered. Traffic accident records for the years of 2004, 2005 and 2006 are used in analyzing accidents. The accident reports are provided by Local Police Department. All of the data and documents are taken from an ongoing research project. Following information are collected from the reports:

- Location of accident (coordinates)
- Type of accident
- Date
- Time
- Accident type for participating vehicle number
- Accident type for occurrence
- Weather condition
- Road and environmental conditions (signal, pavement, policeman, obstacle etc.)
- Road direction type (one or two way)
- Type of pavement
- Pavement surface conditions (dry, wet, icy etc.)
- Problems based on roadway
- Presence of warning sign
- Vertical route conditions
- Horizontal route conditions
- Intersection conditions
- Crossings (school crossing, pedestrian crossing, railroad crossing)
- Other factors (narrow road, bridge, tunnel)
- Information about vehicles (type, model, damage condition, speed etc)
- Information about drivers (age, sex, alcohol, usage of safety belt etc)
- Information about passengers and pedestrians (age, sex, alcohol, usage of safety belt etc)
- Vehicle insurance conditions

All of these data given above are recorded using first MS Excel. Then, coordinates of each accident point are determined using street definition system in MAPINFO software. The data from Excel data base including coordinates of the accident points are transferred to MAPINFO data base. This data base is constituted for accident analysis by inquiring different attribution of each accident. Thus, traffic accident can be evaluated from different points of view and the relations about reasons and results of accidents can be revealed by these analysis.

The data related to coordinates of accidents (locations) are used in cluster analysis. The Figure 1 shows sample processed data on Denizli city GIS map (Murat et al, 2008). The data are analyzed using k-means and fuzzy clustering approaches.

Fig. 1. Sample processed traffic accident data on Denizli city map.

5. Analysis of traffic accidents

In clustering analysis, the observed scales of the variables must be transformed so that their ranges are comparable because the clustering methods are sensitive to scale differences. Therefore, the variables were rescaled between 0 and 1 using equation (18).

Latitude $$Y = (X - X_{min}) / (X_{max} - X_{min}) \tag{18}$$

Longitude $\quad Y = (X - X_{min}) / (X_{max} - X_{min})$

Where Y the feature at site is, X_{min} and X_{max} are the maximum and minimum of the feature within the data set. These rescaled characteristics were employed as the basis for classifying the traffic accidents. To determine the optimum the cluster number, sensitivity of the results from FCM algorithm to variation in the value of cluster numbers (c) is varied from 2 to 9 with increment of 1. The variations of objective function of Fuzzy C-means algorithm for Economically Damaged (ED) and ED+ injured accidents with change in the number of cluster ranging from 2 to 11 are shown in Figure 2. On the other hand, for the Dead and Injured accidents, Figure 3 shows the variations of objective function of FCM algorithm with change in the number of cluster ranging from 2 to 5.

It is seen in Figure 2 and 3 that the values of objective functions of FCM algorithm, in generally, decrease with increase in the number cluster. The optimal number of clusters in the data set is identified by using objective function and fuzzy cluster validation indexes. The variations of cluster indexes for Economically Damaged accidents given in section 2 with change in the number of cluster were calculated and given in Figure 4.

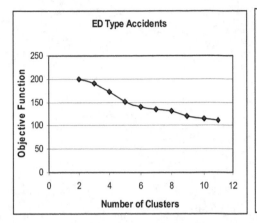
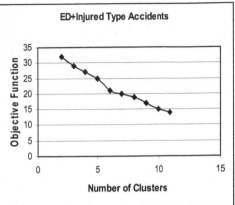

Fig. 2. Variation value of objective function of FCM with change in the number of clusters for ED and ED+Injured type accidents.

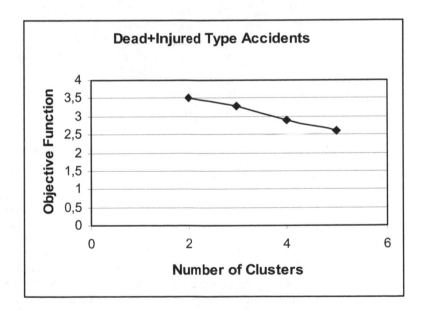

Fig. 3. Variation value of objective function of FCM with change in the number of clusters for Dead and Injured accidents.

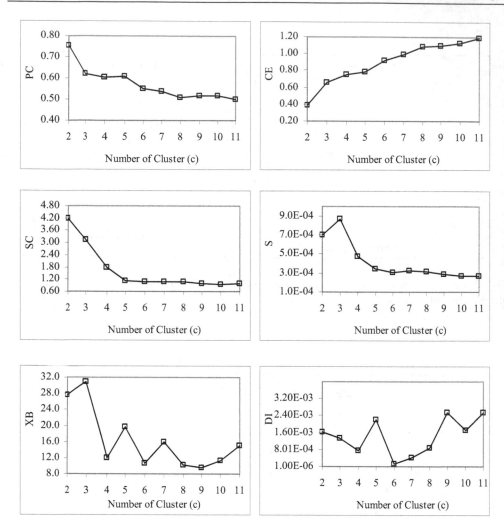

Fig. 4. Variations of cluster indexes with change in the number of cluster

The main drawback of PC is the monotonic decreasing with c and the lack of direct connection to the data. CE has the same problems: monotonic increasing with c and hardly detectable connection to the data structure. It is seen in Figure 4 that SC and S decrease with increase in the number of cluster. On the other hand, SC, S and XB indexes reaches the optimal value of number of cluster $c = 10$ and 11. For Economically Damaged(ED) traffic accident analysis, eleven clusters were chosen as the optimal number of cluster according to optimal values of objective function and validity indexes given in Figure 3 and 4. Table 2 exhibits the coordinates of cluster centers for ED and injured type accidents obtained from fuzzy cluster analysis (Murat and Sekerler, 2009). Similar procedure was carried out for ED+ Injured and Dead and Injured type accidents. Figure 5 shows the location of the corresponding fuzzy clusters for traffic accidents in Denizli city.

The data are also analyzed by conventional K-means clustering approach. In this analysis, seven clusters are obtained. Figure 6 depicts results of k-means clustering approach. Table 3 shows the coordinates of cluster centers and the number of accidents for the clusters determined by conventional k-means clustering analysis.

Cluster No	Coordinates		Number of Accidents
	X	Y	
1	29,082	37,782	1303
2	29,07	37,774	648
3	29,089	37,787	1389
4	29,086	37,772	1349
5	29,097	37,779	1253
6	29,107	37,802	501
7	29,08	37,795	509
8	29,037	37,773	248
9	29,099	37,792	605
10	29,089	37,756	662
11	29,101	37,763	631
	TOTAL		9098

Table 2. Coordinates of Cluster centers given by Fuzzy C-means clustering analysis

Cluster No	Coordinates		Number of Accidents
	x	Y	
1	29,085	37,787	2480
2	29,041	37,772	302
3	29,102	37,798	973
4	29,072	37,778	835
5	29,096	37,780	1589
6	29,095	37,760	1274
7	29,086	37,772	1645
	TOTAL		9098

Table 3. Coordinates of Cluster centers given by conventional k-means analysis

It can be said that analysis of the fuzzy clustering approach has more details than the conventional k-means clustering approach.

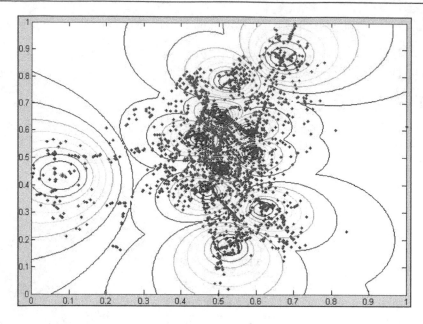

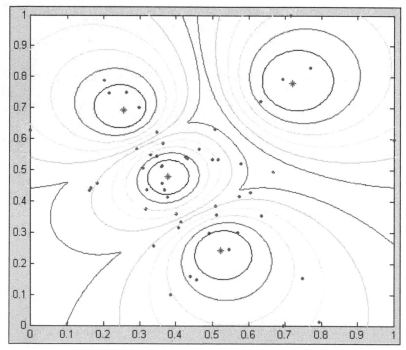

Fig. 5. The location of the corresponding fuzzy clusters for traffic accidents in Denizli city (a) for 11 clusters, (b) for 4 clusters.

As seen on Figure 6, the centers obtained are similar to that obtained by fuzzy clustering approach. But fuzzy clustering approach provided four more clusters comparing to conventional k-means clustering approach. One of the important cluster (center named Ucgen) that has the biggest number of accident is not defined by k-means clustering approach. But it is defined by fuzzy c-means clustering approach.

Total numbers of accidents are defined in both clustering analysis approaches. But the distributions of accidents are different for k-means and fuzzy c-means clustering approaches. This is come from the number of clusters and difference about the analysis.

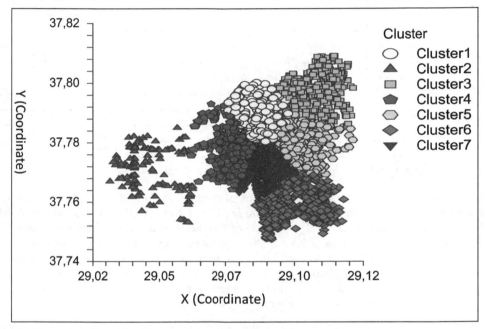

Fig. 6. Clusters obtained by K-means clustering approach.

6. Results and discussion

Using cluster analysis, different types of traffic accidents are analyzed and three types of clusters are carried out as four, seven and eleven clusters respectively. Following table shows the common points that can be considered as black spots for three types of clusters. These points are also determined as the center of each cluster. As seen on Table 3, the number of accidents certified the black spots centers determined.

Location of black spots has an importance in analysis. It should be considered as urban sections and rural areas. But it is difficult to determine a strict line for clustering accidents. Some accidents location can be defined in more than one region or cluster. Therefore, fuzzy clustering approach is preferred. The results show that, Fuzzy clustering approach provided four more black spot centers comparing to k-means clustering approach. Three of them are located in urban areas and one of them is in rural areas.

The black spots that are determined by cluster analysis are examined in detail regarding types of accident occurrence. The geometric and physical conditions of black spots are also examined in detail and the results obtained are summarized as follow.

Intersection or Road Section (Black Spot)	Type of Accident			Cluster No
	Dead+Injured Accidents	Economically Damaged (ED) Accidents	ED+Injured Accidents	
Ucgen	1	229	17	1
Karayolları		46	4	2
Cinar	1	86	1	3
Kiremitci		25	0	4
Yeni Adliye		27	6	5
İstasyon	1	107	12	6
Sevindik		93	8	7
Emniyet	1	76	9	8
Ulus		94	4	9
Hastane-M.Efendi		50	1	10
25. cadde	1	200	26	11
Total	5	1033	88	

Table 3. The common black spots determined by cluster analysis

The first black spot, Ucgen Intersection, is one of the most important intersections in Denizli city center. The main arterials from Ankara, İzmir and Antalya cities are connected at this point. Average Annual Daily Traffic volume of this intersection is very high and congested traffic conditions are seen in peak hours. The Antalya road arm has some problems occurred by geometric design. There is not enough weaving area from the previous intersection for the vehicles that wants to change the lanes in this arm. Most of accidents are occurred because of this fault. Another important problem is related to pedestrian crossings. The pedestrians do not obey the rules while crossing the street.

Karayolları Intersection is determined as the second black spot. The main problem of this intersection is also related to geometric design. This intersection has five approaches. Therefore optimizing signal timing is very hard. Main reasons of accidents in this intersection are related to high speed and sight distance. The speed reduction and monitoring systems can reduce number of accidents and accident severity.

Cınar is another important intersection of the city. This intersection is served most of the daily traffic circulating in the city. There are some problems about optimizing signal timings. On the other hand, some drivers ride as aggressive drivers and cause traffic accidents. There is serious pedestrian traffic in this area and traffic signal is designed as filter for vehicles and pedestrians. Traffic safety problems are seen, because of the design and can be solved by re-calculating the intersection signal timings and changing phase plans.

The main problems in Kiremitci intersection is related to intersection geometry and aggressive drivers. The problem can be solved by re-designing and optimizing signal timings.

One of the different black spot is determined as 25. Cadde. This area is an industrial area that has many roads and intersections. The traffic composition includes heavy and light vehicle traffic flows are seen in this area. Most of the accidents are seen at intersections and all of them are controlled by isolated systems. One of the serious problems is related to design of intersections especially some uncontrolled intersections.

One of the main advantages of fuzzy cluster analysis is to handle the problem in an easiest and practical way. The conventional approaches take very long time and require many trials for the analysis.

Actually, most of reasons of problems occurred in all of these black spots are similar. These are high traffic density, non-optimized signal timing, inconvenient pedestrian crossings, and aggressive driving (caused by non-optimized control), geometric design faults (for weaving areas, taper design etc), inconvenient lane use and lane changing, excessive speed etc. Solutions for these problems can be achieved by developing some policies and intervene the system considering international standards for design. But sustainable solution can be found by generalizing and improving "*traffic concept*" in the society.

The fuzzy clustering approach presented in this study can be used in determination of black spots instead of conventional approaches and traffic safety policies can be developed considering detailed analysis of these black spots. The fuzzy clustering approach can also be used for analyzing other related effective factors on traffic accidents and very interesting results may be obtained based on these analysis.

7. Conclusion

The findings of this research can be used for investigation of different effects on traffic accident occurrence considering characteristics of black spots and centers. Safety levels of black spots can be determined by this way. Some countermeasures can be developed using safety levels of black spots. On the other hand, the risk analysis can be made in detail in these centers and priorities of investment planning can be defined considering level of safety risk. The fuzzy clustering analysis can be extended considering other characteristics (such as accident type, occurrence type etc.) of black spots. Therefore, definition of black spots can be reviewed after these analyses.

8. Acknowledgement

This research was supported by The Scientific and Technical Research Council of Turkey (TUBITAK) under project number 105G090. Part of the analysis presented is made by Mr. Alper Şekerler during preparation of his MSc. dissertation. These supports are appreciated.

9. References

Abdel-Aty M., Radwan E, (2000). Modelling traffic accident occurrence and involvement, *Accident Analysis and Prevention* 32, 633-642.

Abdel-Aty M.,Pange, A., (2007). Crash data analysis: Collective vs. individual crash level approach, *Journal of Safety Research,* 38, 581–587

Abdel-Aty, M. (2003). Analysis of driver injury severity levels at multiple locations using ordered probit models, *Journal of Safety Research* 34, 597- 603.

Bezdek, J. C. (1981)., *Pattern Recognition with Fuzzy Objective Function Algorithms*, Plenum, New York.

Bezdek, J. C.,(1973). *Fuzzy mathematics in pattern classification.*, Ph.D. dissertation, Cornell University, Ithaca, NY.

Dunn, J. C., (1974). A fuzzy relative of the ISODATA process and its use in detecting compact, well-separated clusters., *Journal of Cybernetics*, 3(3), 32-57.

Grubesic, T.H. (2006). On The Application of Fuzzy Clustering for Crime Hot Spot Detection, *Journal of Quantitative Criminology*, Vol. 22, No. 1, 77-105.

http://gisdevelopment.net./application/urban/products/index.htm. 18

Kamalasudhan A, Mitra, S., Huang, B., Chin, H., C., (2000). An Analysis Of Expressways Accident in Singapore available from

Murat, Y.Ş., Fırat, M., Altun, S. (2008). Analysis of Traffic Accidents Using Fuzzy Clustering and Geographical Information Systems, *10th International Conference on Application of Advanced Technologies in Transportation*, May 27- 31, Athens GREECE , 2008. (Proceeding CD)

Murat, Y.Ş., Şekerler, A., (2009). Use of Clustering Approach in Traffic Accident Data Modelling, *Technical Journal of Turkish Chamber of Civil Engineers*, Vol. 20, No 3, July 2009, p 4759-4777. (in Turkish)

Ng, K.S., Hung, W.T., Wong, W.G., (2002). An algorithm for assessing the risk of traffic accident", *Journal of Safety Research*, 33, 387-410.

Saplıoglu, M., Karasahin, M. (2006). Urban Traffic Accident Analysis by using Geographic Information System, *Journal Of Engineering Sciences*, Pamukkale University, Engineering College, Vol. 12, 3, 321-332. (in Turkish)

Şekerler, A., (2008). *Analysis of Traffic Accident Data using Clustering Approach*, Master of Science Thesis, Pamukkale University, Institute of Natural and Applied Sciences, 113 p, Denizli, Turkey. (in Turkish)

Wang, Y., Nihan, N. (2004). Estimating the risk of collisions between bicycles and motor vehicles at signalized intersections, *Accident Analysis and Prevention* 36, 313–321.

Part 2

Transportation and Communication

7

Adaptive Fuzzy Wavelet NN Control Strategy for Full Car Suspension System

Laiq Khan, Rabiah Badar and Shahid Qamar
Department of Electrical Engineering,
COMSATS Institute of Information Technology, Abbottabad
Pakistan

1. Introduction

In the last few years, different linear and non-linear control techniques have been applied by many researchers on the vehicle suspension system. The basic purpose of suspension system is to improve the ride comfort and better road handling capability. Therefore, a comfortable and fully controlled ride can not be guaranteed without a good suspension system. The suspension system can be categorized as; Passive, Semi-active and Active.

The passive suspension system is an open loop control system consisting of the energy storing (spring) and dissipating element (damper). The passive suspension performance depends on the road profile, controlling the relative movement of the body and tires by using various kinds of damping and energy dissipating elements. Passive suspension has considerable restriction in structural applications. The features are resolved by the designers with respect to the design objectives and the proposed application. All the ongoing research in this area mainly caters the following issues to improve the suspension control;

- minimize the effect of road and inertial disturbances, on human body, caused by cornering or braking.
- minimize the vertical car body displacement and acceleration.
- good control on all the four wheels of the car for their optimal contact with road.

All the above objectives lead to rapidly changing operating conditions and the passive suspension system is not as efficient to cope with them by adapting its parameters, simultaneously. So, there would always be a compromise between comfort and safety for passive suspension system.

Semi-active suspension system consists of a sensor that identifies bumps on the road and motion of the vehicle and a controller that controls the damper on each wheel. The semi-active suspension can respond to even small variations in road area and cornering. It offers quick variations in rate of springs damping coefficients. This suspension system does not give any energy to the system but damper is changed by the controller. The controller resolves the rank of damping based on control approach and automatically changes the damper according to the preferred levels. Actuator and sensors are attached to sense the road profile for the control input. The adaptive fuzzy controller for semi-active suspension systems was presented by

(Lieh & Li, 1997) which shows only the acceleration of the vehicle compared to the passive suspension.

On the other hand, active suspension consists of actuator. The controller drives the actuator, which depends on the proposed control law. The active suspension system gives the freedom to tune the whole suspension system and the control force can be initiated locally or globally depending on the system state. The active suspension systems provide more design flexibility and increase the range of achievable objectives. The active suspension passenger seat is proposed by (Stein & Ballo, 1991) for off-road vehicles. Also, the passenger suspension seat was considered by (Nicolas et al., 1997) in their control technique to improve ride comfort. Various control techniques such as optimal state-feedback (Esmailzadeh & Taghirad, 1996), model reference adaptive control (Sunwoo et al., June 1991), backstepping method (Lin & Kanellakopoulos, 1997), fuzzy control (Yoshimura et al., 1999) and sliding mode control (Yoshimura et al., 2001) have been presented in the last few years for optimized control of the active suspension system.

In order to examine these suspension systems, three types of car model have been introduced in the literature; Quarter car model, Half car model and Full car model. In car modeling, quarter car model is the simplest one. Many approaches on quarter car suspension systems have been carried out by (Hac, 1987; Yue et al., 1988) but do not reveal robustness of the system. The robustness of quarter-car suspension system based on stochastic stability has been presented by (Ray, 1991) but this technique needs large feedback gains and an appropriate phase must be chosen. The best performance estimations of variable suspension system on a quarter car model are observed by (Redfield & Karnopp, 1988). Various linear control techniques are applied on a quarter car model in (Bigarbegian et al., 2008) but did not give any information for large gain from road disturbance to vehicle body acceleration. The dynamic behavior and vibration control of a half-car suspension model is inspected by different researchers in (Hac, 1986; Krtolica & Hrovat, 1990; 1992; Thompson & Davis, 2005; Thompson & Pearce, 1998).

The active control of seat for full car model is examined by (Rahmi, 2003). Some control approaches have been examined to minimize the vertical motion, roll and also the chassis motion of vehicle by (Barak & Hrovat, 1988; Cech, 1994; Crolla & Abdel−Hady, 1991). The PID controller is applied on active suspension system by (Kumar, 2008). The combined H_∞ controller with LQR controller on an active car suspension is given by (Kaleemullah et al., 2011), but this controller requires the frequency characterization of the system uncertainties and plant disturbance, which are usually not available. An experimental 1-DOF microcomputerized based suspension system was presented by (White-Smoke, 2011), using actuator force as control input. However, the extension of this model to other practical models is not straightforward.

Fuzzy logic control has been utilized widely for the control applications. Such a control approach has the definite characteristic of being able to build up the controller without mathematical model of the system. Therefore, it has been employed to control active suspension systems (Hedrick & Butsuen, 1990; Hrovat, 1982; Meller, 1978; Smith, 1995).

In (Nicolas et al., 1997), the authors used a fuzzy logic controller to increase the ride comfort of the vehicle. A variety of simulations showed that the fuzzy logic control is proficient to give a better ride quality than other common control approaches for example, skyhook control (Ahmadian & Pare, 2000; Bigarbegian et al., 2008). (Lian et al., Feb. 2005) proposed a fuzzy controller to control the active suspension system. The fuzzy control for active suspension system presented by (Yester & Jr., 1992) considers only the ride comfort. (Rao & Prahlad, 1997) proposed a tuneable fuzzy logic controller, on active suspension system without taking into account the nonlinear features of the suspension spring and shock absorber, also, the robustness problem was not discussed. The neural network control system applied on active suspension system has been discussed by (Moran & Masao, 1994) but does not give enough information about the robustness and sensitivity properties of the neural control towards the parameter deviations and model uncertainties. Also, sliding mode neural network inference fuzzy logic control for active suspension systems is presented by (Al-Holou et al., 2002), but did not give any information about the rattle space limits. (Huang & Lin, 2003; Lin & Lian, 2008) proposed a DSP-based self-organizing fuzzy controller for an active suspension system of car, to reduce the displacement and acceleration in the sprung mass so as to improve the handling performance and ride comfort of the car. (Lian et al., Feb. 2005) proposed a fuzzy controller to control the active suspension system.

However, it is still complicated to design suitable membership functions and fuzzy linguistic rules of the fuzzy logic controllers to give suitable learning rate and weighting distribution parameters in the self-organizing fuzzy controller.

Since, the aforementioned fuzzy logic and neural network controllers on active models, did not give enough information about the robustness, sensitivity and rattle space limits. These techniques were combined with wavelets to solve different control and signal processing problems and collectively known as Fuzzy Wavelet Neural Networks (FWNNs) (Chalasani, 1986; Hac, 1986; Heo et al., 2000; Meld, 1991; Thompson & Davis, 2005; Thompson & Pearce, 1998). The combination of a fuzzy wavelet neural inference system comprises the strength of the optimal definitions of the antecedent part and the consequent part of the fuzzy rules. In this study, fuzzy wavelet neural network control is proposed for the active suspension control. A FWNN combines wavelet theory with fuzzy logic and neural networks. Wavelet neural networks are based on wavelet transform which has the capability to examine non-stationary signals to determine their local details. Fuzzy logic system decreases the complexity and deals with vagueness of the data. Neural networks have self-learning qualities that raises the precision of the model. Their arrangement permits to build up a system with fast learning abilities that can explain nonlinear structures. Different structures of FWNN have been proposed in the literature. Due to its strong estimation and controlling properties FWNN has found extensive applications in the areas of identification and control of non-linear plants (Abiyev & Kaynak, 2008; Adeli & Jiang, 2006; Banakar & Azeem, 2008; Yilmaz & Oysal, 2010).

In this chapter, different softcomputing techniques have been combined with wavelets for the active suspension control of full car model to minimize the vibrations of the vehicle against the road disturbances. The proposed Adaptive Fuzzy Wavelet Neural Network (AFWNN) control integrates the ability of wavelet to analyze the local details of the signal with that of fuzzy logic to reduce system complexity and with the self learning capability of neural networks, which makes the controller efficient for controlling unknown dynamic plants. The results of the proposed models have been compared with passive and semi-active suspension system. The robustness of the system has further been evaluated by comparing the results with Adaptive PID (APID).

This chapter has been arranged as follows; Section2 gives the structural and mathematical details of the proposed AFWNN models. In Section 3 the modeling details and closed loop system have been discussed. Section 4 gives the simulation results and discussion. Finally, section 5 concludes our work.

2. Fuzzy wavelet neural network control

Wavelet neural network is a new and innovative network, which is based on wavelet transforms (Oussar & Dreyfus, 2000). The structural design of the wavelet neural network is laid on a multilayered perceptron. A discrete wavelet function is applied as node activation function in the wavelet neural network. Because, the wavelet space is utilized as a feature space of pattern identification, the feature extraction of signal is recognized by the weighted sum of the inner product of wavelet base and signal vector. Furthermore, network acquires the ability of approximation and robustness. The entire estimation is on the logistic infrastructure. Wavelets can be expressed as follows:

$$\Psi_j(x) = |a_j|^{\frac{-1}{2}} \Psi \left(\frac{x - b_j}{a_j} \right), \quad a_j \neq 0, \quad j = 1, 2, ..., n \tag{1}$$

Where, $\Psi_j(x)$ is the family of wavelets, $x = x_1, x_2, ..., x_m$ shows the input values, $a_j = a_{1j}, a_{2j}, ..., a_{mj}$ and $b_j = b_{1j}, b_{2j}, ..., b_{mj}$ represent the dilation and translation parameters of the mother wavelet $\Psi(x)$, respectively. The $\Psi(x)$ function is a waveform of limited duration and has a zero mean value.

Wavelet neural networks are mainly three layered networks using wavelets as activation function. The output for wavelet neural network is formulated as;

$$y = \sum_{j=1}^{k} w_j \Psi_j(x) \tag{2}$$

Where, $\Psi_j(x)$ is the wavelet function of the *jth* part of hidden layer, because, the wavelet networks contain the wavelet functions in the hidden layer's neurons of the network. w_j are the weights connected between the hidden layer and the output layer.

Wavelet functions have capability of time−frequency localization property (Zhang & Benveniste, 1992). Localization of the *ith* hidden layer of wavelet neural network is found by the dilation and translation parameters of the wavelet function. The dilation parameter controls the spread of the wavelet and the translation parameter determines the center position of the wavelet (Y. Chen & Dong, 2006).

Normally, two techniques are used for signifying multidimensional wavelets. In the first technique, they are created by using the product of one-dimensional wavelet functions. This wavelet neural network technique model is used by (Zhang et al., 1995). In second technique, the Euclidian norms of the input variables are used as the inputs of one-dimensional wavelets (Billings & Wei, 2005; Zhang, 1997).

The proposed AFWNN incorporates wavelet functions in the conventional TSK fuzzy logic system. In the conventional approach, a linear function or constant is used in the consequent part of the linguistic rules for TSK fuzzy system. In the AFWNN, wavelet functions are used in the consequent part to enhance the estimation capability and computational strength of the neuro-fuzzy system by utilizing their time-frequency localization property.

In a TSK fuzzy model, each rule is divided into two regions, represented by the IF-THEN statement. In the IF part of the fuzzy rule, membership functions are given, and in the THEN part of the fuzzy rule a linear function of inputs or a constant is used. These rules are based on either experts knowledge or adaptive learning. The wavelets can collect the information globally and locally easily by means of the multiresolution property (Ho et al., 2001). The proposed AFWNN model has fast convergence and accuracy properties.

The AFWNN rules have the following form;

$$If\ x_1\ isA_{11}\ and\ x_2\ is\ A_{12}\ and\ ...\ x_m\ is\ A_{1m}\ Then\ y_1 = \sum_{i=1}^{m} w_{i1}(1 - q_{i1}^2)e^{-\frac{q_{i1}^2}{2}}$$

$$If\ x_1\ isA_{21}\ and\ x_2\ is\ A_{22}\ and\ ...\ x_m\ is\ A_{2m}\ Then\ y_2 = \sum_{i=1}^{m} w_{i2}(1 - q_{i2}^2)e^{-\frac{q_{i2}^2}{2}}$$

$$\vdots$$

$$If\ x_1\ isA_{n1}\ and\ x_2\ is\ A_{n2}\ and\ ...\ x_m\ is\ A_{nm}\ Then\ y_n = \sum_{i=1}^{m} w_{in}(1 - q_{in}^2)e^{-\frac{q_{in}^2}{2}}$$

Where, $x_1, x_2, ..., x_m,\ y_1, y_2, ..., y_n$ are the input-output variables and A_{ij} is the membership function of ith input and jth rule. Wavelet functions are in the consequent part of the rules. The entire fuzzy model can be attained by finding/learning the parameters of antecedent and consequent part.

The AFWNN structure has been depicted in Figure 1. This structure comprises of combination of the two network structures, i.e., upper side and lower side. Where, upper side encloses wavelet neural network and lower side encloses fuzzy reasoning process.

The whole network works in a layered fashion, as follows;
Layer 1: This is the first layer of fuzzy reasoning as well as the wavelet network. This layer accepts input values. Its nodes transmit input values to the next layer.

Layer 2: In this layer fuzzification process is performed and neurons represent fuzzy sets used in the antecedent part of the linguistic fuzzy rules. The outputs of this layer are the values of the membership functions '$\eta_j(x_j)$'.

Layer 3: In this layer each node represents a fuzzy rule. In order to compute the firing strength of each rule, and min operation is used to estimate the output value of the layer. i.e.,

$$\mu_j(x) = \prod_i \eta_j(x_i) \tag{3}$$

where, $\prod_i$ is the min operation and $\mu_j(x)$ are the input values for the next layer (consequent layer).

Layer 4: In this layer, wavelet functions are represented. The output of this layer is given by;

$$y_l = w_l \psi_l(q) \tag{4}$$

Where, $\psi_l = f(a_{il}, q_{il})$ is a functional such that

$$q_{il} = f(x_i, b_{il}, a_{il})$$

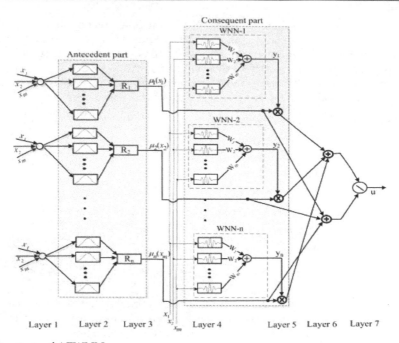

Fig. 1. Structure of AFWNN

Here, 'b_{il}' and 'a_{il}' represent the parameters for the 'ith' input and 'lth' output of the wavelet function. Where, $i = 1, 2, ..., n$ and $l = 1, 2, ..., n$.

Layer 5: This layer estimates the weighted consequent value of a given rule.

Layer 6, 7: In these layers, the defuzzification process is made to calculate the output of the entire network, i.e., it computes the overall output of system. Therefore, the output for the fuzzy wavelet neural network can be expressed as;

$$u = \frac{\sum\limits_{l=1}^{n} \mu_l(x) y_l}{\sum\limits_{l=1}^{n} \mu_l(x)} \tag{5}$$

Where, 'u' is the output for the entire network. The training of the network starts after estimating the output value of the AFWNN.

The AFWNN learning is to minimize a given function or input and output values by adjusting network parameters. Adapted parameters are mean 'g_{ij}' and variance 'σ_{ij}' of membership functions in antecedent part, translation 'b_{ij}' and dilation 'a_{ij}' parameters of wavelet functions and weights 'w_{ij}' are the parameters in the consequent part of the rules.

The AFWNN learning is done by minimizing the performance index. In this study, the gradient descent technique has been used to speed up the convergence and minimize the cost function.

The performance index can be expressed as;

$$J = \frac{1}{2} \sum_{i=0}^{O} e^2$$

$$= \frac{1}{2} \sum_{i=0}^{O} (r_i - u_i)^2 \tag{6}$$

Where, $'r_i'$ and $'u_i'$ are the desired and current output values of the system, respectively. $'O'$ shows the number of the output values of the system, which is one in our case. The update parameters $'w_l'$, $'a_{il}'$, $'b_{il}'$ of the consequent part of network and $'g_{il}'$ and $'\sigma_{il}'$ ($i = 1, 2, ..., m$, $j = 1, 2, ..., n$) of the antecedent part of the network can be formulated as follows;

$$w_l(t+1) = w_l(t) - \gamma \frac{\partial J}{\partial w_l} + \lambda(w_l(t) - w_l(t-1)) \tag{7}$$

$$a_{il}(t+1) = a_{il}(t) - \gamma \frac{\partial J}{\partial a_{il}} + \lambda(a_{il}(t) - a_{il}(t-1)) \tag{8}$$

$$b_{il}(t+1) = b_{il}(t) - \gamma \frac{\partial J}{\partial b_{il}} + \lambda(b_{il}(t) - b_{il}(t-1)) \tag{9}$$

$$g_{ij}(t+1) = g_{ij}(t) - \gamma \frac{\partial J}{\partial g_{ij}} \tag{10}$$

$$\sigma_{ij}(t+1) = \sigma_{ij}(t) - \gamma \frac{\partial J}{\partial \sigma_{ij}} \tag{11}$$

Where, $'\gamma'$ and $'\lambda'$ represent the learning rate and momentum, respectively. $'m'$ and $'n'$ shows the input values and rules number of the network such that $i = 1, 2, ..., m$ and $j = 1, 2, ..., n$.

By using chain rule the partial derivatives shown in the above equations can be expanded as;

$$\frac{\partial J}{\partial w_l} = \frac{\partial J}{\partial u} \frac{\partial u}{\partial y_l} \frac{\partial y_l}{\partial w_l} \tag{12}$$

$$\frac{\partial J}{\partial a_{il}} = \frac{\partial J}{\partial u} \frac{\partial u}{\partial y_l} \frac{\partial y_l}{\partial \psi_l} \frac{\partial \psi_l}{\partial q_{il}} \frac{\partial q_{il}}{\partial a_{il}} \tag{13}$$

$$\frac{\partial J}{\partial b_{il}} = \frac{\partial J}{\partial u} \frac{\partial u}{\partial y_l} \frac{\partial y_l}{\partial \psi_l} \frac{\partial \psi_l}{\partial q_l} \frac{\partial q_l}{\partial b_l} \tag{14}$$

$$\frac{\partial J}{\partial g_{ij}} = \sum_j \frac{\partial J}{\partial u} \frac{\partial u}{\partial \mu_j} \frac{\partial \mu_j}{\partial g_{ij}} \tag{15}$$

$$\frac{\partial J}{\partial \sigma_{ij}} = \sum_j \frac{\partial J}{\partial u} \frac{\partial u}{\partial \mu_j} \frac{\partial \mu_j}{\partial \sigma_{ij}} \tag{16}$$

Equations (12) to (16) shows the contribution of update parameters for change in error. The following sections give a brief detail of different configurations of AFWNN, applied to full car model. Since, the full car active suspension control is a nonlinear problem, the idea is to check different combinations of wavelets and membership functions to increase the nonlinearity of the controller as well so that it could efficiently deal with a nonlinear system.

2.1 AFWNN-1: Structure and parameters update rules for learning

AFWNN-1 structure uses Gaussian membership function in the antecedent part and Mexican hat wavelet in the consequent part. The gaussian membership function is given by;

$$\eta_j(x_i) = e^{-(x_i - g_{ij})^2/\sigma_{ij}^2} \quad i = 1, 2, ..., m, \quad j = 1, 2, ..., n \tag{17}$$

Where, $'\eta_j(x_j)'$ shows the membership function, $'g_{ij}'$ and $'\sigma_{ij}'$ are the mean and variance of membership function of the $jith$ term of ith input variable. $'m'$ and $'n'$ are the number of input signals and number of nodes in second layer, respectively.

The Mexican hat wavelet function is given by;

$$\psi(q_i) = \sum_{i=1}^{m} |a_i|^{-1/2}(1 - q_i^2)e^{-q_i^2/2}$$

where,

$$q_j = \frac{x - b_j}{a_j} \tag{18}$$

Where, $\Psi_j(x)$ is the family of wavelets, $x = x_1, x_2, ..., x_m$ shows the inputs values, $a_j = a_{1j}, a_{2j}, ..., a_{mj}$ and $b_j = b_{1j}, b_{2j}, ..., b_{mj}$ represent the dilation and translation parameters of the mother wavelet $\Psi(x)$, respectively. Figure 2(a) shows Mexican wavelet function.

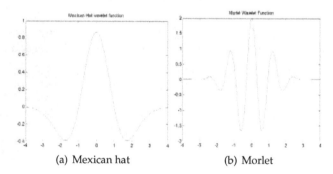

(a) Mexican hat   (b) Morlet

Fig. 2. Wavelet functions

Referring to equations (12) to (16) and simplifying gives the following results;

$$\frac{\partial J}{\partial w_l} = (u(t) - r(t))\mu_l(x).\psi(q_l) \Big/ \sum_{l=1}^{n} \mu_l(x) \tag{19}$$

$$\frac{\partial J}{\partial a_{il}} = \delta_i \frac{(-3.5q_{il}^2 - q_{il}^4 - 0.5)e^{-q_{il}^2/2}}{\sqrt{a_{il}^3}} \tag{20}$$

$$\frac{\partial J}{\partial b_{il}} = \delta_l (3q_{il} - q_{il}^3)e^{-q_{il}^2/2} \Big/ \left(\sqrt{a_{il}^3}\right) \tag{21}$$

$$\frac{\partial J}{\partial g_{ij}} = \sum_j (u(t) - r(t)) \frac{y_j - u}{\sum_j \mu_j} \mu_j(x_i) \frac{2(x_i - g_{ij})}{\sigma_{ij}^2} \tag{22}$$

$$\frac{\partial J}{\partial \sigma_{ij}} = \sum_j (u(t) - r(t)) . \frac{y_j - u}{\sum_j \mu_j(x)} . u_j(x_i) \frac{2(x_i - g_{ij})^2}{\sigma_{ij}^3} \tag{23}$$

where,

$$\delta_l = (u(t) - r(t)) \mu_l(x) . w_l \Big/ \sum_{l=1}^n \mu_l(x)$$

Putting these values in respective equations from equation (7) to equation (11), gives the final update equations for AFWNN-1 as follows;

$$w_l(t+1) = w_l(t) - \gamma(u(t) - r(t)) \mu_l(x) . \psi_l(q) \Big/ \sum_{l=1}^n \mu_l(x) + \lambda(w_l(t) - w_l(t-1)) \tag{24}$$

$$a_{il}(t+1) = a_{il}(t) - \gamma \delta_l \frac{(3.5q_{il}^2 - q_{il}^4 - 0.5)e^{-q_{il}^2/2}}{\sqrt{a_{il}^3}} + \lambda(a_{il}(t) - a_{il}(t-1))$$

$$\Rightarrow a_{il}(t+1) = a_{il}(t) - \frac{\gamma(u(t) - r(t)) \mu_l(x) . w_l(q)}{\sum\limits_{l=1}^n \mu_l(x)} \frac{(3.5q_{il}^2 - q_{il}^4 - 0.5)e^{-q_{il}^2/2}}{\sqrt{a_{il}^3}}$$

$$+ \lambda(a_{il}(t) - a_{il}(t-1)) \tag{25}$$

$$b_{il}(t+1) = b_{il}(t) - \gamma \delta_l \left[|a_{il}|^{-1/2}(-3q_{il} + q_{il}^3)e^{-q_{il}^2/2} \left(\frac{-1}{a_{il}} \right) \right]$$

$$+ \lambda(b_{il}(t) - b_{il}(t-1))$$

$$\Rightarrow b_{il}(t+1) = b_{il}(t) - \frac{\gamma(u(t) - r(t)) \mu_l(x) . w_l(q)}{\sum\limits_{l=1}^n \mu_l(x)} \left[|a_{il}|^{-1/2}(-3q_{il} + q_{il}^3)e^{-q_{il}^2/2} \left(\frac{-1}{a_{il}} \right) \right]$$

$$+ \lambda(b_{il}(t) - b_{il}(t-1)) \tag{26}$$

$$g_{ij}(t+1) = g_{ij}(t) - \sum_j (u(t) - r(t)) \frac{y_j - u}{\sum_j \mu_j} \mu_j(x_i) \frac{2(x_i - g_{ij})}{\sigma_{ij}^2} \tag{27}$$

$$\sigma_{ij}(t+1) = \sigma_{ij}(t) - \sum_j (u(t) - r(t)) . \frac{y_j - u}{\sum_j \mu_j(x)} . u_j(x_i) \frac{2(x_i - g_{ij})^2}{\sigma_{ij}^3} \tag{28}$$

The gradient descent method shows convergence on the basis of the learning rate and the momentum value. The values of the learning rate and momentum are usually taken in interval [0,1]. If the value of the learning rate is high, it makes the system unstable and if its value is small the convergence process is slow. The momentum term 'λ' speeds up the learning process.

2.2 AFWNN-2: Structure and parameters update rules for learning

In AFWNN-2, linear function or constant in the consequent part of the linguistic rules in TSK fuzzy system are replaced with Mexican hat wavelet function. The Mexican Hat wavelet function is given by equation (18), as for AFWNN-1. To illustrate the linguistic term, the Triangular membership function has been used for this neuro-fuzzy system and is given by,

$$\eta_j(x_i) = 1 - \frac{2\,|\,x_i - g_{ij}\,|}{\sigma_{ij}} \quad i = 1, 2, ..., m, \quad j = 1, 2, ..., n \tag{29}$$

Where, '$\eta_j(x_j)$' shows the membership function, 'g_{ij}' and 'σ_{ij}' are the mean and variance of membership function of the '$jith$' term of 'ith' input variable. In order to calculate the updated values for this network simplifying the Equations (12) to (16) give the following results;

$$\frac{\partial J}{\partial w_l} = (u(t) - r(t))\mu_l(x).\psi(q_l) \Big/ \sum_{l=1}^{n} \mu_l(x) \tag{30}$$

$$\frac{\partial J}{\partial a_{il}} = \delta_l \frac{(-3.5q_{il}^2 - q_{il}^4 - 0.5)e^{-q_{il}^2/2}}{\sqrt{a_{il}^3}} \tag{31}$$

$$\frac{\partial J}{\partial b_{il}} = \delta_l(3q_{il} - q_{il}^3)e^{-q_{il}^2/2} \Big/ \left(\sqrt{a_{il}^3}\right) \tag{32}$$

$$\frac{\partial J}{\partial g_{ij}} = \sum_j \left[\left(u(t) - r(t)\right).\frac{y_j - u}{\sum_j \mu_j} \frac{\mu_j}{\eta_j(x_i)}.2\frac{sign(x_i - g_{ij})}{\sigma_{ij}}\right] \tag{33}$$

$$\frac{\partial J}{\partial \sigma_{ij}} = \sum_j \left[\left(u(t) - r(t).\right)\frac{y_j - u}{\sum_j \mu_j}.\frac{\mu_j}{\eta_j(x_i)}\frac{1 - \eta_j}{\sigma_{ij}}\right] \tag{34}$$

By putting these values in Equations (7) to (11) the final update equations are given by;

$$w_l(t+1) = w_l(t) - \gamma(u(t) - r(t))\mu_l(x).\psi_l(q) \Big/ \sum_{l=1}^{n} \mu_l(x)$$
$$+ \lambda(w_l(t) - w_l(t-1)) \tag{35}$$

$$a_{il}(t+1) = a_{il}(t) - \gamma\delta_l \frac{(-3.5q_{il}^2 - q_{il}^4 - 0.5)e^{-q_{il}^2/2}}{\sqrt{a_{il}^3}}$$
$$+ \lambda(a_{il}(t) - a_{il}(t-1))$$

$$\Rightarrow a_{il}(t+1) = a_{il}(t) - \frac{\gamma(u(t) - r(t))\mu_l(x).w_l(q)}{\sum\limits_{l=1}^{n} \mu_l(x)}\frac{(-3.5q_{il}^2 - q_{il}^4 - 0.5)e^{-q_{il}^2/2}}{\sqrt{a_{il}^3}}$$
$$+ \lambda(a_{il}(t) - a_{il}(t-1)) \tag{36}$$

$$b_{il}(t+1) = b_{il}(t) - \gamma\delta_l\left[|a_{il}|^{-1/2}(-3q_{il} + q_{il}^3)e^{-q_{il}^2/2}\left(\frac{-1}{a_{il}}\right)\right]$$
$$+ \lambda(b_{il}(t) - b_{il}(t-1))$$

$$\Rightarrow b_{il}(t+1) = b_{il}(t) - \frac{\gamma(u(t) - r(t))\mu_l(x).w_l(q)}{\sum\limits_{l=1}^{n}\mu_l(x)}\left[|a_{il}|^{-1/2}(-3q_{il}+q_{il}^3)e^{-q_{il}^2/2}\left(\frac{-1}{a_{il}}\right)\right]$$
$$+ \lambda(b_{il}(t) - b_{il}(t-1)) \tag{37}$$

$$g_{ij}(t+1) = g_{ij}(t) - \gamma\sum_j\left[\left(u(t)-r(t)\right).\frac{y_j-u}{\sum\limits_j\mu_j}\frac{\mu_j}{\eta_j(x_i)}.2\frac{sign(x_i-g_{ij})}{\sigma_{ij}}\right] \tag{38}$$

$$\sigma_{ij}(t+1) = \sigma_{ij}(t) - \gamma\sum_j\left[\left(u(t)-r(t).\right)\frac{y_j-u}{\sum\limits_j\mu_j}.\frac{\mu_j}{\eta_j(x_i)}\frac{1-\eta_j}{\sigma_{ij}}\right] \tag{39}$$

Hence, these are the required equations for the update parameters, 'w_l', 'a_{il}', 'b_{il}', 'g_{il}' and 'σ_{il}' respectively.

2.3 AFWNN-3: Structure and parameters update rules for learning

In AFWNN-3 the consequent part uses Morlet wavelet function whereas the antecedent part uses the same Gaussian membership function as that of AFWNN-1. The Morlet wavelet function has been shown in Figure 2(b) and is given by;

$$\Psi_j(x) = cos(5q_j)e^{-\frac{1}{2}(q_j^2)} \tag{40}$$

The Gaussian membership function is given by equation (17); The output value 'y' for the 'lth' wavelet network is given by;

$$y_l = w_l\psi_l(q), \quad \psi_l(q) = \sum_{i=1}^{m} cos(5q_{il})e^{-\frac{1}{2}(q_{il}^2)}$$

$$\Rightarrow y_l = w_l\sum_{i=1}^{m} cos(5q_{il})e^{-\frac{1}{2}(q_{il}^2)}$$

$$\Rightarrow y_l = w_l\sum_{i=1}^{m} cos5\left(\frac{x_i-b_{il}}{a_{il}}\right)e^{-\frac{1}{2}\left(\frac{x_i-b_{il}}{a_{il}}\right)^2} \tag{41}$$

By using equations (12) to (16), the partial derivatives can be solved as follows;

$$\frac{\partial J}{\partial w_l} = (u(t)-r(t))\mu_l(x).\psi(q_l)\Big/\sum_{l=1}^{n}\mu_l(x) \tag{42}$$

$$\frac{\partial J}{\partial a_{il}} = \delta_l\left(\frac{cos(5q_{il})e^{-\frac{1}{2}(q_{il}^2)}q_{il}^2 + 5q_{il}\,sin(5q_{il})e^{-\frac{1}{2}(q_{il}^2)}}{a_{il}}\right) \tag{43}$$

$$\frac{\partial J}{\partial b_{il}} = \delta_l\left(\frac{cos(5q_{il})e^{-\frac{1}{2}(q_{il}^2)}q_{il} + 5\,sin(5q_{il})e^{-\frac{1}{2}(q_{il}^2)}}{a_{il}}\right) \tag{44}$$

$$\frac{\partial J}{\partial g_{ij}} = \sum_j\left[\left(u(t)-r(t)\right)\frac{y_j-u}{\sum\limits_j\mu_j}\mu_j(x_i)\frac{2(x_i-g_{ij})}{\sigma_{ij}^2}\right] \tag{45}$$

$$\frac{\partial J}{\partial\sigma_{ij}} = \sum_j\left[(u(t)-r(t)).\frac{y_j-u}{\sum\limits_j\mu_j(x)}.u_j(x_i)\frac{2(x_i-g_{ij})^2}{\sigma_{ij}^3}\right] \tag{46}$$

Equations (42) to (46) give the required values of $\frac{\partial J}{\partial w_l}$, $\frac{\partial J}{\partial a_{il}}$, $\frac{\partial J}{\partial b_{il}}$, $\frac{\partial J}{\partial g_{ij}}$ and $\frac{\partial J}{\partial \sigma_{ij}}$, showing the contribution of each update parameter for error convergence.

The required updates can be calculated using equations (7) to (11) as follows;

$$w_l(t+1) = w_l(t) - \gamma(u(t) - r(t))\mu_l(x).\psi_l(q) \Big/ \sum_{l=1}^{n} \mu_l(x) + \lambda(w_l(t) - w_l(t-1)) \tag{47}$$

$$a_{il}(t+1) = a_{il}(t) - \gamma\delta_l \left(\frac{\cos(5q_{il})e^{-\frac{1}{2}(q_{il}^2)}q_{il}^2 + 5q_{il}\sin(5q_{il})e^{-\frac{1}{2}(q_{il}^2)}}{a_{il}} \right)$$

$$+ \lambda(a_{il}(t) - a_{il}(t-1))$$

$$\Rightarrow a_{il}(t+1) = a_{il}(t) - \frac{\gamma(u(t)-r(t))\mu_l(x).w_l(q)}{\sum\limits_{l=1}^{n}\mu_l(x)} \left(\frac{\cos(5q_{il})e^{-\frac{1}{2}(q_{il}^2)}q_{il}^2 + 5q_{il}\sin(5q_{il})e^{-\frac{1}{2}(q_{il}^2)}}{a_{il}} \right)$$

$$+ \lambda(a_{il}(t) - a_{il}(t-1)) \tag{48}$$

$$b_{il}(t+1) = b_{il}(t) - \gamma\delta_l \left(\frac{\cos(5q_{il})e^{-\frac{1}{2}(q_{il}^2)}q_{il} + 5\sin(5q_{il})e^{-\frac{1}{2}(q_{il}^2)}}{a_{il}} \right)$$

$$+ \lambda(b_{il}(t) - b_{il}(t-1))$$

$$\Rightarrow b_{il}(t+1) = b_{il}(t) - \frac{\gamma(u(t)-r(t))\mu_l(x).w_l(q)}{\sum\limits_{l=1}^{n}\mu_l(x)} \left(\frac{\cos(5q_{il})e^{-\frac{1}{2}(q_{il}^2)}q_{il} + 5\sin(5q_{il})e^{-\frac{1}{2}(q_{il}^2)}}{a_{il}} \right)$$

$$+ \lambda(b_{il}(t) - b_{il}(t-1)) \tag{49}$$

$$g_{ij}(t+1) = g_{ij}(t) - \gamma \sum_j u(t) - r(t)\frac{y_j - u}{\sum\limits_j \mu_j}\mu_j(x_i)\frac{2(x_i - g_{ij})}{\sigma_{ij}^2} \tag{50}$$

$$\sigma_{ij}(t+1) = \sigma_{ij}(t) - \gamma \sum_j u(t) - r(t)\frac{y_j - u}{\sum\limits_j \mu_j}\mu_j(x_i)\frac{2(x_i - g_{ij})^2}{\sigma_{ij}^3} \tag{51}$$

Hence, these are the required equations for the update parameters w_l, a_{il}, b_{il}, g_{il} and σ_{il}.

2.4 AFWNN-4: Structure and parameters update rules for learning

AFWNN-4 uses Morlet wavelet function along with triangular membership function. The triangular membership function is given by Equation (29). Using Morlet wavelet function the output value 'y' for the 'lth' wavelet is given by;

$$y_l = w_l\psi_l(q), \quad \psi_l(q) = \sum_{i=1}^{m} \cos(5q_{il})e^{-\frac{1}{2}(q_{il}^2)}$$

$$\Rightarrow y_l = w_l \sum_{i=1}^{m} \cos 5\left(\frac{x_i - b_{il}}{a_{il}}\right) e^{-\frac{1}{2}\left(\frac{x_i - b_{il}}{a_{il}}\right)^2} \tag{52}$$

The derivatives given by equations (12) to (16) can be simplified as follows;

$$\frac{\partial J}{\partial w_l} = (u(t) - r(t))\mu_l(x).\psi(q_l) \Big/ \sum_{l=1}^{n} \mu_l(x) \tag{53}$$

$$\frac{\partial J}{\partial a_{il}} = \delta_l \left(\frac{\cos(5q_{il})e^{-\frac{1}{2}(q_{il}^2)}q_{il}^2 + 5q_{il}\sin(5q_{il})e^{-\frac{1}{2}(q_{il}^2)}}{a_{il}} \right) \tag{54}$$

$$\frac{\partial J}{\partial b_{il}} = \delta_l \left(\frac{\cos(5q_{il})e^{-\frac{1}{2}(q_{il}^2)}q_{il} + 5\sin(5q_{il})e^{-\frac{1}{2}(q_{il}^2)}}{a_{il}} \right) \tag{55}$$

$$\frac{\partial J}{\partial g_{ij}} = \sum_j \left[\left(u(t) - r(t) \right).\frac{y_j - u}{\sum_j \mu_j}\frac{\mu_j}{\eta_j(x_i)}.2\frac{sign(x_i - g_{ij})}{\sigma_{ij}} \right] \tag{56}$$

$$\frac{\partial J}{\partial \sigma_{ij}} = \sum_j \left[\left(u(t) - r(t) \right)\frac{y_j - u}{\sum_j \mu_j}.\frac{\mu_j}{\eta_j(x_i)}\frac{1 - \eta_j}{\sigma_{ij}} \right] \tag{57}$$

Equations (53) to (57) give the required values of $\frac{\partial J}{\partial w_l}$, $\frac{\partial J}{\partial a_{il}}$, $\frac{\partial J}{\partial b_{il}}$, $\frac{\partial J}{\partial g_{ij}}$ and $\frac{\partial J}{\partial \sigma_{ij}}$, respectively.

Using Equations (7) to (11) the updates can be found as follows;

$$w_l(t+1) = w_l(t) - \gamma(u(t) - r(t))\mu_l(x).\psi_l(q) \Big/ \sum_{l=1}^{n} \mu_l(x)$$
$$+ \lambda(w_l(t) - w_l(t-1)) \tag{58}$$

$$a_{il}(t+1) = a_{il}(t) - \gamma\delta_l \left(\frac{\cos(5q_{il})e^{-\frac{1}{2}(q_{il}^2)}q_{il}^2 + 5q_{il}\sin(5q_{il})e^{-\frac{1}{2}(q_{il}^2)}}{a_{il}} \right)$$
$$+ \lambda(a_{il}(t) - a_{il}(t-1))$$

$$\Rightarrow a_{il}(t+1) = a_{il}(t) - \frac{\gamma(u(t) - r(t))\mu_l(x).w_l(q)}{\sum_{l=1}^{n} \mu_l(x)} \left(\frac{\cos(5q_{il})e^{-\frac{1}{2}(q_{il}^2)}q_{il}^2 + 5q_{il}\sin(5q_{il})e^{-\frac{1}{2}(q_{il}^2)}}{a_{il}} \right)$$
$$+ \lambda(a_{il}(t) - a_{il}(t-1)) \tag{59}$$

$$b_{il}(t+1) = b_{il}(t) - \gamma\delta_l \left(\frac{\cos(5q_{il})e^{-\frac{1}{2}(q_{il}^2)}q_{il} + 5\sin(5q_{il})e^{-\frac{1}{2}(q_{il}^2)}}{a_{il}} \right)$$
$$+ \lambda(b_{il}(t) - b_{il}(t-1))$$

$$\Rightarrow b_{il}(t+1) = b_{il}(t) - \frac{\gamma(u(t) - r(t))\mu_l(x).w_l(q)}{\sum_{l=1}^{n} \mu_l(x)} \left(\frac{\cos(5q_{il})e^{-\frac{1}{2}(q_{il}^2)}q_{il} + 5\sin(5q_{il})e^{-\frac{1}{2}(q_{il}^2)}}{a_{il}} \right)$$
$$+ \lambda(b_{il}(t) - b_{il}(t-1)) \tag{60}$$

$$g_{ij}(t+1) = g_{ij}(t) - \gamma\sum_j \left[\left(u(t) - r(t) \right).\frac{y_j - u}{\sum_j \mu_j}\frac{\mu_j}{\eta_j(x_i)}.2\frac{sign(x_i - g_{ij})}{\sigma_{ij}} \right] \tag{61}$$

$$\sigma_{ij}(t+1) = \sigma_{ij}(t) - \gamma\sum_j \left[\left(u(t) - r(t).\right)\frac{y_j - u}{\sum_j \mu_j}.\frac{\mu_j}{\eta_j(x_i)}\frac{1 - \eta_j}{\sigma_{ij}} \right] \tag{62}$$

The above equations give the parameters updates for AFWNN-4.

3. System modeling and design

The proposed AFWNN structures have been applied to full car model with eight degree of freedom, being closer to reality, as shown in Figure 3. The eight degrees of freedom are the four wheels displacement ($Z_{f,r}, Z_{f,l}, Z_{r,r}, Z_{r,l}$), seat displacement '$Z_s$', heave displacement '$Z$', pitch displacement '$\theta$' and roll displacement 'ϕ'. The car model comprises of only one sprung mass attached to the four unsprung masses at each corner. The sprung mass is allowed to have pitch, heave and roll and the unsprung masses are allowed to have heave only. For simplicity, all other motions are ignored for this model. The suspensions between the sprung mass and

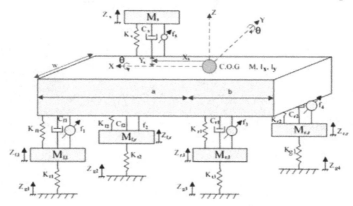

Fig. 3. Full-Car Model

unsprung masses are modeled as non-linear viscous dampers and spring components and the tires are modeled as simple non-linear springs without damping elements. The actuator gives forces that determine by the displacement of the actuator between the sprung mass and the wheels. The dampers between the wheels and car body signify sources of conventional damping like friction among the mechanical components. The inputs of full-car model are four disturbances coming through the tires and the four outputs are the heave, pitch, seat, and roll displacement. For details of the dynamic model the reader is referred to (Rahmi, 2003). Figure 4 depicts the closed loop diagram of the feedback system. The input to the plant is the noisy output of controller. The controller parameters are adapted on the basis of calculated error which is the difference between the desired and actual output of the plant.

The inputs of the plant (full-car model) are four disturbances from the tire. The outputs are Seat, Heave, Pitch and Roll displacements. The states required for controller come from displacement sensors which measure the displacement states of four tires and one more sensor for measuring the displacement of seat. The adaptive control law uses control technique and adaptation mechanism to adapt the controller itself using proposed algorithms. The general class of nonlinear MIMO systems is described by;

$$y^{(r)} = A(x) + \sum_{i=1}^{p} \sum_{j=1}^{s} B_{ij}(x)u_j + \sum_{i=1}^{p} \sum_{j=1}^{s} G_{ij}(x)z_j \tag{63}$$

Where, $x = [y_1, \dot{y}_1, \cdots, y_1^{(r_1-1)}, \cdots, y_p, \dot{y}_p, \cdots, y_p^{(r_p-1)}]^T \epsilon R^r$ is the overall state vector, which

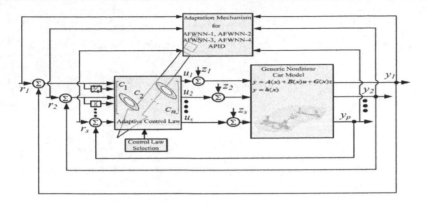

Fig. 4. Overall control system design

is assumed available and $r = r_1 + r_2 + \cdots + r_p$.

$u = [u_1, u_2, \cdots, u_s]^T \epsilon R^s$ is the control input vector, $y = [y_1, \cdots, y_p]^T \epsilon R^p$ is the output vector and $z = [z_1, \cdots, z_s]^T \epsilon R^s$ is the disturbance vector. $A_i(x)$, $i = 1, \cdots, p$ are continuous non-linear functions, $B_{ij}(x)$, $i = 1, \cdots, p; j = 1, \cdots, s$ are continuous non-linear control functions and $G_{ij}(x)$, $i = 1, \cdots, p; j = 1, \cdots, s$ are continuous non-linear disturbance functions.

Let us refer;

$$A = [A_1(x)\, A_2(x)\, \cdots\, A_p(x)]^T \qquad (64)$$

The control matrix is:

$$B(x) = \begin{bmatrix} b_{11}(x) & \dots & b_{1s}(x) \\ \vdots & \ddots & \vdots \\ b_{p1}(x) & \dots & b_{ps}(x) \end{bmatrix}_{p \times s}$$

The disturbance matrix is:

$$G(x) = \begin{bmatrix} g_{11}(x) & \dots & g_{1s}(x) \\ \vdots & \ddots & \vdots \\ g_{p1}(x) & \dots & g_{ps}(x) \end{bmatrix}_{p \times s}$$

$$y^{(r)} = [y_1^{(r_1)}, y_2^{(r_2)}, \cdots, y_p^{(r_p)}]^T$$

$$y^{(r)} = A(x) + B(x).u + G(x).z \qquad (65)$$

$$A(.) \epsilon R^{p \times p}; \quad B(.) \epsilon R^{p \times s}; \quad G(.) \epsilon R^{p \times s}$$

The generic non-linear car model is,

$$\dot{y} = f(x) + B(x).u + G(x).z$$

$$y = h(x)$$

Where, $f(x) \in R^{(16 \times 16)}$, $B(x) \in R^{(16 \times 4)}$, $G(x) \in R^{(16 \times 4)}$, state vector $x \in R^{(16 \times 1)}$, $u \in R^{(4 \times 1)}$ and $z \in R^{(4 \times 1)}$.

These matrices can be shown in state-space form, with state vector x, represented in row matrix form.

$$f(x) = [A_1(x) \quad A_2(x) \quad A_3(x) \quad \ldots \quad A_{16}(x)]$$

$$x = [x_1 \quad x_2 \quad x_3 \quad \ldots \quad x_{16}]^T$$

$A_1(x)$ to $A_8(x)$ are velocity states and $A_9(x)$ to $A_{16}(x)$ are acceleration states of four tires, seat, heave, pitch and roll.

The disturbance inputs for each tire individually are represented in the form of z matrix.

$$z = [z_1 \quad z_2 \quad z_3 \quad z_4]^T$$

z_n are n disturbances applied to full-car model. u_n are n control inputs to full-car model, so to regulate the car model disturbances. y_n are n states of car. r_n are n desired outputs for the controller to achieve.

Each **controller** in this work has two inputs. One of the inputs is 'r_n' and delay of it is given to second input . The y_n states are fed to the controller as an error, so to adapt the update adaptation law for the desired regulation. Based on this error the adaptation law is formulated using AFWNN-1, AFWNN-2, AFWNN-3 and AFWNN-4. The algorithms develop a back-propagation algorithm for training the controller to achieve the desire performance.

In this work for the full-car model **four states of tires** are used by the four controllers as an error to adapt the adaptation law. As the purpose of controller is to regulate the disturbances so r_n's are zero, the second input of controllers is a delayed version of first input. The adaptation law of the controller provides the control inputs u_1, u_2, u_3 and u_4 to plant so as to regulate the plant. The four disturbances z_1, z_2, z_3 and z_4 are coming from road through tires into suspension system and to the body of the vehicle.

Two cases have been considered. In the **first case**, only the states of the four tires y_1, y_2, y_3 and y_4 displacement are used as an error to the controller. Which develops the control law according to that error. These control inputs u_1, u_2, u_3 and u_4 are provided to the plant from each controller (placed on each tire) to achieve the desired performance of the plant (full-car model) i.e. both better passenger comfort (better seat and heave displacement) and better vehicle stability (better heave, pitch and roll displacement). In the **second case**, an additional controller is applied under the driver seat to improve the passenger comfort. In this case, another state y_5 is used as an error input to the controller. This additional control input will help in reducing the disturbance effect and improving the passenger comfort.

Table 1 gives the description of different constants and their respective values used for simulation.

4. Simulation results and discussion

Four different types of fuzzy wavelet neural network control techniques in addition to the APID and semi-active control have been applied to full car suspension model. AFWNNC-1

Constants	Description	Values	Units
k_{f1}, k_{f2}	Front-left and Front-right suspension stuffiness, respectively.	15000	N/m
k_{r1}, k_{r2}	Rear-left and rear-right suspension stuffiness, respectively.	17000	N/m
k_s	Seat spring Constant	15000	N/m
c_s	Seat damping Constant	15000	N/m
$c_{s1} - c_{s4}$	Front-left, Front-right, rear-right and rear-left tire damping, respectively.	2500	N.sec/m
$k_{t1} - k_{t4}$	Front-left, Front-right, rear-right and rear-left tire suspension, respectively.	250000	N/m
a	Distance between front axle suspension and C.O.G.	1.2	m
b	Distance between rear axle suspension and C.O.G.	1.4	m
X_s	Horizontal distance of seat from C.O.G.	0.3	m
Y_s	Vertical distance of seat from C.O.G.	0.25	m
$M_{f,l}, M_{f,r}$	Front-left and Front-right unsprung mass, respectively.	25	kg
$M_{r,l}, M_{r,r}$	Rear-left and rear-right unsprung mass, respectively.	45	kg
M_s	Seat Mass	90	kg
M	Vehicle body mass	1100	kg
I_x	Moment of inertia for pitch	1848	$kg.m^2$
I_y	Moment of inertia for roll	550	$kg.m^2$
Cshy1	Shyhook damper constant	-2500	N.sec/m

Table 1. Vehicle Suspension Parameters

and AFWNNC-2 use Mexican hat as wavelet in the consequent part and gaussian and triangular as membership function in the antecedent, respectively.   AFWNNC-3 and AFWNNC-4 use Morlet as wavelet in the consequent part and gaussian and triangular as membership function in the antecedent, respectively. Two rules each having two membership functions have been used for simulation. For each AFWNN, 18 parameters have been adapted being the mean and variance of the antecedent part and translation, dilation and weights of the consequent part. Three types of road profiles have been examined to check the robustness

Sr. No.	Control Algo.	Seat	Front		Rear	
			Left	Right	Left	Right
1	APID	0.9	1	0.6	0.5	0.8
2	AFWNN-1	0.001	0.4	0.09	0.7	0.2
3	AFWNN-2	0.0054	0.08	0.09	0.08	0.09
4	AFWNN-3	0.003	0.08	0.007	0.009	0.008
5	AFWNN-4	0.003	0.0009	0.001	0.004	0.006

Table 2. Learning rates 'γ' for controls

of the applied algorithms. These road profiles have been used in context of roll, pitch, heave and seat displacement and acceleration. Four controllers have been applied to each car tire and one has been taken for seat. The learning rates for each controller have been shown in Table 2. These values have been set for learning rates based on hit-and-trial keeping in view the fact that a positive change in the error rate leads to increase the value of 'γ' and vice versa. For simplicity of implementation the moment term has been neglected.

The performance index used for evaluation of different algorithms is given by,

$$I = \frac{1}{2} \int_0^T (Z_P^T Q Z_P) dt \tag{66}$$

where, 'Z_p' is the vector for displacement or acceleration, 'Q' is the identity matrix. The Root Mean Square (RMS) value for displacement and acceleration of heave, pitch, roll and seat has been calculated by,

$$z_{disp.}^{rms} = \sqrt{\frac{1}{T} \int_{t=0}^T [h(t)]^2} \tag{67}$$

$$\ddot{z}_{acc.}^{rms} = \sqrt{\frac{1}{T} \int_{t=0}^T [\ddot{h}(t)]^2} \tag{68}$$

Figure 5 shows different road profiles used for simulation.

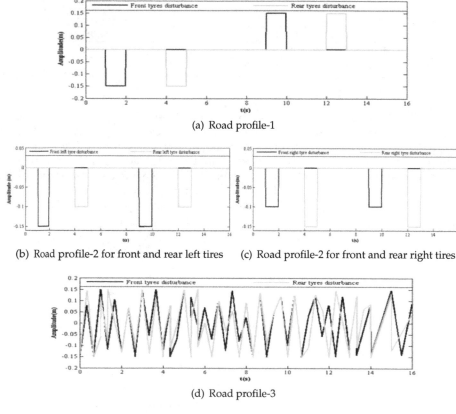

(a) Road profile-1

(b) Road profile-2 for front and rear left tires   (c) Road profile-2 for front and rear right tires

(d) Road profile-3

Fig. 5. (a) Road profile-1 (b) Road profile-2 (c) Road profile-3

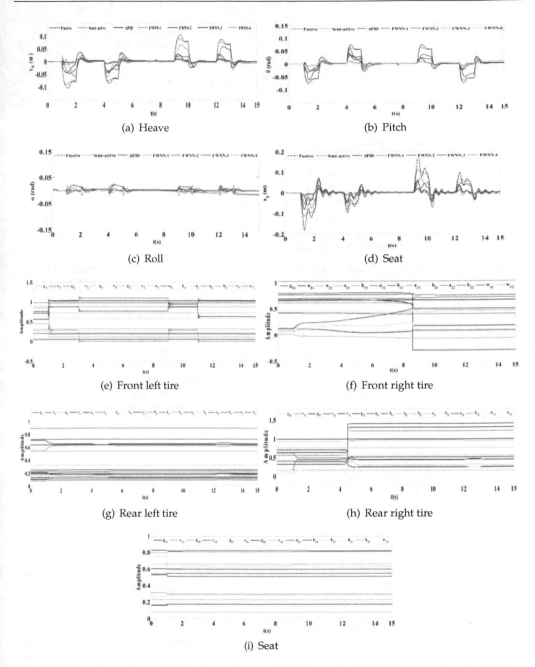

Fig. 6. (a) Heave amplitude (b) Pitch amplitude (c) Roll amplitude (d) Seat amplitude (e)-(i) Update parameters for antecedent and consequent part of AFWNN-4 for all five controllers

4.1 Road profile-1

Road profile-1 involves one pothole and one bump, each having duration of one second with a time delay of 8 secs., for front and rear tires. Mathematically, road profile-1 is given by;

$$z_1(t) = \begin{cases} -0.15 & 1 \leq t \leq 2 \, and \, 4 \leq t \leq 5 \\ 0.15 & 9 \leq t \leq 10 \, and \, 12 \leq t \leq 13 \\ 0 & \text{otherwise} \end{cases} \qquad (69)$$

i.e., the road profile contains a pothole and a bump of amplitudes $-0.15m$ and $0.15m$, respectively. This road profile is helpful to calculate heave of a vehicle. Figure 5(a) depicts the road profile-1. Figures 6(a)-(d) show the regulation results for heave, roll, pitch and seat displacement for active suspension as compared to passive and semi-active suspension. It is clear from the figures that there is improvement in the results for active suspension. The settling time has been reduced and the steady state response is improved. In case of heave and seat the passive control approaches the rattle space limits whereas AFWNN-4 has optimal results for all the four cases showing the least variation from steady state.

In passive and semi-active suspension suspension, the maximum values of displacements for heave is $0.106m$ and $0.088m$, for roll $0.016m$ and $0.009m$, for pitch is $0.075m$ and $0.061m$ and for seat is $0.15m$ and 0.11, respectively. Due to high nonlinear nature of AFWNN-4 these values get improved as $0.004m$, $0.006m$, $0.012m$ and 0.02 for heave, roll pitch and seat, respectively.

Table3 shows the results for percent improvement and RMS values for displacement and acceleration, for road profile-1. It can be seen that maximum improvement has been achieved in case of heave with AFWNN-4. Figures 6(e)-(i) show the antecedent and consequent parameters variation for AFWNN-4 for all the five controls. Parameters variation for front and rear right tires is large whereas front and rear left tire has low parameters variation. It was found that the control effort by front and right tires was greater as compared to seat and the left side tires controls.

4.2 Road profile-2

Road profile-2 has been taken as two potholes of different amplitudes as shown in Figures 5(b)-(c). The road profile-2 is given as follows:

$$z_2(t) = \begin{cases} -0.15 & 1 \leq t \leq 2 \, and \, 9 \leq t \leq 10 \\ -0.10 & 4 \leq t \leq 5 \, and \, 12 \leq t \leq 13 \\ 0 & \text{otherwise} \end{cases} \qquad (70)$$

Road profile-2 involves two different potholes of amplitudes $-0.15m$ and $-0.10m$ for front and rear left and rear and front right, respectively. This road profile is very helpful for the calculation of pitch and roll of the vehicle.

Figures 7(a)-(d) reveal that APID shows satisfactory results whereas the result are very good in case of AFWNN-4. The maximum improvement has been found in case of roll for this road profile, which corresponds to the control of vehicle around horizontal axis. Figures 7(e)-(i) give the update parameters results for AFWNN-4 showing large variations for rear left and rear right tires. Table 4 shows the results for road profile-2 in terms of percent improvement and RMS values of displacement and acceleration. The passive and semi-active suspension show poor performance in terms of passenger comfort and vehicle stability.

#	Road Profile	Control Algo.	Performance Index	RMS		% Improvement w.r.t.	
				Disp.	Acc.	Passive	Semi-active
1	Heave	Passive	6.03515	0.0404	3.476	-	-
		Semi-active	5.3037	0.03729	3.2567	-	-
		APID	4.92835	0.0166	3.1395	70	62
		AFWNN-1	4.6587	0.0158	3.0524	75	65
		AFWNN-2	4.3854	0.0148	2.965	77	65
		AFWNN-3	1.9529	0.00403	1.9763	93	89
		AFWNN-4	1.8006	0.004	1.8977	94	93
2	Roll	Passive	1.6822	0.00545	1.8342	-	-
		Semi-active	1.4578	0.00443	1.7075	-	-
		APID	1.3194	0.00263	1.6244	53	05
		AFWNN-1	0.7863	0.0021	1.2540	54	10
		AFWNN-2	0.7213	0.0020	1.2011	57	15
		AFWNN-3	0.4600	0.0031	0.9590	57	25
		AFWNN-4	0.2494	0.0022	0.7063	62	35
3	Pitch	Passive	3.6786	0.0308	2.7122	-	-
		Semi-active	3.5407	0.0274	2.6610	-	-
		APID	2.9947	0.0094	2.4473	50	38
		AFWNN-1	1.5545	0.01	1.7632	54	40
		AFWNN-2	1.1381	0.01004	1.2011	69	62
		AFWNN-3	0.9288	0.005	1.3629	80	73
		AFWNN-4	0.7834	0.0041	1.2517	84	80
4	Seat	Passive	3.8449	0.04695	2.7726	-	-
		Semi-active	1.8379	0.04101	1.9168	-	-
		APID	0.8508	0.02	1.3043	55	28
		AFWNN-1	0.7966	0.017	1.2621	70	49
		AFWNN-2	0.6492	0.031	1.1319	72	51
		AFWNN-3	0.066	0.0052	0.3631	87	77
		AFWNN-4	0.0295	0.0039	0.2428	88	81

Table 3. Performance Comparison for road profile-1

4.3 Road profile-3

Road profile-3 is white noise as shown in Figure 5(a).

$$z_3(t) = \begin{cases} \sum_{i=1}^{N} A_i sin(\Omega_i s - \Psi_i) & 0 \le t \le 16 \\ 0 & \text{otherwise} \end{cases} \tag{71}$$

Where, value of 'A_i' is the road amplitude, 'Ω_i' is the number of waves and 'Ψ_i' is the phase angle, $i = 1, 2, ..., N$ ranging from 0 to 2π.

The control problem is that the suspension travel should be $|\ z\ |$ less than $|\ \bar{z}\ |$ from the amplitude of disturbance i.e., $\pm 0.15m$. The maximum displacement of the road profile is $\pm 0.15m$.

#	Road Profile	Control Algo.	Performance Index	RMS		% Improvement w.r.t.	
				Disp.	Acc.	Passive	Semi-active
1	Heave	Passive	4.2056	0.0339	2.9	-	-
		Semi-active	3.8635	0.09855	2.778	-	-
		APID	3.1469	0.01542	2.5087	57	36
		AFWNN-1	2.9745	0.01397	2.439	60	47
		AFWNN-2	3.0190	0.0144	2.453	80	72
		AFWNN-3	1.2864	0.0036	1.604	83	78
		AFWNN-4	1.1303	0.0040	1.503	87	82
2	Roll	Passive	1.7504	0.0099	1.8710	-	-
		Semi-active	1.5832	0.00679	1.7794	-	-
		APID	1.2140	0.00438	1.5582	36	25
		AFWNN-1	0.8991	0.0022	1.3410	57	46
		AFWNN-2	0.7176	0.0020	1.1980	63	46
		AFWNN-3	0.5925	0.0024	1.0886	74	66
		AFWNN-4	0.5011	0.0019	1.0010	95	92
3	Pitch	Passive	2.5485	0.0257	2.2575	-	-
		Semi-active	2.2184	0.0193	2.1063	-	-
		APID	1.9173	0.0119	1.9582	60	53
		AFWNN-1	1.8417	0.0080	1.9190	50	10
		AFWNN-2	1.6864	0.0067	1.8365	60	52
		AFWNN-3	0.8484	0.0031	1.3026	78	74
		AFWNN-4	0.8831	0.0024	1.3290	81	78
4	Seat	Passive	2.6620	0.0391	2.3011	-	-
		Semi-active	1.8148	0.03065	1.9049	-	-
		APID	0.7233	0.1850	1.2026	49	30
		AFWNN-1	0.7014	0.1631	1.1731	69	40
		AFWNN-2	0.7325	0.1432	1.2019	69	43
		AFWNN-3	0.0533	0.0046	0.3265	83	69
		AFWNN-4	0.0317	0.0024	0.2516	85	72

Table 4. Performance comparison for road profile-2

The time delay between front and rear wheels is given by;

$$\delta(t) = \frac{(s_1 + s_2)}{V} \tag{72}$$

Where, $s_1 = 1.2m$ and $s_2 = 1.4m$ are the values of distance between front and rear wheels and 'V' is the vehicle velocity. Figures 8(a)-(d) show the results for displacement for different car parameters for each algorithm. There is a performance degradation in case of AFWNN-2 for pitch. Figures 8(e)-(i) show the update parameters for consequent and antecedent part of AFWNN-4. Table 5 shows the performance comparison for road profile-3 for different parameters. The best results have been obtained in case of AFWNN-4 for seat in this case. The minimum displacement for seat correspond to the passenger comfort which shows that AFWNN-4 gives optimal results for passenger comfort for comparatively rough road profiles. It can be seen that the performance difference between AFWNN-1 and AFWNN-2 is small as compared to that of AFWNN-1 and AFWNN-3 or AFWNN-4 which shows that incorporation of Morlet wavelet has improved the performance consistency, significantly.

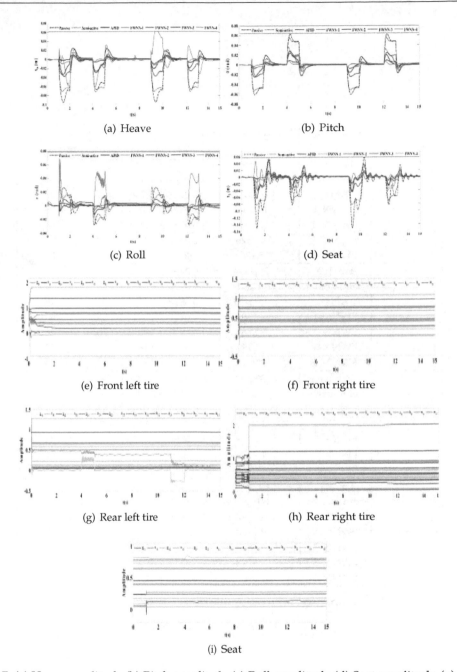

Fig. 7. (a) Heave amplitude (b) Pitch amplitude (c) Roll amplitude (d) Seat amplitude (e)-(i) Update parameters for antecedent and consequent part of AFWNN-4 for all five controllers

♯	Parameters	Control Algo.	Performance Index	RMS		% Improvement w.r.t.	
				Disp.	Acc.	Passive	Semi-active
1	Heave	Passive	34.0666	0.0682	8.254	-	-
		Semi-active	33.4707	0.06684	8.1815	-	-
		APID	14.2367	0.0239	5.336	64	53
		FWNN-1	12.5589	0.02607	5.0117	64	55
		FWNN-2	12.8224	0.0262	5.064	65	64
		FWNN-3	8.0526	0.0318	4.013	79	73
		FWNN-4	5.1264	0.00956	3.202	87	83
2	Roll	Passive	25.3794	0.0495	7.1243	-	-
		Semi-active	18.4609	0.0372	6.0762	-	-
		APID	13.0721	0.0223	5.1131	52	45
		FWNN-1	0.1497	0.0190	4.5010	65	60
		FWNN-2	7.6561	0.1903	3.9085	70	66
		FWNN-3	5.0197	0.0430	3.1682	81	78
		FWNN-4	3.9790	0.0219	2.8209	88	85
3	Pitch	Passive	3.8752	0.0216	2.7839	-	-
		Semi-active	3.1087	0.0192	2.4934	-	-
		APID	2.1505	0.0073	2.0739	40	44
		FWNN-1	1.7559	0.0045	1.8760	59	56
		FWNN-2	2.0279	0.0060	2.0739	50	45
		FWNN-3	1.4126	0.166	1.6808	68	64
		FWNN-4	0.7421	0.1403	1.2176	76	73
4	Seat	Passive	84.3201	0.1233	12.985	-	-
		Semi-active	60.0559	0.1098	10.9590	-	-
		APID	14.4606	0.0486	0.0486	65	35
		FWNN-1	9.3490	0.02607	0.3142	72	45
		FWNN-2	6.3870	0.0262	0.0221	73	46
		FWNN-3	3.8223	0.0318	0.0278	80	67
		FWNN-4	2.2046	0.0102	2.0998	90	92

Table 5. Performance comparison for road profile-3

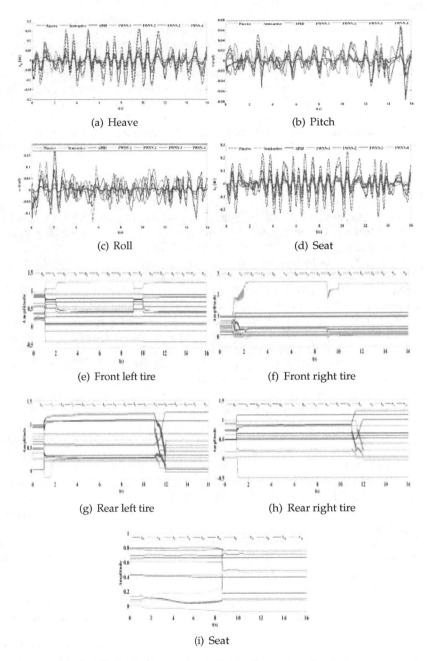

(a) Heave

(b) Pitch

(c) Roll

(d) Seat

(e) Front left tire

(f) Front right tire

(g) Rear left tire

(h) Rear right tire

(i) Seat

Fig. 8. (a) Heave amplitude (b) Pitch amplitude (c) Roll amplitude (d) Seat amplitude (e)-(i) Update parameters for antecedent and consequent part of AFWNN-4 for all five controllers

5. Conclusion

The detailed mathematical modeling of different adaptive softcomputing techniques have been developed and successfully applied to a full car model. The robustness of the presented techniques has been proved on the basis of different performance indices. Unlike, the conventional PID, the proposed algorithms have been compared with each other and APID controller. The simulation results and their analysis reveal that proposed AFWNNC gives better ride comfort and vehicle handling as compared to passive or semi-active and APID control. The performance of the active suspension has been optimized in terms of seat, heave, pitch and roll displacement and acceleration. The results show that AFWNNC-4 gives optimal performance for all rotational and translational motions of the vehicle persevering the passenger comfortability.

6. References

Abiyev, R. H. & Kaynak, O. (2008). Fuzzy wavelet neural networks for identification and control of dynamic plants - a novel structure and comparative study, *IEEE Transactions on Industrial Electronics* 55(8): 3133–3140.

Adeli, H. & Jiang, X. (2006). Dynamic fuzzy wavelet neural network model for structural system idetification, *Journal of Structural Engineering* 132(1): 102–112.

Ahmadian, M. & Pare, C. (2000). A quarter-car experimental analysis of alternative semi-active control methods, *Journal of Intellignet Material Systems and Structures* 11(8): 604–612.

Al-Holou, N., Lahdhiri, T., Joo, D. S., Weaver, J. & Al-Abbas, F. (2002). Sliding mode neural network inference fuzzy logic control for active suspension systems, *IEEE Transactions on Fuzzy System* 10(2): 234–236.

Banakar, A. & Azeem, M. F. (2008). Artificial wavelet neural network and its application in neuro-fuzzy models, *Applied Soft Computing* 8: 1463–1485.

Barak, P. & Hrovat, H. (1988). Application of the lqg approach to design of an automotive suspension for three−dimensional vehicle models, *Proceedings of international conference of advanced suspensions*, ImechE, London.

Bigarbegian, M., Melek, W. & Golnaraghi, F. (2008). A novel neuro-fuzzy controller to enhance the performance of vehicle semi-active suspension systems, *Vehicle System Dynamics* 46(8): 691–711.

Billings, S. A. & Wei, H. L. (2005). A new class of wavelet networks for nonlinear system identification, *IEEE Trans. Neural Netw.* 16(4): 862–874.

Cech, I. (1994). A full−car roll model of a vehicle with controlled suspension, *Vehicle System Dynamics* 23(1): 467–480.

Chalasani, R. M. (1986). Ride performance potential of active suspension system part 11: Comprehensive analysis based on a full car model, *Proceedings of symposium on simulation and control of ground vehicles and transportation systems*, ASME, AMD, Anaheim, CA.

Crolla, D. A. & Abdel−Hady, M. B. A. (1991). Active suspension control: Performance comparisons using control laws applied to a full vehicle model, *Vehicle System Dynamics* 20(2): 107–120.

Esmailzadeh, E. & Taghirad, H. D. (1996). Active vehicle suspensions with optimal state-feedback control, *Journal of Mechanical Engineering Science* 200(4): 1–18.

Hac, A. (1986). Stochastic optimal control of vehicles with elastic body and active suspension, *Journal of Dynamic Systems, Measurement and Control* 108(2): 106–110.

Hac, A. (1987). Adaptive control of vehicle suspensions, *Vehicle System Dynamics* 16(2): 57–74.

Hedrick, J. K. & Butsuen, T. (1990). Invariant properties of automotive suspensions, *Proceedings of the Institution of Mechanical Engineers. part D: Journal of Automobile Engineering* 204(1): 21–27.

Heo, S. J., Park, K. & Hwang, S. H. (2000). Performance and design consideration for continuosly controlled semi-active suspension systems, *International Journal of Vehicle Design* 23(3/4): 376–389.

Ho, D. W. C., Zhang, P.-A. & Xu, J. (2001). Fuzzy wavelet networks for function learning, *IEEE Transactions on Fuzzy Systems* 9(1): 200–211.

Hrovat, D. (1982). A class of active lqg optimal actuators, *Automatica* 18(1): 117–119.

Huang, S. J. & Lin, W. C. (2003). A self-organizing fuzzy controller for an active suspension system, *Journal of Vibration Control* 9(9): 1023–1040.

Kaleemullah, M., Faris, W. F. & Hasbullah, F. (2011). Design of robust h_∞, fuzzy and lqr controller for active suspension of a quarter car model, *4th International conference on mechatronics(ICOM)*, Kuala Lampur, Malaysia.

Krtolica, R. & Hrovat, D. (1990). Optimal active suspension control based on a half-car model, *Proceedings of the 29th IEEE conference on decision and control*, Vol. 2, HI, USA, pp. 2238–2243.

Krtolica, R. & Hrovat, D. (1992). Optimal active suspension control based on a half-car model: analytical solution, *IEEE Transactions on Automatic Control* 37(4): 528–532.

Kumar, M. S. (2008). Development of active suspension system for automobiles using pid controller, *Proceedings of the World Congress on Engineering*, Vol. 2, London, UK.

Lian, R. J., Lin, B. F. & Sie, W. T. (Feb. 2005). Self-organizing fuzzy control of active suspension systems, *International Journal of System Science* 36(3): 119–135.

Lieh, J. & Li, W. J. (1997). Adaptive fuzzy control of vehicle semi-active suspensions, *Proceedings of ASME Dynamic Systems Control Division* 61: 293–297.

Lin, J. & Lian, R. J. (2008). Dsp-based self-organising fuzzy controller for active suspension systems, *Vehicle System Dynamic* 46(12): 1123–1139.

Lin, J. S. & Kanellakopoulos, I. (1997). Nonlinear design of active suspension, *IEEE Control Systems Megazine* 17(3): 45–59.

Meld, R. C. (1991). Performance of lowbandwidth, semi-active damping concepts for suspension control, *Vehicle System Dynamics* 20(5): 245–267.

Meller, T. (1978). Self-energizing, hydro pneumatic leveling systems, *SAE* (780052).

Moran, A. & Masao, N. (1994). Optimal active control of nonlinear vehicle suspensions using neural networks, *JSME International Journal* 37(4): 707–718.

Nicolas, C. F., Landaluze, ., Castrillo, E., Gaston, M. & Reyero, R. (1997). Application of fuzzy logic control to the design of semi-active suspension systems, *Proceedings of 6th IEEE International Conference on Fuzzy Systems*, Barcelona, Spain.

Oussar, Y. & Dreyfus, G. (2000). Initialization by selection for wavelet network training, *Neurocomputing* 34: 131–143.

Rahmi, G. (2003). Active control of seat vibrations of a vehicle model using various suspension alternatives, *Turkish Journal of Engineering and Enviormental Sciences* 27: 361–373.

Rao, M. V. C. & Prahlad, V. (1997). A tunable fuzzy logic controller for vehicle-active suspension system, *Fuzzy Sets System* 85: 11–21.

Ray, L. R. (1991). Robust linear-optimal control laws for active suspension system, *Journal of Dynamic Systems, Measurement and Control* 114(4): 592–599.

Redfield, R. C. & Karnopp, D. C. (1988).   Optimal performance of variable component suspensions, *Vehicle System Dynamics* 17(5): 231–253.

Smith, M. C. (1995). Achievable dynamic response for automotive active suspension, *Vehicle System Dynamics* 24: 1–33.

Stein, G. J. & Ballo, I. (1991). Active vibration control system for the driver's seat for off-road vehicles, *Vehicle System Dynamics* 20(2): 57–78.

Sunwoo, M., Cheok, K. C. & Huang, N. (June 1991).   Model reference adaptive control for vehicle active suspension systems, *IEEE Transactions on Industrial Electronics* 38(3): 217–222.

Thompson, A. G. & Davis, B. R. (2005).   Computation of the rms state variables and control forces in a half-car model with preview active suspension using spectral decomposition methods, *Journal of Sound and Vibration* 285(3): 571–583.

Thompson, A. G. & Pearce, C. E. M. (1998).   Physically realizable feedback controls for a fully active preview suspension applied to a half-car model, *Vehicle System Dynamics* 30(1): 17–35.

White-Smoke (2011).
        URL: *http://white-smoke.wetpaint.com/page/Heave,+Pitch,+Roll,+Warp+and+Yaw*

Y. Chen, B. Y. & Dong, J. (2006).   Time-series prediction using a local linear wavelet neural network, *Neurocomput.* 69(4-6): 449–465.

Yester, J. L. & Jr. (1992). Fuzzy logic control of vehicle active suspension, *M.S. thesis, Electrical and Computer Engineering Department* .

Yilmaz, S. & Oysal, Y. (2010).   Fuzzy wavelet neural network models for prediction and identification of dynamical systems, *IEEE Transactions on Neural Networks* 21(10): 1599–1609.

Yoshimura, T., Kume, A., Kurimoto, M. & Hino, J. (2001). Construction of an active suspension system of a quarter car model using the concept of sliding mode control, *Journal of Sound and Vibration* 239(2): 187–199.

Yoshimura, T., Nakaminami, K., Kurimoto, M. & Hino, J. (1999).   Active suspension of passengers cars using linear and fuzzy-logic controls, *Control Engineering Practice* 7(1): 41–47.

Yue, C., Butsuen, T. & Hedrick, J. K. (1988).   Alternative control laws for automotive active suspensions, *American Control Conference*, IEEE, Atlanta, USA, pp. 2373–2378.

Zhang, J., Walter, G. G., Miao, Y. & Lee, W. N. W. (1995). Wavelet neural networks for function learning, *IEEE Trans. Signal Process* 43(6): 1485–1497.

Zhang, Q. (1997). Using wavelet networks in nonparametric estimation, *IEEE Trans. Neural Netw.* 8(2): 227–236.

Zhang, Q. & Benveniste, A. (1992).   Wavelet networks, *IEEE Trans. Neural Network* 3(6): 889–898.

8

Fuzzy-Logic Analysis of the FDR Data of a Transport Aircraft in Atmospheric Turbulence

C. Edward Lan[1] and Ray C. Chang[2]
[1] Department of Aerospace Engineering, University of Kansas, KS,
[2] Department of Aviation Mechanical Engineering,
China University of Science and Technology,
USA
Taiwan (R.O.C.)

1. Introduction

The aerodynamics of a jet transport in severe atmospheric turbulence, in particular involving plunging motion, is complex in that unsteady aerodynamic effects are significant and not well known. For instance, the aircraft response may lag behind the change in angle of attack and/or control surface deflections. Because of the change in angle of attack, the wing vortex wake may be pulsating. Coupled with the aircraft motion, the pulsating vortex wake would significantly affect the tail aerodynamics and hence, the aircraft stability and control characteristics. These are just a few possible phenomena in aircraft response to be identified. Unfortunately, these aerodynamic characteristics cannot be identified with existing ground testing techniques. Therefore, at present the only option to estimate the aircraft aerodynamic characteristics in severe atmospheric turbulence is to analyze the data from Flight Data Recorders (FDR). Traditional methods of system identification in aerodynamics, such as the maximum likelihood method (MMLE) (Maine & Iliff, 1986), the least-square or the stepwise regression method (Klein, 1981), or the Extended Kalman Filter (EKF) (Minkler & Minkler, 1993; Gelb 1982), have not been demonstrated to be applicable to estimating the unsteady aerodynamics based on these FDR data. Therefore, a more robust model identification technique would be needed. In addition, the established aerodynamic models should be directly usable in flight simulation. To satisfy these goals, the Fuzzy Logic Modeling (FLM) technique is adopted in the present application. The technique used here has been applied to model identification of a fighter aircraft from flight test data (Wang, et al. 2001; Wang, et al. 2002); aerodynamic estimation of transport aircraft from Flight Data Recorder (FDR) data (Lan & Guan 2005; Weng, et al. 2008; Chang, et al. 2009); identification of uncommanded motions from wind-tunnel dynamic free-to-roll test data (Lan, et al., Jan. 2008; Lan, et al., May 2008); and non-aerodynamic problems with the FDR data (Lee & Lan 2003; Lan, et al. 2006), just to name a few.

In the following, the present fuzzy logic algorithm will be described in some detail. It follows with some simple verification examples in Section 3. In Section 4, application of the

FLM algorithm in aerodynamic model identification for a jet transport in severe atmospheric turbulence will be described in detail. Unsteady aerodynamics will be emphasized. Conclusions will follow in Section 5.

2. Fuzzy logic modeling

The general idea of the FLM technique is to set up the relations between system input and output variables. There are two approaches in the FLM technique. One is the fuzzy set approach, involving fuzzy sets, membership functions, weighting factors, and the if-then fuzzy rules (Zadeh 1973). The process involves three stages: fuzzification, fuzzy rule inference and defuzzification. The second approach is the internal function approach, involving the internal functions, membership functions, and the output cells (Takagi & Sugeno 1985). The same three stages mentioned above can also be identified. Since the first approach does not provide continuous derivatives needed in aerodynamics, the second approach will be utilized in the present paper.

Basically, the present FLM algorithm represents a multi-dimensional, nonlinear interpolation scheme without requiring explicit functional forms between the input and output variables. In application, complex motions or relations involving many variables can be treated. Conceptually, each motion variable is divided into a number of ranges in which values of the membership functions are assigned. Each combination of membership functions, one from each motion variable, constitutes a fuzzy cell. Each fuzzy cell contributes to the prediction of the value of outcome equal to its internal function with an associated weighting factor. The latter represents an assembly of the membership grades of all variables. The final prediction of outcome is equal to the weighted average of contributions of all fuzzy cells. This overview will be repeated later by way of equations or formulas.

Two main tasks are involved in the present FLM process. One is the identification of the coefficients of the internal functions. The other one is structure identification to identify the optimal structure of fuzzy cells of the model, in other words, the optimal number of membership functions for each variable. Details of fuzzification, fuzzy rule inference and defuzzification stages in the present FLM technique are described in the following (Wang, et al. 1998, 2001, 2002).

2.1 Fuzzification

In this stage, many internal functions are defined to cover the ranges of the influencing variables (i.e. input variables). The ranges of the input variables are all transformed into the domain of [0,1]. The membership grading also ranges from 0 to 1.0, with "0" meaning no effect from the corresponding internal function, and "1" meaning a full effect. These internal functions are assumed to be linear functions of input variables as follows:

$$P^i = y_i(x_1, x_2, \cdots, x_r, \cdots x_k) = p_0^i + p_1^i x_1 + \cdots + p_r^i x_r + \cdots p_k^i x_k \tag{2.1}$$

where p_r^i, r=0, 1, 2,..., k, are the coefficients of internal functions y_i, and k is number of input variables; i=1, 2, ..., n, and n is the total number of fuzzy cells.

The recorded data in FDR, such as flight altitude (h), calibrated airspeed (CAS), angle of attack (α), accelerometer readings (a_x, a_y, and a_z), and Euler angles (θ, ϕ, and ψ), etc is chosen as the variables in the compatibility analysis and eventually forming the data for specific fuzzy models. In the present Chapter, y_i is defined to be an estimated aerodynamic coefficient of force or moment, and x_r are the variables of the input data. The numbers of the internal functions (i.e. cell's numbers) are quantified by the total number of membership functions (see below).

The values of each fuzzy variable, such as the angle of attack, are divided into several ranges, each of which represents a membership function with $A(x_r)$ as its membership grade. One membership function from each variable constitutes a fuzzy cell. For the ith cell, the corresponding membership grades are represented by $A_r^i(x_r)$, r=1, 2,..., k. In other words, the membership functions allow the membership grades of the internal functions for a given set of input variables to be assigned. For a given system with input variables $x_1, x_2, \cdots, x_r, \cdots x_k$ of one data point, the recorded values of each input variables are normalized by using $(x_r - x_{r,min})/(x_{r,max}-x_{r,min})$ to transform them into the ranges of [0, 1]. The range, $(x_{r,max} - x_{r,min})$, represents the scaling factor and usually is assumed to have a larger range than what actually appears in the data with numerous data points to be more generally applicable for the resulting model. In the present application in aerodynamics, it is empirically assumed to be 1.8 times larger. Generally, overlapped straight lines, triangles or parabolas are frequently the shapes used to represent the grades.

The membership functions partition the input space into many fuzzy subspaces, which are called the fuzzy cells. The total number of fuzzy cells is $n = N_1 \times N_2 \times \cdots \times N_r \times \cdots \times N_k$. For a variable x_r, the number of membership function is N_r. Each fuzzy cell is in a different combination from others formed by taking one membership function from each input variable.

Let N be the number of membership functions and j be the index for the j-th membership functions. Then the membership grades for triangular and parabolic shapes can be described as follows:

2.1.1 Triangular membership functions

1)N = 2:

$$A(x_r) = x_r, \quad j=1$$

$$A(x_r) = 1 - x_r, j=2$$

2)$N \geq 3$:

For j =3 to N- m, where m is equal to the greater number of 0 and integer of (N-2)/2:

$$A(x_r) = x_r/d_u, \quad 0 \leq x_r \leq d_u$$
$$A(x_r) = (1 - x_r)/(1- d_u), \quad d_u \leq x_r \leq 1$$
where $d_u = \Delta x_1*(j - 2)$, and $\Delta x_1 = 1.0/(N - m - 1)$.
For $j \geq N - m$
$$A(x_r)=(d_d - x_r)/d_d, \quad 0 \leq x_r \leq d_d$$
$$A(x_r)= (d_d - x_r)/(d_d - 1), \quad d_d \leq x_r \leq 1$$
where $d_d = \Delta x_2*(j - N + m)$, and $\Delta x_2 = 1.0/(m+1)$.

2.1.2 Parabolic membership functions

1)N=2:

$$A(x_r) = x_r, \quad j = 1$$

$$A(x_r) = 1 - x_r, j = 2$$

2)N ≥ 3:

For j = 3 to N-m, where m is again equal to the greater number of 0 and the integer of (N-2)/2:

$$A(x_r) = -x_r^2 / d_u^2 + 2x_r / d_u, 0 \le x_r \le d_u$$

$$A(x_r) = -(x_r^2 - 2d_u x_r + 2d_u - 1) / (1 - 2d_u + d_u^2), d_u \le x_r \le 1$$

where $d_u = \Delta x_1*(j - 2)$, and $\Delta x_1 = 1.0/(N - m - 1)$.

$$j > N - m$$

$$A(x_r) = x_r^2 / d_d^2 - 2x_r / d_d + 1.0, 0 \le x_r \le d_d$$

$$A(x_r) = (x_r^2 - 2d_d x_r + d_d^2) / (1 - 2d_d + d_d^2), d_d \le x_r \le 1$$

where $d_d = \Delta x_2*(j - N + m)$, and $\Delta x_2 = 1.0/(m+1)$.

The membership functions are illustrated in Fig. 1 for triangular shapes and Fig. 2 for parabolic shapes. In Fig. 1, although the membership functions are continuous functions, there are discontinuities in slopes at some points. However, differentiation of membership

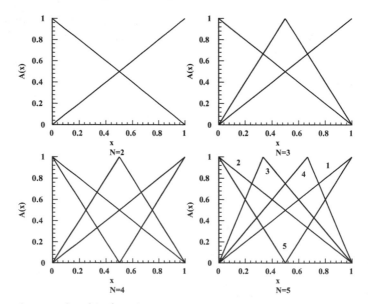

Fig. 1. Triangular membership functions

functions is not performed in estimating derivatives. In the present application, aerodynamic derivatives are all estimated with a central difference scheme, which will be presented later. Because overlapped triangular membership function is simple and involves less computing time, it is the method to represent the grades of membership functions in the present FLM technique. Comparison of computed results based on these two types of membership function will be illustrated later.

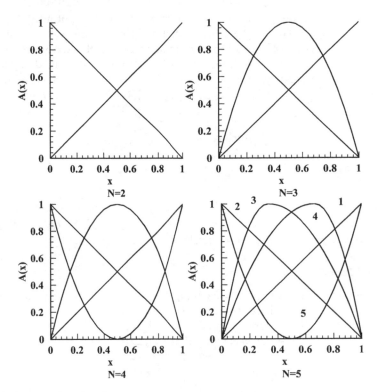

Fig. 2. Parabolic membership functions

2.3 Fuzzy rule inference

A fuzzy cell is formed by taking one membership function from each variable, as indicated earlier. The total number of cells is the number of possible combinations by taking one membership function from each input variable. For every cell, it has a fuzzy rule to guide the input and output relations. For the jth data point, the rule of the ith cell is stated (Wang, et al. 1998) as:

if $x_{1,j}$ is $A_1^i(x_{1,j})$, and if $x_{2,j}$ is $A_2^i(x_{2,j})$, ... and if $x_{k,j}$ is $A_k^i(x_{k,j})$ for the jth data point, then the cell output is equal to its internal function:

$$P^i(x_{1,j},x_{2,j},\cdots,x_{r,j},\cdots x_{k,j}) = p_0^i + p_1^i x_{1,j} + \cdots + p_r^i x_{r,j} + \cdots p_k^i x_{k,j} \qquad (2.2)$$

where $i = 1,2,...,n$ the index of the cells, n is the total number of cells of the model; $P^i(x_{1,j}, x_{2,j}, \cdots, x_{r,j}, \cdots x_{k,j})$ is the internal function with parameters $p_0^i, p_1^i, ..., p_r^i, ... p_k^i$ to be determined, and $A_k^i(x_{k,j})$ denotes the membership grade for $x_{k,j}$. Each function covers a certain range of input variables.

2.4 Defuzzification

In each fuzzy cell, the contribution to the outcome (i.e. the cell output) is based on the internal function, Eq. (2.2). The final prediction of the outcome is the weighted average of all cell outputs after the process of reasoning algorithm. Because of this weighting among many factors over large ranges of possibilities, the word "fuzzy" is derived to describe the method. However, its prediction is never "fuzzy". The output is estimated by the center of gravity method. For the jth input ($x_{1,j}, x_{2,j}, ..., x_{r,j}, ..., x_{k,j}$), the output is as follows:

$$\hat{y}_j = \frac{\sum_{i=1}^{n} product\left[A^i(x_{1,j}), \cdots, A^i(x_{k,j}) \right] p^i}{\sum_{i=1}^{n} product\left[A^i(x_{1,j}), \cdots, A^i(x_{k,j}) \right]} \tag{2.3}$$

In Eq. (2.3) $product\left[A^i(x_{1,j}), ..., A^i(x_{k,j}) \right]$ is the weighted factor of the ith cell; and the index j of the data set, where $j=1,2,..., m$, and m is the total number of the data records; and the "product" stands for product operator of its elements in this Chapter.

2.5 Parameter identification

Given a set of membership functions for each input variable, the unknown coefficients of the internal functions are determined by using the Newton gradient-descent method. The accuracy of the established aerodynamic model through the fuzzy-logic algorithm is estimated by the sum of squared errors (SSE) and the squared multiple correlation coefficients (R^2):

$$SSE = \sum_{j=1}^{m} (\hat{y}_j - y_j)^2 \tag{2.4}$$

$$R^2 = 1 - \frac{\{\sum_{j=1}^{m} (\hat{y}_j - y_j)^2\}}{\{\sum_{j=1}^{m} (\overline{y} - y_j)^2\}} \tag{2.5}$$

In Eqs. (2.4) and (2.5), where $\hat{y}_j$, the output of the fuzzy-logic model at data point j, is estimated by Eq. (2.3); y_j is the data point used for the model training at point j; $\overline{y}$ is the mean of the sample data, and m is the total number of data points. The model training is to determine the unknown coefficients of the internal functions, $p_r{}^i$, by maximizing the value of R^2. These coefficients are determined by the following iterative formula to minimize the sum of squared error (Eq. 2.4):

$$p_{r,t+1}^i = p_{r,t}^i - \alpha_r \frac{\partial(SSE)}{\partial p_r^i} \tag{2.6}$$

$$\frac{\partial(SSE)}{\partial p_r^i} = 2\sum_{j=1}^m (\hat{y}_j - y_j) \frac{\partial \hat{y}_j(x_{1,j},...,x_{k,j},p_r^i,...,p_k^n)}{\partial p_r^i} \tag{2.6a}$$

$$\frac{\partial \hat{y}_j}{\partial p_r^i} = \frac{product[A_1^i(x_{1,j}),...,A_k^i(x_{k,j})]x_{r,j}}{\sum\limits_{i=1}^n product\left[A_1^i(x_{1,j}),\cdots,A_k^i(x_{k,j})\right]} \tag{2.6b}$$

where α_r is the convergence factor or the step size in the gradient method; subscript index t denotes the iteration sequence, and $x_{r,j}=1.0$ if r=0 in Eq. (2.6b). Usually, the magnitude of α_r is chosen based on that of the gradient. Eq. (2.6), together with Eq. (2.6a), would result in summing contributions to the total *p-coefficients* from all data points. Instead, simplification is applied to result in a point-iteration approach, so that in each iteration over the dataset, the *p-coefficients* represent only the contribution from one data point. After simplification, Eq. (2.6) becomes

For $r = 0$,

$$p_{0,t+1}^i = p_{0,t}^i - 2\alpha_0(\hat{y}_j - y_j) \times \frac{product[A_1^i(x_1),\cdots,A_k^i(x_{k,j})]}{\sum\limits_{s=1}^n product[A_1^s(x_{1,j}),\cdots,A_k^s(x_{k,j})]} \tag{2.6c}$$

and for $r = 1, 2, ..., k$,

$$p_{r,t+1}^i = p_{r,t}^i - 2\alpha_r(\hat{y}_j - y_j) \times \frac{product[A_1^i(x_1),\cdots,A_k^i(x_{k,j})]x_{r,j}}{\sum\limits_{s=1}^n product[A_1^s(x_{1,j}),\cdots,A_k^s(x_{k,j})]} \tag{2.6d}$$

The iteration during the search sequence stops when one of the following three criteria is satisfied (Wang, et al. 1998, 1999):

$$1) \text{ Cost}= SSE_t < \varepsilon_1 \tag{2.7}$$

$$2) \text{ RER}= \frac{SSE_t - SSE_{t-1}}{SSE_t} < \varepsilon_2 \tag{2.8}$$

$$3) \; t = t_{max} \tag{2.9}$$

In the above criteria, Cost= SSE_t is the sum of squared errors (SSE) in current iteration to be denoted by "Cost" and RER=(cost_current - cost_previous)/cost_current (i.e. the relative error) for simplicity in descriptions; ε_1 and ε_2 are the required precision criteria; and t_{max} is a specified maximum iteration number. The convergence of modeling is achieved only when the first two criteria (Eqs. 2.7 and 2.8) are satisfied.

Given membership functions and the training data, this parameter identification procedure can be applied to establish a fuzzy-logic model, i.e. determining the p-coefficients in Eq. 2.2. One important reason for the fuzzy logic algorithm, as described above, to work well in nonlinear, robust interpolation is that it employs numerous internal functions to cover the whole ranges of input variables.

2.6 Model structure identification

In the fuzzy-logic model, the model structure is indicated by the number of membership functions for each variable. For a fuzzy-logic model with multiple variables, the structure is the combination of the numbers and forms of the membership functions assigned to all input variables. Since the sequence defines the one-to-one relationship between the numbers and the forms for each variable, the structure can be uniquely described by numbers of the membership functions.

The model structure is determined by maximizing the correlation coefficient, Eq. (2.5). A search forward algorithm has been employed for the identification. At each search stage, there may be many fuzzy-logic models with different structure combinations. The search stage numbers are denoted by N_s. Out of all the possible intermediate fuzzy-logic models at each search stage, for an efficient search, only some structures are developed and evaluated. Two selection criteria, to be given below, are used to choose these structures. With the incremental sequence and the selection criteria, the search forward algorithm is summarized as follows (Wang, et al. 1998):

1. Specify the input variables x_r, $r = 1, 2,..., k$ and the output variable y;
2. Assume an initial structure, also called parent structure as $(N_{10}, N_{20}, \cdots, N_{r0}, \cdots, N_{k0})$;
3. Begin at the search stage number $N_s = 1$, form all possible structures starting from the parent structure by adding one more membership function a time only to one input variable. Those all possible structures are called child structures as $(N_{10} + 1, N_{20}, \cdots, N_{r0}, \cdots, N_{k0})$, $(N_{10}, N_{20} + 1, \cdots, N_{r0}, \cdots, N_{k0})$, $\cdots$, $(N_{10}, N_{20}, \cdots, N_{r0}, \cdots, N_{k0} + 1)$. Perform the identification of internal coefficients in Eq. (2.1) for each child structure and then calculate the R^2 by using Eq. (2.5);
4. Select the top 5 child structures among all calculated values of R^2 as new parent structures for next search step $N_s = N_s + 1$;
5. Go back to step 2) starting from the new parent structures and repeat the same procedures in steps 2) and 3) until the best structure is identified;
6. Pick out the maximum value of R^2 among the child structures in each searching stage as R^2_{max}. The structure with the largest R^2_{max} corresponding to all picking values is the optimal structure within a sensible N_s.

The above process is illustrated in Fig. 3. In the structure identification, parameter identification to determine the p-parameters according to Eq. (2.6) is also needed. But the number of iteration to determine the p-parameters is limited to 2000, so that the best structure is decided on a relative basis. After this last step, Eq. (2.6) is applied iteratively until both the values of R^2 and RER reach the requirements in the final parameter identification.

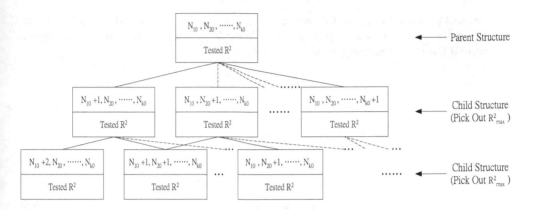

Fig. 3. Identification process for the best structure

3. Some verification examples

In application, the more complex the problem is, the more usefulness of the present algorithm would clearly exhibit. A complex problem in identifying the aerodynamic models of a jet transport in severe atmospheric turbulence will be presented in Section 4. Here, a simpler problem, yet complex enough for a conventional parameter identification method, will be used to show the robustness and reliability of the present algorithm. The idea is to assume the aerodynamic derivatives are known from the wind-tunnel forced oscillation test and the aerodynamic model data are generated from these derivatives. The algorithm is to obtain a numerical model containing the p-coefficients and the aerodynamic derivatives are then estimated for comparison with the test data.

For this purpose, the rolling moment coefficient model will be examined. It is assumed to be a function of

$$\alpha, \beta, \phi, p, r, k, \dot{\beta} \tag{3.1}$$

where $k = \omega b/2V$, the reduced frequency and ω is the oscillation frequency in the test.

3.1 Wind-tunnel data

Define the rolling motion, $\phi(t)$, in wind-tunnel testing being described as follows.

$$\beta = \alpha_n \sin \phi(t)$$

$$\dot{\beta} = p \sin \alpha_n$$

$$\alpha = \alpha_n \cos \phi(t)$$

$$\phi(t) = -\Delta\phi\cos(\overline{k}\overline{t}) \tag{3.2}$$

where α_n is the nominal angle of attack used in wind tunnel testing and p is the roll rate. Since the rolling moment coefficient is also affected by yawing motion, $\psi(t)$, the latter in wind-tunnel testing is assuming to be:

$$\beta = -\psi\cos\alpha_n$$

$$\dot{\beta} = -\dot{\psi}\cos\alpha_n,$$

$$\dot{\psi} = r, \text{ the yaw rate}$$

$$\alpha = \alpha_n$$

$$\psi(t) = -\Delta\psi\cos(\overline{k}\overline{t}) \tag{3.3}$$

According to the linear theory, the rolling moment coefficient is calculated from:

$$C_l = C_{l\beta}\beta + C_{lp}\overline{p} + C_{lr}\overline{r} + C_{l\dot{\beta}}\overline{\dot{\beta}} \tag{3.4}$$

where the bar over a variable indicate a dimensionless one. For example, $\overline{p} = pb/2V$, where V is the airspeed. The verification will be performed at two conditions: one at small oscillation amplitudes, and the other one at large amplitude. These conditions are given in the following.

3.1.1 Small amplitudes at two reduced frequencies

3.1.1.1 α = 5 deg., $\Delta\phi$ = 5 deg., $\Delta\psi$ = 5 deg., k=0.12

The wind-tunnel data for a test model show: $C_{l\beta}$ = -0.0688; C_{lp}= -0.17; C_{lr} = 0.06; $C_{l\dot{\beta}}$ =-0.04

Therefore,

$$(C_{lp})_{osc} = C_{lp} + C_{l\dot{\beta}}\sin\alpha = -0.1735$$

$$(C_{lr})_{osc} = Clr - C_{l\dot{\beta}}\cos\alpha = 0.0998$$

3.1.1.2 α = 20 deg.; $\Delta\phi$ =5 deg., $\Delta\psi$ = 5 deg., k=0.08

The wind-tunnel data show: $C_{l\beta}$ = -0.2493; C_{lp}= -0.10; C_{lr} = 0.233; $C_{l\dot{\beta}}$ =-0.17

Therefore,

$$(C_{lp})_{osc} = C_{lp} + C_{l\dot{\beta}}\sin\alpha = -0.1581$$

$$(C_{lr})_{osc} = C_{lr} - C_{l\dot{\beta}}\cos\alpha = 0.3927$$

3.1.2 Large amplitudes

3.1.2.1 $\alpha = 5$ deg., $\Delta\phi = 30$ deg., $\Delta\psi = 15$ deg., k=0.12

3.1.2.2 $\alpha = 20$ deg.; $\Delta\phi = 15$ deg., $\Delta\psi = 15$ deg., k=0.08

All derivatives are taken to be the same as in the small amplitude case.

3.2 Modeling results

Based on Eq. (3.4), two sets of data are generated at k=0.12 and 0.08, which are then combined into one for modeling. In linear aerodynamic theory, the rolling moment coefficient is known to be independent of the roll angle (ϕ). Two models are set up with $\phi = 0$ or without ϕ in Eq. (3.1), and ϕ given by Eq. (3.2) to test the robustness of the algorithm. To calculate the response, input data in the form of Eq. (3.4) for a cosine harmonic oscillation are prepared. The output from the model is then Fourier-analyzed to obtain the in-phase and out-of-phase response. The out-of-phase response is the damping component and is what to be presented below. Only the small-amplitude results are presented, because the large-amplitude results are very similar.

3.2.1 $\alpha = 5$ deg., $\Delta\phi = 5$ deg., $\Delta\psi = 5$ deg., k=0.12

Assume $\phi(t) \neq 0$ and is given by Eq. (3.2). The modeling results are:

$$C_{l\beta} = -0.0688; \; (C_{lp})_{osc} = -0.1736; \; (C_{lr})_{osc} = 0.0999$$

On the other hand, if ϕ is assumed 0 in the model data, the modeling results are:

$$C_{l\beta} = -0.0688; \; (C_{lp})_{osc} = -0.1736; \; (C_{lr})_{osc} = 0.0999$$

It is seen that the results are identical at $\alpha = 5$ degrees in both cases, and agree with the original wind-tunnel data very well. Same results are obtained if ϕ is absent in the model structure.

3.2.2 $\alpha = 20$ deg.; $\Delta\phi = 5$ deg., $\Delta\psi = 5$ deg., k=0.08

Again, assume $\phi(t) \neq 0$ and is calculated with Eq. (3.2). The modeling results are:

$$C_{l\beta} = -0.2493; \; (C_{lp})_{osc} = -0.1581; \; (C_{lr})_{osc} = 0.3926$$

If $\phi = 0$ or it is absent in the model data, the modeling results are:

$$C_{l\beta} = -0.2494; \; (C_{lp})_{osc} = -0.1584; \; (C_{lr})_{osc} = 0.3925$$

The results at $\alpha = 20$ degrees are nearly identical, except the last digit and also agree with the original data well.

3.2.3 Large-amplitude test cases

The large-amplitude test cases produce similarly accurate results as compared with the wind-tunnel data. Therefore, the results will not be repeated.

3.2.4 Concluding remarks

In the above example the model prediction practically shows the same results as the wind-tunnel data with or without the extra $\phi(t)$-variable in the model. It illustrates one important concept in the present fuzzy logic aerodynamic modeling that more variables than what are known in the present linear theory may be included in the model without affecting the results of prediction. In the case of nonlinear theory, including more variables in the model allows presently unknown phenomena to be captured at the expense of more computing time.

3.3 Modeling of wind-tunnel unsteady aerodynamic data

Verification with other methods is difficult to conduct because of the unavailability of suitable data and published results. However, the present algorithm has been verified with wind-tunnel experimental data. The wind-tunnel data used consist of static, forced oscillation, and some cases with rotary balance data, in numerous sets. These data sets at various angles of attack and reduced frequencies are combined to set up six (6) aerodynamic models. The resulting models can predict aerodynamic hysteresis quite well (Wang, et al. 1998, 1999). To save space, all these correlation results will not be presented, except one pitching moment curve. Fig. 4 presents the comparison of experimental data and modeling prediction. As indicated earlier, the modeling results predict only the mean approximation in the least-square sense and are seen here to re-produce well the hysteresis in the test data. Note that k is defined as $\omega\bar{c}/V$ in this case. The arrows indicate the direction of changes in C_m as α varies in Fig. 4. As will be explained later, if the hysteresis curve is counterclockwise, as shown at low α's, the oscillatory pitch damping derivative is stable (i.e. negative in sign). On the other hand, if it is clockwise, as shown at high α's, the damping derivative is unstable (i.e. positive in sign).

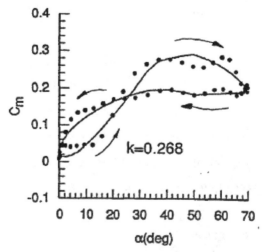

Fig. 4. Comparison of experimental forced oscillation data with modeling results in pitching moment coefficient

4. Application to aircraft aerodynamic modeling

4.1 Flight data

The twin-jet transport in the present study encountered clear-air turbulence in cruise flight at the altitude around 10,050 m. As a result, several passengers and cabin crews sustained injuries, because of which this event was classified as an accident. The present study was initiated to examine possible concepts of accident prevention in the future. The dataset used for the modeling are extracted from the FDR during turbulence encounter lasting for 92 seconds.

The main aircraft geometric and inertial characteristics are taken, or estimated, as shown in Table 1:

Geometric data		Moments of inertia	
W (take-off)	1,431,800 N (321900 lb)	I_{xx}	10,710,000 kg-m² (7,899,900 slugs-ft²)
S	260 m² (2798.7 ft²)	I_{yy}	14,883,800 kg-m² (10,978,000 slugs-ft²)
$\bar{c}$	6.608 m (21.68 ft)	I_{zz}	25,283,271 kg-m² (18,648,470 slugs-ft²)
b	44.827 m (147.08 ft)	I_{xz}	0.0 kg-m² (0.0 slugs-ft²)

Table 1. The main aircraft geometric and inertial characteristics

The required operational parameters in FDR dataset for generating aerodynamic model data are time (t), CAS, pressure altitude (h), roll attitude (ϕ), pitch attitude (θ), magnetic heading (ψ), longitudinal acceleration (a_x), lateral acceleration (a_y), vertical acceleration (a_z), angle of attack (α), aileron deflection (δ_a), elevator (δ_e), rudder (δ_r), stabilizer (δ_s), engine EPR, outside air temperature, wind speed, wind direction, and fuel flow rate. Since only the normal acceleration is recorded in 8-Hz resolution (i.e. 8 points per second), all other parameters are interpolated with a monotone cubic spline to the same sampling rate. Based on the principle in flight data analysis, to estimate stability (or sensitivity) derivative with a flight variable, the corresponding flight variable must be sufficiently excited in the flight. This principle can be satisfied by choosing a large time period so that flight variables have sufficient variation during the time period, or by combining different flights if a model to represent a particular aircraft is desired.

4.2 Compatibility analysis

Typically, the longitudinal, lateral, and vertical accelerations (a_x, a_y, a_z) along the (x, y, z)-body axes of aircraft, angle of attack α, and the Euler angles (ϕ, θ, and ψ), as well as all control deflections are available and recorded in the FDR of all transport aircraft. Since the recorded flight data may contain errors (or called biases), compatibility analysis is performed to remove them by satisfying the following kinematic equations:

$$\dot{\phi} = p + q\sin\phi\tan\theta + r\cos\phi\tan\theta \tag{4.1}$$

$$\dot{\theta} = q\cos\phi - r\sin\varphi \tag{4.2}$$

$$\dot{\psi} = (q\sin\phi + r\cos\phi)\sec\theta \tag{4.3}$$

$$\dot{V} = (a_x - g\sin\theta)\cos\alpha\cos\beta + (a_y + g\sin\phi\cos\theta)\sin\beta + (a_z + g\cos\phi\cos\theta)\sin\alpha\cos\beta \quad (4.4)$$

$$\dot{\alpha} = [(a_z + g\cos\theta\cos\phi)\cos\alpha - (a_x - g\sin\theta)\sin\alpha]/(V\cos\beta) + q - \tan\beta(p\cos\alpha + r\sin\alpha) \,(4.5)$$

$$\dot{\beta} = \cos\beta(a_y + g\cos\theta\sin\phi)/V + p\sin\alpha - r\cos\alpha$$
$$-\sin\beta[(a_z + g\cos\theta\cos\phi)\sin\alpha - (a_x - g\sin\theta)\cos\alpha]/V \quad (4.6)$$

where g is acceleration due to gravity, V is flight speed, β is sideslip angle, p is roll rate, q is pitch rate, and r is yaw rate in Eqs. (4.1) ~ (4.6). Let the biases be denoted by $b_{a_x}, b_{a_y}, b_{a_z}, b_p, b_q, b_r, b_V, b_\alpha, b_\beta, b_\theta, b_\varphi, b_\psi$, respectively for a_x, a_y, a_z, etc. These biases are estimated by minimizing the squared sum of the differences between the two sides of the above equations. These equations in vector form can be written as:

$$\dot{\vec{z}} = \vec{f}(x) = \vec{f}(x_m - \Delta x) \quad (4.7)$$

where

$$\vec{z} = (V, \alpha, \beta, \theta, \phi, \psi)^T \quad (4.8)$$

$$\vec{x}_m = (a_x, a_y, a_z, p, q, r, V, \alpha, \beta, \theta, \phi, \psi)^T \quad (4.9)$$

$$\Delta \vec{x} = (b_{a_x}, b_{a_y}, b_{a_z}, b_p, b_q, b_r, b_V, b_\alpha, b_\beta, b_\theta, b_\phi, b_\varphi)^T \quad (4.10)$$

where the subscript "m" indicates the measured or recorded values. The cost function is defined as:

$$J = \frac{1}{2}(\dot{\vec{z}} - \vec{f})^T Q(\dot{\vec{z}} - \vec{f}) \quad (4.11)$$

where Q is a weighting diagonal matrix with elements being 1.0 except the one for the slowly varying flight speed being 10.0 and $\dot{\vec{z}}$ is calculated with a central difference scheme with $\vec{z}_m$, which is the measured value of $\vec{z}$. The steepest descent optimization method is adopted to minimize the cost function. As a result of the analysis, variables not present in the FDR, such as β, p, q and r, are also estimated.

The force and moment coefficients are obtained from the following flight dynamic equations (Roskam 2003) about the airplane body axes:

$$ma_x = C_x \bar{q} S + T_x \quad (4.12)$$

$$ma_y = C_y \bar{q} S + T_y \quad (4.13)$$

$$ma_z = C_z \bar{q} S + T_z \quad (4.14)$$

$$C_l \bar{q} S b = I_{xx}\, \dot{p} - I_{xz}(\dot{r} + pq) - (I_{yy} - I_{zz})qr \quad (4.15)$$

$$C_m \bar{q} S \bar{c} = I_{yy} \dot{q} - I_{xz}(r^2 - p^2) - (I_{zz} - I_{xx})rp - T_m \tag{4.16}$$

$$C_n \bar{q} S b = I_{zz} \dot{r} - I_{xz}(\dot{p} - qr) - (I_{xx} - I_{yy})pq \tag{4.17}$$

where m is the aircraft mass; $\bar{q}$ the dynamic pressure; S the wing reference area; C_x, C_z, and C_m the longitudinal aerodynamic force and moment coefficients; C_y, C_l, and C_n the lateral-directional aerodynamic force and moment coefficients; I_{xx}, I_{yy}, and I_{zz} the moments of inertia about x-, y-, and z-axes, respectively; I_{xy}, I_{xz}, and I_{yz} the products of inertia; and T_x, T_y, T_z, and T_m the thrust terms about x-, y-, z-axes, and in equation of pitching moment, respectively in Eqs. (4.12) ~ (4.17).

The above equations are used to determine all aerodynamic coefficients based on accelerometer readings (a_x, a_y, and a_z), Euler angles (ϕ, θ, and ψ), angular rates (p, q and r), and thrusts (T_x, T_y, T_z, and T_m). The angular rates are estimated through compatibility analysis. Since thrust was not measured during flight for most flight vehicles, those values and the effects on the forces and pitching moments in equations of (4.12), (4.13), (4.14), and (4.16) should be predicted by a thrust model (see Section 4.4).

4.3 Equivalent harmonic motion

The reduced frequency is a parameter to indicate the degree of unsteadiness in unsteady aerodynamics and is estimated in this paper by fitting the local trajectory with a harmonic motion. In the static case, the reduced frequency is 0. Large values of the reduced frequency imply the importance of unsteady aerodynamic effect. For longitudinal aerodynamics, the equivalent harmonic motion is the one based on the angle-of-attack variation following the classical unsteady aerodynamic theory of Theodorsen (Theodorsen 1935). For lateral-directional aerodynamics, it is based on the time variation of roll angle (Wang, et al. 1998).

For the longitudinal motion, the time history of the angle of attack (α) and time rate of angle of attack ($d\alpha/dt$, or $\dot{\alpha}$) is fitted with one of a harmonic motion at any instant as follows (Wang, et al. 1998):

$$\alpha(t) = \bar{\alpha} + \alpha \cos(\omega t + \bar{\phi}) \tag{4.18}$$

$$\dot{\alpha}(t) = -a\omega \sin(\omega t + \bar{\phi}) \tag{4.19}$$

where those terms on the left hand side of Eqs. (4.18) and (4.19) are given and the unknowns are the local mean angle of attack ($\bar{\alpha}$), the local amplitude of the harmonic motion (a), the phase lag ($\bar{\varphi}$), and the angular frequency (ω). These unknowns are calculated through an optimization method by minimizing the following cost function (least squares)

$$J = \sum_{i=1}^{n} \left[\alpha_i - (\bar{\alpha} + a\cos(\omega t_i + \bar{\phi}))\right]^2 + \left[\dot{\alpha}_i - (\bar{\alpha} + a\omega\sin(\omega t_i + \bar{\phi}))\right]^2 \tag{4.20}$$

In Eq. (4.20), where α_i is the measured value at point i and n is the number of the data points used in the optimization. For the case in the present study, $n = 20$ is found to be the best choice by correlating with a cosine wave with a constant frequency. The 20 points preceding and including the current time are employed in Eq. (4.20). The least-square method is found to converge well and gives reasonably accurate results. The lateral-directional equivalent reduced frequency is computed in the same manner.

The local equivalent reduced frequency in the longitudinal motion is defined as,

$$k_1 = \frac{\omega \bar{c}}{V} \tag{4.21}$$

where $\bar{c}$ is the mean chord length of wing airfoil section. The lateral-directional equivalent reduced frequency is defined as

$$k_2 = \frac{\omega b}{2V} \tag{4.22}$$

where b is the wing span.

4.4 Fuzzy-Logic thrust model

As shown before, the thrust terms appear in the force equations and the pitching moment equation (Eqs. 4.12~4.14 and 4.16; but in the current application, $T_y = T_z = 0$.). Since the values of thrust for aircraft in flight cannot be directly measured in the current state of the art, they are not recorded in the FDR. The manufacturers of engines agreed that using such parameters as the Mach number, airspeed, flight altitude, temperature, the rpm of the pressure compressors and engine pressure ratios is adequate to estimate the engine thrust. A realistic thrust model is quite complex and cannot be represented by any simple equation. Since such thrust model is not available for the present study, a realistic one tied to the recorded engine performance parameters is developed with the fuzzy-logic algorithm.

For a commercial aircraft, most likely only the axial force and the pitching moment are affected by thrust. This assumption will be made in this Chapter. Theoretically, clear-air turbulence (i.e. random change in u, w (or α) and v (or β)) affect the engine performance through its effects on static and dynamic distortions at the engine face. However, its effects are not known and cannot be estimated, and therefore ignored in the present application.

For the present purpose, data from the flight manual for the fuel flow rates ($\dot{m}_f$) at various altitudes (h), weights (W), Mach numbers (M), calibrated airspeed (CAS), engine pressure ratios (EPR), in cruise flight are utilized. Note that the drag polar for a given aircraft is generally not known to most researchers. To estimate it and hence the thrust magnitude in cruise, the assumption of a design lift-to-drag ratio (L/D) of 17.5 is made. This value of lift-to-drag in cruise is assumed based on the past design experience for twin-jet transports. In the flight manual, various weights, altitudes, Mach numbers, CAS, EPR, and fuel flow rates in cruise are tabulated. The lift coefficient can be calculated at each flight condition immediately. As a result, the drag coefficient can be estimated from the assumption of lift-to-drag ratio. Therefore, the design thrust in cruise at various Mach numbers can be estimated. For the Pratt & Whitney turbofan engines, thrust (T) is defined by EPR, so that the thrust model is set up as:

$$T = f(h, W, M, \text{CAS}, \text{EPR}, \dot{m}_f) \tag{4.23}$$

For GE or CFM turbofan engines, the rpm of the low-pressure compressor (N_1) is used to set the level of thrust, so that the thrust model is set up as:

$$T = f(h, W, M, \text{CAS}, N_1, \dot{m}_f) \tag{4.24}$$

In the present study, the P&W turbofan engines powering the twin-jet transport under study will be illustrated. The actual thrust in operation is obtained by using the recorded variables in the FDR, in particular the fuel flow rates.

The following climb equation (Lan & Roskam 2008) is to be satisfied in the least square sense over a 5-second internal:

$$\frac{W}{g}\frac{dV}{dt} = T - D - W\sin\gamma \tag{4.25}$$

and

$$\frac{D}{W} = \frac{D}{L}\cos\gamma \tag{4.26}$$

All these equations are still valid in descent with negative climb angles (γ). The above equations are further employed for parameter identification in the process of modeling.

Once the thrust model is generated as a function of h, W, M, CAS, EPR, and $\dot{m}_f$ with the flight conditions of climbing, cruise, and descent, one can estimate the thrust magnitude by inserting these flight variables from the FDR into the model.

4.5 Fuzzy-Logic unsteady aerodynamic models

Modeling means to establish the numerical relationship among certain variables of interest. In the fuzzy-logic model, more complete necessary influencing flight variables can be included to capture all possible effects on aircraft response to atmospheric disturbances. For longitudinal aerodynamics, the models are assumed to be of the form:

$$C_x, C_z, C_m = f(\alpha, \dot{\alpha}, q, k_1, \beta, \delta_e, M, p, \delta_s, \bar{q}) \tag{4.27}$$

where the left hand side represents the coefficients of axial force (C_x), normal force (C_z), and pitching moment (C_m), respectively. All variables on the right hand side of Eq. (4.27) have been defined in the previous section. It should be noted that the stabilizer angle (δ_s) is included here, because it varies, though slowly, in flight to provide pitch trim (i.e. reducing the total static pitching moment to 0.0). The roll rate is included here because it is known that an aircraft under high aerodynamic loads at transonic speeds may have its longitudinal stability derivatives affected when additional disturbance due to roll rate is imposed.

For the lateral-directional aerodynamics,

$$C_y, C_l, C_n = f(\alpha, \beta, \phi, p, r, k_2, \delta_a, \delta_r, M, \dot{\alpha}, \dot{\beta}) \tag{4.28}$$

where the left hand side represents the coefficients of side force (C_y), rolling moment (C_l) and yawing moment (C_n), respectively.

4.6 Numerical results and discussions

In the present study, the accuracy of the established unsteady aerodynamic models with six aerodynamic coefficients by using FLM technique is estimated by the sum of squared errors (SSE) and the square of multiple correlation coefficients (R^2). Fig. 5 presents the aerodynamic coefficients of normal force C_z, pitching moment C_m, rolling moment C_l, and yawing moment C_n predicted by the unsteady aerodynamic models. The predicted data by the final refined models have good agreement with the flight data. The C_m-data scattering is most likely caused by turbulence-induced buffeting on the structure, in particular on the horizontal tail. Once the aerodynamic models are set up, one can calculate all necessary derivatives to analyze the stability.

The fuzzy-logic aerodynamic models are capable of generating the continuous derivatives for the static and dynamic stability study of a twin-jet transport in turbulence response. Firstly, how the fuzzy-logic prediction is achieved will be illustrated with one numerical example in the C_z calculation. At first, the range for each variable is defined to be larger than what actually occurred in the present set of C_z-data as follows:

$[\alpha]=[-13,12]$, $[\dot{\alpha}]=[54,50]$, $[q]=[-20,10]$, $[k_1]=[0,0.6]$, $[\beta]=[-7,3]$, $[\delta_e]=[-10,6]$, $[M]=[0,1.6]$, $[p]=[-24,38]$, $[\delta_s]=[-3,3]$, $[\bar{q}]=[4.964, 21.746]$

For the first cell $(1,1,1,1,1,1,1,1,1,1)$, the coefficients in Eq. (2.1) after model training are found to be:

$p_k^1 =$ (2.61755, 1.26662, 1.42338, 2.07962, -0.44241, 2.78017, 1.78150, 1.30818, 1.82872, 1.67592, 1.13787).

Assume that in the following flight conditions C_z is to be predicted:

α=6.91015 deg.; $\dot{\alpha}$=2.95510 deg/sec; q=1.16609 deg/sec; k_1= 0.01965; β= -1.55252; δ_e = 0.68120 deg; M=0.77279; p= -2.62359 deg/sec; δ_s=-0.13930 deg, $\bar{q}$ =11.0545 kpa

These values of variables are converted to [0, 1]. For example,

$x_\alpha = [6.91015-(-13)]/[12-(-13)] = 0.79641$

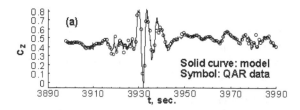

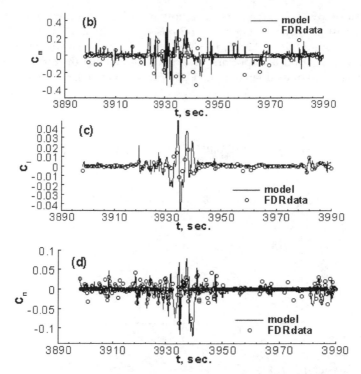

Fig. 5. Predicted aerodynamic coefficients in normal force and moments for a twin-jet transport encountering severe atmospheric turbulence at cruise altitudes around 10,050 m

Other variable values are converted in the same way. It follows that the cell internal function becomes

P_1=2.61755+(1.26662)*(0.79641)+(1.42338)*(0.54764)+(2.07962)*(0.70554)-(0.44241)*(0.03275)+(2.78017)*(0.54475)+(1.7815)*(0.66758)+(1.30818)*(0.48299)+(1.82872)*(0.34478+(1.67592)*(0.47678)+(1.13787)*(0.3730)=11.04817

The membership grades for the first cell are exactly equal to x_r, being 0.79641, 0.54764, etc. Their product can be calculated to be 1.08536E-004. Therefore, the contribution of the first cell to the total output is

11.04817*1.08536E-004=1.19912E-003

The total output from all cells can be calculated to be 5.9962; while the denominator in Eq. (2.3) is calculated to be 7.46459. Therefore, the final prediction is 0.8033. Comparing with data of 0.81038, this prediction has an error of –0.88%.

To examine the stability characteristics, it is imperative to understand the flight environment in detail. The corresponding flight data are presented in Fig. 6. Note that a_z is the same as a_n, the normal acceleration. The variation of normal acceleration is presented in Fig. 6(a), showing the highest a_n being 1.75 g around t = 3930 sec and the lowest being 0.02 g around t = 3932 sec. Fig. 6(b) shows that α is approximately in phase with a_n. When a_n is the highest (around t = 3930 sec), the aircraft rapidly plunging downward with the altitude (h) reaching the lowest as shown in Fig. 6(c); and α is highest about 6.5 deg. in Fig. 6(b). At the same time, M is around 0.77 in Fig. 6(d). Since α reaches a value about 6.5 deg in transonic flight, compressibility effect is important. It should be noted that the turbulent vertical wind field was not measured or estimated in the FDR; but is included in the totalα.

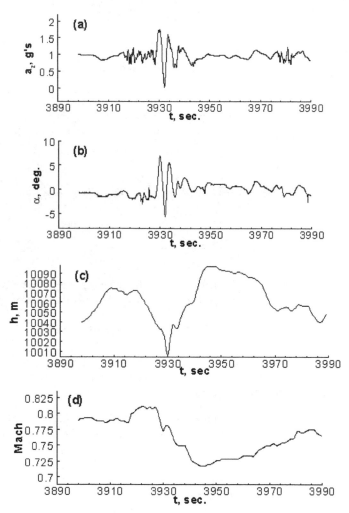

Fig. 6. The time history of flight variables for a twin-jet transport in severe atmospheric turbulence at the altitude around 10,050 m in transonic flight

The aerodynamic derivatives extracted from the unsteady aerodynamic models can be calculated with a central difference scheme. The longitudinal stability derivative ($C_{m\alpha}$) is extracted from the model of C_m. It is evaluated with the central difference approach as follows:

$$C_{m\alpha} = [C_m \, (\alpha + \Delta\alpha, \, ---) - C_m \, (\alpha - \Delta\alpha, \, ---)]/2\Delta\alpha \qquad (4.29)$$

where $\Delta\alpha = 0.5$ degree represents that α is perturbed by 0.5 degree while keeping all other variables unchanged.

The roll damping (C_{lp}) is extracted from the models of C_l with the central difference approach as follows:

$$C_{lp} = [C_l \, (---, p + \Delta p, \, ---) - C_l \, (---, p - \Delta p, \, ---)]/2\Delta p \qquad (4.30)$$

where Δp is in deg/sec. Similarly, all other aerodynamic derivatives are calculated by using the same method.

4.6.1 Effects of membership shape functions

Before presenting the full aerodynamic characteristics, it is desirable to examine the effect of membership shape functions. The normal force coefficient, $C_z = C_N$, and its derivatives in α and $d\alpha/dt$ play an important role in the plunging motion. Therefore, only these two derivatives are compared in Fig. 7. R^2 for the triangular and parabolic shapes are 0.9787 and 0.9786, respectively. Although the values of R^2 are close to each other, details in the derivatives do differ, in particular in $C_{N\dot{\alpha}}$ in plunging motion, probably because in the neighborhood of the peak values of the shape functions, the difference in the membership grades tends to be small. As a result, the effect of parabolic shape functions would smooth out the variation.

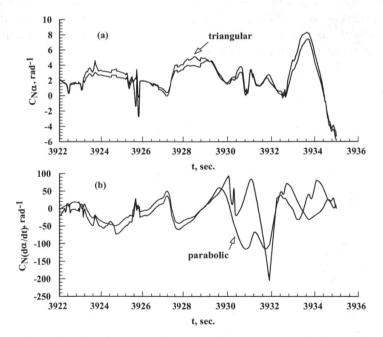

Fig. 7. Effects of membership shape functions on estimated α- and $d\alpha/dt$- derivatives of C_N of a transport aircraft in atmospheric turbulence with plunging motion

From a physical point of view, it is expected that in plunging motion the $C_{N\dot{\alpha}}$ -derivative, which basically represents the virtual mass effect in unsteady aerodynamics (Sheu & Lan, 2011), should vary sharply. Note that the dynamic derivative, $C_{N\dot{\alpha}}$, is dimensionless (see below). In addition, with parabolic shape functions, modeling tends to take longer to converge. Therefore, in the following all derivatives are based on the model with the triangular membership shape functions.

4.6.2 Stability derivatives for the whole time period

The time period between 3927.5 sec and 3932.5 sec is emphasized in evaluating the stability characteristics, because of the plunging motion that affects the flight safety the most. All derivatives are converted to dimensionless ones in accordance with internationally known definition. For example, C_{lp} is defined as $\partial C_l / \partial (pb/2V)$ and C_{mq} as $\partial C_m / \partial (q\bar{c}/2V)$, where $\bar{c}$ is the mean chord length. Therefore, the units of all aerodynamic derivatives are in rad^{-1}. The main longitudinal and lateral-directional stability derivatives along the flight path are presented in Fig. 8. It should be noted that these derivatives are evaluated at the instantaneous conditions, instead of about the trim conditions as have been traditionally done. From the point of view in static stability, initially, the configuration has longitudinal stability ($C_{z\alpha}$ >0 and $C_{m\alpha}$ <0) as shown in Fig. 8(a), stable longitudinal damping (C_{mq} <0) in Fig. 8(b), lateral stability ($C_{l\beta}$ < 0) and directional stability ($C_{n\beta}$ > 0) in Fig. 8(c), small roll damping (C_{lp} < 0) and insufficient directional damping (C_{nr} small or positive) in Fig. 8(d). During the plunging motion, in the period between t = 3928.5 sec. and t = 3930.5 sec, $C_{m\alpha}$ > 0 and $C_{l\beta}$ > 0, so that the static stability becomes unstable. The aerodynamic instability is most likely caused by the motion that produces a time-dependent pressure distribution on the aircraft surface involving compressibility effects.

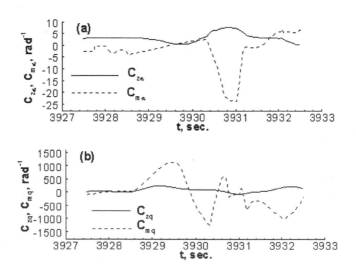

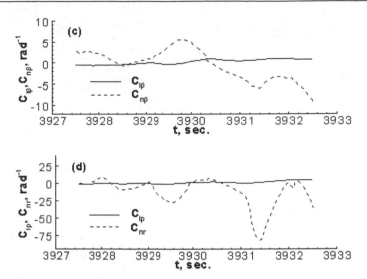

Fig. 8. The time history of main longitudinal and lateral-directional of the static stability derivatives along the flight path

Fig. 9 presents the time history of main longitudinal and lateral-directional oscillatory derivatives along the flight path involving the $\dot{\alpha}$ and $\dot{\beta}$-derivatives. Note that in Fig. 9(a), the oscillatory derivatives are defined as:

$$(C_{mq})_{osc} = C_{mq} + C_{m\dot{\alpha}} \tag{4.31}$$

$$(C_{zq})_{osc} = C_{zq} + C_{z\dot{\alpha}} \tag{4.32}$$

In Fig. 9(c), the oscillatory derivatives are defined as

$$(C_{lp})_{osc} = C_{lp} + C_{l\dot{\beta}} \sin\alpha \tag{4.33}$$

$$(C_{nr})_{osc} = C_{nr} - C_{n\dot{\beta}} \cos\alpha \tag{4.34}$$

During the plunging motion, the values have some differences between oscillatory and damping derivatives in Fig. 9(a) (C_{mq} and $(C_{mq})_{osc}$) and 9(c) (C_{nr} and $(C_{nr})_{osc}$) due to the effects of the dynamic derivatives (i.e. $\dot{\alpha}$ and $\dot{\beta}$-derivatives). The effects of $\dot{\alpha}$-derivative on $(C_{zq})_{osc}$, and $\dot{\beta}$-derivative on $(C_{lp})_{osc}$ are small. However, the effect of $\dot{\alpha}$-derivative on $(C_{mq})_{osc}$ is to improve the stability in pitch after t = 3929.5 sec; while the effects of $\dot{\beta}$-derivative is to cause the directional characteristics more unstable (i.e. $(C_{nr})_{osc}$ more positive). These results indicate that the turbulent crosswind has the effects on directional stability and damping. Although the dynamic derivatives tend to be small for the present configuration, these are much helpful to understand the unknown factors of instability characteristics. To be stable, $(C_{zq})_{osc} < 0$, $(C_{mq})_{osc} < 0$, $(C_{lp})_{osc} < 0$, and $(C_{nr})_{osc} < 0$. Physically, if it is unstable, the motion will be divergent in oscillatory motions.

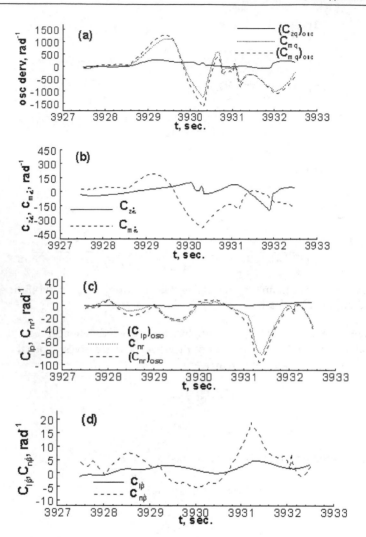

Fig. 9. The time history of main longitudinal and lateral-directional oscillatory derivatives along the flight path

All derivatives in Eqs. (4.31) ~ (4.34) are estimated individually with the aerodynamic models and added afterwards to retain the nonlinearity. In wind-tunnel testing, these derivatives are not separately measured; instead they are determined in combination. As an example, assuming that it is desired to extract the response in C_N and C_m at average conditions given by $k_1 = 0.02$, $\beta = -1.5$, $\delta_e = 0.0$, M= 0.78, p = -3.0 deg/sec, $\delta_s = -0.5$, V=817 ft./sec., $\bar{q}$ =234 psf (see Eq. 4.27). The corresponding flight condition is approximately the one during the plunging motion. The angle of attack is assumed to vary harmonically (e.g. a cosine function) with a reduced frequency equal to k_1. From the fuzzy-logic models, the response can be determined to be as shown in Fig. 10. The arrows represent the directions of change in α. According to a linear theory for C_N and C_m as functions of α, $\dot{\alpha}$, q and $\dot{q}$ (see Eq. 3.4 for the example of an expression based on a linear theory), the following in-phase and out-of-phase integrals are given by: using C_N as an example,

$$\text{In-phase: } \int_0^{2\pi} C_N \alpha d\theta \tag{4.35}$$

$$\text{Out-of-phase: } \int_0^{2\pi} C_N (d\alpha / d\theta) d\theta \tag{4.36}$$

After integration, Eq. (4.36) should produce Eq. (4.32) with C_z interpreted as C_N. In addition, as shown in Fig. 10(a), the direction of the hysteretic curve is clockwise, and Eq. (4.36) should produce a positive value based on the linear theory. The sign of the integral (4.35), is represented by the slope of the hysteretic curve. Similarly, for the pitching moment, Fig. 10(b), the direction of the hysteretic curve is counterclockwise and hence the out-of-phase integral should produce a negative value according to the linear theory (i.e. stable damping). The example illustrates the fact that the present fuzzy-logic models can produce results to simulate the forced-oscillation testing. Typically, the linear results are used in design; while the nonlinear results can be used in performance and simulation.

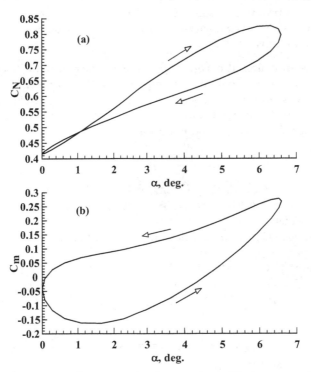

Fig. 10. Aerodynamic response due to a cosine harmonic oscillation at a reduced frequency of 0.02 in α as extracted from the fuzzy logic models.

4.7 Flight dynamic application

As indicated in Introduction, the aerodynamic models generated by the FLM algorithm can serve as the forcing functions and be coupled with the dynamic equations of motion for flight simulation or flight reconstruction in accident investigation. However, it was found that the flight dynamic equations require reformulation to improve numerical damping and avoid numerical divergence (Sheu & Lan 2011). As a result of numerical integration, the turbulent vertical wind can also be estimated from the difference in the total α as measured by the aircraft α-sensor and the motion-produced α by numerical integration. The numerical example presented in the quoted reference is based on the same flight data examined in this Section.

5. Conclusions

The main objective in this paper was to illustrate the nonlinear unsteady aerodynamic models based on the FLM technique having the capability to evaluate the variations in stability of commercial aircraft with adverse weather effects. The present FLM technique was explained in detail and verified with simple examples and wind-tunnel data. It was shown that the FLM technique was capable of handling nonlinear and unsteady aerodynamic environment exhibited for a twin-jet transport in severe atmospheric turbulence with sudden plunging motion in transonic flight. The predicted results showed that the models could produce reasonable aerodynamic coefficients and several derivatives for the assessment of stability characteristics, especially for the study of unknown factors in adverse weather conditions.

At the present time, any aircraft encountering severe atmospheric turbulence is considered uncontrollable. Since the aerodynamics represented by the fuzzy-logic models is realistic, they can be coupled with the numerical integration of flight dynamic equations to study possible improvement in controllability. However, to develop the control law, it is imperative to include the unsteady and nonlinear aerodynamic effects.

6. References

Chang, R. C.; Ye, C. E.; Lan, C. E. & Guan, W. L. (2009). Flying Qualities for a Twin-Jet Transport in Severe Atmospheric Turbulence, *AIAA Journal of Aircraft*, Vol. 46, No. 5, pp. 1673-1680.

Gelb, A. (1982). *Applied Optimal Estimation*, The M. I. T. Press, Cambridge, Massachusetts, USA.

Klein, V.; Batterson, J. G. & Murphy, P. C. (1981), Determination of Airplane Model Structure from Flight Data by Using Modified Stepwise Regression, NASA Technical Publication No. 1916, National Aeronautics and Space Administration, USA.

Lan C E & Guan M., (2005). Flight Dynamic Analysis of a Turboprop Transport Airplane in Icing Accident, AIAA Paper 2005-5922, American Institute of Aeronautics and Astronautics, Reston, Virginia, USA.

Lan, C. E.; Chang, R. C. & Guan, W. L., (2006). Evaluation of Structural Integrity of Transport Aircraft Based on Flight Data," *Journal of Aeronautics, Astronautics and Aviation*, Series A, Vol. 38, No. 3, Sept. 2006, pp. 159-166.

Lan, C. E.; Bianchi, S. & Brandon, J. M. (2008). Effects of Bearing Friction of a Free-to-Roll Rig on Transonic Lateral, Aerodynamics, *Journal of Aircraft*, Vol. 45, No. 1, Jan.-Feb. 2008, pp. 298-305.

Lan, C. E.; Bianchi, S. & Brandon, J. M. (2008). Estimation of Nonlinear Aerodynamic Roll Models for Identification of Uncommanded Rolling Motions, *Journal of Aircraft*, Vol. 45, No. 3, May–June 2008, pp. 916-922.

Lan, C. E. & Roskam, J. (2008). *Airplane Aerodynamics and Performance*, DAR corporation, Lawrence, KS 66044, USA.

Lee, Y. N. & Lan, C. E. (2003). Estimation of Engine Integrity through Fuzzy Logic Modeling, AIAA paper 2003-6817, American Institute of Aeronautics and Astronautics, Reston, Virginia, USA.

Maine, R. E. & Iliff, K. W. (1986). Application of Parameter Estimation to Aircraft Stability and Control, NASA Reference Publication No. 1168, National Aeronautics and Space Administration, USA.

Minkler, G. & Minkler, J. (1993). *Theory and Application of Kalman Filter*, Magellan Book Company, Tucson, Arizona, USA.

Roskam, J. (2003). Airplane Flight Dynamics and Automatic Flight Controls, Part I, published by DAR Corporation, Lawrence, Kansas, USA.

Sheu, D. & Lan, C. E. (2011). Estimation of Turbulent Vertical Velocity from Nonlinear Simulations of Aircraft Response, *Journal of Aircraft*, Vol. 48, No. 2, pp. 645-651.

Wang, Z.; Lan, C. E. & Brandon, J. M. (1998). Fuzzy Logic Modeling of Nonlinear Unsteady Aerodynamics, AIAA Paper 98-4351, American Institute of Aeronautics and Astronautics, Reston, Virginia, USA.

Wang, Z.; Lan, C. E. & Brandon, J. M. (1999). Fuzzy Logic Modeling of Lateral-Directional Unsteady Aerodynamics, AIAA Paper 99-4012, American Institute of Aeronautics and Astronautics, Reston, Virginia, USA.

Wang, Z.; Li, J.; Lan, C. E. & Brandon, J. M. (2001). Estimation of Unsteady Aerodynamic Models from Flight Test Data," AIAA Paper 2001-4017, American Institute of Aeronautics and Astronautics, Reston, Virginia, USA.

Wang, Z.; Lan, C. E. & Brandon, J. M. (2002). Estimation of Lateral-Directional Unsteady Aerodynamic Models from Flight Test Data, AIAA Paper 2002-4626, American Institute of Aeronautics and Astronautics, Reston, Virginia, USA.

Weng, C. T. & Lan, C. E. (2008). Aerodynamic Analysis of a Landing Transport Airplane in Windshear, a monograph published by VDM Vertag Dr. Muller, Germany.

Takagi, T. & Sugeno, M. (1985). Fuzzy identifications of systems and its applications to modeling and control, *IEEE Transactions on Systems, Man and Cybernetics*, Vol. SMC-15, No. 1, pp. 116-132.

Theodorsen, T. (1935). General Theory of Aerodynamic Instability and the Mechanism of Flutter, NACA Report 496, National Advisory Committee for Aeronautics, Hampton, Virginia, USA.

Zadeh, L. A. (1973). Outline of a New Approach to the Analysis of Complex Systems and
    Decision Processes, *IEEE Transactions on Systems, Man, and Cybernetics*, Vol. SMC-3,
    No. 1, pp. 28-44.

9

Fuzzy Logic for Multi-Hop Broadcast in Vehicular Ad Hoc Networks

Celimuge Wu, Satoshi Ohzahata and Toshihiko Kato
University of Electro-Communications
Japan

1. Introduction

A Vehicular Ad hoc Network (VANET) is a form of mobile ad hoc network in which vehicles are equipped with wireless communication devices. Vehicular ad hoc networks have been attracting the interest of both academic and industrial communities on account of their important role in Intelligent Transportation Systems (ITS). VANETs are expected to be able to significantly reduce the number of road accidents. When vehicles travel at a high speed on roads, drivers have very little time to react to the vehicle in front of them. By using vehicular ad hoc networks, emergency information can be propagated along the road to notify drivers ahead of time so that necessary actions can be taken to avoid accidents. Vehicular ad hoc networks also make the driving more efficient by disseminating traffic warning information and service information.

In this chapter, we consider VANET broadcast protocols which work as a basis of many vehicular applications especially safety applications. Providing reliable and efficient multi-hop broadcast in vehicular ad hoc networks is very challenging. First, in vehicular ad hoc networks, vehicles are usually deployed in a dense manner. Therefore, a simple broadcast scheme cannot work well because of redundant broadcasts. Second, wireless communications are unreliable and vehicles can move at a high speed. Consequently, it is difficult to reduce the redundant broadcast while maintaining a high packet dissemination ratio.

As a solution, we explain an approach which uses a fuzzy logic to enhance multi-hop broadcast in vehicular ad hoc networks. Due to the high node density, vehicle movement and fading feature of wireless communications, providing a reliable and efficient multi-hop broadcast in vehicular ad hoc networks is still an open research topic. Using only a subset of neighbor nodes to relay broadcast messages is a main concept for providing efficiency. Meanwhile, in order to ensure a high reliability, multiple metrics of inter-vehicle distance, node mobility and signal strength should be jointly considered in the relay node selection. However, these metrics conflict with each other and these conflicts depend on the vehicle mobility, vehicle distribution and fading condition. The mathematical model of the optimal relay problem is complex to derive and a solution based on it would be too expensive for practical application. Therefore, we employ fuzzy logic to handle these imprecise and uncertain information. We use a fuzzy logic based method to select relay nodes by jointly considering inter-vehicle distance, node mobility and signal strength. The selected relay nodes can provide a reliable data forwarding with a high efficiency. In this chapter, we give a detailed description of the fuzzy logic based method with simulation results.

The basic idea of the approach has been published by IEEE (Wu et al. (2010)). However, in this chapter, we use a more realistic model to evaluate the approach and present our new simulation results. We explain the approach with new and more detailed information.

2. Multi-hop broadcast in vehicular ad hoc networks

The simplest way to disseminate information is flooding. In the flooding, each node rebroadcasts a packet upon the first reception. Obviously, in a high-density network, the flooding introduces too many redundant broadcasts and consequently incurs collisions and results in a low dissemination rate. There have been a lot of protocols to reduce the redundant broadcasts in a high-density network. These protocols can be classified into two categories of sender-oriented protocols and receiver-oriented protocols. In the sender-oriented protocols, a sender node specifies relay nodes. In contrast, in the receiver-oriented protocols, upon reception of a message, a receiver node determines own action (whether rebroadcast the message or not) in an autonomous manner.

2.1 Receiver-oriented protocols

Several receiver based broadcast protocols have been proposed. Wisitpongphan & Tonguz (2007) have proposed three broadcast schemes: weighted p-persistence, slotted 1-persistence, and slotted p-persistence schemes. In these protocols, upon reception of a message, a node calculates a broadcast probability according to the distance from the sender node. Generally, a larger distance from the sender node results in a higher broadcast probability. Suriyapaiboonwattana et al. (2009) have proposed a protocol which uses an adaptive wait time and adaptive probability to trigger the rebroadcast. Slavik & Mahgoub (2010) have proposed a protocol in which all nodes rebroadcast a received message with a certain probability. Mylonas et al. (2008) have proposed a Speed Adaptive Probabilistic Flooding algorithm to determine the rebroadcast probability according to vehicle speed. However, in the receiver-based protocols, each node determines whether rebroadcast or not in an autonomous manner. Therefore, redundant broadcasts cannot be eliminated entirely.

2.1.1 Weighted p-persistence, slotted 1-persistence and slotted p-persistence scheme

Wisitpongphan & Tonguz (2007) have proposed three probabilistic and timer-based broadcast suppression techniques. They are weighted p-persistence, slotted 1-persistence and slotted p-persistence Scheme.

In the weighted p-persistence scheme, upon reception of a packet from node t, node r checks the packet ID and rebroadcasts with probability p_{tr} if node r receives the packet for the first time. Otherwise, the node discards the packet. The probability, p_{tr}, is calculated on a per packet basis using

$$p_{tr} = \frac{D_{tr}}{R},$$ (1)

where D_{tr} is the relative distance between nodes t and r, R is the average transmission range. The larger the D_{tr}, the higher the probability will be.

In slotted 1-persistence scheme, upon reception of a packet, a node checks the packet ID. If the node receives the packet for the first time and fails to detect any rebroadcast from other nodes in an assigned time slot $T_{S_{tr}}$, the node rebroadcasts the packet. If the node can detect a rebroadcast of the packet from any other nodes, the node discards the packet. $T_{S_{tr}}$ is calculated as

$$T_{S_{tr}} = S_{tr} \times \tau, \tag{2}$$

where τ is the estimated one-hop delay, which includes the medium access delay and propagation delay. S_{tr} is the assigned slot number, which is calculated by

$$S_{tr} = \lceil N_s(1 - \frac{min(D_{tr}, R)}{R}) \rceil, \tag{3}$$

where N_s is the number of slots.

Similar to slotted 1-persistence scheme, in the slotted p-persistence scheme, upon reception of a packet, a node checks the packet ID. If the node receives the packet only once in the assigned time slot $T_{S_{tr}}$ which is calculated as Eq. (2), the node rebroadcasts with the predetermined probability p. Otherwise, the node discards the packet.

2.2 Sender-oriented protocols

In the sender-oriented protocols, since the sender node specifies relay nodes, the redundant broadcasts can be minimized. The relay node selection method directly affects the performance of a sender-oriented protocol. Generally, the relay node selection is based on the information collected from the exchange of hello messages. Qayyum et al. (2002) have proposed a multipoint relay (MPR) broadcast scheme (here we call MPR Broadcast) in which relay nodes are selected using two-hop neighbor information. Djedid et al. (2008) have proposed a broadcast protocol which selects relay nodes based on Connected Dominating Set. However, these protocols do not consider node mobility in the relay node selection. As a result, the selected relay node can become sub-optimal and can lose the message due to the node movement.

In our previous work (Wu et al. (2010)), we have proposed a relay node selection which considers the additional radio coverage and node movement (here we call EMPR Broadcast). However, EMPR Broadcast does not consider the fading feature of wireless channels. In a wireless channel, a node can receive a hello message from a neighbor which is at a distance where stable communication is impossible. If the neighbor node is selected as a relay node, a packet loss would occur at the neighbor node.

Sahoo et al. (2009) have proposed BPAB, a Binary Partition Assisted emergency Broadcast protocol for vehicular Ad hoc networks. BPAB intends to use the farthest node to relay messages. However, in a fading channel, the farthest node can lose the messages. Therefore, we have to choose the nodes which have stable signal strength as relay nodes. In short, multiple metrics of inter-vehicle distance, mobility and signal strength should be considered in the relay node selection.

2.2.1 MPR

Qayyum et al. (2002) have proposed a multipoint relay (MPR) broadcast scheme (here we call MPR Broadcast). MPR can substantially reduce the message overhead as compared to the flooding. In MPR broadcast, each node selects a set of its neighbor nodes as "multipoint relays" (MPR). Only the selected MPR nodes are responsible for forwarding the messages. The neighbors of node N which are not in its MPR set, receive and process broadcast messages but do not retransmit broadcast messages received from node N. MPR broadcast provides an efficient mechanism for disseminating messages by reducing the number of transmissions.

Every node attaches its one hop neighbors to the hello messages. In this way, every node is aware of its two-hop neighbors. Each node selects its MPR set from its one-hop neighbors. This set is selected such that these nodes cover (in terms of radio range) all two-hop neighbor nodes. The MPR set of N, denoted as $MPR(N)$, is then an arbitrary subset of the one-hop neighbor of N. $MPR(N)$ satisfies the following condition: every node in the two-hop neighborhood of N must have a link towards $MPR(N)$. The smaller a MPR set (in term of the number of nodes in the set), the less the message overhead.

The following is a heuristic for the selection of MPR nodes.

1. Start with an empty multipoint relay set $MPR(x)$.
2. First select those one-hop neighbor nodes in $N(x)$ as multipoint relays which are the only neighbor of some node in $N^2(x)$, and add these one-hop neighbor nodes to the multipoint relay set $MPR(x)$.
3. While there still exist some node in $N^2(x)$ which is not covered by $MPR(x)$:
   (a) For each node in $N(x)$ which is not in $MPR(x)$, compute the number of nodes that the node covers among the uncovered nodes in the set $N^2(x)$.
   (b) Add the node which has the maximal this number to $MPR(x)$.

MPR can optimize the message dissemination by minimizing the number of messages flooded in the network. The technique is particularly suitable for large and dense networks. However, MPR cannot be used in vehicular ad hoc networks without enhancement because MPR does not consider node mobility at all. In vehicular ad hoc networks, because of node movement, the neighbor information can be imprecise, resulting in the selected relay nodes fail to receive the packets.

2.2.2 EMPR

In addition to the radio coverage, EMPR (Wu et al. (2010)) considers node mobility in the relay node selection. EMPR algorithm introduces predicted MPR fitness (PMF) to evaluate a node whether it is suitable for relaying broadcast packet or not. A sender node selects the neighbor which has the maximal PMF as a relay node from the possible candidate nodes.

Upon reception of a hello message from node x, sender node s calculates the corresponding multipoint relay fitness ($MF(x)$) as

$$MF_i(x) = \frac{|AC_i(x)|}{|N_i(s) \cup N_i(x)|} \tag{4}$$

where i indicates the current value. $N_i(x)$ denotes neighbor set of node x, $|N_i(x)|$ denotes number of x's one hop neighbors. $AC(x)$ is defined as

$$AC(x) = \overline{N(s)} \cap N(x). \tag{5}$$

Eq. (4) could give a higher value for a node that has larger additional radio coverage.

In order to provide different weights to different level of movements, EMPR algorithm introduces discount rate θ which is calculated as

$$\theta = \begin{cases} \sqrt{\frac{|AC_i(x) \cap AC_{i-1}(x)|}{|AC_i(x) \cup AC_{i-1}(x)|}}, & \text{if } AC_i(x) \cup AC_{i-1}(x) \neq \phi \\ 0, & \text{otherwise,} \end{cases} \tag{6}$$

where $i - 1$ indicates the previous value (the value is updated on the reception of a hello message). Eq. (6) could give a larger value for the same directed vehicles and smaller value for vehicles that moving toward opposite direction. If a node x has opposite moving direction to the sender, corresponding θ will be smaller than other vehicles which have the same direction because its additional radio coverage ($AC(.)$) is changing frequently.

Upon reception of a hello from its neighbor, a sender node updates a neighbor's PMF as follows.

$$PMF_i(x) \leftarrow (1 - \mu)PMF_{i-1}(x) + \mu \times \theta \times MF_i(x). \tag{7}$$

Every node maintains a PMF ($PMF_{i-1}(x)$) and AC ($AC_{i-1}(x)$) for every one-hop neighbor. In Eq. (7), the $PMF_{i-1}(x)$ is initialized to 0. Similarly, $AC_{i-1}(x)$ is initialized to ϕ in Eq. (6). The sender node uses these values, the current MF ($MF_i(x)$) and AC ($AC_i(x)$) to calculate the latest PMF ($PMF_i(x)$) as shown in Eq. (6) and Eq. (7). The node then updates the $PMF_{i-1}(x)$ and $AC_{i-1}(x)$. $PMF(x)$ is reset to zero if the sender fails to hear any hello message from node x in three times the hello interval.

In Ref. (Wu et al. (2010)), a retransmission method also has been proposed. However, in this chapter, we do not consider the retransmission issue.

2.3 Challenges

Receiver-oriented approaches cannot reduce the redundant broadcasts entirely. As a result, it is difficult to guarantee a high data dissemination ratio. In this chapter we consider using a sender-oriented approach. However, in the sender-oriented approach, when a relay node fails to receive a packet, the data delivery fails. Therefore, selecting efficient and reliable relay nodes is the most important issue for sender-oriented protocols.

3. Why fuzzy logic

In vehicular ad hoc networks, redundant rebroadcasts incur packet collisions and a higher end-to-end delay due to the increase of MAC layer contention time. It is important to reduce the broadcast redundancy by selecting a small subset of nodes to relay a broadcast packet. However, the relay node selection uses the information collected from the exchange of hello messages. In a highly mobile network, the selected relay node can move out the transmission range of the sender node. Moreover, a node can receive a hello message from a neighbor which is at a distance where stable communication is impossible. If an inappropriate neighbor node is selected as a relay node, the neighbor node fails to receive the message.

Therefore, in the relay node selection, multiple metrics of inter-vehicle distance, node mobility and signal strength should be considered jointly. However, it is difficult to establish a satisfactory relay node evaluation criterion for the following reasons. First, the network information (inter-vehicle distance, node mobility and signal strength) known by each node is inaccurate, incomplete and imprecise. Second, since these metrics may conflict with each other, it results in uncertainty.

As shown in Fig. 1, if we select the farthest node as a relay node, it minimizes the number of relays (efficiency up). But that relay node may lose the packet because the signal is weak (reliability down). Moreover, due to the node movement, the relay node might move out the transmission range of the sender node. These conflicts depend on the vehicle mobility, vehicle distribution and fading condition. Therefore, the mathematical model of the optimal relay problem is complex to derive and a solution based on it would be too expensive for practical application. Fortunately, fuzzy logic can handle imprecise and uncertain information. Therefore, we use a fuzzy logic based method to identify those relay nodes that will give the best results.

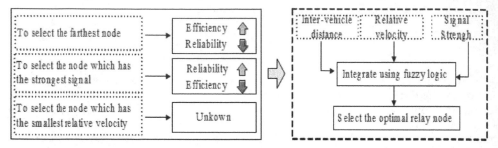

Fig. 1. Using fuzzy logic to consider multiple metrics jointly.

In fuzzy set theory (Klir et al. (1997)), elements have degrees of membership. Fuzzy set theory represents incomplete or imprecise information by defining set membership as a possibility distribution. Based on fuzzy set theory, fuzzy logic deals with the concept of approximate rather than precise factors. For example, we can define a person's height as being 0.5 "high" and 0.5 "low", rather than "completely high" or "completely low". Fuzzy logic has been broadly used for industrial communities due to its efficient handling of approximate reasoning which is similar to human reasoning. In contrast to numerical values in mathematics, fuzzy logic uses non-numeric linguistic variables to express the facts. Fuzzy logic uses fuzzy membership functions to represent the degrees of a numerical value belonging to linguistic variables.

Typically, a fuzzy logic based system consists of three steps: input, process and output steps. In the input step, numerical values are converted to linguistic variables. The process step collects fuzzy rules which are defined in the form of IF-THEN statements and applies the rules to get the result in a linguistic format. The output step converts the linguistic result into a numerical value.

A fuzzy logic based system is flexible because the system can satisfy different requirements by tuning the fuzzy membership function and fuzzy rules. A flexible design is very important for vehicular ad hoc networks due to the variance of channel status and vehicle movement for different road conditions.

4. A multi-hop broadcast protocol based on fuzzy logic

In this section, we present an approach which uses a fuzzy logic to enhance multi-hop broadcast in vehicular ad hoc networks.

4.1 Protocol design

The protocol uses a sender-oriented approach. As shown in Fig. 2. In order to reduce rebroadcast redundancy in high-density networks, the protocol uses only a subset of nodes in the network to relay broadcast packets. We assume every node knows its own position which can be acquired from GPS like positioning services. Vehicles exchange information through hello messages. Every vehicle places its own position information to hello messages and therefore vehicles know positions of their neighbors. A neighbor node is removed from the neighbor list if a node fails to receive any hello message from the neighbor node in 3 times the hello interval. The hello interval is set to 1 second. Before broadcasting a packet, a sender node attaches the identifiers (IP addresses) of the relay nodes to the packet. Upon reception of a packet, a node rebroadcasts the packet only if itself is included in the relay node list.

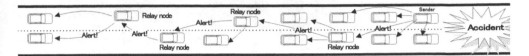

Fig. 2. Multi-hop broadcast by using relay nodes.

Every node maintains a distance factor, mobility factor and signal strength factor for each neighbor. These factors are updated upon reception of a hello message. Before sending a data packet, each node evaluates one-hop neighbors by using fuzzy logic to combine these factors. Based on the evaluation result, the nodes which have high evaluation values are selected as relay nodes.

4.2 Broadcast zone and the number of relay nodes

The sender node specifies relay nodes. It is important to ensure selected relay nodes reaching all intended receivers while minimizing the number of rebroadcasts. To solve this issue, the concept of "broadcast zone" is introduced. In the protocol, a sender node selects one relay node from each broadcast zone.

A sender node first groups neighbor vehicles according to [road_no, sender_pos, direction]. As shown in Fig. 3, "road_no" denotes the road number, "sender_pos" denotes the sender position and "direction" can be "outbound" or "inbound." We call a triad [road_no, sender_pos, direction] a "broadcast zone". For example, the triad [1, (x, y, z), outbound] shows the area which is on the road No.1 and in the "outbound" direction of position (x, y, z).

We note that "outbound" and "inbound" are predefined for each road. For a loop-free road, since the start point and end point can be defined, we define the direction from the start point to the end point as "outbound," and define the direction from the end point to the start point as "inbound." For a loop road, we define the clockwise direction as "outbound" and the counter-clockwise direction as "inbound." As shown in Fig. 3, for road No.1, the direction from A to B is the outbound direction, and the direction from B to A is the inbound direction. In here, "outbound" and "inbound" depend on the position of the vehicles but be independent to the driving directions of the vehicles. We say V1 is at the outbound direction of node V2. In contrast, V2 is at the inbound direction of node V1.

Before broadcasting a data message, the source node specifies the intended area as a list of broadcast zones. The sender node selects one relay node in each of the specified broadcast zones. In the example in Fig. 3, to disseminate information in all directions, node S has to select 4 relay nodes.

In a large scale network, we do not need to let a data message traverse through the whole network. In this case we can specify a border for each broadcast zone by specifying the most distant (from the sender node) position of the intended area. Another way is to define a life time for each message by specifying the hop count or TTL (Time To Live). In this section, without loss of generality, we consider all nodes in the network as the intended receivers.

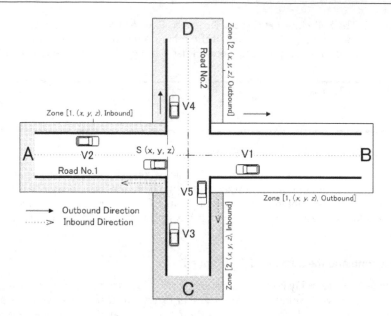

Fig. 3. A street road topology.

4.3 Neighborhood status update using hello messages

In the protocol, upon reception of a hello message from a neighbor, a node evaluates the neighbor according to the inter-vehicle distance, mobility and signal strength respectively. In this way, through exchanging hello messages, each node maintains an evaluation result for each neighbor. When selecting a relay node, these evaluation results are used.

4.3.1 Distance

Upon reception of a hello message from a neighbor X, a node calculates a Distance Factor (DF) as Eq. (8). In Eq. (8), $d(X)$ is the distance between the current node and node X. R is the average transmission range. Here we assume every node has the same transmission power and the transmission power is constant.

$$DF(X) = \begin{cases} \frac{d(X)}{R}, & d(X) <= R \\ 1, & d(X) > R \end{cases} \tag{8}$$

Eq. (8) gives a higher value for a node which has larger distance from the sender node. When the Distance Factor is large, a message can reach the destination region with a small number of rebroadcasts. Therefore, a larger distance factor is desirable to provide a high efficiency.

4.3.2 Mobility

Upon reception of a hello message from a neighbor X, a node calculates a Mobility Factor (MF) as Eq. (9). MF indicates the mobility level of the neighbor node. Here, $d_i(X)$ is the distance between the current node and the neighbor node at time i. α is a smooth factor which is used to smooth out short-term errors. The value of α is set to 0.7 based on out experimental results. MF is initialized to 0.

$$MF(X) \leftarrow (1 - \alpha) \times MF(X) + \alpha \times (1 - \frac{|d_i(X) - d_{i-1}(X)|}{R}). \tag{9}$$

As shown in Eq. (9), the lower the relative movement, the larger is the mobility factor. Since each neighbor is evaluated periodically (upon reception of a hello message), a large mobility factor is required to ensure a specified relay node is still in the transmission range of the sender node when a data packet is sent at the sender node.

4.3.3 Signal strength

Upon reception of a hello message from a neighbor X, a node calculates a Received Signal Strength Indication Factor (RSSIF) as Eq. (10). In Eq. (10), RxPr denotes the received signal power, and RXThresh is the reception threshold. RSSIF indicates the average signal strength of the neighbor node. Here RSSIF is initialized to 0.

$$RSSIF(X) \leftarrow (1 - \alpha) \times RSSIF(X) + \alpha \times (1 - \frac{RXThresh}{RxPr}). \tag{10}$$

Eq. (10) calculates the average signal strength from a neighbor node. In here, we use the RSSI factor to estimate the received signal strength at the neighbor node. A high RSSIF factor can ensure the packet reception at the neighbor node when the neighbor node is selected as a relay node.

4.4 Relay node selection based on fuzzy logic

4.4.1 Procedure

As mentioned above, each node evaluates its neighbors in term of distance, mobility and signal strength by exchanging hello messages. When there is a need to send a packet, a node employs the fuzzy logic to calculate an average relay fitness value for each neighbor based on the neighbor's distance, mobility and signal strength. The node then selects a relay node for each broadcast zone.

For each broadcast zone, a sender node selects the node that has maximal fitness value to relay the packet. The calculation steps for the relay fitness value for each neighbor are as follows.

- **Fuzzification** Use predefined linguistic variables and membership functions to convert the distance factor, mobility factor and RSSI factor to corresponding fuzzy values.
- **Mapping and combination of IF/THEN rules** Map the fuzzy values to predefined IF/THEN rules and combine the rules to get the rank of the neighbor as a fuzzy output value.
- **Defuzzification** Use predefined output membership function and defuzzification method to convert the fuzzy output value to a numerical value.

4.4.2 Fuzzification

"Fuzzification" is the process of converting a numerical value to a fuzzy value using a predefined fuzzy membership function. The fuzzy membership function of distance factor is defined as Fig. 4. The linguistic variables defined for the distance factor are {Large, Medium,

Small}. The sender node uses the membership function and the distance factor to calculate what degree the distance factor belongs to {Large, Medium, Small}. As shown in Fig. 4, when the distance factor is 0.2, we get a fuzzy value {Large:0, Medium:0.4, Small:0.6}. Fig. 5 shows

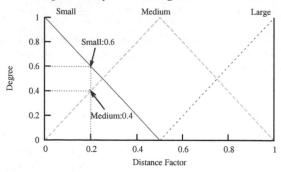

Fig. 4. Distance membership function.

the fuzzy membership function defined for the mobility factor. The sender node uses the mobility factor and this membership function to calculate what degree the mobility factor belongs to {Slow, Medium, Fast}. Fig. 6 shows the fuzzy membership function defined for the

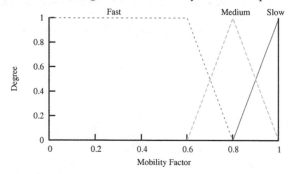

Fig. 5. Mobility membership function.

RSSI factor. The sender node uses the RSSI factor and this membership function to calculate what degree the RSSI factor belongs to {Good, Medium, Bad}.

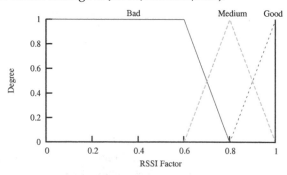

Fig. 6. Signal strength membership function.

4.4.3 Rule base

Based on the fuzzy values of distance factor, mobility factor and RSSI factor, the sender node uses the IF/THEN rules (as defined in Table 1) to calculate the rank of the node. The linguistic variables of the rank are defined as {Perfect, Good, Acceptable, NotAcceptable, Bad, VeryBad}. In Table 1, Rule1 defines the following rule. **IF** *Distance* is Large, *Mobility* is Slow and *Signal*

	Distance	Mobility	Signal Strength	Rank
Rule1	Large	Slow	Good	Perfect
Rule2	Large	Slow	Medium	Good
Rule3	Large	Slow	Bad	NotAcceptable
Rule4	Large	Medium	Good	Good
Rule5	Large	Medium	Medium	Acceptable
Rule6	Large	Medium	Bad	Bad
Rule7	Large	Fast	Good	NotAcceptable
Rule8	Large	Fast	Medium	Bad
Rule9	Large	Fast	Bad	VeryBad
Rule10	Medium	Slow	Good	Good
Rule11	Medium	Slow	Medium	Acceptable
Rule12	Medium	Slow	Bad	Bad
Rule13	Medium	Medium	Good	Acceptable
Rule14	Medium	Medium	Medium	NotAcceptable
Rule15	Medium	Medium	Bad	Bad
Rule16	Medium	Fast	Good	Bad
Rule17	Medium	Fast	Medium	Bad
Rule18	Medium	Fast	Bad	VeryBad
Rule19	Small	Slow	Good	NotAcceptable
Rule20	Small	Slow	Medium	Bad
Rule21	Small	Slow	Bad	VeryBad
Rule22	Small	Medium	Good	Bad
Rule23	Small	Medium	Medium	Bad
Rule24	Small	Medium	Bad	VeryBad
Rule25	Small	Fast	Good	VeryBad
Rule26	Small	Fast	Medium	VeryBad
Rule27	Small	Fast	Bad	VeryBad

Table 1. Rule Base

Strength is Good **THEN** *Rank* is Perfect.

When the distance factor is large, we can reduce the number of hops for broadcast. When the mobility is slow, the relay nodes are not likely to move out the transmission range of the sender node. A high Signal Strength can ensure a packet will be received by the relay nodes. This is why the Rank of the Rule1 is Perfect.

Compared with the Rule1, when any one of three factors (Distance, Mobility and Signal Strength) drops to the next level, we set the Rank to be "Good" (Rule2, Rule4 and Rule10). Similarly, when any two of three factors drop to the next level, we set the rank to be "Acceptable" (Rule5, Rule11 and Rule13). When any one of three factors drops to the worst level, we set the Rank to be "NotAcceptable" (Rule3, Rule7 and Rule19). The same for the case when all three factors are at the medium level (Rule 14). When two or all three factors drop to the worst level, we set the Rank to be "VeryBad" (Rule9, Rule18, Rule21, Rule24, Rule 25, Rule26 and Rule27). For other rules, we set the Rank to be "Bad" (Rule6, Rule8, Rule12, Rule15, Rule16, Rule17, Rule20, Rule22 and Rule23). In this way, we define 27 rules in total. These rules cover all possible combinations of fuzzy values in different factors.

In a rule, the IF part is called the "antecedent" and the THEN part is called the "consequent". Since there can be multiple rules applying for the same fuzzy variables, we have to combine their evaluation results. Here we use Min-Max method to match and combine the rules. In the Min-Max method, for each rule, the minimal value of antecedent is used as the final degree. When combining different rules, the maximal value of consequents is used.

For example, as shown in Fig. 7, we assume a neighbor's distance, mobility and RSSI factor belong to the corresponding linguistic variables as {Large:1, Medium:0, Small:0},{Slow:0.8, Medium:0.2, Fast:0},{Good:0.5, Medium:0.5, Bad:0} respectively. In this case, these fuzzy sets match Rule1, Rule2, Rule4 and Rule5. For Rule1, the degree for {Large} (Distance) is 1, the degree for {Slow} (Mobility) is 0.8 and the degree for {Good} (Signal Strength) is 0.5. In the Min-Max method, we take the minimal value of antecedent members and therefore the degree of the antecedent will be 0.5. Similarly, the degrees of antecedents for Rule2, Rule4 and Rule5 will be 0.5, 0.2 and 0.2 respectively. As both Rule2 and Rule4 lead to the Rank {Good}, we take the maximal value of consequents and therefore the degree of the Rank Good will be 0.5. In this way, all rules are combined to get a fuzzy result.

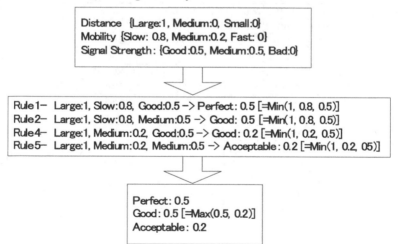

Fig. 7. An example for fuzzy rule evaluations.

4.4.4 Defuzzification

Defuzzification is used to produce a numeric result based on a predefined output membership function and corresponding membership degrees. Fig. 8 shows the defined output membership function. Here Center of Gravity (COG) method is used to defuzzify the fuzzy result.

As shown in Fig. 8, we cut the output membership function in a straight horizontal line according to the corresponding degree, and remove the top portion. For the example given

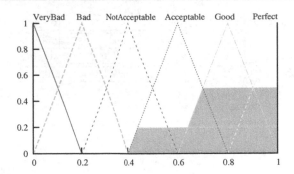

Fig. 8. Output membership function and an example for $\mu(x)$.

above, when the degree for Rank {Acceptable} is 0.2, the degree for Rank {Good} is 0.5 and the degree for Rank {Perfect} is 0.5, the result function will be as shown in Fig. 8. The center of gravity is calculated as

$$COG = \frac{\int \mu(x)x dx}{\int \mu(x) dx},\qquad(11)$$

where $\mu(x)$ is the result function and x is the value of X-axis. In this protocol, the calculated COG represents the fitness of the neighbor being a relay node. For each broadcast zone, the sender node calculates a fitness value for each neighbor node and then selects the node which has the maximal fitness value.

4.5 Simulation results

Network Simulator 2 (ns-2.34) (ns-2 (2010)) was used to conduct simulations. We used a Freeway model (Bai et al. (2003)) to generate the network topology (see Table 2). We used a freeway which has two lanes in each direction. All lanes of the freeway were 2000 m in length. The maximum allowable vehicle velocity was 40m/s. We used Nakagami propagation model. Parameters of the Nakagami model are shown in Table 3. These parameters result packet delivery ratios as shown in Fig. 9. We used these parameter values because they model a realistic wireless channel of vehicular ad hoc networks (Khan et al. (2009)).

Topology	Freeway scenario, 2000m, 4lanes
Number of nodes	100 to 600
Mobility generation	Bai et al. (2003)
Number of sources	2
Number of receivers	The number of all nodes in the network
Number of packets	50 packets at each source
Packet size	512 bytes
Data rate	10 packet per second
MAC	IEEE 802.11 MAC (2Mbps)
Propagation model	Nakagami Model
Simulation time	150 s

Table 2. Simulation Environment

Other simulation parameters were the default settings of ns-2.34. From 20s, two source nodes generated 50 packets with a rate of 10 packets per second. These two nodes (randomly

gamma0_	gamma1_	gamma2_	d0_gamma_	d1_gamma_
1.9	3.8	3.8	200	500
m0_	m1_	m2_	d0_m_	d1_m_
1.5	0.75	0.75	80	200

Table 3. Parameters of Nakagami Model

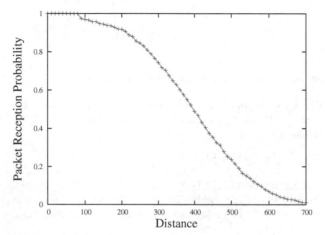

Fig. 9. Packet reception probability for various distances.

selected) were neighbors and being close to each other. This is to simulate a condition of two collided vehicles send data messages at the same time. Simulation time was 150s. We launched simulations with 50 different vehicle deployments and different vehicle movements, and analyzed the average value.

The protocol (Fuzzy) was compared with Flooding, Weighted p-persistence (Wisitpongphan & Tonguz (2007)), MPR Broadcast (Qayyum et al. (2002)) and EMPR Broadcast (Wu et al. (2010)). We did not use retransmission in all these protocols.

4.5.1 Number of broadcasts

Fig. 10 shows the number of broadcasts per data packet for various number of nodes. Flooding generates too many redundant broadcasts in a high density network. As a result, many packets are lost due to packet collisions.

Since the Weighted p-persistence uses a probabilistic broadcast method to reduce the redundant rebroadcast, the Weighted p-persistence performs better than the flooding. However, the number of broadcasts also increases linearly with the increase of node density. Therefore, redundant rebroadcasts cannot be eliminated entirely. In the MPR Broadcast, EMPR Broadcast and the Fuzzy protocol, only the nodes which have been selected as relay nodes, rebroadcast the packets. Therefore, the redundant broadcast can be reduced efficiently.

4.5.2 Packet dissemination ratio

Fig. 11 shows packet dissemination ratio for various number of nodes. In flooding, as the number of nodes increases, the dissemination ratio decreases. This is because many nodes try

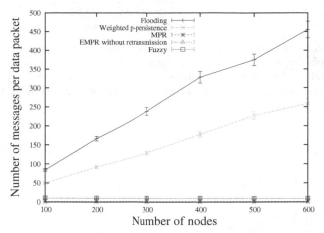

Fig. 10. Number of broadcasts per data packet for various number of nodes.

to broadcast at the same time and this introduces collisions and a drop in packet dissemination ratio.

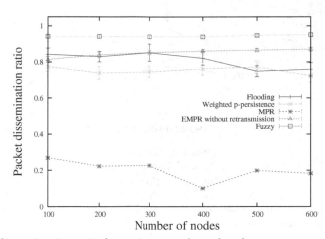

Fig. 11. Packet dissemination ratio for various number of nodes.

The Weighted p-persistence scheme works better than the flooding by reducing the number of broadcasts. However, since a probabilistic method is used, the number of broadcasts also increases as the node density increases, leading to a drop in performance. In the MPR Broadcast, although the number of broadcasts can be efficiently reduced, we observe a poor dissemination ratio. This is because a sender node usually selects the farthest node. However, in a fading channel, the furthest node always fails to receive the broadcast packet. In MPR, since the node mobility is not considered in the relay node selection, a packet loss also occurs at the selected relay node due to the vehicle movement. The EMPR Broadcast performs better than the MPR Broadcast because it considers node mobility in the relay node selection. In the EMPR Broadcast, a sender node selects a relay node which has a low relative mobility and large additional coverage. As the number of nodes increases, the choices increase and therefore the performance of the EMPR Broadcast improves slightly.

The Fuzzy protocol evaluates relay fitness values of relay nodes considering inter-vehicle distance, node mobility and received signal strength. We use Fig. 12 to show the distribution of relay fitness values for various distances and relative velocities. In here, the received signal power on a certain distance is calculated by averaging received signal powers of 10,000 packets in the same distance.

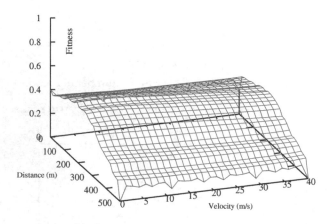

Fig. 12. Relay fitness for various distances and relative velocities.

By jointly considering inter-vehicle distance, node mobility and signal strength, the Fuzzy protocol can deal with node mobility and fading while providing large progress on the dissemination direction. As a result, the Fuzzy protocol provides better packet dissemination ratio (above 94%) than other protocols. The very small number of packet losses are because of the packet collisions. It is possible to get a higher packet reception ratio if we use a retransmission mechanism. However, this is beyond the scope of this work.

4.5.3 End-to-end delay

Fig. 13 shows end-to-end delay for various number of nodes. In the end-to-end delay calculation, we only count the successfully delivered packets. In Flooding, as the node density increases, the delay increases drastically. This is because of the increase of MAC layer contention time with the increase of the number of rebroadcasts. Another reason is the effect of packet losses. When the node density is high, the redundant broadcasts introduce many collisions and consequently the nodes that provide larger progress on distance lose the data packets. As a result, the packets are delayed because they are delivered through sub-optimal paths (longer paths).

In Weighted p-persistence, the end-to-end delay also increases with the increase of the node density because Weighted p-persistence cannot eliminate redundant broadcasts completely.

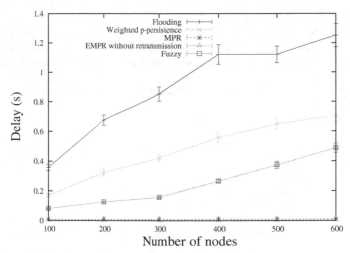

Fig. 13. End-to-end delay for various number of nodes.

MPR shows the lowest delay. This is because MPR chooses the farthest node as a relay node. The low delay of MPR is also because many data messages are lost at the relay node.

EMPR Broadcast and the Fuzzy protocol show comparable delays. Although the selected relay nodes are usually not the farthest possible nodes, the Fuzzy protocol shows lower end-to-end delays. This is because the Fuzzy protocol reduces the contention time at each node by reducing the number of rebroadcasts. The Fuzzy protocol shows an increase of the end-to-end delay with the increase of the number of nodes. This is because with the increase of node density, the number of hello messages increases, resulting in a slight increase of MAC layer contention time at each node. However, this is acceptable because the Fuzzy protocol does show a low delay even when the network density is high.

5. Conclusions

Efficient and reliable relay node selection is important for providing multi-hop broadcast services in vehicular ad hoc networks. Due to the network dynamics of vehicular ad hoc networks, the optimal mathematical model of the relay node selection problem is difficult to derive. As a solution, in this chapter, we presented a fuzzy logic protocol to enhance the multi-hop broadcast in vehicular ad hoc networks. By employing the fuzzy logic into the relay node selection, the protocol considers the inter-vehicle distance, node mobility and signal strength jointly. As a result, a high level of reliability and efficiency are provided. We used computer simulations to evaluate the protocol's performance. The simulation results confirmed that the Fuzzy protocol offers a significant performance advantage over existing alternatives by selecting better relay nodes. The fuzzy logic based approach is easy to implement and can be configured to any scenario by tuning the fuzzy membership parameters.

6. Acknowledgement

This work was supported by JSPS KAKENHI Grant-in-Aid for Young Scientists (B) #23700072.

7. References

Wu, C.; Kumekawa, K. & Kato T. (2010). A Novel Multi-hop Broadcast Protocol for Vehicular Safety Applications. *Journal of Information Processing*, Vol. 18, pp.930–944, 2010.

Clausen, T. & Jacquet P. (2003). Optimized Link State Routing Protocol (OLSR). *RFC 3626*, Vol. 18, Oct., 2003.

The Network Simulator - ns-2. *http://www.isi.edu/nsnam/ns/*, Accessed on June 23. 2010.

Wisitpongphan, N. & Tonguz, K.O. (2010). Broadcast Storm Mitigation Techniques in Vehicular Ad Hoc Networks. *IEEE Wireless Communications*, Vol. 14, No.6, pp.84–94, 2007.

Suriyapaiboonwattana, K.; Pornavalai, C. & Chakraborty, G. (2009). An adaptive alert message dissemination protocol for VANET to improve road safety. *Proceedings of IEEE Intl. Conf. on Fuzzy Systems*, Jeju Island, Korea, pp.1639–1644, 2009.

Slavik, M. & Mahgoub I. (2010). Stochastic Broadcast for VANET. *Proceedings of IEEE Consumer Communications and Networking Conference*, pp.1–5, 2010.

Mylonas, Y.; Lestas M. & Pitsillides A. (2008). Speed adaptive probabilistic flooding in cooperative emergency warning. *Proceedings of 4th Annual Intl. Conf. on Wireless Internet*, Maui, Hawaii, pp.1–7, 2008.

Qayyum, A.; Viennot L. & Laouiti A. (2002). Multipoint Relaying for Flooding Broadcast Messages in Mobile Wireless Networks. *Proceedings of 35th Annual Hawaii Intl. Conf. on System Sciences*, Big Island, Hawaii, pp.3866–3875, 2002.

Djedid, L.O.; Lagraa N.; Yagoubi M. & Tahari K. (2008). Adaptation of the MCDS broadcasting protocol to VANET safety applications. *Proceedings of Intl. Conf. on Innovations in Information Technology*, pp.534–538, 2008.

Sahoo, J.; Wu E.H.K.; Sahu P.K. & Gerla M. (2009). BPAB: Binary Partition Assisted Emergency Broadcast Protocol For Vehicular Ad Hoc Networks. *Proceedings of 18th Intl. Conf. on Computer Communications and Networks*, San Francisco, USA, pp.1–6, 2009.

Klir, G.J.; Clair, U.S. & Bo, Y. (1997). *Fuzzy set theory: foundations and applications*, Prentice-Hall Inc., ISBN:978-0133410587.

Bai, F.; Sadagopan N. & Helmy A. (2003). Important: A Framework to Systematically Analyze The Impact of Mobility on Performance of Routing Protocols for Adhoc Networks. *Proceedings of 22nd Annual Joint Conf. of the IEEE Computer and Communications Societies*, San Francisco, USA, pp.825–835, 2003.

Wu, C.; Ohzahata S. & Kato T. (2010). Fuzzy logic based multi-hop broadcast for high-density vehicular ad hoc networks. *Proceedings of IEEE Vehicular Networking Conference*, New Jersey, USA, pp.17–24, 2010.

Khan, A.; Sadhu S. & Yeleswarapu M. (2009). A comparative analysis of DSRC and 802.11 over Vehicular Ad hoc Networks. *Project Report*, Department of Computer Science, University of Californai, Santa Barbara, pp.1–8, 2009.

10

Condition Ranking and Rating of Bridges Using Fuzzy Logic

Saptarshi Sasmal, K. Ramanjaneyulu and Nagesh R. Iyer
CSIR-Structural Engineering Research Centre,
CSIR Complex, TTTI Post, Taramani,
India

1. Introduction

Bridges are the crucial components of highway networks. In recent years, there has been growing awareness about the problems associated with the existing old bridges. Many of the existing bridges in service today were designed for less traffic, smaller vehicles, slower speeds and lighter traffic. Hence, they have become inadequate according to the current loading standards/codes of practice for design of highway bridges. Even in the case of newer bridges, deterioration caused by unforeseen service condition, adverse environmental actions and inadequate maintenance is causing great concern to bridge engineers. Bridge authority has the responsibility to maintain its bridges in a safe condition. To ensure safe and durable service, it is usual to perform periodic in-situ inspections. These inspections involve visual observations, non-destructive testing and partial destructive testing. The data collected from site and processed in laboratory, would be used to decide about suitable repair, strengthening or demolition of existing bridges. It is also evident that engineers and decision makers have to deal with large number of deficient bridges in years to come and it will be extremely demanding to decide the most deserving one to allot fund for timely retrofitting. Further, it is necessary to formulate a systematic method to assess the present and future needs of the existing bridges which would help the decision makers in identifying the most deserving bridges for improvement during a given period.

In view of this, several countries have initiated development of bridge management systems for assisting their decision makers in finding optimal strategies for maintenance, rehabilitation and replacement of bridges. Furthermore, it also has to ensure value for money by carrying out preventive work at appropriate time so that future maintenance needs are also kept at a minimum level. In a broader sense, the funding body has to consider the justification and priority for money to be spent on a multitude of expenditure areas. Decision makers and/or society at large should be able to choose whether to spend money on rehabilitating a bridge or to demolish it. The bridge engineers and the policy makers are being increasingly pressed to justify the funding order proposed to maintain the bridges. It shows the importance of an exclusive bridge management system. Bridge management is a rational and systematic approach for organising and carrying out the activities related to planning, design, construction, maintenance, rehabilitation and replacement of bridges.

To decide upon all these matters, a systematic and logical way for prioritization of the bridges under consideration and rating of the most deserved one is needed (as shown in Fig. 1). The bridge condition rating is the datum for any bridge management system. The usefulness of a bridge management system and the accuracy of bridge rating rely upon the bridge condition data which constitute subjective judgment and intuition of the bridge inspector. So, a procedure like fuzzy logic would be useful to handle the uncertainty, imprecision and subjective judgment.

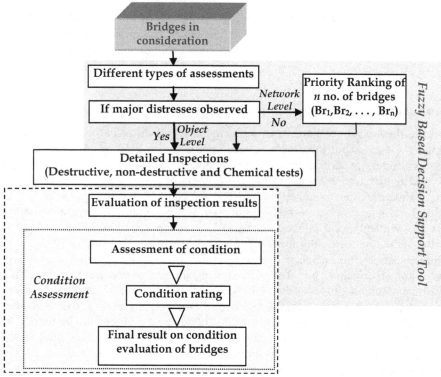

Fig. 1. Schematic representation of condition assessment of bridges

Before proceeding further, it is important to know the decision making tools useful for this type of problem. To provide the ready reference to the readers, few of the mostly used and appropriate models are discussed below.

2. Different decision making methods

One of the most crucial problems in many decision making methods is the precise evaluation of data. Very often, in real-life decision making applications, data are imprecise and fuzzy [Ben-Arieh and Triantaphyllou (1992), Tseng and Klein (1992)]. A decision maker may encounter difficulty in quantifying and processing linguistic statements. Therefore, it is desirable to develop decision making methods which can handle fuzzy data. It is equally important to evaluate the performance of the following decision making methods. Among the decision making methods, the Weighted Sum Model (WSM) is probably the best known and most widely used method of decision making, especially in single dimensional problem. If there are M alternatives and N criteria in a decision making problem, then the best alternative, A*, is the one which satisfies (in the maximisation case) the following expression (Fishburn, 1967)

$$A^*_{WSM} = \max_i \sum_{j=1}^{N} a_{ij} W_j \quad \text{for i= 1,2,....,M} \tag{1}$$

where, a_{ij} is the measure of performance of the ith alternative in terms of the jth decision criterion, and W_j is the weight of importance of the jth criterion. Further, Weighted Product Model (WPM) is very similar to WSM. The main difference is that it uses multiplication, instead of addition, to rank alternatives. Each alternative is compared with the others by multiplying a number of ratios, one for each criterion. Each ratio is raised to the power of the related weight of the corresponding criterion. Generally, in order to compare the two alternatives A_K and A_L, the following formula (Bridgman, 1922; Miller and Starr, 1969; Chen and Hwang, 1992) can be used.

$$R\left(\frac{A_K}{A_L}\right) = \prod_{j=1}^{N} \left(\frac{a_{Kj}}{a_{Lj}}\right)^{W_j} \tag{2}$$

where, N is number of criteria, a_{ij} is actual value (performance) of ith alternative in terms of jth criterion and W_j is weight of importance of the jth criterion. The analytic hierarchy process (AHP) was developed by Saaty (1980), based on an axiomatic foundation that has established its mathematical viability (Harker and Vargas 1990; Saaty, 1994). The diverse applications of the technique are due to its simplicity and ability to cope with complex decision making problems. The AHP methodology has been widely used for solving problems where definite quantitative measures are not available to support correct decisions. Zahedi (1986) provided an exhaustive survey of AHP methodology and its applications. The AHP attracted the interest of many researchers for long because of its easy applicability and interesting mathematical properties. In this chapter also, AHP, the well-proven technique, is used as a decision making tool because of its inherent strength in tackling complex problems.

2.1 Formation of Analytic Hierarchy Model (AHM) for AHP

The AHP deals with the construction of an M × N matrix (where M is the number of alternatives and N is the number of criteria) using the relative importance (weights) of the alternatives in terms of each criterion. The vector $X_i = (a_{i1}, a_{i2}, a_{i3}, ..., a_{iN})$ for the ith alternative (i=1,2,3,...,M) is the eigenvector of an N × N reciprocal matrix which is determined through a sequence of pair-wise comparisons. Also, the elements in such a vector add-up to one. The AHP uses relative values instead of actual ones. Therefore, the AHP can be used in single- and multi-dimensional decision making problems. The analytic hierarchy model (AHM) begins with representing a complex problem as a hierarchy. At the top level of the hierarchy, the goal (objective) upon which the best decision should be made is placed. The next level of the hierarchy contains attributes or criteria that contribute to the quality of the decisions. Each attribute may be decomposed into more detailed attributes (indices). After the hierarchical network is constructed, one can determine the weights (importance measures) of the elements at each level of the decision hierarchy, and synthesize the weights to determine the relative importance (weights) of decision alternatives. First, a comparison matrix, which includes first (lowest) level elements of the hierarchy, is constructed. Then, a ratio scale through pair-wise comparison of each pair of criteria with respect to the overall goal is performed. The relative importance (weight) of each criterion is estimated using an eigenvector approach or other methods. Then, the relative importance (weight) of each alternative with respect to each criterion is determined using similar pair-wise comparisons. Here, it is important to note that the efficiency of AHP greatly depends on the accuracy with which pair-wise weights of items are assigned during the formation of comparison matrix. For pair-wise assignment of weights for items, there is a need for a scale for relative quantification of items.

2.2 Scales for quantifying pair-wise comparisons

One of the most vital and crucial steps in decision-making methods is the accurate estimation of the pertinent data. Very often, these data are not known in terms of absolute values. Therefore, many decision-making methods attempt to determine the relative importance (weight) of each alternative involved in a given decision-making problem. Consider the case of having a single decision criterion and a set of N alternatives denoted as A_i (i = 1, 2, 3,..., N). The decision maker wants to determine the relative performance of the alternatives under each criterion. Here, one may consider the N alternatives as the members of a fuzzy set. Then, the degree of membership of element (i.e. alternative) A_i expresses the degree to which alternative A_i meets the criterion. This is also the approach considered by Federov et al. (1982) and Chen and Hwang (1992) and was also discussed by Saaty (1994). All the methods which use the pair-wise comparison approach eventually express the qualitative answers of a decision maker as some numbers. Pair-wise comparisons are quantified by using a scale. Such a scale is one-to-one mapping between the set of discrete linguistic choices available to the decision maker and a discrete set of numbers which represent the importance or weight of the previous linguistic choices. There are two major approaches in developing such scales. The first approach is based on the linear scale and the other is based on exponential scale [Roberts (1979), Lootsma (1991)]. It is easier to use linear scale to translate the weight of an item/element over the other. Therefore, in this study, the linear scale has been used to assign the importance/weight of items or elements under each decision layer.

2.3 Real Continuous Pair-wise (RCP) and Closest Discrete Pair-wise (CDP) matrices

A procedure is required for obtaining comparison matrix from the relative importance (weights) for a group of elements, using a suitable scale, based on pair-wise comparisons. It involves the formulation of real continuous pair-wise (RCP) and the closest discrete pair-wise (CDP) matrices. Reciprocal matrices with pair-wise comparisons were used for extracting all the pertinent information from a decision maker. Each entry in these matrices represents numerically the value of a pair-wise comparison between two alternatives with respect to a single criterion. For a problem that has 'p' objectives, a scale is constructed for rating these objectives as to their importance with respect to the decision as seen by the analyst. Let w_1, w_2, w_3, ..., w_p be the real membership values of a fuzzy set with p members. Comparing objective k with objective l, the ratios α_{kl} can be assigned, and the RCP matrix (p × p) is constructed as

$$RCP = A_{p \times p} = [\alpha_{kl}] = \left[\frac{w_k}{w_l}\right] \quad k,l = 1,p \quad (3)$$

The entry α_{kl} in RCP matrix represents the exact (and thus unknown) value of the comparison when the kth member is compared with the lth member. Each element β_{kl} ($\beta_{kl} \in \Phi$) in the CDP matrix can be determined and the matrix will be formed such that $|(\alpha_{kl} - \beta_{kl})|$ is minimum. Any other norm may also be assumed as

$$\left|\frac{\alpha_{kl}}{1+\alpha_{kl}} - \frac{\beta_{kl}}{1+\beta_{kl}}\right| \quad (4)$$

3. Condition evaluation of existing bridges through prioritization

The Analytic Hierarchy Process (AHP) is mainly applied to the decision making problem with multiple evaluation criteria and uncertainty conditions. After hierarchical decomposition from different layers and through the quantitative judgment, the AHP is thus made a synthetic evaluation to reduce risk of wrong decision making. The AHP uses eigenvalue method to find the weights of different items. The eigen equation is adopted to construct the comparison matrix (Yu and Cheng, 1994, Liang et al., 2001) for finding the relative importance (weights) and orders of multiple objectives to an objective and the concept has already been successfully used to solve different types of decision making problems. The methodology involves the following operations.

3.1 Relative importance (weights) of items

A decision-maker provides the upper triangle of the comparison matrix (as shown in Table 1), while reciprocals are placed in the lower triangle which do not need any further judgment. The diagonal elements of the matrix are always equal to one. Assuming that any item group consists of A_1, A_2, A_3, ...A_n items, the comparison matrix is constructed and then relative weights of items (A_{ij}) of the group are evaluated by comparing objective i with objective j, the ratios α_{kl} can be assigned, and the real continuous pair-wise (RCP) matrix of order $p \times p$ is constructed. It can be proved that consistent reciprocal matrix '[A]' has rank 1 with non-zero eigenvalue (λ) = n. Then, we have

$$[A]w = nw \text{ Where, w is an eigenvector} \quad (5)$$

The same equation also states that in the perfectly consistent case (i.e. A_{ij} = A_{ik} A_{kj}), the vector w, with the membership values of the elements 1,2,3,....,n is the principal right-eigenvector (after normalisation) of matrix [A].

3.2 Check for consistency of comparison matrices

In most of the real world problems, the pair-wise comparisons are not perfect, that is, the entry A_{ij} might deviate from the ratio of the real membership values W_i and W_j (i.e. W_i /

W_j). In a non-consistent case, the expression $A_{ij} = A_{ik} \times A_{kj}$ does not hold good for all the possible combinations. Now, the new matrix [A] can be considered as a perturbation of the previous consistent case when the entries A_{ij} change slightly, then the eigenvalues change in the similar fashion (Saaty, 1994). Moreover, the maximum eigenvalue is close to n (greater than n), while the remaining eigenvalues are close to zero. Thus, in order to find the membership values in the non-consistent cases, one should find an eigenvector that corresponds to the largest eigenvalue λ_{max}. That is to say, one must find the principal right-eigenvector W that satisfies

$$AW = \lambda_{max} W \qquad \text{where } \lambda_{max} \approx n \qquad (6)$$

The consistency ratio (CR) is obtained by first estimating λ_{max} of matrix [A] Then, Saaty (1994) defined the consistency index (CI) of the matrix '[A]' as

$$CI = (\lambda_{max} - n)/(n-1) \qquad (7)$$

Then, the consistency ratio (CR) is obtained by dividing CI with the random consistency index (RCI) as shown in Table 2 (proposed by Saaty, 1994). Each RCI is an average random consistency index derived from a sample of size 500 of randomly generated reciprocal matrices. If the previous approach yields a CR greater than 0.10 then a re-examination of the pair-wise judgments is recommended until a CR less than or equal to 0.10 is achieved.

B	A_1	A_2	A_3	....	A_n
A_1	A_{11}	A_{12}	A_{13}	....	A_{1n}
A_2	A_{21}	A_{22}	A_{23}	....	A_{2n}
A_3	A_{31}	A_{32}	A_{33}	....	A_{3n}
....	....	....	....	....	....
A_n	A_{n1}	A_{n2}	A_{n3}	....	A_{nn}

Table 1. Comparison Matrix

n	1	2	3	4	5	6	7	8	9	≥10
RCI	0	0	0.58	0.90	1.12	1.24	1.32	1.41	1.45	1.56

Table 2. RCI values of sets of different order 'n'

3.3 Fuzzy synthetic evaluation of estimation indices for items

Most of the decision making in the real world takes place in a situation in which the pertinent data and the sequence of possible actions are not precisely known. Therefore, it is very important to adopt fuzzy data to express such situations in decision making problems. In order to fuzzify the crisp decision making methods, it is important to know how fuzzy operations are used on fuzzy numbers. Fuzzy operation in decision making was first introduced by Dubois and Prade (1979) and Boender et al. (1989) presented a fuzzy version of the AHP. For fuzzy numbers, triangular fuzzy numbers (that is, fuzzy numbers with lower, modal and upper values) are preferred, because they are simpler than trapezoidal fuzzy numbers. A fuzzy number M on R $\in$ (-∞, +∞) is defined by Dubois and Prade, 1979 to be a fuzzy triangular number if its membership function $\mu_m: R \to [0,1]$ is equal to

$$\mu_m(x) = \begin{cases} \dfrac{1}{m-l}x - \dfrac{l}{m-l} & x \in [l, m] \\[2ex] \dfrac{1}{m-u}x - \dfrac{l}{m-u} & x \in [m, u] \\[2ex] 0 & \text{otherwise} \end{cases} \tag{8}$$

where, $l \le m \le u$, and l and u stand for the lower and upper values of the support for the decision of the fuzzy number M, respectively, and m for the modal value. In this study, the basic mathematical operations on fuzzy triangular numbers developed by Laarhoven and Pedrycz (1983) are followed. In decision problems, the maximum and minimum membership function suggested by Zadeh (1973) are adopted and expressed in the following form.

$$\mu(x) = \begin{cases} 1 & f(x) \le \inf(f) \\[1ex] \dfrac{\sup(f) - f(x)}{\sup(f) - \inf(f)} & \inf(f) < f(x) < \sup(f) \\[1ex] 0 & f(x) \ge \sup(f) \end{cases} \tag{9}$$

and

$$\mu(x) = \begin{cases} 1 & f(x) \ge \sup(f) \\[1ex] \dfrac{f(x) - \inf(f)}{\sup(f) - \inf(f)} & \inf(f) < f(x) < \sup(f) \\[1ex] 0 & f(x) \le \inf(f) \end{cases} \tag{10}$$

where $\sup(f)$ and $\inf(f)$ are the superior and inferior values of $f(x)$ respectively. It is understandable that Eq. (9) is a membership function with monotonic decrease whereas Eq. (10) is a membership function with monotonic increase. The significance of Eq. (9) is that the less the value is, more requirement for repair whereas the meaning of Eq. (10) is just the opposite of Eq. (9). An evaluation method can be developed by separating bridge deterioration into D (degree), E (extent), R (relevance) and U (urgency) for assessment. A combination of visual inspection, field and laboratory testing may be employed for determining the item estimation indices of bridges considered for condition assessment. Based on inspection results of all the items, the condition index (CoI) is calculated by using

$$\text{CoI} = \frac{\sum (Ic_i \times w_i)}{\sum w_i} \tag{11}$$

Where, w_i is the weight of each bridge item and is greater than 1, and Ic_i is calculated as

$$Ic_i = \frac{\sum Ic_{ii}}{n} \tag{12}$$

in which n is the number of relevant inspection items for a particular bridge, and Ic_{ii} is the item condition estimation index for each item and is calculated as

$$Ic_{ii} = D \times E \times R^a \times U^a \tag{13}$$

3.4 Condition ranking of existing bridges

If $R_{n,m}$ (in which n= 1,2....no of criteria layers, and m=1,2,...of items in each index layer) denotes the membership degrees of estimation indices of the items under index layer and $\bar{W}_n$ stands for the relative weights of items under index layer (calculated by using Eq. 3), then the relationship between $R_{n,m}$ and $\bar{W}_n$ can be presented by

$$\bar{D}_n = \bar{W}_n R_{n.m} \tag{14}$$

where the value $\bar{D}_n$ in Eq. 14 is the fuzzy synthesis evaluation matrix. The purpose of $\bar{D}_n$ is to construct the membership function for each alternative of evaluation set. The membership degrees of estimation indices, $R_{n.m}$, can be formulated based upon the decision makers choice in using the pessimistic- or optimistic- functions as stated in Eqs. 9 and 10, respectively.

Based on the fuzzy mathematics theory, the fuzzy synthesis evaluation result, $\bar{B}$, of any factor can be expressed as

$$\bar{B} = \bar{A}_n . \bar{D}_n \tag{15}$$

where, $\bar{A}_n$ is the weight vector. The prioritization or optimum repair order can be determined by using Eq. (15). The more the value of $\bar{B}$ has, the better the priority selection to decision making objective is.

4. Application of fuzzy logic for condition rating of bridges

The aim of the bridge condition rating is to evaluate the structural strength and serviceability condition of an existing bridge. Fuzzy set theory was specially defined to analyse the linguistic data within the formal mathematical framework. After the publication on fuzzy sets by Zadeh (1965), fuzzy mathematics was used extensively for numerous applications. Brown and Yao (1983) described the methodology of application of fuzzy sets in structural engineering. Tee et al. (1988) suggested a fuzzy mathematical approach for evaluation of bridges. Shiaw and Huang (1990) adopted the limit state design principle combined with fuzzy evaluation and random variable analysis to determine the bearing capacity index and degree of safety for bridges. Jwu et al. (1991) used fuzzy mathematics to determine the reliability of a wharf structure. In order to enhance the evaluation performance, the grade partition method was suggested. Tee and Bowman (1991) presented bridge condition assessment model that is based on resolution identity of fuzzy sets. Qian (1992) used the concept of fuzzy sets to evaluate the damage grade of existing bridges. Yu and Cheng (1994) presented a fuzzy based interactive comparison matrix approach for making group decision with multiple objectives. Wang (1996) provided a multi-target and multi-person evaluation method for structural durability. Melhem and Aturaliya (1996) proposed a model for condition rating of bridges using an eigenvector based priority setting. Liang et al. (2001) used fuzzy mathematics to build a damage evaluation methodology for existing reinforced concrete bridges. Liang et al. (2002) proposed grey and regression models for predicting the remaining service life of existing reinforced concrete bridges. Zhao and Chen (2002) developed a fuzzy rule-based inference system for bridge damage diagnosis and prediction which aims at providing bridge designers with valuable information about the impact of design factors on bridge deterioration. Kawamura and Miyamoto (2003) presented a new approach for developing a concrete bridge rating expert system for deteriorated concrete bridges, using multi-layer neural networks. To evaluate the condition of different structures using fuzzy logic, the proposed methods are either too simplistic [Qian (1992); Liang et al. (2001)] or very complex [Jwu et al. (1991); Kawamura and Miyamoto (2003)]. In this chapter, a systematic procedure and formulations have been proposed for condition rating of existing bridges using fuzzy mathematics combined with eigenvector based priority setting technique. From the review of literature, authors felt that the existing methodologies for condition rating of existing bridges may be difficult to follow for a practical application. In view of this, in this chapter, a methodology for condition rating of bridges is described in steps that can easily be followed for practical applications. The methodology and its application are demonstrated through a case study and the details are presented in the chapter.

4.1 Unified approach for condition rating of existing bridge

Some important issues and the methodology for the development of a systematic, fast and reliable evaluation system for rating of existing reinforced concrete bridges have been illustrated in the following sections.

4.1.1 Inspection data

Towards a systematic rating of existing bridges, the essential requirement is the input data from the bridge inspector that consist of the ratings and importance factors for the relevant elements of bridge which would reflect the overall condition of a bridge as a whole.

4.1.2 Inspector's observation and rating of elements

Bridge inspection involves the use of various evaluation techniques in order to assess the physical condition of bridges. The Bridge Inspector's Training manual 90 (FHWA 1991), published by the US Department of Transportation, provides the basic guidelines for bridge inspection. Bridge components and their constituent elements, different types of bridge deterioration and the common causes are discussed in this manual. It also provides procedures for rating the condition of various elements. In this study also, as specified in Bridge Inspector's Training manual, bridge is divided into three major components, namely, 'deck', 'superstructure' and 'substructure'. Each component is further divided into number of elements. The deck, superstructure and substructure have 13, 16 and 20 elements respectively as shown in Table 3. The bridge inspector is required to assess the condition of each element individually. The rating evaluation for that particular component is carried out based on the rating of the constituent elements. This process is repeated for all the three components towards final rating of the bridge. To a large extent, rating of the elements is based on the experience, intuition and personal judgment of the inspector. Nevertheless, although the condition assessment of each element requires the inspector's personal judgment, general guidelines on how to assess the condition of the various elements are described in the inspector's manual. Hence, while two competent bridge inspectors may differ on the rating of a given element, but their difference in the rating would not be significant.

Deck	R	Superstructure	R	Substructure	R
1. Wearing Surface	8	1. Bearing devices	5	1. Bridge seats	6
2. Deck condition	9	2. Stringers	×	2. Wings	5
3. Kerbs	6	3. Girders	4	3. Back wall	6
4. Median	9	4. Floor beams	7	4. Footings	×
5. Sidewalks	8	5. Trusses	×	5. Piles	7
6. Parapets	9	6. Paint	5	6. Erosion	8
7. Railings	6	7. Machinery	×	7. Settlements	9
8. Paint	7	8. Rivets-Bolts	×	8. Pier-cap	2
9. Drains	8	9. Welds	2	9. Pier-column	5
10. Lighting	9	10. Rust	4	10. Pier-footing	3
11. Utilities	8	11. Timber decay	×	11. Pier-piles	6
12. Joint leakage	5	12. Concrete cracks	5	12. Pier-scour	5
13. Expansion joints	9	13. Collision damage	6	13. Pier-settlement	6
		14. Deflection	5	14. Pier-bents	4
		15. Member alignment	7	15. Concrete cracks	5
		16. Vibrations	6	16. Steel corrosion	8
				17. Timber decay	×
				18. Debris seats	5
				19. Paint	6
				20. Collision damage	5
				Note: × - not applicable	

Table 3. Decomposition of a bridge into elements with observed ratings (R)

4.1.3 Evaluation of importance factors

In a bridge condition evaluation, rating of each element under a particular component does not influence the component's overall structural condition rating in a similar degree. A well trained inspector or the concerned expert determines the structural importance of different elements of all components of a bridge. The importance factor of element is not constant but varies with the degree of distress sustained by the element under consideration. Hence, determination of structural importance factors for various bridge elements is not an easy task. The knowledge gained by the bridge inspectors and experts through many years of design and inspection experience can not be obtained directly through structural analysis, although analysis can provide general trends of the behaviour of damaged members.

So, the importance factors for the elements at various deterioration stages should be evolved from the response of competent bridge inspectors/experts. These membership functions for structural importance were originally constructed through a survey among a number of bridge engineers and inspectors (Tee et al., 1988). Then, the collected data was statistically processed and the mean was presented by Melhem and Aturaliya (1996). As membership functions for structural importance corresponding to different ratings of elements/components is not bridge specific, membership functions for structural importance reported by Melhem and Aturaliya (1996) are used in the present study for structural importance factors of the elements under each component of the bridge. In this study, a scale of 1-9 has been considered for rating of the elements. An element with rating value of 9 signifies the best possible condition without distress and the descending rating numbers represent the increased degree of distress. The fuzzy membership values of structural importance for the elements of deck, superstructure and substructure are given in Tables 4, 5 and 6 respectively. From Tables 4 - 6, it may be noted that the mean value of the importance of an element increases as the physical condition deteriorates. For example, importance of deck concrete with rating 1 is 0.96, whereas its importance is 0.42 when the rating is 9.

4.2 Fuzzification of input data obtained from bridge inspectors

If R_n is a fuzzy set, representing rating of an element (where 'n' represents rating number i.e. n =0,1,.....9), the general form of the membership function can be formed as follows:

$$R_n = \mu_m(r_m) \mid r_m \qquad (m = 0,1,2,....,9) \qquad (16)$$

where, $\mu(r)$ is a membership function representing the degree of membership of any fuzzy set and $0 \le \mu \le 1$. The function as described in Eq. (16) quantifies the ambiguity associated with the rating of any element of a bridge. Any rating number can be represented using fuzzy membership function (Emami et al. 1998).

SL No.	Rating Item	Mean values of Structural Importance									
		0	1	2	3	4	5	6	7	8	9
1	wearing coat	1	0.90	0.80	0.70	0.61	0.51	0.45	0.33	0.23	0.17
2	deck concrete	1	0.96	0.92	0.89	0.85	0.81	0.77	0.72	0.50	0.42
3	curbs	1	0.85	0.70	0.55	0.40	0.25	0.20	0.14	0.10	0.08
4	median	1	0.85	0.70	0.54	0.39	0.24	0.21	0.14	0.11	0.09
5	sidewalks	1	0.88	0.76	0.64	0.52	0.40	0.33	0.25	0.17	0.14
6	parapets	1	0.88	0.76	0.63	0.51	0.39	0.33	0.26	0.19	0.19
7	railing	1	0.88	0.76	0.65	0.53	0.41	0.35	0.26	0.19	0.16
8	paint	1	0.87	0.74	0.61	0.48	0.35	0.31	0.24	0.18	0.15
9	drains	1	0.90	0.80	0.70	0.61	0.51	0.45	0.35	0.29	0.22
10	lighting	1	0.86	0.72	0.57	0.43	0.29	0.27	0.20	0.16	0.15
11	utilities	1	0.85	0.70	0.55	0.40	0.25	0.23	0.17	0.13	0.11
12	joint leakage	1	0.91	0.82	0.72	0.63	0.54	0.49	0.41	0.34	0.28
13	expansion joint	1	0.92	0.85	0.77	0.70	0.62	0.55	0.47	0.38	0.30

Table 4. Mean values of the structural importance for the deck elements for different rating

SL No.	Rating / Item	Mean values of Structural Importance									
		0	1	2	3	4	5	6	7	8	9
1	bearing device	1	0.96	0.92	0.07	0.83	0.79	0.71	0.60	0.47	0.42
2	stringers	1	0.96	0.92	0.07	0.83	0.79	0.72	0.61	0.50	0.44
3	girders	1	0.98	0.97	0.95	0.94	0.92	0.85	0.75	0.64	0.58
4	floor beams	1	0.98	0.96	0.94	0.92	0.90	0.83	0.72	0.60	0.54
5	trusses	1	0.97	0.94	0.90	0.87	0.84	0.77	0.67	0.56	0.51
6	paints	1	0.90	0.80	0.70	0.60	0.49	0.43	0.35	0.29	0.24
7	machinery	1	0.94	0.88	0.82	0.76	0.70	0.66	0.58	0.52	0.44
8	rivet or bolts	1	0.96	0.91	0.87	0.82	0.78	0.71	0.61	0.49	0.42
9	weld cracks	1	0.97	0.95	0.92	0.90	0.87	0.83	0.73	0.63	0.56
10	rusts	1	0.95	0.90	0.84	0.79	0.74	0.64	0.54	0.40	0.31
11	timber decay	1	0.97	0.93	0.90	0.86	0.83	0.75	0.65	0.51	0.43
12	concrete crack	1	0.96	0.91	0.87	0.82	0.78	0.70	0.59	0.49	0.40
13	collision damage	1	0.94	0.88	0.83	0.77	0.71	0.64	0.53	0.42	0.35
14	deflection	1	0.95	0.89	0.84	0.78	0.73	0.66	0.59	0.50	0.43
15	alignment	1	0.94	0.88	0.83	0.77	0.71	0.64	0.54	0.44	0.37
16	vibrations	1	0.95	0.88	0.81	0.75	0.69	0.63	0.54	0.43	0.36

Table 5. Mean values of the structural importance for the superstructure elements for different rating

SL No.	Rating / Item	Mean values of Structural Importance									
		0	1	2	3	4	5	6	7	8	9
1	bridge seats	1	0.95	0.90	0.86	0.81	0.76	0.68	0.57	0.45	0.40
2	wings	1	0.92	0.73	0.75	0.66	0.58	0.51	0.41	0.33	0.29
3	backwall	1	0.85	0.86	0.80	0.73	0.66	0.58	0.48	0.40	0.35
4	footings	1	0.95	0.90	0.84	0.79	0.74	0.67	0.57	0.46	0.42
5	piles	1	0.94	0.89	0.83	0.78	0.72	0.66	0.56	0.46	0.39
6	erosion	1	0.94	0.87	0.81	0.74	0.68	0.60	0.51	0.40	0.35
7	settlement	1	0.96	0.92	0.87	0.83	0.79	0.70	0.60	0.50	0.45
8	piers, caps	1	0.95	0.89	0.84	0.73	0.78	0.65	0.56	0.46	0.41
9	piers, columns	1	0.96	0.91	0.87	0.82	0.78	0.70	0.60	0.49	0.43
10	piers, footing	1	0.95	0.90	0.84	0.79	0.74	0.67	0.57	0.47	0.42
11	piers, piles	1	0.95	0.90	0.84	0.79	0.74	0.68	0.59	0.48	0.38
12	piers, scour	1	0.95	0.89	0.84	0.78	0.73	0.65	0.53	0.43	0.45
13	Piers settlement	1	0.96	0.91	0.87	0.82	0.78	0.70	0.62	0.51	0.42
14	pile, bends	1	0.95	0.90	0.85	0.80	0.75	0.67	0.58	0.48	0.42

SL No.	Item	Rating									
		Mean values of Structural Importance									
		0	1	2	3	4	5	6	7	8	9
15	concrete crack	1	0.94	0.88	0.82	0.76	0.70	0.62	0.51	0.37	0.32
16	steel corrosion	1	0.95	0.90	0.84	0.79	0.74	0.66	0.54	0.43	0.36
17	timber decay	1	0.96	0.93	0.89	0.86	0.82	0.72	0.62	0.50	0.44
18	debris, seats	1	0.89	0.78	0.68	0.57	0.46	0.40	0.33	0.25	0.21
19	paint	1	0.90	0.79	0.69	0.58	0.48	0.41	0.34	0.26	0.22
20	collision damage	1	0.94	0.87	0.81	0.74	0.68	0.59	0.48	0.34	0.28

Table 6. Mean values of the structural importance for the bridge substructure elements for

Usually, the membership values for each rating value are assumed without indication of any specific reason. If membership functions for rating values of 0 and 1 are specified, the membership functions for other rating values can be evaluated using consecutive fuzzy addition rule (Kaufmann & Gupta, 1985). In this study, the rating membership functions for '0' and '1' are assumed as follows:

R_0 = {1.00 | 0, 0.76 | 1, 0.55 | 2, 0.35 | 3, 0.16 | 4, 0.00 | 5, 0.00 | 6,.......... ,0.00 | 9} and

R_1 = {0.00 | 0, 1.00 | 1, 0.45 | 2, 0.00 | 3, 0.00 | 4, 0.00 | 5, 0.00 | 6,.......... ,0.00 | 9}

Using fuzzy addition, rating membership functions for '2' is calculated as

R_2 = {0.00 | 0, 0.45 | 1, 1.00 | 2, 0.70 | 3, 0.45 | 4, 0.20 | 5, 0.00 | 6,.......... ,0.00 | 9}

R_9 = {0.00 | 0, 0.09 | 1, 0.18| 2, 0.28 | 3, 0.39 | 4, 0.51 | 5, 0.62 | 6, 0.74| 7, 0.87| 8, 1.00 | 9}

Fuzzy membership functions for rating values 0 - 9, as obtained above, are shown in Fig. 2.

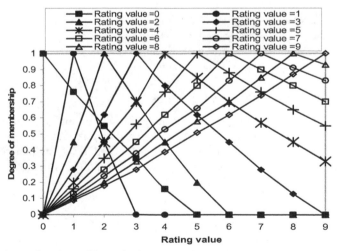

Fig. 2. Degree of membership of fuzzified rating values

4.3 Overall condition rating of a bridge

After getting the fuzzified rating and importance of all the elements, it is required to process those sets to arrive at the rating set for the components. In the similar way, the final rating for the bridge can be evaluated by processing the rating and importance sets of components. Generally, the processing of these rating and importance sets is executed using Fuzzy Weighted Average (FWA) or resolution identity technique. Brief details of these two techniques are given below:

4.3.1 Fuzzy Weighted Average (FWA) technique

Using a structural damage rating scheme according to the local, global and cumulative damage of the structure, resulting damage rating, R, can be evolved (Bertero & Bresler, 1977), using a weighted average approach, as

$$R = \frac{\sum (w_i \phi_i \Omega_i)}{\sum (w_i \delta_i \tau_i)} \tag{17}$$

where, w_i is the importance factor for the ith structural element,

ϕ_i is the service history coefficient for structural response (or demand),
Ω_i is the structural response (or demand) in the ith element due to load,
δ_i is the service history influence coefficient for capacity, and
τ_i is the resistance (or capacity) in the ith element

For a bridge structure, Eq. (2) can be simplified for obtaining the rating as

$$R = \frac{\sum_{i=1}^{p} (w_i \times r_i)}{\sum_{i=1}^{p} w_i} \tag{18}$$

where, w_i is the importance coefficient of the ith object, r_i is the local rating of the ith object and R is the global or overall rating index when w_i and r_i stand for the bridge components, R is the component rating when w_i and r_i stand for the bridge elements. Detailed discussions on this methodology are given elsewhere (Sasmal et al., 2004a, 2004b).

4.3.2 Fuzzy resolution identification technique

A fuzzy set can be easily decomposed into its level sets or intervals through resolution identity as suggested by Dong and Wong (1987). If A is a fuzzy set of universe (U), then an α-level set or alpha cut of A is a non-fuzzy set denoted by A_α which comprises of all elements of U whose grade of membership in A is greater than or equal to α.

A_α can be expressed in symbolic form as:

$$A_\alpha = \{u \mid \mu_A(u) \geq \alpha\} \tag{19}$$

In mathematical form, the fuzzy set A can be decomposed into its level sets through the resolution identity such that

$$A = \sum_{\alpha=0}^{1} \alpha A_\alpha \text{ or, } A = \int_0^1 \alpha A_\alpha \tag{20}$$

where, αA_α is the product of a scalar α with the set A_α, and the symbol $\int_0^1$ (or $\sum_\alpha$) is the union of the A_α, with α ranging from 0 and 1.

The minimum (pessimistic) and maximum (optimistic) values of the intervals for a specific level set correspond respectively to the lower and upper limits of fuzzy membership function at that α-level. The set describing the rating of a component at a particular level of α would be

$$R_\alpha = \frac{\sum_{i=1}^{n} W_{i\alpha} R_{i\alpha}}{\sum_{i=1}^{n} W_{i\alpha}} \tag{21}$$

where, $R_{i\alpha}$ is the rating value for the ith element at α-level, $W_{i\alpha}$ is the importance value for the ith element at α-level. Therefore, the most pessimistic and optimistic range of the resulting set at each α-level would form all possible combinations using the discretised non-fuzzy values. Hence, the resolution identity technique provides a convenient way of generalizing various concepts associated with non-fuzzy sets to fuzzy sets.

From the above mentioned techniques for processing fuzzy sets, the FWA technique is simpler and faster. As FWA technique does not require discretisation of fuzzy set, accurate result may be achieved with less computational effort provided that the sets representing the rating or importance of different elements are convex. Otherwise, adjustments have to be made to the resulting fuzzy set to ensure its convexity for making the task of transforming a computed fuzzy set into natural language expression easier. Further, another adjustment that is often made to a fuzzy set is the normalization operation to ensure that at least one of the elements of the set contains the degree of membership of one, as suggested by Mullarky and Fenves (1985). On the other hand, accuracy of resolution identity technique depends on refinement of the concerned sets through α-level which has a direct impact on computational time. Therefore, in this study, a methodology has been proposed by judiciously using the advantages of both the techniques.

4.4 Combined technique for condition rating of existing bridges

In this present approach, the results obtained from eigenvector based priority setting approach combined with FWA for rating of the bridge components are taken as the input for the resolution identity module. It is to be mentioned here that the number of alternatives increase with the increase in the objects (here, components) considered. For example, if a bridge is considered to consist of three main components, such as, 'deck', 'superstructure' and 'substructure' with different ratings and importance factors, number of alternatives produced for each α-level is $2^{3+3} = 64$ to determine the most optimistic and pessimistic values. Further, for 11 α-levels (from 0 to 1.0 in step of 0.1), total number of calculations are

704. The same increases enormously with the increase in number of objects (here, components or elements of the bridge). If the procedure mentioned above is implemented for a bridge which is assumed to be divided into 10 components, the number of calculations required to get the resultant rating fuzzy set would be $2^{10+10} \times 11 = 11534336$. In fact, the availability of high speed microcomputers has made this approach attractive and practical for actual bridge inspection, management and planning applications.

Further, question may arise that why the resolution identity technique alone can not be applied for the whole bridge rating system by avoiding FWA technique. The simple answer is that component rating can be evolved by the simple FWA technique because there is no need for tackling non-convexity of the assigned sets unless it is essential. Otherwise, for the whole rating evaluation, number of calculations would be enormous. For a bridge having 3 components with 13, 16 and 20 elements (as described in Table 3) under the components, the total number of calculations required for the final result using resolution identity alone would be in the order of 1.2×10^{13}. Hence, a combined technique is proposed in this study to get the accurate result without much increase in computing time.

In the approach proposed in this study, priority setting values of elements are calculated to evaluate the power of importance of each element in describing the condition of a particular component. The usual techniques available for condition rating combine the rating and importance of elements to arrive at the rating of each component. But, the importance factor, as mentioned earlier, is very much dependent on the prevailing condition (rating) of the particular element. Thus, a minor element with worse condition may unnecessarily reduce the rating value of that component under which the element is grouped. This problem can be tackled by the introduction of power of importance which is independent of the prevailing condition of elements. As mentioned earlier, imprecision, subjective judgment and uncertainty are associated with bridge inspection data. Because of uncertainty, the bridge inspector may not exactly know the prevailing condition (rating) of a particular element of a bridge. Moreover, importance factor for an element depends on its rating. But, decision on rating is a difficult proposition. Under these circumstances, several models were introduced for decision making in a fuzzy environment. In this study, Multi-Attributive Decision Making (MADM) model has been adopted as a decision tool.

4.5 Multi-Attributive Decision Making (MADM) model

Multi-Attributive Decision Making (MADM) model is one of the methods in decision studies where the factors towards a priority decision are many (multi-criteria). The assessment of bridge rating can be viewed as a Multi-Attributive Decision Making model because of its many components and sub-components (elements). In this study, an attempt has been made to use MADM model, to get the priority vector of elements depending on their importance over the others which would lead to a reliable decision (rating) from the bridge inspection data. The general MADM model can be expressed as follows:

Let $L = \{L_i | i = 1,2,3,....,p\}$ be a set of goals and $C = \{c_j | j=1,2,3,....,n\}$ be a finite set of decision alternatives from which the acceptability of the alternatives is judged. The objective is to select the one, from these alternatives, that best satisfies the set of goals, $L_1,.......L_p$. The objective function can be expressed in the form of fuzzy set as follows:

$$L_i = [\mu_{i,1}(c_1)|c_1,\ \mu_{i,2}(c_2)|c_2,\ \mu_{i,3}(c_3)|c_3,\ ,\ \mu_{i,n}(c_n)|c_n\ ]_{i\ =\ 1,\ p} \tag{22}$$

in which $\mu(c_i)$ is the membership grade corresponding to alternative c_i. The solution would be the optimal alternative which has the highest degree of acceptability with respect to all relevant goals L_i. Towards this, several models have been introduced, in recent years, for fuzzy MADM but the eigenvector based priority setting approach is considered as one of the best alternatives.

4.6 Application of priority vector in MADM model for condition rating

For the general MADM problem described using Eq. (22), a positive, non-zero number in the priority vector (W) corresponding to each object indicates the power of importance (α_i) of that object in the decision process. By applying the associated powers $\alpha_1, \alpha_2, \alpha_3,\dots \alpha_p$ to the fuzzy objective sets $L_1, L_2, L_3,\dots, L_p$ respectively, the following can be obtained:

$$L_i^{\alpha_i} = [\mu_{i,1}^{\alpha_i}(c_1)\ |\ c_1,\ [\mu_{i,2}^{\alpha_i}(c_2)\ |\ c_2,\ [\mu_{i,3}^{\alpha_i}(c_3)\ |\ c_3,\ \dots\dots\ [\mu_{i,n}^{\alpha_i}(c_n)\ |\ c_n];_{\ i\ =\ 1,\ p} \tag{23}$$

The decision function D is then obtained from the intersection of the fuzzy sets representing the goals as

$$D = L_1^{\alpha_1} \cap L_2^{\alpha_2} \cap L_3^{\alpha_3} \ \dots\dots\dots \cap L_p^{\alpha_p} \tag{24}$$

$$\text{Or, } D = [D_1(c_1)|\ c_1,\ D_2(c_2)|\ c_2,\ D_3(c_3)|\ c_3,\ \dots\dots\dots,\ D_n(c_n)|\ c_n] \tag{25}$$

where, $D_1(c_1), D_2(c_2), D_3(c_3), \dots\dots\dots, D_n(c_n)$ are the decision values corresponding to the alternatives $c_1, c_2, c_3,\dots,c_n$, and are given by Aturaliya (1994) as :

$$D_j(c_j) = \min[\mu_{1,j}^{\alpha_1}(c_j)\ |\ c_1,\ [\mu_{2,j}^{\alpha_2}(c_j)\ |\ c_2,\ [\mu_{3,j}^{\alpha_3}(c_j)\ |\ c_3,\ \dots\dots\dots,\ [\mu_{p,j}^{\alpha_p}(c_j)\ |\ c_p];_{\ j\ =\ 1,\ n} \tag{26}$$

The final decision is the one that corresponds to maximum of all decision values. Hence, the final decision becomes

$$D_{final} = \max[D_j(c_j)\ |\ c_j];\quad j = 1,n \tag{27}$$

For the bridge rating application, let $e_1, e_2, e_3,\dots,e_p$ be the elements considered under each component of the bridge. The fuzzy set for a given condition rating r_i of element e_i can be expressed as the objective (goal) L_i, as

$$L_i = [R]_{ei} = \{\mu_{i,1}|\ r_1,\ \mu_{i,2}|\ r_2,\dots\dots,\ \mu_{i,9}|\ r_9\} \tag{28}$$

where $i = 1$, p and $\mu_{i,n}$ is the membership value of element e_i at r_n.

Therefore, decision value (D) for rating of any element can be evaluated from Eq. 25 as

$$D = [d_1|\ r_1,\ d_2|\ r_2,\ d_3|\ r_3,\ \dots\dots\dots,\ d_n|\ r_n] \tag{29}$$

The final rating of each of the major bridge components is found from the decision values as

$$D_{final} = \max\ \{\ d_1|\ r_1,\ d_2|\ r_2,\ \dots\dots\dots,d_9|\ r_9\}$$

$$= [d_m| \, r_m] \tag{30}$$

Hence, the rating of the particular component would be 'm' that represents any integer value between 1 and 9.

5. A case study for illustration of the proposed methodology

Computer programs have been developed based on the formulations presented in the preceding sections for condition evaluation of existing bridges and rating of the most deserved one. Based on the formulation discussed in the previous sections and the computer program developed in this study using the formulations, a study has been made for priority ranking of bridges. The data corresponding to five RC bridges (Br1, Br2, Br3, Br4 and Br5) has been adopted. In order to use the AHP to rank these bridges, at first an Analytic Hierarchy Model (AHM) with three layers, such as, objective layer (OL), criteria layer (CL) and index layer (IL) is constructed, as shown in Fig. 3. This hierarchy model is constructed by the authors based on the information available from FHWA (1991) and Liang et al. (2003) to demonstrate the proposed methodology. It is worthy to mention that the proposed methodology can be used for any hierarchy model. Therefore, it may be noted that the appropriate item(s) under any layer (as shown in Fig. 3) may be added or deleted depending on the requirement for assessing the condition of concerned bridges.

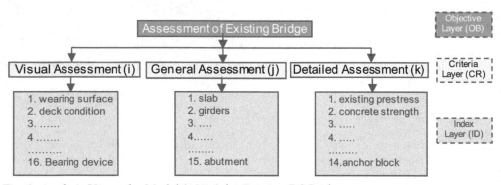

Fig. 3. Analytic Hierarchy Model (AHM) for Existing RC Bridge

After establishing the model, a set of relative importance (weights) between each single factor evaluation (item) is set-up for controlling the reliability of layer ranking. Combination of relative importance (weights) to each single item forms a comparison matrix. Condition evaluation of the considered bridges through prioritization and the rating of the most deserved bridge are arrived using the methodology described in the preceding sections. The whole procedure has been described in following sections for better illustration and understanding.

5.1 Formulation of comparison matrices for each layer and check for consistency

The first step is to carry out pair-wise comparisons of items under each layer of the AHP model as shown in Fig. 3. In this study, criteria layer is divided into three parts, namely, visual assessment, general assessment and detailed assessment. The items which can be evaluated through visual inspection are grouped under visual assessment. The items which need a detailed inspection, comprehensive observation and thorough study are grouped under general assessment. Further, the items which would require rigorous testing, both at site and in the laboratory using sophisticated instrumentation are grouped under detailed assessment. The comparison matrices for different components are formed (Triantaphyllou et al., 1997; Sasmal et al. 2006). The relative importance of any item with respect to the other, under any layer, may change depending on location, societal importance and decision objectives. The eigen solutions of the comparison matrices are carried out for different criteria layers to check for the consistency (in other words, check for acceptance of the comparison matrix) of the elements assigned for different items under criteria layer. The largest eigenvalue (λ_{max}) of the comparison matrix corresponding to each layer is obtained by solving Eq. 6 and this eigenvalue is used for calculating the consistency ratio (CR). The values for consistency index (CI) are obtained by using Eq. 7 and the consistency ratio (CR) is obtained by dividing CI with random consistency index (RCI). The values of λ_{max}, CI, RCI and CR for different items under criteria layer are presented in Table 7 and the values of CR for different items (index layers) under criteria layer are within the acceptable limit (<10%). Hence, the comparison matrix assigned for index layers are accepted for further study.

	λ_{max}	CI =$(\lambda_{max}$-n)/(n-1)	RCI	CR = (CI/RCI)100%
Visual assessment (16)	17.3951	0.0930	1.56	5.962
General assessment (15)	16.1770	0.0841	1.56	5.391
Detailed assessment (14)	15.1707	0.0901	1.56	5.776

Table 7. Check for consistency of pair-wise assigned weights

5.2 Calculation of relative weights of different index layers on criteria layer

The relative weights for components of index layers (i), (j) and (k) are established using the Eq. 3. The relative importance (weights) of items under index layers (i, j and k) obtained in this study are presented in Table 8. From the table, it is clear that there are considerable differences in relative weights of items in each index layer which signify their importance on the functionality of a bridge as a whole. It is also worthy to mention here that a large variation of relative weights of items signifies the necessity for correct, logical and realistic assignment of the weights for formation of comparison matrix using AHP.

5.3 Formulation of higher layer comparison matrix using AHP

Next step is to form the pair-wise comparison matrix for criteria layer to get the optimum goal in objective layer. Following the scheme described above, relative weights of each item of the criteria layer has to be evaluated. Table 8 shows both the comparison matrix between criteria layers and the relative weights of each criteria layer on objective layer. It signifies that the relative weight of detailed assessment on condition assessment of existing bridge is much more than that of the visual assessment. But, it may be noted that the relative weights of different assessments on condition assessment of overall bridge may change with the type of bridge, specific site condition and the degree of accuracy of different assessment procedures. Hence, the comparison matrix has to be modified accordingly.

Index layer (i) Visual assessment		Index layer (j) General assessment		Index layer (k) Detailed assessment	
Item	Relative weight	Item	Relative weight	Item	Relative weight
i1	0.0342	j1	0.0338	k1	0.0233
i2	0.0194	j2	0.0165	k2	0.0572
i3	0.0152	j3	0.0421	k3	0.0225
i4	0.0591	j4	0.0252	k4	0.1373
i5	0.0189	j5	0.0200	k5	0.0298
i6	0.0134	j6	0.0704	k6	0.0684
i7	0.0439	j7	0.0250	k7	0.1875
i8	0.0179	j8	0.0169	k8	0.1816
i9	0.1442	j9	0.0483	k9	0.0840
i10	0.0282	j10	0.0233	k10	0.0457
i11	0.0645	j11	0.1563	k11	0.0425
i12	0.2012	j12	0.0375	k12	0.0369
i13	0.1881	j13	0.0867	k13	0.0212
i14	0.0719	i14	0.2081	k14	0.0621
i15	0.0367	j15	0.1900		
i16	0.0431				

Table 8. Relative weights of items under index layer on criteria layer

5.4 Fuzzy synthesis and evaluation of membership functions

This step deals with the assessment of condition of bridge items under index layer (in this case, i, j and k). In this study, the assessment of items has been carried out by determining the estimation indices of the items as described in preceeding section. The estimation indices of the items for different bridges (Br1, Br2, Br3, Br4 and Br5) are presented in Table 9. In this table, the relative weights of components, are calculated using the procedure described above. In this study, the optimistic membership evaluation function has been used for developing membership functions. Using the estimation indices of items as tabulated in Table 9, the membership degrees, $R_{n,m}$ (n=1 to 3; m = 1 to 16/15/14) of each items are calculated for the bridges (Br1, Br2, Br3, Br4, Br5) considered for assessment.

5.5 Fuzzy synthesis evaluation matrix and priority ranking values

The relationship between the membership degrees $R_{n,m}$ (in which n= 1,2....no of criteria layers, and m=1,2,...no of items in each index layer) of each single factor (alternative) evaluation index and weight, $\bar{W}_n$, is $\bar{D}_n = \bar{W}_n R_{n.m}$ as per Eq. (14), where the value $\bar{D}_n$ in Eq. (14) is the fuzzy synthesis evaluation matrix. The proposition of $\bar{D}_n$ is to construct the membership function for each alternative of evaluation set. Based on the fuzzy mathematics theory, the fuzzy synthesis evaluation result, $\bar{B}$, of any factor can be expressed as in Eq. 15.

In this case, $\bar{B}$ = $[0.456636 \quad 0.256391 \quad 0.296120 \quad 0.525126 \quad 0.43876]$

Estimation Criterion	Subsystem weight	Item No.	Estimation items	Item weight	Estimation indices of items of bridge				
					Br1	Br2	Br3	Br4	Br5
Visual assessment (i)	0.126	1	wearing surface	0.0342	0	0	0	2	1
		2	deck condition	0.0194	2	0	12	9	3
		3	kerbs	0.0152	0	2	2	1	0
		4	median	0.0591	0	4	0	0	2
		5	sidewalks	0.0189	0	2	2	2	0
		6	parapets	0.0134	2	0	1	1	0
		7	railing	0.0439	4	2	0	0	0
		8	paints	0.0179	3	4	2	2	1
		9	drains	0.1442	6	6	4	6	0
		10	lighting	0.0282	9	9	0	0	0
		11	utilities	0.0645	2	2	4	4	6
		12	joint leakage	0.2012	0	0	3	9	12
		13	expansion joint	0.1881	1	4	4	6	2
		14	bearing device	0.0719	3	3	12	18	3
		15	wing masonry	0.0367	4	2	0	0	2
		16	others	0.0431	12	9	2	4	9
General assessment (j)	0.297	1	stringers	0.0338	×	×	×	×	×
		2	girders	0.0165	27	18	0	18	6
		3	slab beams	0.0421	×	×	×	×	×
		4	trusses	0.0252	×	×	×	×	×
		5	chloride content	0.0200	12	0	0	2	9
		6	rivet bolts	0.0704	×	×	×	×	×
		7	concrete crack	0.0250	36	12	36	2	9
		8	pier settlement	0.0169	27	27	12	18	3
		9	erosion	0.0483	12	18	2	18	3
		10	substructure protection	0.0233	18	36	0	3	27
		11	pier	0.1563	18	0	12	3	9
		12	pier shaft	0.0375	0	12	0	0	0
		13	friction layer	0.0867	0	9	0	0	0
		14	abutment	0.2081	12	6	9	3	2
		15	others	0.1900	0	2	3	12	9

Estimation Criterion	Subsystem weight	Item No.	Estimation items	Item weight	Estimation indices of items of bridge				
					Br1	Br2	Br3	Br4	Br5
Detailed assess-ment (k)	0.577	1	existing prestress	0.0233	36	12	0	36	27
		2	concrete strength	0.0572	27	18	36	36	48
		3	foundation mat	0.0225	12	0	12	18	9
		4	vibration	0.1373	18	9	0	36	27
		5	prevention earthquake block	0.0298	18	0	0	0	18
		6	steel corrosion	0.0684	0	36	0	0	12
		7	deflection	0.1875	12	18	36	48	12
		8	footing	0.1816	18	0	3	12	6
		9	collision damage	0.0840	0	0	0	0	12
		10	piles	0.0457	×	×	×	×	×
		11	pier-column	0.0425	12	2	9	6	9
		12	pier footing	0.0369	18	3	12	3	18
		13	prestressing cable corrosion	0.0212	36	12	0	18	36
		14	anchor block	0.0621	27	12	0	36	48

× Represents the non-availability of estimation data

Table 9. Estimation indices of items of the bridges considered for condition assessment

The fuzzy synthesis evaluation result, $\bar{B}$, actually shows the relative condition of existing bridges considered. Therefore, the values under $\bar{B}$ can also be treated as the priority vector for condition assessment of the bridges. As the optimistic membership evaluation function is used in this study (given in Eq. 10), the higher value in fuzzy synthesis evaluation result for a bridge in comparison to the other ones signifies greater degree of distress. In this study, the condition of Br4 among the five bridges considered here can be treated as most deficient and similarly, Br2 would be the best. The condition priority order of the bridges considered here for illustration is shown in Fig. 4. From the figure, it may be noted that the priority order of the bridges considered is as follows:

$$=[Br4, Br1, Br5, Br3, Br2]$$

5.6 Condition rating of the most deserved bridge

Using the fuzzy mathematics, ratings of different component of the bridge, Br4, are calculated using FWA. Importance(weight) of different elements has been considered as reported in (Aturaliya, 1994). Fuzzy sets for rating of the components, i.e, deck, superstructure and substructure are shown in Table 10 and corresponding importances (weights) are shown in Table 11.

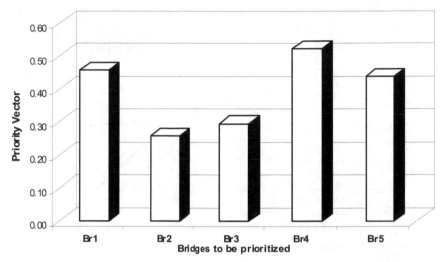

Fig. 4. Priority ranking values of the bridges considered for condition assessment

Components	Rating membership									
	0	1	2	3	4	5	6	7	8	9
1. Bridge Deck	0.00	0.33	0.67	1.00	0.83	0.67	0.50	0.33	0.17	0.00
2. Superstructure	0.00	0.25	0.50	0.75	1.00	0.88	0.75	0.63	0.50	0.38
3. Substructure	0.00	0.25	0.50	0.75	1.00	0.88	0.75	0.63	0.50	0.38

Table 10. Computed fuzzified rating values for different components of the bridge

Components	Importance factors									
	0	1	2	3	4	5	6	7	8	9
1. Bridge Deck	1.00	1.00	0.90	0.80	0.70	0.61	0.51	0.45	0.33	0.23
2. Superstructure	1.00	1.00	0.96	0.92	0.87	0.83	0.79	0.71	0.60	0.47
3. Substructure	1.00	1.00	0.80	0.70	0.60	0.50	0.35	0.25	0.15	0.10

Table 11. Importance membership functions of the components

As described earlier, the resolution identity technique is adopted in this study to get the final rating of the bridge when the component ratings (from the elemental values) are computed using eigenvector based priority setting technique using MADM combined with FWA method. Hence, for arriving at the final rating of the most deserved bridge, the basic data considered are the calculated ratings of the components and computed weights as shown in Tables 8 and 9. The fuzzy membership functions of rating and weights of different components (deck, superstructure and substructure) thus obtained, are discretised using resolution identity technique. Here, each set is discretised into 11 α-levels (from 0.0 to 1.0 in step of 0.1). For better illustration, the resolution identification of the fuzzy set representing the rating of the deck component of the bridge concerned is shown in Fig. 5. Further discussion can be found elsewhere [Sasmal el al. (2005)].

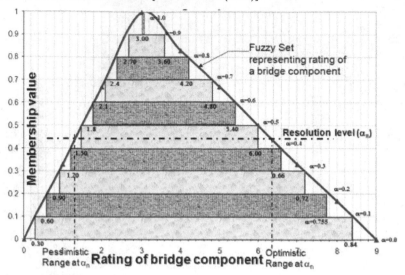

Fig. 5. Resolution identification of the fuzzy set representing rating of the deck component

At each α-level, there would be 64 combinations to get the most optimistic (maximum) and pessimistic (minimum) range of the fuzzy set at that α-level. For 11 α-levels (as considered in this study) the optimistic and pessimistic ranges of the resultant set and the membership representation of the resultant rating (RR) derived from the pessimistic and optimistic ranges using resolution identity technique is shown in Fig. 5. The resultant rating of the bridge, as a whole, has been defuzzified using MATLAB, to get the rating value of the bridge. For this particular case, the defuzzification has been executed using the centroidal method and the rating value is obtained as '**4.6668**'. From the result, it is clear that the rating of the bridge (Br4) falls in between 4 and 5 but closer to 5. It may be the decision maker's discretion in considering the rating value depending on the practical condition and other factors like the environmental condition, importance of the bridge as a whole on the societal service etc. As mentioned earlier, a scale of 0-9 has been considered in this study. So, the condition of the bridge (Br4) falls between 4 and 5 which perhaps reflect the moderate condition. Since, the condition rating of the most deserved bridge among the bridges considered in this study is in between 4 and 5, hence the other bridges are comparatively in better condition.

6. Concluding remarks

- In bridge engineering, systematic identification of the order of degree of deficiency of the bridges that are considered for their condition assessment is a usual problem. Until now, no systematic approach seems to be available for priority ranking of existing bridges.

- In view of this, a methodology based on AHP has been used, in this chapter, for ranking of the existing bridges towards their assessment of prevailing condition which would help in fixing their repair order.
- The comparison matrices for different layers of hierarchy are formulated for arriving at the relative weights of the items under each layer. An eigen solution is carried out for each comparison matrix to extract the largest eigenvalue which is further used for checking the consistency of the formulation of the comparison matrices. Estimation indices of individual bridge components have to be arrived based on the bridge inspector's observation and the results of field and laboratory testing. Thus, the estimation indices would suffer from subjective judgement and uncertainty. Hence, an optimistic fuzzy membership function has been used to scale the indices of all the components of the bridges uniformly. Based on the fuzzy synthesized evaluation matrix, the priority ranking of the bridges has been evolved.
- For evaluating the condition rating of the most deserved bridge determined from the prioritization, it is found that as the number of elements of bridge components increase the complexity in arriving at a unique rating number using Fuzzy Weighted Average (FWA) also increases. Hence, a resolution identity method is incorporated in the methodology to take care of the problems that may arise due to non-convexity and requirement of normalisation of the concerned sets.
- Further, for the component rating, the Multi-Attributive Decision Making (MADM) model based on priority vector of the constituent elements of the component is also considered because it gives a more realistic representation of the condition of the component.
- A computer programs have been developed based on the proposed methodology for condition evaluation through prioritization and rating of bridges. It is found that the methodology is capable of handling any number of bridges without any limitation on consideration of components, and elements and rating scale. Thus, the proposed methodology would certainly help the engineers and policy makers concerned with bridge management to arrive at a systematic judgment and to formulate methodical steps towards retrofitting, rehabilitation or demolition of bridge in future years.
- It is worthy to mention here that though the condition evaluation through fuzzy logic based AHP may be used as an useful tool for decision making, it should be utilised with adequate care because the whole procedure is dependent on different estimation indices of controlling parameters which have to be taken from inspector's observation and results of field and laboratory testing.

7. References

Aturaliya, S.P. (1994). *Bridge condition rating based on fuzzy set theory and Eigenvector approach*, Masters thesis, Department of Civil Engineering, Kansas State University, Manhattan, Kansas.

Ben-Arieh, D. & Triantaphyllou, E. (1992). Quantifying data for group technology with weighted fuzzy features, *Int. J. of Production Research*, Vol. 30, pp. 1285-1299.

Bertero, V.V. & Bresler, B. (1977). Design and engineering decisions: Failure criteria (Limit State): Developing methodologies for Evaluating the earth quake safety of Existing

Buildings, *Report No. UCB-EERC-77/06*, Earthquake Engineering Research Centre, University of California at Berkeley, February, 114-142.

Boender, C.G.E, de Graan, J.G. & Lootsma, F.A. (1989). Multi-criteria decision analysis with fuzzy pair-wise comparisons, *Fuzzy Sets and Systems*, Vol. 29, pp. 133-143.

Bridgman, P. W. (1922). Dimensional analysis. New Haven, CT: Yale University Press.

Brown, C.B., & Yao J.T.P. (1983). Fuzzy sets and structural engineering, *J. Structural Engineering ASCE*, Vol. 109, No. 5, pp. 1211-1235.

Chen, S.J. & Hwang, C.L. (1992). Fuzzy multiple attribute decision making: methods and applications, *Lecture Notes in Economics and Mathematical Systems*, No. 375, Berlin: Springer.

Dong W.M. & Wong F.S. (1987). Fuzzy weighted average and implementation of the extension principle, *Fuzzy sets and systems*, Vol. 21, No. 2, pp. 183-199.

Dubois, D. & Prade, H. (1979). Fuzzy real algebra: Some results, *Fuzzy Sets and Systems*, Vol. 2, pp. 327-348.

Emami, M.R. Turksen, I.B. & Goldenberg, A.A. (1998). Development of a systematic methodology of fuzzy logic modelling, *IEEE Transactions on Fuzzy Systems*, Vol. 6, No. 3, pp. 346-361.

Federal Highway Administration (FHWA). *Bridge inspectors training manual 90*, U.S. Department of Transportation, Bureau of Public Road, Washington, D.C., 1991.

Federov, V.V., Kuz'min, V.B. & Vereskov, A.I. (1982). Membership degrees determination from Saaty matrix totalities, edited by M.M. Gupta and E. Sanchez, *Approximate Reasoning in Decision Analysis*, Amsterdam: North-Holland.

Fishburn, P.C. (1967). Additive utilities with incomplete product set: *Applications to priorities and assignments*. Baltimore, MD: ORSA Publication.

Harker, D.T. & Vargas, L.G. (1990). Theory of ratio scale estimation: Saaty's Analytic Hierarchy Process, *Management Science*, Vol. 36, pp. 269-273.

Jwu, T.H., Harn, Y. & Liou, W.M, (1991). Fuzzy Evaluation of Wharf Structures at Harbour, Report of *Investigation of Corrosion Failure and Its Protection Strategy for Harbour Wharf*, Institute of Engineering and Technology of Ten-Jin Waterway, Department of Transportation, China.

Kawamura, K. & Miyamoto, A. (2003). Condition state evaluation of existing reinforced concrete bridges using neuro-fuzzy hybrid system, *Computers and Structures*, Vol. 81, pp. 1931-1940.

Kaufmann, A. & Gupta, M.M. (1985). *Introduction to fuzzy arithmetic, Theory and Applications*, New York: Van Nostrand Reinhold.

Laarhoven, P.J. M. & Pedrycz, W.A. (1983). A fuzzy extension of Saaty's priority theory, *Fuzzy Sets and Systems*, Vol. 11, pp. 229-241.

Liang M.T., Wu J.H. & Liang C.H. (2001). Multiple layer fuzzy evaluation for existing reinforced concrete bridges, *J Infrastructure System*, Vol. 7, No. 4, pp. 144-159.

Liang, M.T, Chang, J.W. & Li, Q.F. (2002). "Grey and regression models predicting the remaining service life of existing reinforced concrete bridges", *J. Grey System*, Vol. 14, No. 4, pp. 291-310.

Liang, M.T., Lin, C.M. & Yeh, C.J. (2003). Comparison matrix method and its applications to damage evaluation for existing reinforced concrete bridges, *J. Marine Science & Technology*, Vol. 11, No. 2, pp. 70-82.

Lootsma, F.A. (1991), *Scale sensitivity and rank preservation in a multiplicative variant of the AHP and SMART,* Report 91-67, Faculty of Technical Mathematics and Informatics, Delft University of Technology.

Melhem, H.G. & Aturaliya, S. (1996). Bridge condition rating using an Eigenvector of priority setting, *J. Microcomputers in Civil Engineering,* Vol. 11, No. 6, pp. 421-432.

Miller, D.W. & Starr, M.K. (1969). Executive decisions and operations research. Englewood Cliffs, NJ: Prentice-Hall, Inc.

Mullarky, P.W. & Fenves, S.J. (1985). Fuzzy logic in a geotechnical knowledge-based system: cone, Proc., *NSF workshop on civil engineering applications of fuzzy sets,* Purdue University, Indiana.

Qian, Y.J. (1992). *Evaluation and diagnosis of existing reinforced concrete bridges,* Ph. D. Dissertation, Southwest Chiaotung University, Xian, China.

Roberts, F.S., Measurement theory, reading, MA, 1979 (Addison-Wesley).

Saaty, T. L. (1980). *The Analytic Hierarchy Process,* McGraw Hill: New York.

Saaty, T.L. (1994). Fundamentals of decision making and priority theory with the AHP, RWS Publications, Pittsburgh.

Sasmal, S., Ramanjaneyulu, K., Gopalakrishnan, S. & Lakshmanan, N. (2004a). *Condition assessment of existing bridges through prioritization in a fuzzy environment,* SERC Research Report No. RCS-MLP10741-RR-2004-2, May 2004.

Sasmal, S., Ramanjaneyulu, K., Gopalakrishnan, S. & Lakshmanan, N. (2004b). Condition ranking of existing bridges using analytic hierarchy approach, in Proceedings of International Conference on *World of Innovations in Structural Engineering* (WISE-2004), organised by ACCE at Hyderabad during December 1th to 3rd, 2004, 344-352.

Sasmal, S., Ramanjaneyulu, K., Gopalakrishnan, S. & Lakshmanan, N. (2005). Condition rating of bridges using fuzzy mathematics, Proc., Int. Conf. on *Advances in Concrete Composites and Structures* (ICACS-2005), India, 943-952.

Sasmal, S., Ramanjaneyulu, K., Gopalakrishnan, S. & Lakshmanan, N. (2006). Fuzzy logic Based condition rating of existing reinforced concrete bridges, *J. Performance of Constructed Facilities- ASCE,* l 20(3), 2006, 261-273.

Shiaw, S.S. & Huang, W.D (1990). Synthesis evaluation of fuzzy and random Properties for bridge bearing capacity, *J of Chiaotung Institute* at Chung Ching, 1, 64-71.

Tee. A.B., Bowman, M.D. & Sinha, K.C. (1988). A fuzzy mathematical approach for bridge condition evaluation, *J. Civil Engineering systems,* Vol. 5, No. 1, pp. 17-25.

Tee. A.B. & Bowman, M.D. (1991). Bridge condition assessment using fuzzy weighted averages, *Journal of Civil Engineering systems,* Vol. 8, No. 1, pp. 49-57.

Tseng, T.Y., & Klein, C.M. (1992). A new algorithm for fuzzy multi-criteria decision making, *Approx. Reasoning,* Vol. 6, pp. 45-66.

Triantaphyllou, E., Kovalerchuk, B., Mann jr. L. & Knapp G.M. (1997). Determining the most important criteria in maintenance decision making, *J. Quality in Maintenance Engg.,* Vol. 3, No. 1, pp. 16-28.

Wang, H.D. (1996). Basic Study on Durability Evaluation of Reinforced Concrete Structure, Ph. D. Dissertation, Department of Civil Engineering, Dalian University of Technology, China.

Yu, L. & Cheng, M. (1994). A new method to group decision making with multiple objectives-interactive comparison matrix approach, *J. System Engineering,* Vol. 9, No. 2, pp. 28-35.

Zadeh, L.A. (1973). The concept of a linguistic variable and its application in approximate reasoning, *Information Science, part I*: Vol. 8, No. 3, pp. 199-249.

Zadeh L.A. (1965). Fuzzy sets, *Information & Control*, Vol. 8, pp. 338-353.

Zhao, Z. & Chen C. (2002). A Fuzzy system for concrete bridge damage diagnosis, *Computers and Structures*, Vol. 80, pp. 629-641.

Zahedi, F. (1986). The analytic hierarchy process – a survey of the method and its applications, *Interfaces*, Vol. 16, No. 4, pp. 96-108.

11

Fuzzy Logic Applied to Decision Making in Wireless Sensor Networks

Antonio M. Ortiz and Teresa Olivares
Albacete Research Institute of Informatics
Spain

1. Introduction

This chapter presents a real application of fuzzy logic applied to decision making in Wireless Sensor Networks (WSNs). These networks are composed by a large number of sensor devices that communicate with each other via wireless channel, with limitations of energy and computing capabilities. The efficient and robust realization of such large, highly dynamic and complex networking environments is a challenging algorithmic and technological task.

Networking is important because it provides the glue that allows individual nodes to collaborate. Radio communication is the major consumer of energy in small sensor nodes. Thus, the optimization of networking protocols can greatly extend the lifetime of the sensor network as a whole.

Organizing a network, composed in many cases by a high number of low-resourced nodes, is a difficult task since the algorithms and methods have to save as much energy as possible while offering good performance. Power saving has been the main driving force behind the development of several protocols that have recently been introduced.

The design and implementation of routing schemes that are able to effectively and efficiently support information exchange and processing in WSNs is a complex task. Developers must consider a number of theoretical issues and practical limitations such as energy and computation restrictions.

Self-organization algorithms also provide network load balance to extend network lifetime, improving efficiency, and reducing data loss. Another feature to bear in mind is network monitoring, necessary to control topology changes and the addition or elimination of nodes in the network.

We propose the use of fuzzy logic in the decision-making processes of the AODV routing protocol, in order to select the best nodes to be part of the routes. In this chapter, fuzzy logic improve the selection of routing metrics. It details parameter selection and definition, and fuzzy-rule set design. Finally, we show a complete series of results, where our intelligent proposal is compared to AODV, the routing protocol for mesh networks used by the ZigBee standard, and with AODV-ETX, an interesting metric commonly used in wireless networks.

From results obtained we can afford that AODV-FL (AODV with Fuzzy Logic) consumes less energy, since it sends less discovery messages resulting in fewer collisions; the number of hops for the routes created is lower with respect to AODV and the end-to-end delay is also reduced.

Therefore, the use of fuzzy logic as a metric in network routing improves the performance of the overall network.

2. Wireless Sensor Networks

Wireless Sensor Networks are composed by a set of sensor nodes, it is, embedded systems that can take data from the environment such as temperature, humidity or atmospheric pressure among others, and that can communicate via wireless (Yick et al., 2008; Zhao & Guibas, 2004). Usually, data is gather in an special node, know as Base Station, central node or sink. This node is usually connected to a PC or a high capacity device. When data is taken by sensors, nodes process the information and send it to the Base Station by using diverse communication protocols.

This kind of networks can be used in any environment where continuous monitoring is necessary, and node deployment may not follow any order. Algorithms and protocols used, must be able to work autonomously, in order to efficiently satisfy application requirements.

Due to node nature and the particular applications executed in WSNs, there are several special characteristics that define this kind of networks, as well as those inherit from traditional wireless systems:

- **Limitations:** nodes composing WSNs are small and do not permit the incorporation of powerful processors and high capacity storage devices. Furthermore, the available energy, provided by batteries, limits node-operation time.
- **Scalability:** the large number of nodes that can be deployed to fulfil a certain task, can be much larger than traditional local-area networks, so the communication techniques for WSNs must keep its functionality and efficiency as the number of network nodes grows.
- **Self-configuration:** WSNs should be able to self-configure due to manual configuration of hundreds or thousands of devices may not be possible. Moreover, the network have to self-adapt to possible changes related to the incorporation, elimination, and change of location of the nodes.
- **Simplicity:** as a consequence of node limitations and network size, applications and protocols must be as simple as possible.
- **Specificity:** there is a big variety of parameters and available options when designing a WSN that makes designs high application dependant, and this is why most of the proposals available in the literature are focused to determined applications.

All these features make WSNs a challenging field, and several universities, enterprises and research centres are working on the design and development of effective and efficient applications and protocols for these networks.

2.1 Devices

Nodes composing WSNs are quipped with a motherboard that incorporates: micro-controller, work and secondary memory, wireless interface and input/output system. Sensors are usually plugged in the input/output system, but some recent nodes already incorporate several sensors in the motherboard (see Fig. 1).

Fig. 1. Maxfor Tip node (*Maxfor Technology INC. http://http://www.maxfor.co.kr*, 2011)

Since the wireless interface is the component with highest energy consumption, communication protocols should be energy efficient, with the aim of increasing, as much as possible, the network lifetime.

Data collected by nodes are usually sent to a central node or Base Station, that have higher computation capabilities that sensor nodes, higher storage capacity and used to be connected to a wired network in order to be able to access network data by using a common Internet connection.

There is a wide variety of sensors that fulfil the requirements of any application, such as temperature, humidity, atmospheric pressure, presence, energy consumption or CO_2.

2.2 Applications

There exists a wide range of applications for wireless sensor networks. The variety in parameters that can be read by sensors makes the number of applications to grow every day. The application range includes industrial monitoring, building and home automation, medicine, environmental monitoring, urban sensor networks or energy management among others (Vasseur, 2010). These networks can also be used for security, military defense, disaster monitoring and prevention, etc.

Applications based on sensor networks are usually focused on monitoring parameters along time, in zones where it is not possible to deploy a wired network. This parameter monitoring collects data by using wireless nodes equipped with several sensors, and the information is normally sent to a central node that gathers the information of all network nodes. Figure 2 shows a WSN node attached to a vine in the Wisevine project (*Wisevine project, http://www.wisevine.info/*, 2011).

Due to the high number of nodes that can be deployed, and its battery-based nature, nodes must be able to self-organize by themselves, in order to perform efficient and automatic

Fig. 2. WSN node attached to a vine in the Wisevine project.

communications. Self-organization is an important issue in the world of sensor networks that ensures the correct operation of the networks and its efficiency.

2.3 Architectures

Architectures in WSNs are defined with the objective of organize protocols and communication services that can be executed by sensor nodes. This structure helps developers to create products that are completely functional when combining with other protocols, services and devices in the system (Forouzan, 2006).

Wireless sensor networks have adopted (with some changes) the five-layer architecture used in TCP/IP networks, as a result of the simplification of the OSI architecture. The most important changes are related to the inter-layer communication. While in TCP/IP there exists several interfaces that allow inter-layer communications, the architectures for WSNs incorporate global services to allow transparent inter-layer communication. The most popular architectures used in the field of sensor networks are 6LoWPAN and ZigBee.

2.3.1 6LoWPAN

IPv6 over Low power Wireless Personal Area Networks (Z. Shelby and C. Bormann, 2009) is an architecture that defines the use of IPv6 addressing for WSNs, allowing so the inclusion in the global network, favouring the access to network nodes from everywhere. Same as ZigBee, 6LoWPAN uses IEEE 802.15.4 for the definition of physical and medium access layers, while in the network layer it uses IPv6 addressing adapted to WSNs by using the LowPAN layer, that provides encapsulation and the necessary methods to allow the co-existence of 802.15.4 and IPv6. Transport layer can use UDP or ICMP, depending on the requirements of the particular application.

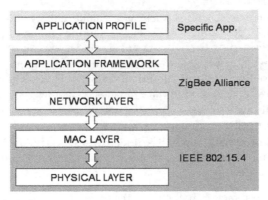

Fig. 3. ZigBee protocol stack.

2.3.2 ZigBee

The ZigBee Alliance *ZigBee Specification, ZigBee Alliance* (2011) and the IEEE 802.15.4 *IEEE Standard for Part 15.4: Wireless Medium Access Control (MAC) and Physical Layer (PHY) specifications for Low-Rate Wireless Personal Area Networks (WPANS)* (2011) Task Group are leading the efforts to define a standard protocol stack for the implementation of wireless sensor networks. IEEE 802.15.4 is focused on the standardization of the MAC and physical levels, while ZigBee defines network layer and application framework (see Fig. 3).

The ZigBee network layer includes three different topologies, namely, tree, mesh, and cluster-based topologies. This chapter is focused on mesh topology networks for which ZigBee uses the Ad hoc On demand Distance Vector protocol (AODV), that will be detailed below.

2.4 Self-organization and routing

The correct operation of both wired and wireless networks requires some kind of network organization. Most of networking systems follow some kind of organization, well centralized or distributed to make data to effectively reach the destination. In wired networks, routers and switches define the network structure, but in wireless networks, and particularly in WSNs where hundreds or thousands of nodes have to be organized without any specific device to perform organization, the nodes themselves have to implement efficient self-organization mechanisms.

Self-organization in WSNs covers several tasks such as topology discovering, medium access control, data routing, and specific application controls. Self-organization can be defined as *the execution of local tasks by the individuals that take part in the network in order to get a global objective without using any centralized control* (Zvikhachevskaya & Mihaylova, 2009).

One of the most important tasks in self-organization in WSNs is routing, since it allows the network to stablish the routes necessary to correct and efficiently deliver network data to the destination in a reliable manner (Royer & Toh, 1999).

The special features of WSNs make that the development of routing schemes for this kind of networks must consider the following aspects (Pantazis et al., 2009; Yang & Mohammed, 2010):

- **Resource limitations:** restrictions such as available energy, memory and processing capabilities should be considered in order to extend, as much as possible, the network lifetime without overloading the network and the nodes themselves.

- **Node heterogeneity:** it is possible the coexistence of different node models in the same network. So, the routing protocol should solve the problems that can arise when nodes with different hardware or radio interface have to collaborate.

- **Transmission medium:** problems regarding the wireless channel such as interferences, signal attenuation or collisions must be considered.

- **Coverage and connectivity:** since the node coverage is limited, the connectivity of all the network must be ensured, avoiding node isolation, and enabling multi-hop communication if necessary.

The consideration of these factors will ensure the achievement of the routing protocols, but it is important to consider some requirements such as scalability, fault tolerance, efficiency or quality of service, in order to get the desired result when using the routing approach.

Next, AODV routing protocol is analysed in order to illustrate its main features and drawbacks.

3. Ad-hoc On demand Distance Vector routing (AODV)

AODV is a pure on-demand routing protocol which bases route discovery on a route request and route reply query cycle and the metric used is the number of hops from the source to the destination. In general terms, when a source node aims to send data to a destination node, the source broadcasts a route-request packet in order to discover a route to the destination. Intermediate nodes will forward the route-request, and eventually, any node which has a route to the destination or the destination itself will reply (unicast) with a route-reply message to the source. Once the source has received the route-reply, it is ready to send data to the destination. Routes are maintained and if any error occurs during the route valid time (or lifetime), a route-error message is propagated in order to avoid the use of broken links and out-of-date routes.

Messages used in AODV during route discovery and maintenance processes are:

- **Route Request (RREQ):** this kind of messages are used to discover network routes. An RREQ contains: ID, source and destination addresses, sequence number, hop count, time-to-live (TTL), and control flags. RREQ ID, combined with the source address, uniquely identifies an RREQ.

- **Route Reply (RREP):** it is used to answer route-request messages. It contains source and destination addresses, route lifetime, sequence number, hop count and control flags.

- **Route Error (RRER):** these messages are used to notify of link failures, and avoid their use. They contain the addresses and corresponding destination sequence number of all active destinations that have become unreachable due to the link failure. A node receiving an RRER message, will invalidate the corresponding entries in its routing table.

In AODV, the route discovery process starts when a source node intends to communicate with a destination node. If the route is unknown, data packets are buffered, and the source node broadcasts an RREQ intended for the destination node. A node receiving an RREQ will verify the destination address to check if it is the destination node, or if it has a route to the

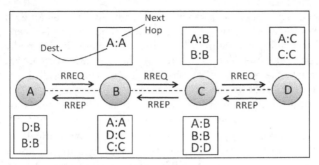

Fig. 4. AODV route discovery example.

destination. In this case, it will send (unicast) an RREP to the originator of the received RREQ. Otherwise, the intermediate node will save the request in order to forward an eventual RREP, and the RREQ will be re-broadcast if TTL (Time-To-Live) value is greater than zero. Figure 4 shows an example of the messages sent during route discovery between the source node (A) and the destination node (D).

To control network-wide broadcasts of RREQs, the source node uses an expanding ring search technique, which allows a search of increasingly larger areas of the network if a route to the destination is not found. In order to avoid loops and forwarding storms, both RREQ and RREP packets are forwarded just once unless an intermediate node receives an RREQ or RREP with the same source and destination addresses, but with a lower number of hops. In that case, it will be forwarded in order to discover the route with the lowest number of hops. Eventually, the source node will receive an RREP if there is a route to the destination. Then, buffered data packets can be sent to the destination node using the newly-discovered route.

In the case of a link failure, implied nodes will generate an RRER message in order to notify communicating nodes about the invalidation of the routes using that link.

3.1 AODV drawbacks

Due to its on-demand-based nature, AODV presents several problems that are mainly related to high packet drop ratios and high routing overheads (Alshanyour & Baroudi, 2008). These problems cause packet loss, collisions, high end-to-end delay and high latency, among others.

- **Packet overhead**: AODV requires an enormous number of packets to complete path discovery and perform routing tasks (Lin, 2005; Sklyarenko, 2006). RREQ broadcasts represent a high network load, and this load is increased when packets have to be re-injected due to high channel occupancy and collisions. As the node density increases, the number of messages sent and received per node appears to increase quadratically (Sklyarenko, 2006). This occurs because when nodes broadcast RREQ messages, those messages are received by more nodes, and these nodes occupy the channel rebroadcasting them. As more nodes come together, the channel scheduling becomes more difficult.

- **Redundant discovery**: routes frequently become saturated causing blocks, thereby leading to new route discoveries. These route discoveries increase the routing overhead, thus aggravating the problem (Pirzada & et al., 2007). Moreover, the path discovery overhead and the routing overhead are sometimes very high, with the consequent time and energy costs to complete routing tasks.

- **High route discovery delay**: as a reactive protocol, AODV has an evident weakness: its latency, since routes are discovered on demand. The route discovery process can take some time and this delay can be increased due to problems in the medium access, such as busy channel and collisions. The time taken by the network to create routes exhibits cubic growth in relation to the number of network nodes (Sklyarenko, 2006). AODV's end-to-end delay is also a weakness of this protocol since it becomes very high when a big proportion of the network nodes have to send messages. This problem is caused by collisions during the routing discovery process, and during data forwarding (Nefzy & Song, 2007).
- **High memory demand**: along with time, memory is also critical and AODV requires all nodes to reserve sufficiently large memory spaces to store possible routing entries for active sources and destinations (Lin, 2005; Ramachandran et al., 2005). This is a problem that limits scalability in WSNs and is due to nodes being resource constrained (Manjula et al., 2008). The throughput of AODV is compromised due to high packet loss (Pirzada & et al., 2007). Since data delivery is a critical issue for some applications such as health and monitoring, packet loss has to be minimized.
- **Duplicated messages**: the route discovery process also has some problems due to the absence of a delay between receiving and forwarding discovery packets. For example, a node that has just forwarded an RREQ from a source node, may receive the same RREQ with a lower number of hops, and it will have to forward it again, thus increasing energy consumption and network traffic.
- **Deficient metric**: another problem in AODV, is the metric used to make routing decisions. AODV forms routes using only the number of hops as a metric. Even though one may agree that AODV can always choose the route that minimizes the delay (Boughanmi & Song, 2007), it does not take into account other important parameters, such as available node energy, route traffic, or the signal strength of the received packets, among others.

In order to solve some of these problems, next section details the use of fuzzy logic in WSNs, as a backgraund of the proposal detailed in Section 5

4. Fuzzy Logic and Wireless Sensor Networks

In the literature, there exists several techniques oriented to improve the performance of routing approaches for WSNs. Most of these techniques are focused on changing the metric used to optimize parameters in order to determine the best path between source and destination, reduce the number of packets used, or reduce the end-to-end delay, among others.

The use of fuzzy logic to optimize the metric used in routing approaches for WSNs is a promising technique since it allows combine and evaluate diverse parameters in an efficient manner. Moreover, several proposals have shown that the use of fuzzy logic in this kind of networks is a good choice due to the execution requirements can be easily supported by sensor nodes, while it is able to improve the overall network performance.

Fuzzy logic is used in (Bacour et al., 2010) to perform link quality estimation. The system takes as input the information about link capacity to transport information, asymmetry, stability and channel quality. The experiments in a network in which all nodes are reachable from the base station show improvements in terms of reliability and stability.

In (Wang et al., 2009) is presented a method based on fuzzy logic and implemented in ZigBee nodes, with the aim of reducing the on/off frequency of an air conditioner system. To do that, they use as input variables the temperature, humidity, fan speed, and engine speed. The experiments show good results compared to a traditional control system based on discrete temperature values.

An example of the use of fuzzy logic in routing for WSNs is LEACH-FL (Ran et al., 2010), where the selection of cluster-heads is based on several variables: node battery level, node density and distance to the base station. The experiments show that the use of fuzzy logic helps to reduce the energy consumption, so extending the overall network lifetime. Another example of fuzzy logic in WSN routing is (Ortiz et al., 2011) where the metric of the Tree Routing protocol used in ZigBee is replaced with the output of a fuzzy-logic based mechanism that allows a reduction in the path length, in the network discovery time and in the number of forwarding nodes.

In summary, the fuzzy logic is a powerful tool to be used in WSN approaches, since it provides effective parameter combination, and it is able to be executed in the low-resourced nodes that compose these networks. The next section details AODV-FL, a routing approach for wireless sensor networks that makes use of the fuzzy logic to evaluate several parameters that are considered during the route-creation process.

5. Ad-hoc On demand Distance Vector Routing with Fuzzy Logic (AODV-FL)

The use of fuzzy logic in the decision-making processes is detailed herein in order to select the best nodes to be part of the routes, and the incorporation of a timer when a new RREQ is received, to be able, if necessary, to evaluate several RREQs received (with the same ID and sequence number) and just forward the best of all those, instead of sometimes forwarding a worse RREQ and later a better one, as the traditional AODV does. With this timer we aim to reduce the number of messages used to discover routes, and so the network congestion caused by this high number of messages.

The lack of an efficient metric to evaluate node conditions in AODV has been solved by the definition of a new metric based on the combination of different node and network parameters by using a fuzzy-logic system. The idea is to specify the input parameters in natural language and, with the help of a fuzzy-rule set, to define the relationship among different inputs with the output, which represents the suitability or quality of a node to be selected as a part of the incoming route.

The input parameters to be considered are:

- **Number of hops**: this is the length of the path. In general, a lower number of hops will represent a better route, but this is not true at all, since it is possible that some nodes in the route have low battery or bad Received Signal Strength Indicator (RSSI), so it is very important to consider more variables to decide the route. This input fuzzy set is shown in Fig. 5a. The maximum number of hops observed in our experiments has been 5. Fuzzy sets have been declared to deal with any extreme situation that can occur during the execution. These fuzzy sets can be customized depending on each particular network size.
- **Local Battery level**: this parameter must be considered in order to avoid nodes with low battery taking part in data paths since they can cause failures in communication. Route construction considering nodes with high energy levels will help to save the energy of low-battery nodes and will cooperate to balance network lifetime. Moreover, the consideration of the battery level will ensure data transmission, preventing nodes in the

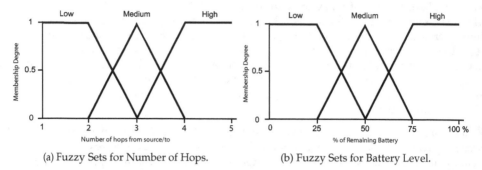

(a) Fuzzy Sets for Number of Hops.   (b) Fuzzy Sets for Battery Level.

Fig. 5. Input Fuzzy sets.

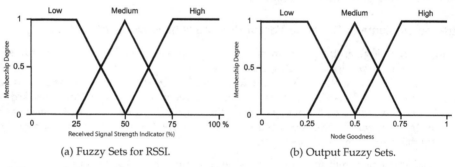

(a) Fuzzy Sets for RSSI.   (b) Output Fuzzy Sets.

Fig. 6. Input and Output Fuzzy sets.

route from running out of battery. Fuzzy sets for battery level are shown in Fig. 5b. The X-axis represents (as %) the remaining battery of the node.

- **RSSI (Received Signal Strength Indicator)**: the strength of the received signal is an indicator of the quality of communications between two nodes. In order to ensure quality communications and prevent data loss, data paths will consist of nodes that are able to communicate with a certain level of signal quality. Figure 6a shows the fuzzy sets declared for this variable. The X-axis represents (as %) the strength of the received signal.

The output of the fuzzy system (see Fig. 6b) represents the suitability of a node to be considered for inclusion in the route.

The geometric pattern of triangles is commonly used to determine the appropriate membership functions and control rules in many theory applications (Wang et al., 2009). In this paper, the geometric pattern of triangles to define input and output variables has been adopted.

Input and output sets are combined through a set of rules in order to obtain the corresponding output. Table 1 depicts the fuzzy-rule base used in the experiments. The objective of the fuzzy rules is to serve as a basis to determine, during the route discovery process, the best node to

Nhops	Bat.	RSSI	Output	Nhops	Bat.	RSSI	Output	Nhops	Bat.	RSSI	Output
Low	Low	Low	**Low**	Med	Low	Low	**Low**	High	Low	Low	**Low**
Low	Low	Med	**Low**	Med	Low	Med	**Low**	High	Low	Med	**Low**
Low	Low	High	**Med**	Med	Low	High	**Med**	High	Low	High	**Med**
Low	Med	Low	**Low**	Med	Med	Low	**Low**	High	Med	Low	**Low**
Low	Med	Med	**Med**	Med	Med	Med	**Med**	High	Med	Med	**Low**
Low	Med	High	**High**	Med	Med	High	**Med**	High	Med	High	**Med**
Low	High	Low	**Med**	Med	High	Low	**Low**	High	High	Low	**Low**
Low	High	Med	**High**	Med	High	Med	**Med**	High	High	Med	**Med**
Low	High	High	**High**	Med	High	High	**High**	High	High	High	**Med**

Table 1. Fuzzy rule base

forward its request/reply packet, with the objective of reducing packet overhead and energy consumption.

The input parameters, sets and rules shown herein, are just an example for the particular application and network model used in our experiments. Note that both fuzzy sets and rules, as well as considered parameters, can be customized depending on the application requirements, node features, network size and capabilities.

In AODV-FL, a node receiving an RREQ calculates the fuzzy-logic value associated to that RREQ, and if it is the first RREQ received (no RREQ with the same ID and sequence number has been received), it starts a timer. During the duration of the timer, if the node receives more RREQs with the same ID and sequence number, the stored request will be updated if the calculated FL-value for the received RREQ is higher than the one stored. When the timer expires, the node will forward the received RREQ with the highest FL value.

The destination node, or any intermediate node having a route to the destination, will reply with an RREP to the best RREQ received (for a given ID and sequence number).

Flow charts for AODV and AODV-FL are shown in Figs. 7 and 8. There are two main differences between both proposals: first, the change of metric, the number of hops used in AODV, for the output of the FL-evaluation process in AODV-FL; and second, the use of a timer to allow the reception (if necessary) of several RREQs from the same source node, and select the best (fuzzy-logic evaluation based) RREQ to be forwarded, thus avoiding multiple forwarding for the same RREQ. This event is frequent in AODV when using a realistic MAC protocol, because sometimes a node may receive first an RREQ with $numhops = x$ and later another RREQ with $numhops = x - n$, and both will be forwarded. In contrast, the timer implemented in AODV-FL allows nodes to wait for more RREQs (with the same ID and sequence number) when the first one is received. This timer is randomly calculated by considering one-hop packet delivery time and the *MaxBackOff* parameter from the MAC layer.

With these premises we aim to:

- Reduce the number of packets sent, so reducing the global energy consumption.
- Improve route formation by selecting, at each hop, the best available node, ensuring route stability and avoiding data loss.
- Maintain routing table size, not making the use of extra memory space.

Fig. 7. AODV decision flowchart.

- Provide adaptability: AODV-FL is able to deal with different networks in various applications, it is just necessary to tune the fuzzy parameters to be used, as well as the fuzzy sets and rules.

Figure 9 shows an example of message exchange during a part of route discovery for both AODV and AODV-FL. The topology used in this example is shown in Fig. 9a, in which the dotted line shows the connections in terms of the coverage of each node. $SOURCE$ node aims to send data to $DEST$ node, and broadcasts an RREQ. Lett's detail the operation of AODV, and our proposal, AODV-FL:

- **AODV**: (shown in Fig. 9b) nodes 1 and 3 receive the RREQ from $SOURCE$ and both aim to forward it. Let's suppose that CSMA/CA (implemented in MAC layer) makes node 1 own the channel, so it forwards the RREQ, and node 3 buffers it to forward it later. Nodes 2 and 3 receive that packet, and just node 2 will forward it since node 3 has buffered an RREQ with a lower number of hops. Suppose that node 2 finds the channel free, and forwards the RREQ. Nodes 1, 3 and 4 receive it. Nodes 1 and 3 discards the packet since it does not improve the hop count stored for that RREQ. Remember that node 3 has an RREQ buffered.

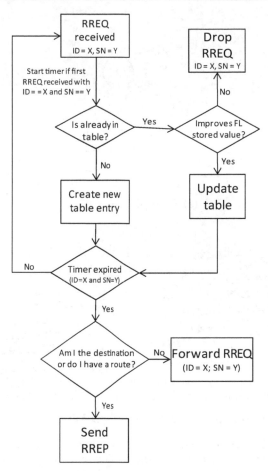

Fig. 8. AODV-FL decision flowchart.

So nodes 3 and 4 compete to forward the RREQ. Let's suppose once again that node 4 owns the channel and forwards the RREQ which is received by nodes 2, 3 and $DEST$. Nodes 2 and 3 discard it and $DEST$ generates an RREP and sends it to node 4. This RREP will be forwarded by nodes 2 and 1 until it reaches $SOURCE$. Now, node 3 finds the channel free, so it forwards the RREQ that received from $SOURCE$. Nodes 1, 2 and 4 receive this packet. Nodes 1 and 2 discard it since it does not improve their hop counts, and node 4 forwards it since it improves the hop count (previously 3, now 2). $DEST$ receives this RREQ and generates a new RREP, because it improves the stored hop count. The new route now has 3 hops instead of the 4 hops of the previous route. Then (not shown) Node 4 will forward the RREP to 3, which will forward it to $SOURCE$ (not shown in Fig. 9b).

- **AODV-FL**: (shown in Fig. 9c) nodes 1 and 3 receive the RREQ from $SOURCE$ and both start a timer in order to wait to receive more RREQs with equal ID and sequence number. Let's suppose that the timer in node 1 finishes first(note that timers are set with a random time proportional to the number of different RREQs received). So node 1 forwards the packet. Nodes 2 and 3 receive the RREQ; node 3 discards it since it does not improve its

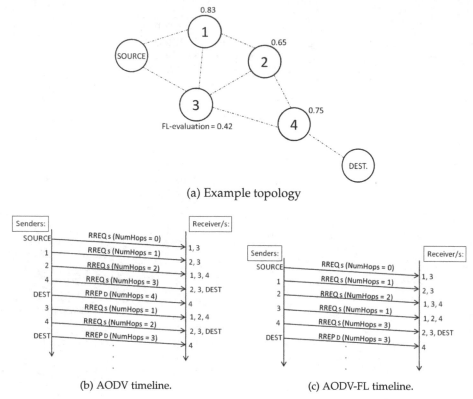

(a) Example topology

(b) AODV timeline.   (c) AODV-FL timeline.

Fig. 9. Message exchange example for AODV and AODV-FL.

FL-value, and node 2 starts a timer. Let's suppose that the timer of node 2 finishes before the one in node 3. So node 2 forwards the RREQ, which is received by nodes 1, 3, and 4. Node 1 discards it, since it has already forwarded that RREQ; node 3 discards it, and node 4 starts a timer. Now, the timer in node 3 finishes and it forwards the RREQ from SOURCE. Node 4 ignores it, due to as it does not improve the stored FL-value (node 2, 0.75). When the timer in node 4 expires, it forwards the RREQ. DEST receives the RREQ and generates an RREP for node 4. Node 4 will forward (not shown in Fig. 9b) the RREP to node 2 since the best RREQ received by node 4 came from node 2. Now the route has 4 hops instead of the 3 selected by AODV, but it is important to consider the low FL-value obtained by node 3, which may be a sign of packet loss.

The example shows the efficiency of route discovery with AODV-FL, which even selects routes with more hops but that are able to avoid data loss. AODV selected the shortest route, but node 3 may present battery or signal strength problems that cause packet loss, with the consequent energy consumption caused by re-injection. Besides the reliability of the routes created by AODV-FL, it is important to consider the energy saving achieved: only with six nodes, AODV-FL reduces the number of packets by 25%. This packet reduction will rise when the network size increases.

Parameter	Value
max MAC Frame Size	80 bytes
MAC Frame Overhead	14 bytes
MAC Buffer Size	32 frames
min Exponential Backoff	3
max Exponential Backoff	5
max CSMA Backoffs	4
max Frame Retries	3

Table 2. MAC parameters used in the experiments with AODV, AODV-FL and AODV-ETX

6. Experiments

In order to evaluate the performance of our proposal, we have implemented AODV, AODV-FL, AODV-ETX (AODV using ETX-based metric), and CSMA/CA in the Omnet++ (*Omnet++ Network Simulation Framework*, 2011) module for wireless sensor simulation. The use of a realistic MAC protocol will provide us with reliable results in order to include our proposal in a real wireless sensor network.

In AODV-ETX Ni et al. (2008), the hop-count metric is replaced with a new metric based on expected transmissions, ETX (Expected Transmissions Count) Couto et al. (2003) aims to find high-throughput paths on multihop wireless networks, by minimizing the expected total number of packet transmissions required to successfully deliver a packet to the ultimate destination.

In the experiments, nodes decide whether to discover a route and send data to a random destination with a probability of 25%. Routes are established on demand and the experiments consists on the sending nodes executing the discovery process and sending one data packet. Nodes are deployed randomly with a separation between nodes which varies between 1 and 50 meters. The number of nodes varies from 25 to 200, and each experiment has been executed 50 times to get reliable results.

In order to ensure route discovery, and taking into account that CSMA/CA is used to perform channel access, when the MAC layer reports *MAX NUMBER OF BACKOFF* or *MAX FRAME RETRIES* achieved for a particular packet, this packet will be re-injected by the network layer. Table 2 shows the main MAC parameters used in the experiments.

To make a fair comparison, the results for AODV-ETX do not show the process of ETX calculation which is carried out prior to the first RREQ send.

6.1 Results

The variables to be evaluated are: energy consumption, number of RREQ and RREP packets sent, number of collisions, end-to-end delay, and number of hops.

The energy consumption is a key element in WSNs; energy saving is a key objective of protocols for this kind of networks. Figure 10 shows (as %) the average energy saving achieved by AODV-FL and AODV-ETX with respect to the original AODV. The energy consumption of AODV-FL and AODV-ETX have been normalized according to the energy consumed in AODV.

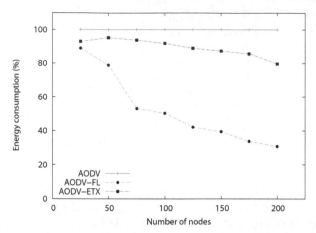

Fig. 10. AODV-FL and AODV-ETX energy saving with respect to AODV energy consumption.

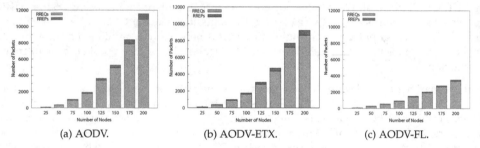

(a) AODV.   (b) AODV-ETX.   (c) AODV-FL.

Fig. 11. Messages sent during route discovery phase for AODV, AODV-ETX and AODV-FL.

The energy consumed by AODV-FL is considerably lower than that consumed by AODV and AODV-ETX. This reduction will allow WSNs running AODV-FL to increase their lifetime. This energy saving is given due to the reduction in the number of packets sent during the route discovery phase. The number of RREQs and RREPs directly affects energy consumption, and is an important factor to be considered in the evaluation. Figure 11 depicts the average number of discovery messages sent by AODV (a), AODV-ETX (b) and AODV-FL (c) during the experiments.

The RREQ evaluation carried out by AODV-FL before packet forwarding, drastically reduces the number of discovery packets necessary to perform route creation. The high number of RREQs and RREPs sent in AODV and AODV-ETX, besides a higher energy consumption, it also leads to a high number of collisions. In AODV-FL, the RREQ evaluation, performed prior to forwarding, decreases the number of RREQ forwardings, and so reduces the number of collisions. The average number of collisions during the experiments is shown in Fig. 12, which confirms that the reduction in the number of RREQ and RREPs obtained by AODV-FL also reduces the number of collisions.

Collisions directly affect the communication delay since nodes have to re-inject collided packets. Networks with real-time requirements, such as industrial and building monitoring

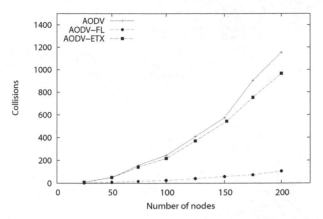

Fig. 12. Number of collisions.

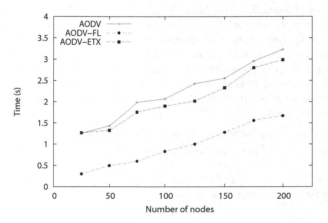

Fig. 13. End-to-end delay.

ones, require low end-to-end communication time, which includes route discovery, and data delivery. Figure 13 shows the average end-to-end delay since the first RREQ is sent until the last data packet arrives to the destination.

The delay introduced with the timer in AODV-FL is not a failing, because the high number of collisions makes AODV and AODV-ETX spend a lot of time re-injecting packets, around 40 to 60% more than AODV-FL.

Another important result is the number of hops. The example in Section 5 shows that AODV-FL may not select the route with lowest number of hops, while AODV does. In that example, AODV firstly selects a non-optimum route (in terms of the number of hops) and later the best route. Figure 14 shows the average number of hops (route length) for the routes created with the first RREP received by the source node for AODV, AODV-ETX and AODV-FL.

The number of hops for the routes created when the source nodes receive the first RREP is higher for AODV with respect to AODV-FL. This is so because in AODV the source nodes may

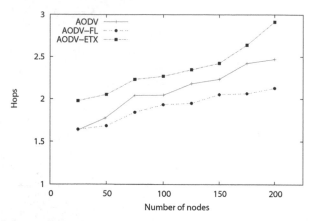

Fig. 14. Route length (number of hops).

receive a non-optimal route first and later the optimal one. Note that for small networks (50 nodes or less), the average number of hops is similar for both proposals, but when the network size increases, so does the number of alternative routes, and the probability of receiving a non-optimal route first in AODV increases. This fact can be a disadvantage for networks with real-time requirements due to as source nodes will either have to wait and see if a better RREP is received, or send data using a route that can be non-optimum. As for AODV-ETX, it obtains higher route lengths due to it selects paths not considering the number of hops, but the expected transmissions.

All these results show that AODV-FL is more effective than the original AODV, and the ETX-based approach in all the experiments, reducing the energy consumption by up to 70%. The performance of the route discovery has also been improved, not only in the number of packets (around 60-70% reduction), but also in the path lengths (20% reduction) and end-to-end delay (40-50% reduction).

7. Conclusions and future research

Monitoring applications in wireless sensor networks require effective, robust and scalable routing protocols, above all in applications with resource-constrained nodes. This chapter details the use of fuzzy logic to improve the routing protocol used by the ZigBee standard in mesh networks, AODV. The use of fuzzy logic as a metric in network routing improves the performance of real networks. AODV-FL uses this metric, achieving an energy reduction of 70% in network route creation, due to a considerable reduction in the number of RREQs generated, reducing collisions and the end-to-end delay. In contrast with other proposals that require additional memory or processing costs, the use of fuzzy logic does not imply an extra load on the system, and it improves the performance of the intelligent dense monitoring of physical environments.

Experimental comparisons with AODV and AODV-ETX endorse the suitability of AODV-FL for implementation in real wireless sensor networks.

Future research can be oriented to the addition of new parameters to the fuzzy logic system, studying the performance achieved by these new variables, such as the number of child nodes, or node density. The use of fuzzy logic in other layers, such as the MAC layer, will help to provide priority in the contention period to those nodes with better conditions.

In summary, fuzzy logic is a powerful approach that has demonstrated to be effective when combining with other disciplines such as routing approaches for WSNs. The potential of fuzzy logic goes beyond traditional control systems and can be used on many research fields, allowing multidisciplinary approaches and performance improvements.

8. References

Alshanyour, A. M. & Baroudi, U. (2008). Bypass AODV: Improving Performance of Ad Hoc On-Demand Distance Vector (AODV) Routing Protocol in Wireless Ad Hoc Networks, *Proceedings of the First International Conference on Ambient Media and Systems (Amby-Sys)*.

Bacour, N., Koubaa, A., Youssef, H., Jamaa, M. B., do Rosario, D., Alves, M. & Becker, L. B. (2010). F-LQE: A Fuzzy Link Quality Estimator for Wireless Sensor Networks, *Proceedings of the European Conference on Wireless Sensor Networks (EWSN)*.

Boughanmi, N. & Song, Y. (2007). Improvement of ZigBee Routing Protocol Including Energy and Delay Constraints, *Proceedings of the Junior Research Workshop on Real-Time Computing*.

Couto, D. D. J. D., Aguayo, D., Bicket, J. & Morris, R. (2003). A High-Throughput Path Metric for Multi-Hop Wireless Routing, *Proceedings of the 9th Annual International Conference on Mobile Computing and Networking (MobiCom)*.

Forouzan, B. A. (2006). *Transmisión de datos y redes de comunicaciones*, Mc. Grawn Hill.

IEEE Standard for Part 15.4: Wireless Medium Access Control (MAC) and Physical Layer (PHY) specifications for Low-Rate Wireless Personal Area Networks (WPANS) (2011). http://standards.ieee.org/getieee802/download/802.15.4c-2009.pdf.

Lin, C. (2005). AODV Routing Implementation for Scalable Wireless Ad-Hoc Network Simulations (SWANS). JIST/SWANS, http://jist.ece.cornell.edu/.

Manjula, S. H., Abhilash, C. N., Shaila, K., Venugopal, K. R. & Patniak, L. M. (2008). Performance of AODV Routing Protocol using Group and Entity Mobility Models in Wireless Sensor Networks, *Proceedings of the International Multiconference of Engineers and Computer Scientists*.

Maxfor Technology INC. http://http://www.maxfor.co.kr (2011).

Nefzy, B. & Song, Y. (2007). Performance Analysis and Improvement of ZigBee Routing Protocol, *Proceedings of the 7th IFAC International Conference on Fieldbuses and Networks in Industrial and Embedded Systems*.

Ni, X., Lan, K. & Malaney, R. (2008). On the Performance of Expected Transmission Count (ETX) for Wireless Mesh Networks, *Proceedings of the 3rd International Conference on Performance Evaluation Methodologies and Tools (VALUETOOLS)*.

Omnet++ Network Simulation Framework (2011). http://www.omnetpp.org/.

Ortiz, A. M., Olivares, T. & Orozco-Barbosa, L. (2011). Smart Routing Mechanism for Green ZigBee-based Wireless Sensor Networks, *Proceedings of the 16th IEEE Symposium on Computer and Communications (ISCC)*.

Pantazis, N. A., Nikolidakis, S. A. & V., D. D. (2009). Energy-efficient routing protocols in wireless sensor networks for health communication systems, *Proceedings of the 2nd International Conference on PErvasive Technologies Related to Assistive Environments*, PETRA, pp. 34:1–34:8.

Pirzada, A. A. & et al. (2007). High performance AODV routing protocol for hybrid wireless mesh networks , *Proceedings of The Fourth Annual International Conference on Mobile and Ubiquitous Systems: Computing, Networking and Services (MobiQuitous)*.

Ramachandran, K. N., Buddhikot, M. M., Chandranmenon, G., Miller, S., Belding-Royer, E. M. & Almeroth, K. C. (2005). On the Design and Implementation of Infraestructure Mesh Networks, *Proceedings of the IEEE Workshop on Wireless Mesh Networks (WiMesh)*.

Ran, G., Zhang, H. & Gong, S. (2010). Improving on LEACH Protocol of Wireless Sensor Networks Using Fuzzy-Logic, *Journal of Information and Computational Science* 7(3).

Royer, E. & Toh, C. K. (1999). Self-Organization in Communication Networks: Principles and Design Paradigms, *IEEE Personal Communications* 6(2): 46–55.

Sklyarenko, G. (2006). AODV Routing Protocol. Seminar Technische Informatik. Institute für Informatik, Freie Universität Berlin.

Vasseur, J. P. (2010). Terminology in Low power And Lossy Networks. Internet draft, Networking Working Group. http://tools.ietf.org/html/draft-ietf-roll -terminology-04.

Wang, T. M., Liao, I. J., Liao, J. C., Suen, T. W. & Lee, W. T. (2009). An Intelligent Fuzzy Controller for Air-Condition with ZigBee Sensors, *International Journal in Smart Sensong and Intelligent Systems* 2.

Wisevine project, http://www.wisevine.info/ (2011).

Yang, Z. & Mohammed, A. (2010). A survey of routing protocols of wireless sensor networks, *Proceedings of the Sustainable Wireless Sensor Networks*.

Yick, J., Mukherjee, B. & Ghosal, D. (2008). Wireless Sensor Network Survey, *Computer Networks* 52.

Z. Shelby and C. Bormann (2009). 6LoWPAN: The Wireless Embedded Internet. Wiley.

Zhao, F. & Guibas, L. (2004). *Wireless Sensor Networks, an Information Processing Approach*, Elsevier.

ZigBee Specification, ZigBee Alliance (2011). http://www.zigbee.org/.

Zvikhachevskaya, A. & Mihaylova, L. (2009). Self-organisation in wireless sensor networks for assisted living, *Proceedings of the IET Assisted Living Conference*.

12

Fuzzy Logic on a Polygenic Multi-Agent System for Steganalysis of Digital Images

Samuel Azevedo, Rummenigge Rudson
and Luiz Gonçalves
Universidade Federal do Rio Grande do Norte,
DCA-CT-UFRN, Campus Universit[ario,
Lagoa Nova, Natal, RN,
Brazil

1. Introduction

Digital cryptography has being a solution for protecting transmission of data in applications such as electronic commerce (Luciano 2003), electronic vote (Kofler 2003), and digital Television (Macq 1995). However, an interceptor monitoring network flow could easily break purely encoded data and clear the contents of cryptographed messages. Steganography techniques came up in order to help improving this protection. The goal of steganography is to hide data into a covering message (envelop) in such a way that an interceptor has no way to notice the presence of a hidden message in its covering envelop. Note that one can combine both cryptography and steganography in order to achieve better security. For example an image can be enriched with visually imperceptible extra information that, when eventually noticed, could be understood as an eventual noise. This damaged image could serve thus as a camouflaging body that brings protected data to the other side of the communication process. Any media object can be used as the covering message, such as text, audio, video, network packages, and file systems. Digital images are known to be the most used media objects for this purpose due to its inherent artistic appeal.

In steganography, specifically, the carrying message is a digital object (image, audio, video etc) that envelops hidden data. When a potential covering object carries hidden data it can be called a steganographed object. In order to extract hidden information from this object, one has to know that a conspicuous object is steganographed, what is the steganographic algorithm used to hide data, and the password that will be generally requested by the algorithm.

On the other side, if one would like to reveal the data which is hidden, it should use steganalysis techniques in order to detect whether a message has hidden data or not. This is just the subject approached in this work. Although it is undeniable that everyone has the right to protect some information there are some situations where it is necessary to reveal its contents, for example breaking of privacy is important in criminal investigations.

Besides detecting the presence of hidden messages, a useful steganalysis technique should also estimate the length of the messages and also somehow possibly to detect which steganographic algorithm is used to hide information. Since one knows the algorithm to hide or to reveal the message contents, and the steganographed object, one may try some common known attacks to break the password like the brute force password guessing.

When new cryptographic or steganographic techniques arise, new cryptoanalysis or steganalysis also are developed addressing the new characteristics of the problem. So, one can say that there is a race between cryptographers and cryptoanalyzers and between steganographers and steganalysers. A technological advance in one side forces the other to overcome it.

Other characteristic of the problem is that when new steganalysis techniques are developed, new steganographic techniques arise immune to the existent attacks. Therefore steganalysis systems demand flexibility to adapt to the new steganographies. This flexibility can be obtained by learning or by using software engineering techniques that ease the alteration of the system in a handful time (such as modularization, documentation, etc).

In this work we approach steganalysis for digital images, which represent a vast distribution of data around the Internet. Due to the very complex nature of the problem, it is generally required to perform steganalysis on a huge volume of data. Of course it would be adequate to perform this in an autonomously way by using a computational system. Autonomy and flexibility are characteristics present in software entities called agents. By the complexity of the problem, these agents would be more appropriately approached in a Multi-Agent System (MAS), which is a system where several specialized or redundant agents interact (through cooperation, negotiation, and exchanging information, for example) to achieve their goals.

Since MAS are systems that approach social interaction between agents, we need to model the way these interactions will be performed. It is common to use metaphors from nature as heuristics in order to solve computational problems in a less complex way. A good heuristic for this solution would be inspired in social interaction of insect communities. Social insects present important characteristics of MAS such as cooperation, distribution of multiple tasks, and coordination. Our work is inspired in the polygenic societies of bees from the species Melipona Bicolor where several queens of a hive can cooperate in the coordination of all the workers. We initially apply such coordination model to our MAS, where each worker is a classifier, and further apply fuzzy logic to solve the classification of heterogeneous classifiers to a same sample.

Therefore, our proposal and main contribution is a multi-agent system for digital image steganalysis that is based on the paradigm of the community of polygenic bees using fuzzy logic. With such approach we aim to solve the problem of automatic steganalysis for digital media with a case study on digital images. The architecture proposed here is designed to detect if a file is suspicious of carrying hidden contents allowing to attempt to extract them with other techniques (such as brute force password guessing). Experimental results validate the system, showing the applicability of the MAS to steganalysis of image data.

2. Background and methods

In order to better understand our problem, some background must be addressed in different areas of knowledge including cryptology, machine learning, MAS, heuristics, image segmentation, and fuzzy logic.

2.1 Machine learning

"Machine Learning is the AI field which aims to develop computational techniques about learning as well as the construction of systems capable to acquire knowledge in an automatic way." (Rezende 2003)

Among the machine learning paradigms, we have (Sanches 2004):

- *Symbolic paradigm* – builds a symbolic representation of the problems´ solution through the analysis of examples, the machine learning most known methods of this paradigm are *decision trees* and *semantic networks*.
- *Statistical paradigm* – composed by the classification methods that try to analyze statistics in order to find an statistical model approximated to the problem; a known method of this paradigm is the *Bayesian Learning* algorithm.
- *Paradigm based in examples* – classifies one instance (or sample) through its comparison with other previously classified samples, returning as result the class of the classified instance that is more similar to it; the most known method of this paradigm is the K-nn which returns the class that appears the most in the k nearest neighbors to a consulted sample.
- *Connectionist paradigm* – based upon the biological metaphor of neural connections of the nervous system, it try to train a network of neurons with samples in a way that the weights of its connections are adjusted to solve the problem of classification.
- *Evolutionary or genetic paradigm* – this is also based in biological metaphor, in this case the genetic evolution; it consists in realizing crossings and mutations in a set of classifiers to solve a problem; during N interactions (or generations), the classifiers with best performance in each generation prevail and the next generation of classifiers is generated by variations of these; the genes are the parameters of the classifiers, that can be of any of the other paradigms, but instead of regular training to accurate they parameters, these parameters are changed through evolution.

Every learning method presents, after training, an error or accuracy rate. Other important rates are the True Positive and True Negative rates that indicate respectively the rates of positive and negative cases correctly detected. Many times, one wish to improve these rates and one of the improving strategies are the ensembles or clustering of classifiers. In steganalysis, a critical rate is the False Negative, which indicates the percent of cases that were incorrectly classified regular images but in fact contained hidden data.

2.2 Multi-agent systems

Agents are autonomous software entities that act in a certain environment and are capable of taking decisions as which actions to perform in order to reach any goal (Russel 1995).

A multi-agent system is a complex system in which several specialized or redundant agents interact, cooperating, negotiating, and exchanging information in order to reach any optimal goal.

MAS are systems that contain a set of software agents working together that interact between them and with the environment through some communication channel. Agents have areas of influence in the environment that may or not overlap (Wooldridge 2001). They can interact through the use of negotiation, coordination, or cooperation. Bid, argumentation or game theory can also be used by agents (Macedo 2001).

A society of agents may be composed by homogeneous or heterogeneous agents. The coordination problem is how to manage the interdependencies of tasks and resources between agents. Wooldridge classifies four models of coordination: global-partial planning, joint intentions, mutual modeling, and social rules.

In our problem, we use a heuristic of social bees to coordinate the collective work of agents, and the we approach in this MAS a fuzzy clustering algorithm to enhance the detection of hidden data into images.

Fig. 1. M. Bicolor queens in reproduction process. Two or more bees can put much more eggs thus diminishing a lot the efforts for getting a mature colony.

2.3 Heuristics

Heuristics can be devised base on approaches as genetic algorithm, memetic algorithms, simulated annealing and insect colonies as ant and bees. Algorithms that use metaphors based on colonies aim to imitate some behavior of those in order to search solutions for complex problems. Biologically, social insects may be monogenic or polygenic. That means, it can exist societies that present a single or several queens at the same time (Aponte 2003). Bees of the specie Meliponine Bicolor (see Figure 1) can be polygenic.

2.4 Image segmentation

Since steganography aims to hide the existence of data within data, it´s important to find computer vision techniques that are able to see this hidden information in images. The most simple steganographic algorithms aim to hide data in the less significant bit of each pixel, these generally are imperceptive to human eye, but they generate distortions in images easily detected by common image segmentation algorithms.

Although there are general purpose techniques and algorithms for image segmentation, they often must be combined with domain knowledge to effectively solve a vision problem; thus, image segmentation must be approached by many perspectives (Pavidlis 1982).

Methods based in edge detection, histogram statistics and clustering, and transform domain error prediction, are found in many of the current solutions for steganalysis, as the discussed in section 2.6.

In our work, we use some of the methods above to compose the features that compose an instance for the machine learning algorithms. These features use statistical information such as mean, variance, asymmetry and kurtosis. Mean is the first statistical momentum, variance, asymmetry and kurtosis are, respectively the second, third and fourth momentums over the mean. The equation bellow shows the general formula to find the kth momentum (the mean is the first momentum, but its value is 0). The equation also can be read as $E[(X - E[X])k]$ where X is a random variable, and $E[X]$ is the expected value.

$$\mu_k = \left\langle (x - \langle x \rangle)^k \right\rangle = \int_{-\infty}^{+\infty} (x - \mu)^k f(x)dx.$$

2.5 Fuzzy logic

Since the publication of "Fuzzy sets" (Zadeh 1965), many studies have been done to apply fuzzy logic in diverse fields. In machine learning, fuzzy logic has been applied to algorithms from different paradigms as well as to ensembles of classifiers, for example: Support Vector Machines (Lin 2002); neural networks (Carpenter 1992), (Jang 1993); and decision trees (Acampora 2011). López-Ortega (2011) points out that fuzzy clustering and MAS lead to high quality decisions.

In software agency, we can see the use of fuzzy knowledge based systems (Arroyo 2011) to implement the decision making process and actions of software agents. Also, we can observe the use of fuzzy logic theory for agents coordination (Goodarzi 2011), (Hagras 2010).

In steganalysis, the most common use of fuzzy logic is presented in the use of fuzzy machine learning algorithms and in fuzzy clustering (see the related work in 2.6 for further details). One of the main contributions of this work is the design of a novel fuzzy clustering approach using coordination of agents.

2.6 Cryptology

Steganography is a subarea of information security that includes several other inner areas meaning covert written (Katzenbeisser 2000). In general, its focus is the inclusion of information in a media data that is not suspect. In fact, it is the art of occluding data in data (Artz 2001). When two communication sides A and B want to exchange a secret message, they use an occulting message (or covering object, envelop, mule) applying some steganography technique that may use or not some key k obtaining in this way a steganographic message that is undistinguishable from the previous. This last is sent through the communication channel. There are several techniques for doing steganalysis as:

1. **Substitution system** – redundant parts of the media are substituted by the data that one wants to occult;
2. **Techniques in the transform domain** – insert secret data in the signal transform domain (frequency domain);
3. **Specter scattering** – the specter of distribution of the information is scattered;

4. **Statistical methods** – produces steganographed data through statistical manipulation of covering data;

5. **Distortion techniques** – produces distortions in a covering media in order to get steganographed data, compares the original covering media with the modified in order to extract them.

An important characteristic in steganography is determining the capacity of an object to hide information, we can observe this concept in what Moskowitz (2002) calls Capability:

"Capability = (P;D) where P is the payload size and D is a detectability threshold. We sometimes expand the capability to a triple (P; D; R) where R is a measure of robustness of the stego channel."

The quoted author also states there for steganography in the least significant bit of images, the payload is limited from 0 to 50% of the size of the carry image, otherwise changing the cover to a negative.

Steganalysis goal is to attack or monitor a communication channel in order to detect existing information that is occulted in messages or to forge some occult message, interrupt communication, and to extract occulted data.

Different approaches to steganalysis can be found in the literature as visual attack (Fridrich, 2002, 2004), statistical analysis (Katzenbeisser 2000), and signature detection (Chandramouli 2004). The first approaches the most elementary methods, as for example the bit substitution systems that may cause visible distortions to images, what reveals the existence of hidden contents. Statistical analysis looks statistical measures in files as the histogram to verify common aberrations. It can use pure statistic methods or some combination with machine learning. In signature detection approaches, any degradation caused by steganography methods can be read as a signature of these methods. These methods generally span suspect files to find signatures in the data noise that can reveal if any steganography approach is used including some times which was the used approach.

There are two categories of steganalysis techniques: specific and universal (or blind) steganalysis. While specific steganalysis is related to attack objects generated by one single steganographic algorithm, universal steganalysis aim to attack stego objects independent of the steganographic algorithm used. Commonly, steganalysis use machine learning algorithms in order to classify whether an object may contain hidden data or not.

In order to create a steganalysis algorithm, one must think in six phases or steps:

1. **Steganalysis goals** - Consists in defining and implementing the category of technique will be performed (specific or universal), and defining which attacks will be realized, as detection of hidden information, data estimation (as for example the length of the hidden data), steganographic algorithm used. The following types of attack don´t need a classifier, and so, if they are isolated attacks it´s not needed to implement the steps 2 to 6, but if combined with the other attacks mentioned above, these steps are still necessary: data extraction (as password guessing from a dictionary), intercept the cover messages (such as sniffing network packages), denial of service (applying noise to an image, disabling the possibility to extract hidden content), and forging a hidden message to confound the communication.

2. **Classifier Method**- one must choose and implement which machine learning algorithms will be used to the classification process. If more than one classifier will be

used, also a clustering technique must be defined to combine the classification results of different algorithms. Sometimes, the architecture of the final algorithm must be redesigned and applied to new trainings and tests in order find improved results. According to the complexity of the features and data that will be analyzed, one may choose a most fitting machine learning solution. This can be performed before features calibration and obtaining data samples, or after these steps.

3. **Features Calibration** - one must select the features used to describe the data that will be applied to the machine learning technique; in the case of images, these features may be statistical data from histogram or from segments of the image, errors found in predicted coefficient values in the transform domain, and so on. This can be achieved by choosing an initial set of features (by literature, empirical experience, experimentation, etc) and testing subsets of these features in the next phases to verify the optimal subset of features. Liu (2008b) describes an interesting methodology for feature mining for steganalysis.

4. **Data Samples** - it's necessary to create a database with samples fitting the features selected, and this database should able to be accessed by the classifier. But two random subsets of samples might be separated, the bigger to the training and smaller to the testing phases. The size of these databases is another issue, the ideal, statistically speaking is that this size should be big enough to represent the population of real cases; but by the nature of the problem, there are no statistics describing how many stego objects are there in the world; so, there are works using from 30 to more than 30000 samples. It's important to say that the samples must be in quantities proportional to the different classes (from non-stego objects/stego objects in the most simple cases; to non-stego objects/stego object for algorithm 1...N in most complex solutions).

5. **Training** - this phase is about training the machine learning mechanisms with the training subset of data, according to the algorithm selected, this step may last a long time.

6. **Testing** - finally, after trained, the classifier may be submitted to the testing dataset, and the accuracy, true positive and true negatives rates must be calculated.

Bakhshandeh (2009) presents a steganalysis technique based on local information and human visual system. By performing segmentation and analysis for clustering these segments, the best segments are chosen for steganalysis. The algorithm they have used for classification is Fuzzy Clustering, simplifying, one may say that they give a fuzzy weight to the results of many classifiers, and use a clustering algorithm to decide the final classification results. Wavelet information is extracted to compose the feature used in a SVM algorithm to classify whether an image has or does not have hidden data. The results are at first sight promising, but if one consider that their experiments were in images carrying hidden data in 100% of theirs spectrum capability for spread spectrum steganography, one would expect to see the results for messages that are smaller the full capability of the cover image, since it's more difficult to detect the presence of smaller data because the resulting alteration is smaller in the cover image data.

In the work of Liu and Sung (Liu 2008) it is presented a steganalysis technique that uses One-Against-All decomposition for SVM to classify whether or not a jpeg image contains hidden data in one of three steganographic techniques, based in detecting errors from predicted DFT, DCT or DWT coefficients. After this classification, they use a Dynamical Evolutionary Neuro-Fuzzy Inference Systems (DENFIS), to estimate the length of the hidden data. The estimative found was very accurate for F5 steganographic algorithm, but not so effective for others.

Amirkhani (2011) highlights that blind steganalysis algorithms use to have each internal similar (or a same) processes for different image categories (smooth, complex, noisy, etc), instead of using the particular characteristics of an image type to attack it. Their framework can make use of any steganalysis technique that are applied to two main modifications: before training, the images must be divided into different content classes; and the result of a classifier must be weighted to a fuzzy value according to the content class trained, after that, the result is combined in order to classify if an image is a regular image or has a hidden content, these two final classes are called by the authors of Cover (regular) and Stego (has hidden content). They experiment this framework with some known steganalysis algorithms and confront their efficacy with several steganographic algorithms, showing discrete increases of accuracy, true positives and true negatives rates. In our approach, we train some of our classifiers for different image types, and other for general image types, in order to further clustering their results.

3. Polygenic MAS fuzzy clustering steganalysis

The MAS system approached here, according to the taxonomy presented by Rezende (2003), may be classified as a heterogeneous agent open system, with low initial granularity.

The main issue is social resolution that aims to solve the problem of steganalysis in a cooperative and distributed way. However, it is also approached the social simulation view for simulating the behavior of polygenic bees. Interaction patterns present in the system are commensalism (in the interactions between classifier and coordinator agents), and proto-cooperation, in interactions between classifier agents.

3.1 Architectural view

Figure 2 presents the general architecture of the proposed solution. The steganalysis process is realized in 2 steps: first, it´s necessary to perform some type of data interception (such as network packets sniffing) – this is not approached in this work; then, the intercepted data may finally be classified with our approach into stego data (data that carries hidden content) or non-stego data (without hidden content).

The polygenic heuristics here is present in the coordinator agents, which can represent the queens of this society. They are responsible to ask for specialized and general classifiers agents to analyze an intercepted image file. These queens also perform the following fuzzy clustering approach:

- According to the training, an **specialized classifier agent** may be more suitable to an image than other, so, it receives a bigger weight when classifying an image which category it was specialized;
- **general classifier agents** are trained to diverse categories of images, and they receive a constant weight parameter;
- The **coordinator agent** (or coordination agent) responsible for an specific file asks for specialized and general agents to classify this file; when there is not enough available agents, this queen instantiates new workers of both types and attributes the classification for them;

- When the attributed workers realize the classification, the queen uses a fuzzy inference system to combine the results of these workers according to their fuzzy weights and finds her classification result.

When more than one coordination agent come to divergent results, they start a negotiation process in order to find the final classification result.

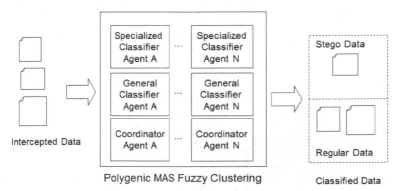

Fig. 2. Polygenic MAS Fuzzy Clustering Steganalysis Architecture.

The specialized and the general classifier agents represent different specialized workers in this metaphor. The communication between the agents is realized through a message board.

The accuracy rate for the general classifier agents and the specialized classifier agents can be fuzzyficated as shown in the graphic bellow. Where L, M and H means Low, Medium and High accurate rates, respectively (Figure 3.a). In order to linearize the classification problem, the classification process will give a probability a given sample is or not a stego object according to the classification (Figure 3.b). The inference method used is a simple Mamdani FIS, and the Figure 4 simplifies its mechanisms.

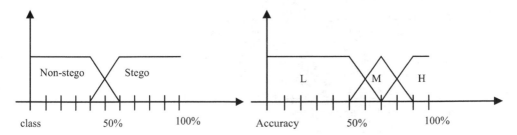

Fig. 3. Fuzzyfication. a) accuracy rates; b) probability of a classified sample being stego object.

3.2 Use case view

Figure 5 presents the use case diagram of the approach. The use cases presented are: monitoring of files, negotiation of final result, coordination of classification, attributing/instantiating agents, and classification; and these actions are realized as described next. The actors that are present at the use case of the system are the monitors (monitor agent), queens (coordinator agents), and laborers (general and specialized classifier agents). The role of **monitor** can be performed by simple users of the system that submit a set of files to be monitored by the system agents to work on them. Alternatively, one can program monitor agents to perform searchers or sniffs in the internet in order to collect and analyze data.

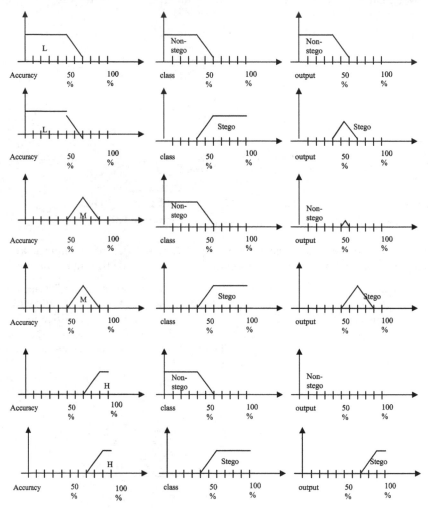

Fig. 4. Fuzzy inference system for classification of stego images (simplification).

After the monitor agent (or user) perform the monitoring of files, random coordination agents are attributed that file and individually start coordination the global classification process. This process, in his turn, needs the attribution or instantiation of general and specialized classifier agents to the task of classifying the monitored file. When a instantiation is needed, the agents are trained and tested in order to receive a weight corresponding to their adequacy in the classification process. So, the roles of general and specialized classification agents are only responsible to classify the data and send this result to the coordination agent, which will use it fuzzy clustering inference algorithm to define the classification result. After the coordination agents find their classification results, if divergent, they negotiate to find a final answer.

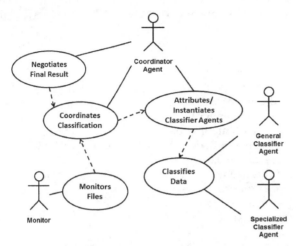

Fig. 5. Use Case Diagram of Polygenic MAS Fuzzy Clustering Steganalysis.

All the inference rules of the negotiation protocol follow:

1. IF TC=OC THEN accord
2. IF TAAR=High and OAAR=High and TC!=OC and TAAR>OAAR THEN TAAR=TAAR+0.01
3. IF TAAR=High and OAAR=High and TC!=OC and TAAR=OAAR and TAFN < OAFN THEN TAAR=TAAR+0.01
4. IF TAAR=High and OAAR=High and TC!=OC and TAAR=OAAR and TAFN >= OAFN THEN TAAR=TAAR-0.01
5. IF TAAR=High and OAAR=High and TC!=OC and TAAR<OAAR THEN TAAR=TAAR-0.01
6. IF TAAR=High and OAAR=Medium and TC!=OC THEN class=TC
7. IF TAAR=High and OAAR=Low and TC!=OC THEN class=TC
8. IF TAAR=Medium and OAAR=High and TC!=OC THEN class=OC
9. IF TAAR=Medium and OAAR=Medium and TC!=OC and TAAR>OAAR THEN TAAR=TAAR+0.01
10. IF TAAR=Medium and OAAR=Medium and TC!=OC and TAAR=OAAR and TAFN < OAFN THEN TAAR=TAAR+0.01
11. IF TAAR=Medium and OAAR=Medium and TC!=OC and TAAR=OAAR and TAFN >= OAFN THEN TAAR=TAAR-0.01
12. IF TAAR=Medium and OAAR=Medium and TC!=OC and TAAR<OAAR THEN TAAR=TAAR-0.01
13. IF TAAR=Medium and OAAR=Low and TC!=OC THEN class=TC
14. IF TAAR=Low and OAAR=High and TC!=OC THEN class=OC
15. IF TAAR=Low and OAAR=Medium and TC!=OC THEN class=OC
16. IF TAAR=Low and OAAR=Low and TC!=OC and TAAR>OAAR THEN TAAR=TAAR+0.01

17. IF TAAR=Low and OAAR=Low and TC!=OC and TAAR=OAAR and TAFN < OAFN
    THEN TAAR=TAAR+0.01
18. IF TAAR=Low and OAAR=Low and TC!=OC and TAAR=OAAR and TAFN >= OAFN
    THEN TAAR=TAAR-0.01
19. IF TAAR=Low and OAAR=Low and TC!=OC and TAAR<OAAR THEN TAAR=TAAR-
    0.01

where,

TAAR - this agent accuracy rate
OAAR - other agent accuracy rate
TC - class according to this agent
OC - class according to the other agent
high - accuracy rate is greater than or equal 0.8
medium - accuracy rate is greater than or equal 0.6 and lesser then 0.8
low - accuracy rate is lesser than 0.6
class - the new result of this agent
accord - finish the negotiation process
TAFN - this agent false negative rate
OAFN - other agent false negative rate

3.3 Description of steganalysis

For the approach described here, we assume that suspicious data is already intercepted and submitted to this approach in order to verify if an object is a stego object or a regular file.

3.3.1 Classifier method

The classifier method used in this work is the Polygenic MAS Fuzzy Clustering. In a MAS architecture, coordination agents use fuzzy clustering inference to group the classification result of specific and general classification agents. Also, negotiation is performed between coordination agents in order to decide the better result.

The classifiers of two specific classification agents are divergent, both because each can be trained for a different type of image, and because each receive a different training subset of the data samples. This last reason also applies to describe the difference between two general classification agents.

The machine learning algorithm chosen for the internal classifier of each agent is a Decision Tree. But different machine learning algorithms would be applied to this architecture in order to search for a more robust classification.

3.3.2 Features calibration

The features that describe each instance or sample are: the four statistical momentums (mean, variance, asymmetry and kurtosis) for both the RGB and the HSBr matrixes, the image category (smooth, regular, complex, noisy), and the name of the class that sample describes (stego/non-stego).

This configuration of features was settled after some tryouts with bigger feature lists, which included:

1. **region-centroid-col**: *central column in a 3x3 pixel region;*
2. **region-centroid-row**: *central line in a 3x3 pixel region;*
3. **region-pixel-count**: *total of pixels in a 3x3 region = 9.*
4. **short-line-density-5**: *counts how many lines with low contrast and size lesser or equal to 5 passes through the region;*
5. **short-line-density-2**: *counts how many lines with high contrast and size greater or equal to 5 passes through the region;*
6. **vedge-mean**: *vertical edge mean;*
7. **vegde-sd**: *vertical edge standard-deviation;*
8. **hedge-mean**: *horizontal edge mean;*
9. **hedge-sd**: *horizontal edge standard-deviation;*
10. **intensity-mean**: $(R + G + B)/3$ *in a region;*
11. **rawred-mean**: *red mean in a region;*
12. **rawblue-mean**: *blue mean in a region;*
13. **rawgreen-mean**: *green mena in a region;*
14. **exred-mean**: *additional red mean:* $(2R - (G + B))$;
15. **exblue-mean**: *additional blue mean:* $(2B - (G + R))$;
16. **exgreen-mean**: *additional green mean:* $(2G - (R + B))$;
17. **value-mean**: *non-linear 3D transformation mean;*
18. **saturation-mean**: *saturation mean in the 3D transform;*
19. **hue-mean**: *hue mean in the 3D transform;*

The features above were used based in literature review, where we choose to operate in special domain instead of transform domain, by empirical experimentation. Though, we observed that the efficiency of the machine learning methods did not decrease by eliminating many of the features above, so they were excluded from the final features list.

3.3.3 Data samples

To create the dataset, we utilized 300 images of landscapes, interiors, animals, buildings, people and food. According to the graphical complexity of each image, they were categorized as smooth, regular, complex or noisy. A random half of these images were kept unmodified, while the other half received hidden data corresponding up to 10% of the carry images size, what represents 20% of the maximum payload a carry image may cover (which is 50% of the total size of the carry image). The average size of the cover images is 800 x 600 pixels. And the stego objects here were created with the steganographic method JPHide/JPSeek (Lathan 2006).

Then, this dataset was once again divided. A random 80% of all the images were separated to compose the training set, and the 20% left composed the testing set.

3.3.4 Training and testing

At runtime, when a specialized classifier agent is instantiated, it receives a random subset from the training set. This subset is selected from all the samples that correspond to one single of the four image categories used in this work (smooth, regular, complex, noisy). Three other specialized classifier agents are created to the other categories. The subset for each of these agents is 20% the size of the training set samples. Similarly, when a general classifier agent is instantiated, it receives a random subset from the training dataset that corresponds to 40% of the total size of the training dataset.

Then, these agents train theirs classifiers and test their performances with 20% of the training dataset (the testing dataset is for testing the approach as a whole). The resulting accuracy rate will be informed to the coordinator agent, generating a weight to that agent decision, and influencing the fuzzy inference mechanism.

The size of these datasets was limited to this small percent in order to produce different agents, with different performances, that will be combined by the polygenic MAS fuzzy clustering approach.

4. Experiments and results

We have developed experiments and tests following the planning experimentation setup discussed by Cobb (1997). Basically, this methodology is resumed in *what measures to take, under what conditions and which material to process in the testes*. The answers are the measures given by the MAS about the classification: correctness rate, false positive and false negative. A set of training data is presented to the system, which is randomly distributed into other data sets for training the classifier agents. The test data is then distributed between the coordinator agents in order for these to coordinate classification activities of the general classifier agents and the specific classifier agents. Finally, the cited rates are obtained and analyzed.

As result of these experiments, the system presents a rate for correct detection of 89,37%, with false positive of 10,63% and false negative of 10,54%.

For JPHide and Seek, Liu (2008) present accuracy rate of 0.8% with OAASVM, and 56% with Adaboost. It is important to say that their dataset is different from the one used here, although we may say that our experiment presented a considerate accuracy rate.

Bakhshandeh (2009) presented accuracy rates from 68,75% to 94,67%, but none of the steganography methods used in their experiment was the same used in our work or in Lius´.

Also, we trained a Decision tree without the Polygenic MAS Fuzzy Clustering Steganalysis, using the entire dataset. And the results were an accuracy rate of 72,45%, false positives of 27,23% and false negatives of 26,92%.

These results show that the Polygenic MAS Fuzzy Clustering Steganalysis approach increased the performance of a machine learning steganalysis.

5. Conclusion

We have proposed a useful technique to detect images that possibly carry encrypted data on its contents. We use a methodology based on polygenic bees (a model based on community) where several agents interact between them. Our model combines this multi-agent system system with fuzzy logic in order to decide whether a digital media object has hidden information, coming up with a decision at the end of processed interactions. In comparison to the rates of correctness of other techniques found in the literature (between 70% to 90%) our rates of about 89% indicates that the proposed approach based on fuzzy logic is a good choice in this direction, being efficient in this task, experimentally comproved.

As future work we intend to to improve this paradigm once the use of MAS can be extended to other learning techniques besides fuzzy logic. A comparison between several techniques will be performed and a possible solution combining two or several of them will also be tried in order to achieve even better performance. For example, we believe that the use of decision trees combined to our fuzzy approach depicgted here can be used hopefully to get better results. So a possible future direction for our work is to test this approach with other techniques and also to use other medias as video, text, and audio, not being addressed in this work. Finallyanother possibility is to develop a more complete system including techniques for extracting the hidden information.

6. References

Acampora 2011 Acampora, G.; Cadenas, J.M.; Loia, V.; Ballester, E.M.;A Multi-Agent Memetic System for Human-Based Knowledge Selection, in IEEE Transactions on Systems, Man and Cybernetics, Part A: Systems and Humans, vol.41, no.5, pp.946-960, Sept. 2011.

Amirkhani 2011 Amirkhani, Hossein; Rahmati, Mohammad: New framework for using image contents in blind steganalysis systems. in Journal of Electronic Imaging, Vol.20, Iss.1, pp.013016, 2011, ISSN: 10179909

Aponte 2003 Aponte, Olga Inés Cepeda: Poliginia e monoginia em Melipona bicolor (Apidae, Meliponini): do coletivo para o individual. DSc Thesis in Biosciences, Universidade de São Paulo, 2003.

Arroyo 2011 Arroyo, A.; Serradilla, F.; Calvo, O. Adaptive fuzzy knowledge-based multi-agent systems on virtual environments. in Expert Systems - Special Issue: New Perspectives on the Application of Expert Systems, v. 28 (4), pp 339–352, September 2011.

Artz 2001 ARTZ, Donovan. Digital Steganography: Hiding Data within Data. IEEE Internet Computings, v.5, n.3, mai.-jun. 2001.

Bakhshandeh 2009 Bakhshandeh, Soodeh; Jamjah, Javad Ravan; Azami, Bahram Zahir: Blind Image Steganalysis Based on Local Information and Human Visual System. in Signal Processing, Image Processing and Pattern Recognition. V. 61: 201-208. SPRINGER-VERLAG, BERLIN, 2009.

Carpenter 1992 Carpenter, G.A.; Grossberg, S.; Markuzon, N.; Reynolds, J.H.; Rosen, D.B.: Fuzzy Artmap: A neural network architecture for incremental supervised learning of analog multidimensional maps in IEEE Transactions on Neural Networks, vol.3, no.5, pp.698-713, Sep 1992.doi: 10.1109/72.159059

Chandramouli 2004 Chandramouli, R.; Subbalakshmi, K.P: Current Trends in Steganalysis: A Critical Survey, Invited session on Multimedia Security, The Eighth International Conference on Control, Automation, Robotics and Vision, ICARCV 2004, December 2004. (invited paper)

Fridrich 2002 Fridrich, J., Goljan, M.: Practical steganalysis of digital images - state of the art. In: Proc. of SPIE Photonics West. Volume 4675. San Jose, California, USA – 2002.

Fridrich 2004 Fridrich, J.; Goljan, M.: On estimation of message length in LSB steganography in spatial domain. Security, Steganography, and Watermarking of Multimedia Contents , 2004.

Goodarzi 2011 Goodarzi, Mohammad; Radmand, Ashkan; Nazemi, Eslam: An Optimized Solution for Multi-agent Coordination Using Integrated GA-Fuzzy Approach in Rescue Simulation Environment, in Advances in Practical Multi-Agent Systems

Studies in Computational Intelligence, 2011, V. 325, pp 377-388, DOI: 10.1007/978-3-642-16098-1_23

Hagras 2010 Hagras, H.; Ramadan, R.; Nawito, M.; Gabr, H.; Zaher, M.; Fahmy, H.: A fuzzy based hierarchical coordination and control system for a robotic agent team in the robot Hockey competition, in IEEE International Conference on Fuzzy Systems (FUZZ), pp.1-8, July 2010. ISSN: 1098-7584.

Jang 1993 Jang, JSR: Anfis - Adaptive-Network-Based Fuzzy Inference System. in IEEE Transactions on Systems Man And Cybernetics, 23(3), pp665-685. May-Jun 1993. DOI: 10.1109/21.256541

Katzenbeisser 2000 Katzenbeisser, Stefan; Petitcolas, Fabien A. P. Information Hiding Techniques for Steganography and Digital Watermarking. Boston: Artech House, 2000.

Kofler 2003 Kofler, R. Krimmer, R. Prosser, A.: Electronic Voting: Algorithmic and implementation Issue. System Sciences, 2003. Proceedings of the 36th Annual Hawaii International Conference on , 6-9 Jan. 2003.

Lin 2002 Lin, Chun-Fu; Wang, Sheng-De.: Fuzzy support vector machines in IEEE Transactions on Neural Networks, vol.13, no.2, pp.464-471, Mar 2002.

Liu 2008 liu, qingzhong; sung, Andrew H.: Detect Information-Hiding Type and Length in JPEG Images by Using Neuro-fuzzy Inference Systems, CISP, vol. 5, pp.692-696, 2008 Congress on Image and Signal Processing, Vol. 5, 2008.

Liu 2008b Liu, Q., Sung, A.H., Chen, Z., Xu, J.: Feature mining and pattern classification for steganalysis of LSB matching steganography in grayscale images. Pattern Recognition, 41 (1), pp. 56-66. 2008.

López-Ortega 2011 López-Ortega, Omar; Rosales, Marco-Antonio: An agent-oriented decision support system combining fuzzy clustering and the AHP, in Expert Systems with Applications, Vol. 38 (7), July 2011, pp 8275-8284, ISSN 0957-4174.

Luciano 2003 Luciano, E. M.; Testa, M. G.; Freitas, H. : As tendências em comércio eletrônico com base em recentes congressos. XXXVIII CLADEA, Lima/Peru, 2003.

Macedo 2001 Macedo, A. P. Cunha: Metodologias de Negociação em Sistemas Multi-Agentes para Empresas Virtuais. Doctors Thesis, Faculdade de Engenharia, Universidade do Porto, 2001.

Macq 1995 Macq, B. M.; Quisquater , J-J. Cryptology for digital TV broadcasting. Proceedings of the IEEE , 1995.

Moskowitz 2002 MOSKOWITZ, Ira S.; CHANG, Liwu; NEWMAN, Richard E. Capacity is the wrong paradigm. In *Proceedings of the 2002 workshop on New security paradigms* (NSPW '02). ACM, New York, NY, USA, 114-126. DOI=10.1145/844102.844124 http://doi.acm.org/10.1145/844102.844124

Pavlidis 1982 Pavlidis, T. Algorithms for graphics and image processing, Springer, Berlin, 1982.

Rezende 2003 Rezende, Solange Oliveira. Sistemas Inteligentes: Fundamentos e Aplicações. Manole Editora. 2003. 525p

Russel 1995 Rusell, Stuart J.; Norving, Peter. Artificial Inteligence: A Modern Approach. Prentice-Hall Series in Artificial Inteligence, 1995.

Sanches 2004 Sanches, M. K.; Geromini, M. R.; Aprendizado de Máquina: Relatório Técnico. Instituto de Ciências Matemáticas e Computação, Universidade de São Paulo, 2004.

Wooldridge 2001 Woolridge, Michael J., Introduction to Multiagent Systems, John Wiley & Sons, Inc., New York, NY, 2001.

Zadeh 1965 Zadeh, L. A.: Fuzzy sets. Information and Control, 8(3), pp. 338-353, 1965.

Part 3

Business, Environment and Energy

13

Fuzzy Logic in Financial Management

Tomasz Korol

Gdansk University of Technology,
Poland

1. Introduction

Fuzzy logic has been widely used in machinery, robotics, and industrial engineering. This chapter introduces the use of fuzzy logic for the needs of financial management. The process of globalization has led to the emergence of a complex network of relationships in the business environment. In a free market economy, this means increased complexity and uncertainty of factors affecting the financial standing of entities. Nowadays many phenomena in finance and economics are fuzzy, but are treated as if they were crisp. In this chapter two such financial research problems are analyzed. The first concerns the issue of consumer credit scoring, while the second the forecasting of the financial situation of firms in short and medium periods (one year and two years forecasts). Predicting both business and consumer bankruptcy, is imprecise and ambiguous. The failure process is affected by many internal and external factors that cannot be precisely and unambiguously defined. Also, the mere allegation that a company or an individual consumer is at risk of bankruptcy must be considered imprecise, and in fact rarely in economic reality are there firms/persons that can be considered as 100% bankrupt. It is difficult to accurately determine the degree of bankruptcy threat using traditional statistical methods such as multivariate discriminant analysis. When the value of the discriminant function is less than the threshold value, we find that a company is at risk of bankruptcy. With the use of fuzzy logic vague and ambiguous concepts can be defined, such as "high risk of bankruptcy" or "low risk of bankruptcy". The presented models are the result of the chapter author's ten years of experience on this issue. They can be used not only for forecasting the level of risk of bankruptcy but also for determining the degree of positive financial standing of the analyzed entity (a company or consumer) - for example, such as "outstanding solvency" or "average solvency" etc. The global financial crisis that began in mid-2008 caused the number of companies in danger of bankruptcy to significantly increase around the world. Furthermore, the highly globalized environment has caused the economies of countries to deteriorate too (for example: such countries as Greece or Iceland risking bankruptcy; the decrease of the USA's credit rating from AAA to AA+ by rating agencies for the first time in history), which directly and indirectly influences the financial situation of both companies and consumers. Therefore, analysts are no longer faced with the dilemma of whether to predict the financial standing of entities (enterprises, consumers, or even countries), but what forecasting method to use in order to minimize forecast errors.

This chapter consists of three sections. In the first the author introduces his financial forecasting methodology and describes the concept of using fuzzy logic in finance. Section 2 is devoted to the author's research on the use of fuzzy logic in consumer credit scoring. Models developed by the author are based on demographic and financial variables of customers of a Central European bank. In the last section, the author presents business bankruptcy prediction models programmed by him. These models are based on financial variables of companies quoted on a stock exchange in Central Europe.

The information contained in this chapter may be used in practice in several aspects:

• in the context of early warning of the deteriorating financial situation of an audited company,
• from the viewpoint of assessing the solvency of partners and customers,
• from the perspective of credit risk assessment by financial institutions,
• in the context of the implementation of financial and economic plans in a company,
• from the perspective of risk assessment, the purchase of shares by individual and institutional investors on stock exchanges,
• in the context of credit scoring the credit applications of consumers by banks,
• from the viewpoint of assessing the consumer bankruptcy threat.

2. Methodology of financial forecasting

2.1 Classification of financial forecasting models

In literature, forecasting models are categorized into three main groups: statistical models, theoretical models, and models using soft computing techniques, which are part of a separate field of science defined as *Computational Intelligence* (a term understood as solving various problems with the help of artificial intelligence). According to literature, 64% of case studies used statistical models, 25% soft computing techniques, and 11% other types of models (Aziz & Dar, 2006).

In statistical models, selected financial ratios that have diagnostic value are estimated and used. The selection of each ratio is based on empirical studies of ex-post groups of entities, consisting of enterprises/consumers with good financial condition and those at risk. Furthermore, the set of indicators is reduced by excluding variables of similar information content, e.g. ratios that are correlated with each other. After defining a set of diagnostic variables, the model's parameters are estimated. Each variable selected receives discriminatory weight. The bankruptcy prediction model is created by a gradual "compaction" of the set of individual ratios, to obtain a single index called a synthetic indicator. "Compaction" is carried out using appropriate statistical and econometrical methods. Using such a model for assessing the risk of bankruptcy is the substitution of the actual value of financial ratios and the calculation of the synthetic indicator of risk. This synthetic index characterizes the financial situation of the audited company/client.

The use of statistical models requires that the variables used in the model meet the following assumptions:

• indicators should have normal distributions,
• indicators must be independent,
• indicators must have a high discriminative ability of separating solvent entities from insolvent ones,

- observations for each individual object (solvent and insolvent companies/clients) must be complete – i.e. should have values for all indicators of all entities,
- object classifications must be clearly defined – belonging to one group excludes its belonging to a second group.

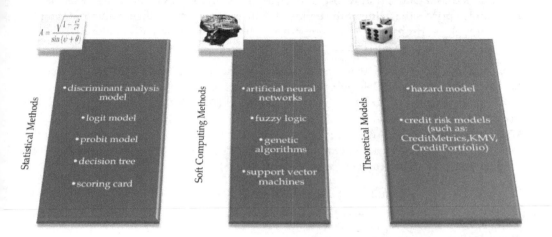

Table 1. Classification of Forecasting Models (the source: based on own studies)

In contrast to the statistical models, methods of soft computing techniques effectively cope with imprecisely defined problems, incomplete data, imprecision, and uncertainty. The issue of consumer and business bankruptcy prediction has all of the above characteristics. In addition, soft computing models are suitable for use in dynamic systems designed to fit certain internal parameters to changing environmental conditions (so-called learning systems). The difference between statistical models and soft computing models is based on aspects such as the precision, reliability, and accuracy of variables used. These elements are the basis of statistical models, while the starting point, e.g. for the fuzzy logic model, is the thesis that precision and certainty carry a cost, and calculating, reasoning, and decision making should exploit tolerance for imprecision and uncertainty wherever possible. Soft computing techniques, in contrast to statistical models, thus tolerate inaccurate data, uncertainty, and approximation. The essence of models based on computational intelligence is the processing and interpretation of data in a variety of capacities. They are able to formulate rules of inference and generalized knowledge about situations where they are expected to predict or classify the object into one of the previously observed categories.

The theoretical models are mainly focused on the use of qualitative information in predicting the bankruptcy of entities. In contrast to the statistical and soft computing methods that rely on the symptoms of going bankrupt, theoretical models focus on finding the causes of the collapse. Theoretical models typically use different statistical techniques for drawing conclusions and quantitative proof of the theoretical argument. Thus, for example in the hazard model, an entity can be seen from the perspective of the player – gambler who plays burdened with a certain probability of loss. The player (company/consumer) continues to function until the moment when its net worth reaches zero (bankruptcy). Another example of the theoretical model is the KMV model, which is based on the use of option pricing theory for the valuation of risky loans and bonds. In the KMV model an entity's net assets are essential. This model assumes that at any time the value of assets can be modelled as a call option whose underlying is the market value of company assets and the exercise price – the value of the entity's liabilities at the time of their maturity. Using the KMV model the probability of a company's value falling below the value of its liabilities (making the firm insolvent) can be determined, .

Literature studies show that the financial situation predictions are dominated by discriminant analysis models, which make up 30.3 percent of all models created among all methods – statistical, soft computing, and theoretical (Aziz & Dar, 2006). Undoubtedly the most popular model for forecasting bankruptcy risk is the statistical model developed by American Professor – E. Altman in 1968. As a pioneer in the use of multivariate discriminant analysis to predict the bankruptcy of companies, he developed a model consisting of a single function with five financial ratios (Altman, 1993):

$$Z = 1.2 * X_1 + 1.4 * X_2 + 3.3 * X_3 + 0.6 * X_4 + 0.999 * X_5 \tag{1}$$

where:

X1 = working capital / total assets
X2 = retained earnings / total assets
X3 = earnings before taxes / total assets
X4 = market value of equity / total long term and short term liabilities
X5 = sales / total assets

Altman proposed the use of three decision areas depending on the value of the Z score:

- if $Z < 1.81$ then it is a signal of a high probability of bankruptcy,
- if $1.81 < Z < 2.99$ then the risk of financial failure of the company is not possible to define (it is a so-called "gray area"),
- if $Z > 2.99$ then there is low probability of bankruptcy.

Predicting the bankruptcy of companies is imprecise and ambiguous. The process of business failure is affected by many internal and external factors that cannot be precisely and unambiguously defined. Also, the mere allegation that a company is at risk of bankruptcy must be considered imprecise, and in fact rarely in economic reality are there companies that can be considered as 100% bankrupt. It is difficult to accurately determine the degree of bankruptcy threat using traditional statistical methods such as multivariate discriminant analysis. When the value of the discriminant function is less than the threshold value, we find that a company is at risk of bankruptcy. With the use of fuzzy logic vague and ambiguous concepts can be defined, such as "high risk of bankruptcy" or "low risk of bankruptcy". The concept of fuzzy sets was introduced by Zadeh in 1965 (Zadeh, 1965). The fuzzy set "A" in a non-empty space X ($A \subseteq X$) can be defined as:

$$A = \{(x, \mu_A(x)) \mid x \in X\} \tag{2}$$

where $\mu_A : X \rightarrow [0,1]$ is a function for each element of X that determines the extent to which it belongs to set A. This function is called a membership function of fuzzy set A.

Classical set theory assumes that any element (company) fully belongs or completely does not belong to a given set (bankrupt or non-bankrupt set of companies). In turn, in the fuzzy set theory an element (company) may partially belong to a certain set, and this membership may be expressed by means of a real number in the interval [0,1]. Thus, the membership function $\mu_A(x) : U \Rightarrow [0,1]$ is defined as follows:

$$\forall_{x \in U} \mu_A(x) = \begin{cases} f(x), x \in X \\ 0, x \notin X \end{cases}$$

where: $\mu_A(x)$ –function defining membership of element x to set A, which is a subset of U; f(x) - function receiving values from the interval [0,1]. The values of this function are called the degrees of membership.

A membership function assigns the degree of membership of each element $x \in X$ to a fuzzy set A, where we can distinguish three situations:

- $\mu_A(x) = 1$ means full membership of element x to the fuzzy set A,
- $\mu_A(x) = 0$ means that no element x belongs to fuzzy set A,
- $0 < \mu_A(x) < 1$ means partial membership of an element x to the fuzzy set A.

Membership functions are usually presented in graphical form. A trapezoidal function $\mu_A(x)$ is often used (see Figure 1). The graph shows information from literature about the accepted values of the cash liquidity ratio. The correct values for this ratio are values in the interval [0.2, 0.5], and incorrect values are in the range of $(0; 0.2) \cup (0.5, \infty)$. When this ratio is lower than 0.2 it is considered that the company has a cash liquidity shortage; in turn, when this amount is higher than 0.5 it is said that the company has excess liquidity, which is also rated as a negative phenomenon (in the case of excess liquidity such companies have too much cash, which is rated as inefficient company management).

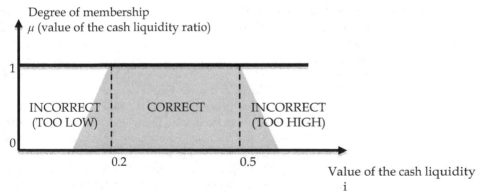

Fig. 1. An Example of the Trapezoidal Membership Function for the Cash Liquidity Ratio

In this case, using the classical set theory to evaluate this financial ratio, there is a sharp boundary between the two sets of ratio values 0.2 and 0.5. If one company recorded a cash liquidity ratio of 0.19, it would be classified as an incorrect value - negative, while if a second company recorded this ratio at the level of 0.2, it would be regarded as a correct value – positive assessment of bankruptcy risk, even though the financial ratio of the two firms differ only by 0.01. The interpretation of the values of individual ratios (e.g. liquidity) is further complicated by the fact that different literature sources give different reference limit values for individual financial ratios.

Application of a fuzzy set changes the assessment of the problem. A cash liquidity ratio with a value of 0.19 is considered as partly correct and partly invalid. The degree of membership to both sets depends on the shape of the membership function.

With such defined subsets, the boundary between the values considered to be positive or negative, is fuzzyficated – a certain ratio value is "partially good" and "partially bad." There is no such possibility in the case of classical logic, i.e. bivalent, in which the value of the ratio is "good" or "bad". Therefore, the use of classical logic in assessing the financial situation of companies affect negatively on the effectiveness of posed forecasts. This occurs especially in ratios which values are close to the threshold of subsets, where an excess of the critical value determines the final evaluation of the ratio (as entirely positive or negative), which is not true, because both values reflect almost the same situation in the enterprise.

The above example concerns the prediction of bankruptcy of companies. But the example for the usefulness of fuzzy logic in assessing the creditworthiness of consumers can also be given. In consumer credit scoring different demographical and financial variables of consumers are taken into account. Bank analysts set individual criteria to each of them in order to evaluate the credit risk of the applicant (setting certain points to each variable). One of the most popular factors is the age of the consumer.

It is generally accepted that the middle aged consumers group is less risky (young people tend to have smaller and less stable income than middle aged men, and old consumers bear higher risk because of their life expectancy). The issue is to set proper age limits into each category. Using the most common classical logic it can be set that middle aged consumers are those in the range of 30-45 years old. In such case a credit applicant who is 29 years old is evaluated on a scoring card worse than the consumer who is only 1 year older. The drawbacks of using classical logic are not only for the bank's clients who may not receive the credit but also for the bank itself that looses the potential profits from refused credit, which could have been given without much larger risk than in case of middle age people. Application of fuzzy logic can improve the efficiency in forecasting the probability of on-time repayment of granted credits. Figure 2 shows that classical logic uses crisp classification of the age of customers – group of young people in age ranges of (0; 30), group of old people in age ranges of (45 and more). With the help of fuzzy logic a bank can set that consumers with an age between 25 and 30 are partially young and middle age ones, and with an age between 45 and 50 are partially middle age and old ones. In the described example, the credit applicants who are 29 years old will be scored very similarly to those who are 30 years old, which would not be possible using credit scoring applications that are based on classical logic.

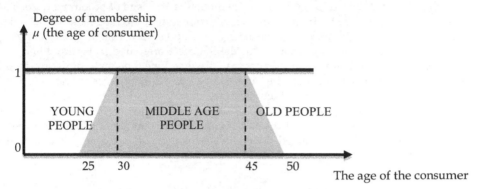

Fig. 2. An Example of the Trapezoidal Membership Function for the Age of Consumers.

2.2 Drawbacks and limitations of traditional forecasting models

Despite the high popularity of traditional bankruptcy prediction models, they are not free of defects and limitations, which rarely receive substantive discussion in literature. The first limitation has already been discussed – the crisp separation between "good" and "bad" values, conditions or situations. Such models use classical logic with no possible partial belonging to a defined group of criteria.

The second issue in assessing the effectiveness of these models is the method of developing a learning dataset (based on which the model shall be estimated) and a testing dataset that consists of entities that did not make it into the learning sample. Elements of the testing sample are unknown to the model. It enables evaluating the effectiveness of the model in conditions similar to those in business practice. In literature, the vast majority of scientists (e.g.: Ooghe & Balcaen, 2006; or Kumar & Ravi, 2007) suggest that the learning dataset was a balanced sample (consisting 50% of entities at risk of bankruptcy, and 50% of entities in good financial condition). This will enable the model to learn to distinguish "good" and "bad" entities. Note, however, that in a market economy the number of firms/consumers at risk of bankruptcy is much smaller than the number of "healthy" entities. Evaluation of the effectiveness of models that use a balanced testing dataset become highly questionable. After all, these models are developed for use in business practice, where the proportion of bankrupts to non-bankrupts is many times smaller. The author of this chapter proved in his previous research that fuzzy logic models are superior over traditional bankruptcy prediction models (both statistical and soft computing techniques) in forecasting risk of bankruptcy of companies in the case of an unbalanced testing dataset (Korol, 2011).

Another controversial aspect on the effectiveness of the most popular analysis methods – multivariate discriminant, logit, and probit , is the possibility of manipulation of the threshold in order to maximize the classification results of these models. This allegation was raised by M. Nwogugu. According to him, the statistical methods do not guarantee reliable results because of the ease at which the threshold which separates "good" and "bad" entities can be manually set (Nwogugu, 2007). Such manipulation, of course, does not increase the effectiveness of the model in business practice after its implementation in a bank, but only in theoretical tests in literature.

The next complaint toward traditional bankruptcy models is the issue of becoming obsolete with the passage of time since their estimation. It is assumed that the models function well for 4-6 years, after which it is necessary to modify and update them (Agarwal & Taffler, 2007). It should be noted, however, that the model life cycle presented in Figure 3 is only generally accepted, but there are no strict rules that exactly define the length of the model's life cycle. Forecasting applications become outdated as a result of changes in the business cycle, changing economic conditions which influence the change of appropriate values of financial ratios of the entities (Altman & Rijken, 2006). Fuzzy logic models, of course, also get outdated, but unlike the traditional models, it is easy to update them according to the changing environment without the need for their re-estimation as in the case of statistical models or most of the soft computing techniques.

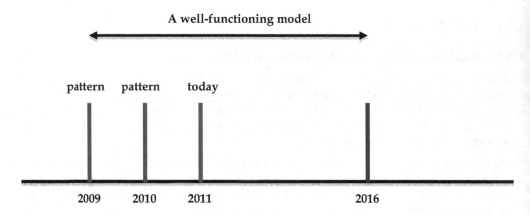

Fig. 3. The Life Cycle of the Bankruptcy Prediction Model.

In relation to statistical models scientists also mention an allegation about the adoption of an assumption about normal distribution of financial ratios of analyzed companies during the estimating of models (Mcleay & Omar, 2000). This assumption is often not observed due to the fact that few variables are characterized by such distribution. However the desire to meet this assumption, significantly limit the number of indicators that truly reflect the financial situation of the company and thus would cause deterioration in the effectiveness of models of this type.

Artificial neural networks, belonging to the soft computing methods, are not subject to the above drawback concerning the normal distribution of financial ratios. This does not mean that they are free from other defects in predicting the financial situation of companies and consumers. The most common complaint encountered in literature is the inability to justify the decisions made. Often the way artificial neural networks forecast are described as a "black-box system" (Bose & Mahapatra, 2001). Analysis of the process for assigning individual variable weights is complex and difficult to interpret. Neural networks do not provide the course of reasoning leading to certain assessment. They only give their outcome, without being able to trace further evidence leading to a final conclusion. This makes it difficult to correctly identify the causes of generated errors by an artificial neural network. Another drawback of the use of artificial neural networks in predicting bankruptcy is an arbitrary method of selecting the network architecture. Although there are general formulas to designate the number of hidden neurons, in literature it is postulated to use an individual and arbitrary approach for each forecasted phenomenon separately.

3. Consumer credit scoring model

3.1 Research assumptions

To conduct this research[1] the author has used the demographical and financial variables of 500 Polish consumers who took consumption credit (400 consumers were "non-bankrupt" – they were repaying the credit with no delays and 100 clients were "bankrupt" – those who had delays in repayment longer than 3 months[2]). This population of consumers was divided into:

- learning dataset - used for developing the model. There were 50 bankrupt consumers and 50 non-bankrupt ones.
- testing dataset "one" – used for testing the model created in conditions of an equal proportion of bankrupt and non-bankrupt customers. There were 50 "good" consumers and 50 credit applicants in danger of going bankrupt.
- testing dataset "two" – consisting of all the customers from testing dataset "one" with the addition of 300 non-bankrupt ones. This enabled testing the ability of the model created to identify customers who have problems with credit repayment among non-bankrupt bank clients in the business practice in proportion of 12,5%/87,5% ("50 bad customers"/"350 good ones").

All customers were described by 10 demographical and financial variables (Table 2). Additionally, all credit takers were marked with 0-1 variables (0-bankrupt, 1-non-bankrupt).

Variable Symbol	Type of Variable
X1	Age
X2	Education
X3	Marital status
X4	Number of children in household
X5	Monthly income
X6	Length of employment (in years)
X7	Type of employment contract
X8	Value of owned car
X9	Net Value of owned apartment/house
X10	Value of other assets

Table 2. Demographical and Financial Variables of Customers.

3.2 Fuzzy logic model

The structure of the developed model is presented in Figure 4. The model consists of four different rule blocks. Rule Block 1 "demographics" evaluates the consumer's demographical

---

[1] All fuzzy logic models were programmed by the author with the use of software – FuzzyTech 5.54d.
[2] In Poland at that time there was no law for consumer bankruptcy. Such law was introduced in 2009.

variables (age, education level, marital status, number of children in household). Rule Block 2 "finance" assesses the financial condition of the consumer based on three variables (monthly income, the length of employment, type of employment contract). Rule Block 3 "financial security" analyzes the financial strength of the customer and eventually the security for the granted credit. Rule Block 4 "the score" uses as entry variables the forecasted output of all three Rule Blocks, which are: demographics variable (there are three states of demographics forecasted at Rule Block 1: weak, average, strong), finance variable (there are three states of financial strength forecasted in Rule Block 2: weak, average, strong), and financial security variable (there are three states of security forecasted at Rule Block 3: weak, average, strong). Based on these three evaluated inputs the model forecasts the final credit scoring output.

The model's output is a variable representing a forecast of the financial situation of an audited consumer. This variable ranges from 0 to 1, while it is assumed that there are three levels of risk: high risk for values smaller than 0.3, medium risk for values from 0.3 to 0.7, and low risk for values larger than 0.7.

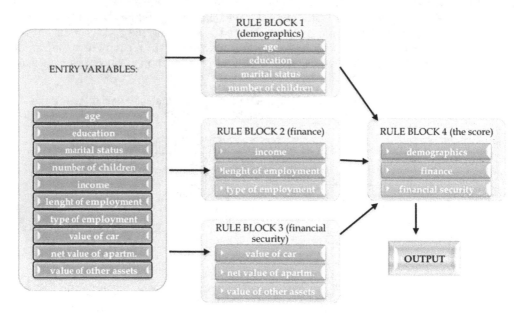

Fig. 4. Structure of the Fuzzy Logic Model for Consumer Credit Scoring.

This model is based on sets of rules written by the author in the form of IF - THEN, where expert knowledge is stored. For each entry variable to the model, the author identified from two to three fuzzy sets (which are subsets of a set of values of the entry variable), and their corresponding membership functions. The fuzzy sets and the shape of membership functions have been arbitrarily designated by the author. The fuzzy sets and the thresholds for all membership functions are presented in Table 3.

Variable	Criteria (thresholds for individual membership functions)
Age (value ranges: 18 years old -65 years old)	Young: less than 33 Middle age: from 27 to 53 Old: more than 48
Number of children (value ranges: 0-5 children)	Few: less than 2.0 Average: from 1.0 to 3.7 Many: more than 3.0
Education level (value ranges: 0-3; where: 0 – elementary education, 1 – high skilled worker, 2 – college education, 3 – university education, doctorate, or high qualified experts)	Basic level: less than 1.0 Average level: from 0.8 to 2.25 High level: more than 1.5
Marital status (value ranges: 0-1; where: 0 – single, 1- married, between 0 and 1 other types of marital status which can improve financial situation of consumer, e.g.: partnership or widow etc.)	Single: less than 0.7 Married: more than 0.7
Monthly income (value ranges: 800 PLN – 5000 PLN)	Low income: less than 2900 PLN Average income: from 1850 PLN to 3950 PLN High income: more than 2950 PLN
Length of employment (value ranges: 0 years – 15 years)	Short: less than 7.5 Medium: from 3.7 to 11.25 Long: more than 7.5
Type of employment contract (value ranges: 0-2, where: 0 – agreement on task job, 1 – agreement on limited duration work, 2 – agreement on indefinite duration job)	Only task job – less than 1.0 Limited duration work – from 0.5 to 1.5 Indefinite duration job – more than 1.0
Value of car (value ranges: 10 000 PLN – 100 000 PLN)	Cheap: less than 55 000 PLN Middle class: from 30 000 PLN to 77 500 PLN Expensive: more than 55 000 PLN
Net value of apartment (value ranges: 0 PLN – 500 000 PLN)	Low: less than 325 000 PLN Average: from 237 500 PLN to 412 500 PLN High: more than 325 000 PLN
Value of other assets (value ranges: 1000 PLN – 20 000 PLN)	Low: less than 4500 PLN Average: from 2700 PLN to 15 250 PLN High: more than 10 500 PLN

Table 3. Threshold Values for Membership Functions of Entry Variables

The exemplary form of the membership functions are presented in Figure 5 for the variable - "Age" and in Figure 6 for variable - "Output". Following set of decision rules was created for Rule Block 1 "Demographics":

If X1 is Young and X2 is Basic and X3 is Single and X4 is Few then Demographics is Weak
If X1 is Young and X2 is Average and X3 is Single and X4 is Few then Demographics is Average

If X1 is Young and X2 is High and X3 is Single and X4 is Few then Demographics is Average
If X1 is Middle age and X2 is Basic and X3 is Single and X4 is Few then Demographics is Weak
If X1 is Middle age and X2 is Average and X3 is Single and X4 is Few then Demographics is Average
If X1 is Middle age and X2 is High and X3 is Single and X4 is Few then Demographics is Average
If X1 is Old and X2 is Basic and X3 is Single and X4 is Few then Demographics is Weak
If X1 is Old and X2 is Average and X3 is Single and X4 is Few then Demographics is Average
If X1 is Old and X2 is High and X3 is Single and X4 is Few then Demographics is Average
If X1 is Young and X2 is Basic and X3 is Married and X4 is Few then Demographics is Weak
If X1 is Young and X2 is Average and X3 is Married and X4 is Few then Demographics is Average
If X1 is Young and X2 is High and X3 is Married and X4 is Few then Demographics is Strong
If X1 is Middle age and X2 is Basic and X3 is Married and X4 is Few then Demographics is Weak
If X1 is Middle age and X2 is Average and X3 is Married and X4 is Few then Demographics is Average
If X1 is Middle age and X2 is High and X3 is Married and X4 is Few then Demographics is Strong
If X1 is Old and X2 is Basic and X3 is Married and X4 is Few then Demographics is Weak
If X1 is Old and X2 is Average and X3 is Married and X4 is Few then Demographics is Average
If X1 is Old and X2 is High and X3 is Married and X4 is Few then Demographics is Strong
If X1 is Young and X2 is Basic and X3 is Single and X4 is Average then Demographics is Weak
If X1 is Young and X2 is Average and X3 is Single and X4 is Average then Demographics is Weak
If X1 is Young and X2 is High and X3 is Single and X4 is Average then Demographics is Average
If X1 is Middle age and X2 is Basic and X3 is Single and X4 is Average then Demographics is Weak
If X1 is Middle age and X2 is Average and X3 is Single and X4 is Average then Demographics is Average
If X1 is Middle age and X2 is High and X3 is Single and X4 is Average then Demographics is Average
If X1 is Old and X2 is Basic and X3 is Single and X4 is Average then Demographics is Weak
If X1 is Old and X2 is Average and X3 is Single and X4 is Average then Demographics is Average
If X1 is Old and X2 is High and X3 is Single and X4 is Average then Demographics is Average
If X1 is Young and X2 is Basic and X3 is Married and X4 is Average then Demographics is Weak
If X1 is Young and X2 is Average and X3 is Married and X4 is Average then Demographics is Average
If X1 is Young and X2 is High and X3 is Married and X4 is Average then Demographics is Strong
If X1 is Middle age and X2 is Basic and X3 is Married and X4 is Average then Demographics is Weak
If X1 is Middle age and X2 is Average and X3 is Married and X4 is Average then Demographics is Average
If X1 is Middle age and X2 is High and X3 is Married and X4 is Average then Demographics is Strong
If X1 is Old and X2 is Basic and X3 is Married and X4 is Average then Demographics is Weak
If X1 is Old and X2 is Average and X3 is Married and X4 is Average then Demographics is Average
If X1 is Old and X2 is High and X3 is Married and X4 is Average then Demographics is Strong
If X1 is Young and X2 is Basic and X3 is Single and X4 is Many then Demographics is Weak
If X1 is Young and X2 is Average and X3 is Single and X4 is Many then Demographics is Weak
If X1 is Young and X2 is High and X3 is Single and X4 is Many then Demographics is Average
If X1 is Middle age and X2 is Basic and X3 is Single and X4 is Many then Demographics is Weak
If X1 is Middle age and X2 is Average and X3 is Single and X4 is Many then Demographics is Average
If X1 is Middle age and X2 is High and X3 is Single and X4 is Many then Demographics is Average
If X1 is Old and X2 is Basic and X3 is Single and X4 is Many then Demographics is Weak
If X1 is Old and X2 is Average and X3 is Single and X4 is Many then Demographics is Weak
If X1 is Old and X2 is High and X3 is Single and X4 is Many then Demographics is Average
If X1 is Young and X2 is Basic and X3 is Married and X4 is Many then Demographics is Weak
If X1 is Young and X2 is Average and X3 is Married and X4 is Many then Demographics is Average
If X1 is Young and X2 is High and X3 is Married and X4 is Many then Demographics is Average
If X1 is Middle age and X2 is Basic and X3 is Married and X4 is Many then Demographics is Weak
If X1 is Middle age and X2 is Average and X3 is Married and X4 is Many then Demographics is Average
If X1 is Middle age and X2 is High and X3 is Married and X4 is Many then Demographics is Average
If X1 is Old and X2 is Basic and X3 is Married and X4 is Many then Demographics is Weak
If X1 is Old and X2 is Average and X3 is Married and X4 is Many then Demographics is Average
If X1 is Old and X2 is High and X3 is Married and X4 is Many then Demographics is Average

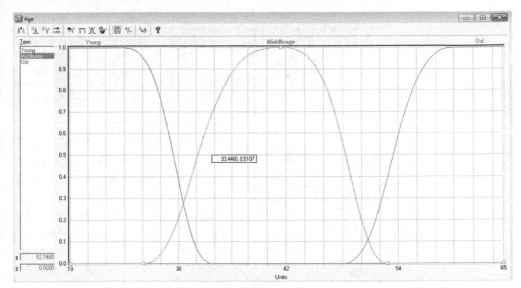

Fig. 5. Defined Membership Functions of Variable "Age".

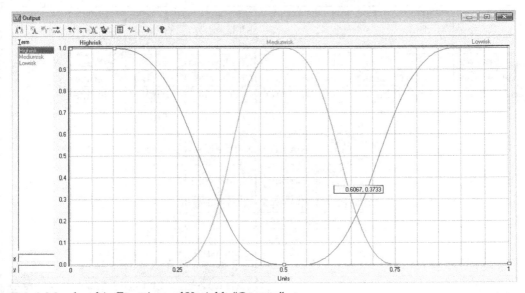

Fig. 6. Membership Functions of Variable "Output".

Based on above set of decision rules the model evaluates a consumer's demographical situation that has direct influence on their credibility. There are four variables analyzed in this rule block: age of consumer, education level, marital status, and number of children in household. The rules are constructed in such a way to consider the different influence each variable has on the strength of a consumer's demographical state. Level of education (values from 0 to 3) is considered to have a positive influence on the credibility of the credit

Rule Block 2 "Finance"				Rule Block 3 "Financial Security"			
If X5 is:	If X6 is:	If X7 is:	Then output "Finance" is:	If X8 is:	If X9 is:	If X10 is	Then output "Financial Security" is:
Low	Short	Task job	Weak	Cheap	Low	Low	Weak
Low	Medium	Task job	Weak	Cheap	Average	Low	Weak
Low	Long	Task job	Average	Cheap	High	Low	Average
Low	Short	Limited dur.	Weak	Cheap	Low	Average	Weak
Low	Medium	Limited dur.	Weak	Cheap	Average	Average	Weak
Low	Long	Limited dur.	Average	Cheap	High	Average	Strong
Low	Short	Indefinite dur.	Weak	Cheap	Low	High	Weak
Low	Medium	Indefinite dur.	Average	Cheap	Average	High	Average
Low	Long	Indefinite dur.	Average	Cheap	High	High	Strong
Average	Short	Task job	Weak	Middle class	Low	Low	Weak
Average	Medium	Task job	Average	Middle class	Average	Low	Average
Average	Long	Task job	Average	Middle class	High	Low	Strong
Average	Short	Limited dur.	Weak	Middle class	Low	Average	Average
Average	Medium	Limited dur.	Average	Middle class	Average	Average	Average
Average	Long	Limited dur.	Average	Middle class	High	Average	Strong
Average	Short	Indefinite dur.	Average	Middle class	Low	High	Average
Average	Medium	Indefinite dur.	Average	Middle class	Average	High	Average
Average	Long	Indefinite dur.	Strong	Middle class	High	High	Strong
High	Short	Task job	Average	Expensive	Low	Low	Weak
High	Medium	Task job	Average	Expensive	Average	Low	Average
High	Long	Task job	Strong	Expensive	High	Low	Strong
High	Short	Limited dur.	Average	Expensive	Low	Average	Average
High	Medium	Limited dur.	Strong	Expensive	Average	Average	Average
High	Long	Limited dur.	Strong	Expensive	High	Average	Strong
High	Short	Indefinite dur.	Strong	Expensive	Low	High	Average
High	Medium	Indefinite dur.	Strong	Expensive	Average	High	Strong
High	Long	Indefinite dur.	Strong	Expensive	High	High	Strong

Table 4. The Set of Decision Rules for Rule Block 2 and Rule Block 3

applicant (the higher level of education the better). In the same positive way marital status (values from 0 to 1) affects the output of Rule Block 1. However, number of children in household (values from 0 to 5) has a negative influence on a consumer's status. A client's age in certain values (range of values for the middle aged category) has a positive affect on the output, and in other cases negatively influences the score (range of values for the young and old category).

The complete block diagram containing all set of decision rules for created Rule Block 2 "Finance", Rule Block 3 "Financial Security" is presented in table 4, and for the output Rule Block 4 "The score" is presented in table 5 (the variables are described in table 2 and 4).

Rule Block 4 "The Score"			
If "Demographics" is:	If "Finance" is:	If "Financial Security" is:	Then final output of the model "The Score" is:
Weak	Weak	Weak	High risk
Weak	Weak	Average	High risk
Weak	Weak	Strong	High risk
Weak	Average	Weak	High risk
Weak	Average	Average	Medium risk
Weak	Average	Strong	Medium risk
Weak	Strong	Weak	Medium risk
Weak	Strong	Average	Medium risk
Weak	Strong	Strong	Low risk
Average	Weak	Weak	High risk
Average	Weak	Average	High risk
Average	Weak	Strong	Medium risk
Average	Average	Weak	Medium risk
Average	Average	Average	Medium risk
Average	Average	Strong	Medium risk
Average	Strong	Weak	Medium risk
Average	Strong	Average	Low risk
Average	Strong	Strong	Low risk
Strong	Weak	Weak	Medium risk
Strong	Weak	Average	Medium risk
Strong	Weak	Strong	Medium risk
Strong	Average	Weak	Medium risk
Strong	Average	Average	Medium risk
Strong	Average	Strong	Low risk
Strong	Strong	Weak	Low risk
Strong	Strong	Average	Low risk
Strong	Strong	Strong	Low risk

Table 5. The Set of Decision Rules for Rule Block 4

In the Rule Block 2 "Finance" there are three variables analyzed: monthly income, the length of employment and the type of employment contract. Based on set of decision rules in this rule block, the model evaluates a consumer's financial strength that has influence on their credibility. It is considered that each variable has different influence on the financial strength of the customer. Monthly income (values from 800 PLN to 5000 PLN) and length of employment (values from 0 to 15 years) are considered to have a positive influence on the financial stability of the customer (the higher value the better). Third variable – the type of employment contract, defines if the customer source of monthly income is stable. There are three types of the contracts specified: task job contract, limited duration contract, indefinite duration contract. The task job contract is considered to be the worst for the stability of the customer's income. The best contract is indefinite duration one.

In case of Rule Block 3 "Financial Security" there are following three variables analyzed: value of the car, net value of the apartment/house, value of other assets. The task of this rule block is to evaluate the loan collateral. The rules are constructed in such a way to analyze the positive influence of all three variables on financial security of the customer. In addition the net value of apartment/house is considered to have dominant role on the output of this rule block, as it is characterized by the highest value and stability than two other variables.

The outputs of rule blocks 1, 2, and 3 are considered as input variables to the Rule Block 4 "The Score". The model's output "The Score" is a variable representing a forecast of the financial situation of an audited consumer. As it was mentioned earlier in this section of chapter, the output variable ranges from 0 to 1, while it is assumed that there are three levels of risk: high risk for values smaller than 0.3, medium risk for values from 0.3 to 0.7, and low risk for values larger than 0.7.

The use of variables (financial and demographical – Figure 4) implemented in this research is consistent with the credit scoring applications in literature. Most authors mainly use age, education, employment/unemployment status, monthly income, and number of children in household in consumer credit scoring models (e.g.: Henley & Hand, 1996; Wiginton, 1980; Thomas, 2000; Tingting, 2006). As described in Section 2 of this chapter, most of the credit scoring applications are statistical models. One of the newest examples of a developed model is the probit model with nine variables (Tingting, 2006). The estimates for each variable in this model are as follows: if consumer was unemployed (1.4207), family income in $00,000 (-0.155), state property exemption in $0,000 (0.1802), if consumer is college-educated (-0.4677), age of consumer (-0.1541), if consumer is male (-0.3354), if consumer is married (-0.0693), if consumer is white (-0.1838), number of children (0.0401). The variables with negative estimates positively influence the risk of bankruptcy (the higher variable value the lower risk of going bankrupt) and variables with positive estimates negatively influence the risk of insolvency (the higher variable value the higher risk). From the form of the model it can be seen that education and status of employment were influencing the output of the model the most[3].

3.3 The results

Model was evaluated based on two types of errors and overall effectiveness:

[3] In the Tingting (2006) paper a few of the variables used seem controversial (e.g. taking the sex or race of a consumer under consideration in the credit scoring procedure).

- Error Type I - $E_1 = D_1$ / BR * 100%, where D_1 – number of consumers who did not repay the credit classified by the model as "good" clients, BR – number of "bad" consumers in the testing set;
- Error Type II - $E_2 = D_2$ / NBR * 100%, where D_2 – number of non-bankrupt consumers classified by the model as a "bad" clients, NBR – number of "good" consumers in the testing set;
- Overall effectiveness – $S = \{1 - [(D_1 + D_2) / (BR + NBR)]\} * 100\%$.

It is necessary to make a note that a I type error is much more costly than a II type error to make. I type error means that a bank classifies a bankrupt consumer as a non-bankrupt one. II type error means that a non-bankrupt entity is classified as a bankrupt one.

The results obtained from testing the developed model against the bankruptcy risk while testing dataset "one" and "two" are presented in Table 6.

Testing Type		Effectiveness
Testing dataset "One" (50 "bad" / 50 "good" consumers)	E1	10% (5 cases)
	E2	8% (4 cases)
	S	91%
Testing dataset "Two" (50 "bad" / 350 "good" consumers)	E1	10% (5 cases)
	E2	11.42% (40 cases)
	S	88.75%

Table 6. Results of Effectiveness of the Fuzzy Logic Model in Consumer Credit Scoring

In the case of testing dataset "one", it can be seen that the fuzzy logic model created evaluated 9 credit applications incorrectly. Among those, 5 cases concerned classification of consumers with the risk of insolvency as "good" borrowers, and remaining 4 mistakes where II type errors, which means that the model classified "good" credit applicants as the high risk operations. The overall effectiveness of this model obtained from that dataset was 91%.

Due to the equal distribution of "bad" and "good" consumers in testing dataset "one", the author treats this research approach as a theoretical possibility test of the predictive power of the method used. From the viewpoint of the practical applicability of the fuzzy logic model in business, the conclusions from the tests conducted on testing dataset "two", which contained 87.5% consumers with good financial condition and 12.5% consumers at risk of insolvency, are more important to analyze. When testing the model with such a proportion of „bad" and „good" consumers, the II type mistakes increased by 3.43 percentage points (from 8% to 11.42%). This caused the decrease of overall effectiveness of the model from 91% to 88.75%. Nevertheless such effectiveness can be rated as high. Unlike the models predicting bankruptcy of firms, it is difficult to conduct comparative analysis of effectiveness of models forecasting bankruptcy of consumers. Models used in literature are theoretical ones, or their authors do not provide results, or they are models for commercial use of restricted character. From the available research, the results of statistical models vary from 72 % (Tingting, 2006) to 77.5 % (Boyle et al., 1992) – figure 7. Comparing the overall effectiveness of the models found in literature to effectiveness of fuzzy logic model created by author, it can be seen that author's model is characterized by:

- 19 percentage points better effectiveness than Tingting's model (in case of balanced testing sample – 91% vs 72%),
- 13.5 percentage points better effectiveness than Boyle's model (in case of balanced testing sample - 91% vs 77.5%),
- 16.75 percentage points better effectiveness than Tingting's model (in case of unbalanced testing sample – 88.75% vs 72%),
- 11.25 percentage points better effectiveness than Boyle's model (in case of unbalanced testing sample – 88.75% vs 77.5%).

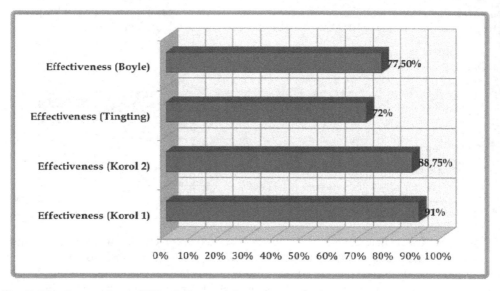

Fig. 7. The Comparison of Effectiveness of Fuzzy Logic Models

4. Business credit scoring model

4.1 Research assumptions

The author of this chapter has created 2 fuzzy logic models in order to verify the influence of the following aspects on the quality of the forecast:

- ability of a fuzzy logic model to predict bankruptcy of companies for one year, two years before,
- proportion of bankrupt and non-bankrupt companies in a testing setdata,
- comparison of the effectiveness of fuzzy logic with the most popular form among artificial intelligence methods – neural network model, and with the effectiveness of the first bankruptcy model of Altman created in 1968, which is still the most popular and widely used in the business world.

To conduct this research the author has used the financial statements of 185 Polish stock equity companies (135 non-bankrupt and 50 bankrupt) from the years 2000-2007. This population of firms was divided into:

- learning dataset - used for developing the models. There were 25 bankrupt companies and 28 non-bankrupt ones. Those 53 companies were from various sectors such as construction, metal industry, food processing, chemicals, telecommunications, etc.
- testing dataset "one" – used for testing the models created in conditions of an equal proportion of bankrupt and non-bankrupt firms. There were 29 "healthy" firms and 25 companies in danger of going bankrupt.
- testing dataset "two" – consisting of all the companies from testing dataset "one" with the addition of 78 non-bankrupt companies. This enabled testing the ability of the models created to identify bankrupt companies among non-bankrupt firms in the business practice in the proportion of 19%/81% ("25 bad enterprises"/"107 good enterprises").

All models were tested by testing dataset "one" and "two" for both two years prior to bankruptcy.

All companies were described by 14 calculated financial ratios for two years before bankruptcy. These ratios are presented in Table 7. Additionally, all firms were marked with 0-1 variables (0-bankrupt, 1-non-bankrupt). Both models were evaluated based on two types of errors and overall effectiveness using the same formulas as in the previous section of the chapter.

Ratio Symbol	Type of Ratio and Calculation Formula
	PROFITABILITY RATIOS
X1	Profit from sales / total assets
X2	Operating profit / revenues from sales
	LIQUIDITY RATIOS
X3	Current assets / short term liabilities
X4	[Current assets - inventories] / short term liabilities
X5	Working capital / total assets
	DEBT RATIOS
X6	Short term liabilities / total assets
X7	Equity / total credits
X8	(net profit + amortization) / Long term and short term liabilities
X10	Gross profit / short term liabilities
X11	(Stockholders equity + long term liabilities) / fixed assets
	ACTIVITY RATIOS
X9	Operating costs / short term liabilities
X12	Net revenues / total assets
X13	Net revenues / short term receivables
	OTHER RATIOS
X14	Log of total assets

Table 7. Financial Ratios Used in the Research

4.2 Early warning models for enterprises

Before programming the bankruptcy prediction models for both years prior to the insolvency of firms with the use of both methods (fuzzy logic and artificial neural networks), the author conducted a correlation analysis for all ratios from Table 7. The objective of this analysis was to choose ratios that were highly correlated with the score and at the same time had a low correlation between each other. The following ratios were taken into the models as entry data nodes:

- one year prior bankruptcy – X3_1, X8_1, X9_1, X10_1,
- two years prior bankruptcy – X1_2, X3_2, X5_2, X7_2, X8_2.

For each entry variable to the model, the author identified two fuzzy sets (which are subsets of a set of values of the entry variable): "positive" and "negative", and their corresponding membership functions. The fuzzy sets and the shape of membership functions have been arbitrarily designated by the author.

In order to set the critical values for membership functions in the models, the author calculated for all ratios the first and the third quartile, and median value separately for "good" and "bad" companies. The value of the third quartile of the "bad" firms was used as the threshold value for membership functions. These values are presented in Table 8.

Ratio Symbol	Threshold value for membership function
One year prior to bankruptcy	
X3_1	1.025
X8_1	0.03
X9_1	2.0
X10_1	(-0.1)
Two years prior to bankruptcy	
X1_2	0.02
X3_2	1.4
X5_2	0.14
X7_2	0.8
X8_2	0.102

Table 8. The Threshold Values for Membership Functions Used in Both Fuzzy Logic Models.

The set of rules used by the fuzzy decision model contains 16 rules for analysis of companies one year prior to bankruptcy and 25 rules for analysis with an increased period of forecast. Extending the length of prediction to two years prior to insolvency required supporting the models (both fuzzy logic and artificial neural networks) with a larger amount of financial information, i.e. financial ratios.

The structure of the fuzzy logic model created for one year and two years prior to bankruptcy is presented in Figure 8 (Figure 8 presents the use of financial ratios for two years analysis, in case of one year analysis the structure is the same, but used financial ratios are different – see table 8). The model consists of four inputs (financial ratios) in one year prior bankruptcy, five inputs (financial ratios) in two years prior financial failure and one rule block in both years. The model's output is a variable representing a forecast of the financial situation of an audited company. This variable ranges from 0 to 1, while it is assumed that the threshold value separating the "good" and "bad" companies is 0.5 (output variable values below 0,5 mean the company is at risk of bankruptcy, while those above 0.5 represent a company safe from bankruptcy). The final result generated by the fuzzy logic model is based on an assessment of four (one year analysis) and five financial ratios (two years analysis). The rule block in the model consists following set of rules for forecasting the economic situation in one year prior financial failure:

If X3_1 <= 1.025 and X8_1 <= 0.03 and X9_1 <= 2 and X10_1 <= (-0.1) then 0
If X3_1 <= 1.025 and X8_1 <= 0.03 and X9_1 <= 2 and X10_1 > (-0.1) then 0
If X3_1 <=1.025 and X8_1 <= 0.03 and X9_1 > 2 and X10_1 > (-0.1) then 0
If X3_1 <=1.025 and X8_1 > 0.03 and X9_1 > 2 and X10_1 > (-0.1) then 1
If X3_1 > 1.025 and X8_1 > 0.03 and X9_1 > 2 and X10_1 > (-0.1) then 1
If X3_1 > 1.025 and X8_1 > 0.03 and X9_1 > 2 and X10_1 <= (-0.1) then 1
If X3_1 > 1.025 and X8_1 > 0.03 and X9_1 <= 2 and X10_1 <= (-0.1) then 1
If X3_1 > 1.025 and X8_1 <= 0.03 and X9_1 <= 2 and X10_1 <= (-0.1) then 0
If X3_1 <=1.025 and X8_1 > 0.03 and X9_1 <= 2 and X10_1 <= (-0.1) then 0
If X3_1 <=1.025 and X8_1 <= 0.03 and X9_1 > 2 and X10_1 <= (-0.1) then 0
If X3_1 <=1.025 and X8_1 > 0.03 and X9_1 > 2 and X10_1 <= (-0.1) then 0
If X3_1 > 1.025 and X8_1 <= 0.03 and X9_1 > 2 and X10_1 > (-0.1) then 1
If X3_1 > 1.025 and X8_1 > 0.03 and X9_1 <= 2 and X10_1 > (-0.1) then 1
If X3_1 > 1.025 and X8_1 <= 0.03 and X9_1 <= 2 and X10_1 > (-0.1) then 0
If X3_1 > 1.025 and X8_1 <= 0.03 and X9_1 > 2 and X10_1 <= (-0.1) then 0
If X3_1 <=1.025 and X8_1 > 0.03 and X9_1 <= 2 and X10_1 > (-0.1) then 0

A set of rules for forecasting the economic situation of companies in two years prior to bankruptcy is as follows:

If X1_2 <= 0.02 and X5_2 <= 0.14 and X8_2 <= 0.102 and X3_2 <= 1.4 and X7_2 <= 0.8 then 0
If X1_2 <= 0.02 and X5_2 <= 0.14 and X8_2 <= 0.102 and X3_2 <= 1.4 and X7_2 > 0.8 then 0
If X1_2 <= 0.02 and X5_2 <= 0.14 and X8_2 <= 0.102 and X3_2 > 1.4 and X7_2 > 0.8 then 0
If X1_2 <= 0.02 and X5_2 <= 0.14 and X8_2 > 0.102 and X3_2 > 1.4 and X7_2 > 0.8 then 1
If X1_2 <= 0.02 and X5_2 > 0.14 and X8_2 > 0.102 and X3_2 > 1.4 and X7_2 > 0.8 then 1
If X1_2 > 0.02 and X5_2 > 0.14 and X8_2 > 0.102 and X3_2 > 1.4 and X7_2 > 0.8 then 1
If X1_2 <= 0.02 and X5_2 <= 0.14 and X8_2 > 0.102 and X3_2 <= 1.4 and X7_2 > 0.8 then 0
If X1_2 <= 0.02 and X5_2 > 0.14 and X8_2 <= 0.102 and X3_2 <= 1.4 and X7_2 > 0.8 then 0
If X1_2 > 0.02 and X5_2 <= 0.14 and X8_2 <= 0.102 and X3_2 <= 1.4 and X7_2 > 0.8 then 0
If X1_2 <= 0.02 and X5_2 <= 0.14 and X8_2 <= 0.102 and X3_2 > 1.4 and X7_2 <= 0.8 then 0
If X1_2 <= 0.02 and X5_2 <= 0.14 and X8_2 > 0.102 and X3_2 <= 1.4 and X7_2 <= 0.8 then 0
If X1_2 <= 0.02 and X5_2 > 0.14 and X8_2 <= 0.102 and X3_2 <= 1.4 and X7_2 <= 0.8 then 0
If X1_2 > 0.02 and X5_2 <= 0.14 and X8_2 <= 0.102 and X3_2 <= 1.4 and X7_2 <= 0.8 then 0
If X1_2 <= 0.02 and X5_2 > 0.14 and X8_2 > 0.102 and X3_2 > 1.4 and X7_2 <= 0.8 then 1
If X1_2 <= 0.02 and X5_2 <= 0.14 and X8_2 > 0.102 and X3_2 > 1.4 and X7_2 <= 0.8 then 0
If X1_2 <= 0.02 and X5_2 > 0.14 and X8_2 <= 0.102 and X3_2 > 1.4 and X7_2 <= 0.8 then 0
If X1_2 <= 0.02 and X5_2 > 0.14 and X8_2 > 0.102 and X3_2 <= 1.4 and X7_2 <= 0.8 then 0
If X1_2 > 0.02 and X5_2 <= 0.14 and X8_2 > 0.102 and X3_2 <= 1.4 and X7_2 <= 0.8 then 0
If X1_2 > 0.02 and X5_2 <= 0.14 and X8_2 <= 0.102 and X3_2 > 1.4 and X7_2 <= 0.8 then 0
If X1_2 > 0.02 and X5_2 <= 0.14 and X8_2 <= 0.102 and X3_2 > 1.4 and X7_2 > 0.8 then 1
If X1_2 > 0.02 and X5_2 > 0.14 and X8_2 <= 0.102 and X3_2 > 1.4 and X7_2 > 0.8 then 1
If X1_2 > 0.02 and X5_2 > 0.14 and X8_2 <= 0.102 and X3_2 <= 1.4 and X7_2 > 0.8 then 1
If X1_2 > 0.02 and X5_2 > 0.14 and X8_2 > 0.102 and X3_2 <= 1.4 and X7_2 <= 0.8 then 1
If X1_2 > 0.02 and X5_2 > 0.14 and X8_2 <= 0.102 and X3_2 > 1.4 and X7_2 <= 0.8 then 1
If X1_2 > 0.02 and X5_2 <= 0.14 and X8_2 > 0.102 and X3_2 > 1.4 and X7_2 > 0.8 then 1

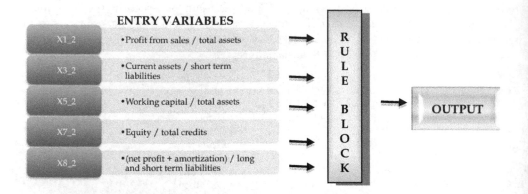

Fig. 8. The Complete Block Diagram of the Fuzzy Logic Model for Business Credit Scoring

The exemplary form of the membership functions are presented in Figure 9 for the variable "X3_2" and in Figure 10 for variable "X8_2".

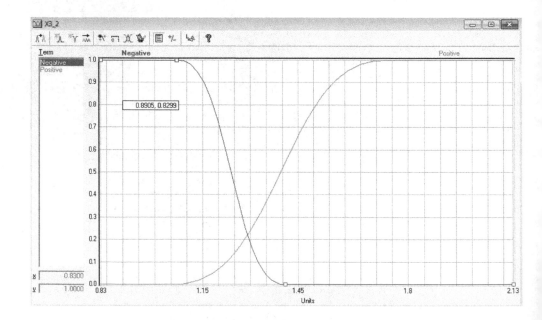

Fig. 9. Membership Functions for Variable "X3_2".

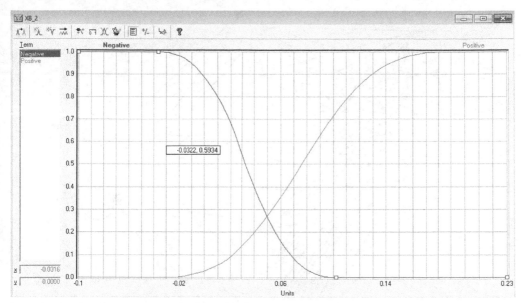

Fig. 10. Membership Functions for Variable "X8_2".

After creating the two fuzzy logic models the author, using the same financial ratios, programmed two artificial neural networks based on the same learning dataset. The aim of such a research approach is to compare the effectiveness of an innovative forecasting method in economics – fuzzy logic (until 2006, the use of fuzzy logic in finance and economics was practically unknown[4]), with the most popular method of soft computing techniques. By using the same population of enterprises to develop models, author is able to verify their effectiveness and to identify the most effective model.

The architecture of developed models by author of this chapter is as follows:

- one year prior to bankruptcy – 4 input neurons (financial ratios: X3_1, X8_1, X9_1, X10_1), 9 hidden neurons where mathematical calculations were made, and 2 output neurons (0 – bankrupt "BR", 1 – non-bankrupt "NBR"),
- two years prior to bankruptcy – 5 input neurons (financial ratios: X1_2, X3_2, X5_2, X7_2, X8_2), 10 hidden neurons, 2 output neurons (0 – bankrupt "BR", 1 – non-bankrupt "NBR") – Figure 11.

In the last stage of this research, the author analyzed the efficiency of the discriminant analysis model created by Altman in forecasting business bankruptcy one year and two years before, based on testing dataset "one" and "two". The form of this model can be found in Section 2 of this chapter. The aim of such comparison is to analyze the usefulness of the first bankruptcy model created in 1968 (which is still the most popular and widely used in the business world) on the same population of companies as in case of developed fuzzy logic and artificial neural network models.

---

[4] Author of this chapter has not found any papers on the use of fuzzy logic in forecasting bankruptcy of entities before 2006.

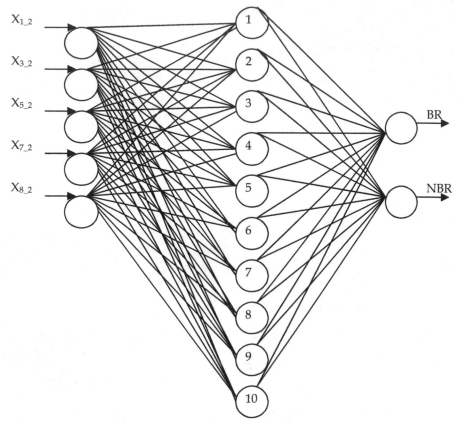

Fig. 11. Architecture of the Artificial Neural Network Model for Evaluating Polish Enterprises in the Analysis of Two Years Prior To Bankruptcy

4.3 The results

The results obtained from testing the two fuzzy logic models and two artificial neural networks developed against the bankruptcy risk of enterprises while testing dataset "one" and "two" are presented in Table 9.

The tests carried out on dataset "one" showed in the analysis one year prior to bankruptcy that the fuzzy logic model obtained 87.03% effectiveness. The same effectiveness was generated by the artificial neural networks model. Table 9 shows, however, that as the forecasting period increases to two years before bankruptcy, the fuzzy logic model is characterized by much better predictive properties than the artificial neural networks model (83.33% vs. 68.51%). In both years of analysis, the discriminant analysis model was worse than the fuzzy logic model (by 9.26 percentage points – one year before, and by as much as 18.52 percentage points – two years before) and artificial neural networks (by 9.26 percentage points – one year before, and by 3.7 percentage points – two years prior to bankruptcy). It is also necessary to point out that in the fuzzy logic model case the decrease of effectiveness with increased period of forecast is the smallest compared to the other two models. The effectiveness of the fuzzy logic model decreased by 3.7 percentage points (from 87.03% one year before bankruptcy to 83.33% two years prior to insolvency). In the case of the artificial neural network effectiveness decreased by 18.52 percentage points (from 87.03% to 68.51%) and in the case of the discriminant analysis model prediction quality decreased by 12.96 percentage points (from 77.77% to 64.81%).

Testing Type	Time	Effectiveness	Method		
			DA (Altman)	ANN (Korol)	FL (Korol)
Testing dataset "one" 25:29	One year before	E1	24% (6)	16% (4)	16% (4)
		E2	20.68 (6)	10.34% (3)	10.34% (3)
		S	77.77%	87.03%	87.03%
	Two years before	E1	28% (7)	24% (6)	4% (1)
		E2	41.37% (12)	37.93% (11)	27.58% (8)
		S	64.81%	68.51%	83.33%

Table 9. The Results of Effectiveness of Fuzzy Logic Model (FL), Artificial Neural Network (ANN) and Discriminant Analysis Model (DA) in Forecasting Business Bankruptcies (parentheses contain the number of misclassified firms).

Similarly at it was in case of consumer credit scoring, due to the equal distribution of bankrupt and non-bankrupt companies in the testing dataset "one", the author treats this research approach as a theoretical possibility test of the predictive power of methods used. From the viewpoint of the practical applicability of these methods in business, the conclusions from the tests conducted on testing dataset "two", which contained 81% companies with good financial condition and less than 19% firms at risk of insolvency, are more important to analyze. Figure 12 shows that in such circumstances, the fuzzy logic model achieved greater overall effectiveness:

- in the analysis one year prior to bankruptcy S1: by 8.34 percentage points better than artificial neural network and by 23.49 percentage points better than the discriminant analysis model (effectiveness: 81.06% vs. 72.72% and vs. 57.57%);
- in the analysis two years prior to bankruptcy S2: by 3.03 percentage points better than artificial neural network model and by as much as 15.90 percentage points better than the discriminant analysis model (effectiveness 65.90% vs. 62.87% and vs. 50%).

It is also worth mentioning that despite a small difference of overall effectiveness S2 in analysis of two years prior to bankruptcy between fuzzy logic model and artificial neural networks (65.90% vs. 62.87%) – figure 12, the artificial neural networks generated six times greater I type errors E1 than fuzzy logic model (24% vs. 4%), and discriminant analysis model made seven times greater errors of such type than fuzzy logic model (28% vs. 4%) – see figure 13. As it was explained before – such errors are much more costly to make by banks than II type errors. Figure 13 shows also that discriminant analysis model additionally generated much greater II type errors E2 than fuzzy logic and artificial neural networks.

Evaluating I type (E1) and II type (E2) errors in one year prior financial failure of enterprises, it can be said that discriminant analysis model made only 8 percentage points greater I type errors than both fuzzy logic and artificial neural network model (24% vs. 16%) – figure 14. But there is a huge difference in II type errors between analyzed models. Figure 14 shows that DA model generated as much as 46.72% of II type errors, while fuzzy logic model only 19.62%.

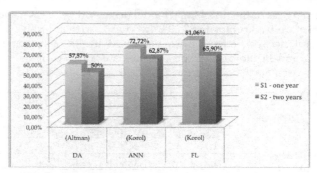

Fig. 12. The Results of Overall Effectiveness of Fuzzy Logic Model (FL), Artificial Neural Network (ANN) and Discriminant Analysis Model (DA) in Forecasting Business Bankruptcies – Testing Dataset "Two" – 25:107.

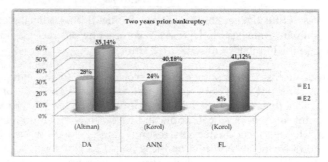

Fig. 13. The Results of Generated I and II Type Errors by Fuzzy Logic Model (FL), Artificial Neural Network (ANN) and Discriminant Analysis Model (DA) in Forecasting Business Bankruptcies – Testing Dataset "Two" – 25:107 – Two Years Prior Bankruptcy.

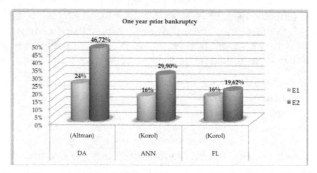

Fig. 14. The Results of Generated I and II Type Errors by Fuzzy Logic Model (FL), Artificial Neural Network (ANN) and Discriminant Analysis Model (DA) in Forecasting Business Bankruptcies – Testing Dataset "Two" – 25:107 – One Year Prior Bankruptcy.

The above conclusions regarding the overall effectiveness, I type and II type errors proved the superiority of developed fuzzy logic models for both years of analyses over the model of discriminant analysis and artificial neural networks.

5. Conclusions

The research conducted showed that it is worth developing such early warning models. All presented fuzzy logic models in the chapter are characterized by high forecasting effectiveness. The author has proven that fuzzy logic can be a very useful and powerful tool in financial analysis, even though the use of fuzzy logic in finance was practically unknown until 2006. Therefore, it is one of the first attempts at using fuzzy logic to predict enterprise and consumer bankruptcy in worldwide literature. The developed bankruptcy prediction models presented in this chapter can be easily used by financial managers as a decisional aid tool in the process of evaluating the financial situation of enterprises and consumers.

It should be emphasized that the fuzzy logic models presented have high practical values. Due to the fact that these models are an „open" application, a person interested in its use can not only use them in their current form, but can also easily modify them for their own needs. For example, a person managing an international company can add exchange rate as a risk factor to the model. The number of model adaptations is virtually unlimited by transforming the set of decision rules for individual needs.

The models presented are superior to even the sophisticated methods of artificial intelligence, such as artificial neural network models, not only in terms of effectiveness achieved, but also in terms of three aspects:

- explicit knowledge,
- ability to explain how to solve the problem (which is in opposition to the model of artificial neural network, which operates on the "black box" principle),
- quick and easy updates to changing economic conditions. In the case of statistical models and artificial intelligence models the desire to change the model involves the need to re-estimate the entire model.

It is necessary to note that the aim of this paper was to evaluate the efficiency of fuzzy logic model in forecasting the financial situation of companies and households and to give the reader "the opened" structure of fuzzy logic model, that can be easily adopted to changed economic situation in the country or even adopted for implementation in different country or region of the world. Therefore, despite the fact that the presented research (both consumer and business credit scoring) is based on financial data from the years 2000 – 2007, it is still valid (the value of variables used did not change significantly in the economy) and useful tool to use nowadays and in future with adopting individual variables (for example – the monthly income of customer etc.). To summarize, this chapter provides the reader with practical models that can be used in financial management. Such models are an useful tool that can be both updated with the passage of time, and adopted for individual needs.

The conclusions of these studies can also be applied to other European, American or Asian companies and consumers.

6. References

Agarwal, V. & Taffler, R. (2007). Twenty-five years of the Taffler z-score model – does it really have predictive ability? *Accounting and Business Research*, Vol. 37, No 4, 2007, pp. 285-300

Altman, E. & Rijken, H. (2006). A point-in-time perspective on through-the-cycle ratings, *Financial Analysts Journal*, No. 62/1, pp. 54-70

Altman, E. (1993). Corporate financial distress, *John Wiley & Sons*, New York

Aziz, M. & Dar, H. (2001). Predicting corporate bankruptcy – where we stand? *Corporate Governance Journal*, Vol. 6, No. 1, pp. 18-33

Bose, I. & Mahapatra, R. (2001). Business data mining – a machine learning perspective, *Information and Management Journal*, No. 39, pp. 211-225

Boyle, M.; Crook, J.; Hamilton, R. & Thomas L. (1992). Methods for credit scoring applied to slow payers, *Oxford University Press*, Oxford, pp. 75-90

Henley, W. & Hand, D. (1996). A k-NN classifier for assessing consumer credit risk, *The Statistician*, No. 65, pp. 77-95

Korol, T. (2011). Multi-Criteria Early Warning System Against Enterprise Bankruptcy Risk, *International Research Journal of Finance and Economics*, issue 61, pp. 141-154

Kumar, P. & Ravi, V. (2007). Bankruptcy prediction in banks and firms via statistical and intelligent techniques – a review, *European Journal of Operational Research*, No. 180, pp. 1-28

Mcleay, S. & Omar, A. (2000). The sensitivity of prediction models to the non-normality of bounded and unbounded financial ratios, *British Accounting Review*, No. 32, pp. 213-230

Nwogugu, M. (2007). Decision-making, risk and corporate governance – a critique of methodological issues in bankruptcy/recovery prediction models, *Applied Mathematics and Computation*, No. 185, pp. 178-196

Ooghe, H. & Balcaen, S. (2006). 35 years of studies on business failure – an overview of the classic statistical methodologies and their related problems, *The British Accounting Review*, No. 38, pp. 63-93

Thomas, L. (2000). Survey of credit and behavioural scoring – forecasting financial risk of lending to consumers, *International Journal of Forecasting*, No. 16, pp. 149-172

Tingting, J. (2006). Consumer credit delinquency and bankruptcy forecasting using advanced econometric modeling, *MPRA Paper*, No. 3187

Wiginton, J. (1980). A note on the comparison of logit and discriminant models of consumer credit behaviour, *Journal of Financial and Quantitative Analysis*, No. 15, pp. 757-770

Wilson, L. & Sharda, R. (1994). Bankruptcy prediction using neural networks, *Decision Support Systems*, No. 11, pp. 548-550

Zadeh, L. (1965). Fuzzy sets, *Information and Control*, No. 8 (3), pp. 338-353.

14

Fuzzy Modeling of Geospatial Patterns

Alejandra A. López-Caloca and Carmen Reyes
Centro de Investigación en Geografía y Geomática
"Jorge L. Tamayo" A.C., CentroGeo,
México

1. Introduction

In computer science, the design of intelligent systems able to manage uncertain, indefinite or incomplete information is called Soft Computing (Zadeh 1994). Its aim is to illustrate real problems that are not manageable by conventional techniques. The main techniques that compose Soft Computing are fuzzy logic, neural networks, evolutionary computing and probabilistics. The works published by Prof. Zadeh on fuzzy sets, fuzzy logic, fuzzy systems, neural networks, soft computing and computing with words have had applications in a great diversity of areas — computational modeling, optimizing, planning, control, geospatial analysis, image classification, prediction and image fusion.

Geospatial modeling and retrieving geographical information has become an important part of different areas of knowledge, such as environmental science, urban planning and criminal spatial patterns, among others. This work examines some of the fuzzy tools most commonly used in geospatial modeling for spatial analysis and image processing. We will present a family of models as an alternative to the fuzzy mathematical representation of spatial patterns. This chapter is primarily concerned with spatial pattern methodologies that attempt to describe the arrangement of phenomena in space. In most cases, these phenomena have either point or area features. Point and area analyses use randomness (or a lack of pattern) as a dividing point between two opposite pattern types — dispersed and clustered. This work also presents a general framework (fuzzy data fusion) to combine information from several individual classifications obtained from satellite images in order to recognize spatial patterns and improve spatial pattern extraction.

2. General framework

The principal ideas and concepts of fuzzy logic (FL), as shown by Zadeh, are that FL is a precise logic of uncertainty and approximate reasoning (Zadeh 1975, 1976). Zadeh (2010) notes two ideas that FL takes from human capabilities. The first refers to an environment of imperfect information that includes uncertainty, incompleteness of information, conflicting information, partiality of truth and partiality of possibility. The second relates to the capability to perform a wide variety of physical and mental tasks without any measurements or computations.

For example, when considering fuzzy concepts, we talk about the lack of sharp class boundaries. Thus, the starting point for FL is the fuzzy set concept, where a fuzzy set is a class with unsharp boundaries. FL deals with three basic concepts: graduation, granulation, and precisiation (Zadeh, 2010). The graduation concept is associated with scale- and membership-degree functions. The granulation concept is useful with regard to imprecision, uncertainty and complexity. For precisiation, two approximations are defined — precisiation and imprecisiation, where the former is based on measurements and the latter on perceptions. In fact, the precisiation of meaning has always played an important role in science. Therefore, graduation is related to precisiation and granulation to imprecisiation.

2.1 Geospatial modeling

The modeling of natural phenomena requires knowledge of the geographic landscape entities that can be conceptualized in space (places, axiomatic geometry, point-set topology, discrete space, raster/vector), spatial attributes and relations (dimension, connectivity, position, size, location, shape), thematic (natural and conventional objects, classifying objects, pattern recognition) and temporal forms (states, processes and dynamic events). The different fields — geography, biology, hydrology, geology, remote sensing, ecology, and others — select the most important aspects of a phenomenon, i.e., representative variables, to generate data (Jacquez et al., 2000) and perform modeling.

Natural objects that are characterized and define variables may be highly regular, in which a large number of cases are shown as an individual, easy-to-identify elements. Others, however, tend to be highly irregular, fragmented, fuzzier, and have boundaries that are difficult to describe (Galton, 2000). A natural pattern is generated by various processes at different space and time scales depending on the phenomena being investigated; hence the interest in fuzzy modeling for research to illustrate geographic problems (Altman, 1994; Usery 1996; Molenaar & Cheng, 2000, Croos & Firat, 2004, Guesgen, 2005).

Problems involving indeterminate boundaries — continuity, heterogeneity, dynamics, scale-dependence (Cheng, 2002; Burroughs, 1996) and contiguity — found in the very nature of objects are described below.

Continuity refers to continuous space, which is seamless, i.e., two regions are not separated but rather are distributed in a continuous way in space. In some cases, their distribution does not permit identifying a very precise border because neither the objects nor isolated processes exist. The problem is to represent these objects in a discrete space (Kavoras, 1996). The nature of the object influences how we become aware of the boundaries and their degree of sharpness (Erwig & Schneider, 1997).

Contiguity measurements evaluate the characteristics of spatial features that are connected, i.e., the evaluation of features that touch one another, that are near one another. Contiguity is desirable to reduce the negative environmental impact on forests, where forest patches affect interior forest habitats.

Spatial heterogeneity is the existence of each object or entity in relation to others, as well as the attributes and qualities of each one of them, and is determined at the moment of mutual interaction. This explains two or various types of vegetation existing in a forest zone and, therefore, describes a heterogeneity problem. The similarity or difference between an entity and its surrounding is a measure of this variation (Reyes-Guerrero, 1986).

Because dynamic geospatial processes and transformations occurring over long periods of time are not uniform, it is necessary to consider changes in their spatial attributes with their temporal dimensional. For example, geometric spatial changes are investigated with what is known as fuzzy change detection (Molenaar & Cheng , 2000). Different classes of spatial changes in frontier areas must be considered with respect to diverse observations at different times (changes in dimension, connectivity, size, shape and non-geometrical spatial attributes). These are often difficult to determine because of a lack of dimensions at the time they occur.

Objects are defined according to a geospatial scale and context. The observation is related to the scale at which the object is described (Couclelis, 1996). When having satellite images with different levels of spatial resolution, the identification of more classes will increase by having more detail on these images. The degree of uncertainty of many geographic objects, with respect to the scale of observation, is proposed on the basis of a neural network structure approach (Silván-Cardenas, 2008) and particular data representation models of objects with scale-induced indeterminate boundaries. Using this approach, fuzzy points and fuzzy lines are considered and the connection between the degree of fuzziness and the scale of representation is discussed.

Spatial data are important to diverse studies; in fact, new technology continually enables generating new data. A number of available methods are applied to spatial data, some of which include spatial classification. Nevertheless, difficulties exist that can be conceptualized and modeled with fuzzy concepts, for example, by eliminating strict ideas of encountering boundaries on the geographic objects studied.

In geo-modeling, the utilization of fuzzy concepts with uncertainty problems (Cheng, 2002, Cheng et al 2004) can be divided in four ways:

a. Spatial Incompleteness. Indetermination is related to objects that cannot be separated, or where there is a lack of information (incompleteness) and imprecision. This can be due to the particular information not covering a specific region or the definition of categories that only makes sense in certain parts of the space (e.g meteorological measurements); in remote sensing, for example, the presence of clouds and shadows on satellite images that do not obstruct observation of the zone.

b. Fuzziness. To construct better real-world models, it is necessary to understand the concept of fuzziness as unsharpness of class boundaries, as well as the role of precision in fuzzy borders. In regionalization studies, regions are defined so that every element in the study universe is distinguishable regardless of whether or not it belongs to the region. Geographical problems can undoubtedly benefit from the fuzzy definition. For example, in the study of urban areas, a characteristic of the city is its lack of clear-cut differences in residential areas as well as in land use, for which incorporating the definition of fuzzy regions is therefore more appropriate (Reyes-Guerrero, 1986).

c. Time Incoherence. Temporal uncertainty with respect to time is common when the phenomena observed occurs when precise knowledge is not available about the instant of such information, and it only can be approximated with certain measurements. The value of the information depends on time, since many observed phenomena have temporal space relations, such as vegetation-season.

d.   Other general problems to be considered regarding spatial data are the lack of data or of definition of the object studied, inexact data, inconsistent data from multiple sources, data processing errors, inadequate generalization operations, limitations in the spatial representation scheme and limitations in data acquisition technology (Burroughs, 1996).

3. Fuzzy spatial clustering

In general, cluster analysis involves a set of data in groups or clusters that is organized so that items in the same group are similar to each other and different from those in other groups. In spatial information in clustering, different types of clustering analyses have been studied, including spatial clustering (clustering of spatial points), regionalization (clustering with geographic contiguity constraints) and point pattern analysis (hot-spot detection with spatial scan statistics). The use of many of these techniques for hot-spot detection is relatively problematic for several reasons, including the relatively arbitrary definition of the number of clusters to be included and the procedures applied to draw hot-spot boundaries. These contour areas indicate high to low robbery occurrence and, therefore, respond to the demand for public safety or provide alternatives to precisely locate schools in geographic distribution plans.

Fuzzy clustering methods allow objects to belong to several clusters simultaneously with different degrees of membership; in this work, we used Fuzzy C-Means clustering (FCM), (Bezdek, 1973). FCM is a data clustering technique that considers each data point belonging to a cluster to a certain degree, as specified by a membership degree. Two geospatial models with different applications are presented—hot-spot crime detection and educational planning.

3.1 Spatial analysis of crime

By definition, a hot-spot is a geographic area that presents a greater concentration of events as compared to its surroundings. It is an important tool for the analysis of point data to describe criminal activities, their geospatial distribution, and especially trends—in order to determine zones more likely to have higher concentrations of criminal events. The algorithms utilized to define a hot-spot may vary significantly when determining optimal and representative clusters—i.e., an adequate grouping must be determined. Generally, analysts must examine a series of possible solutions to spatially determine the optimal configuration; for example, cases using known methods such as hard clustering.

The strict assignment of parameters in the hard-clustering algorithm prevents identifying the optimal number of groups and, therefore, the result is not always realistic. Grubesic (2006) focuses on fuzzy grouping in the case of delinquency.

In order to disclose spatial crime patterns, Lopez-Caloca et al. (2009) tested criminal spatial patterns in the Mexican city of Hermosillo, as well as moving robberies (vehicle theft and public transportation robbery), fixed robberies (household or commercial establishment robberies) and violent robberies. Geo-referenced data from police records are available for each of the events reported during 2005 and 2006. The advantage of fuzzy clusters is a closer estimation of the delimitation of boundaries based on the information, with which to analyze processes in the region.

The FCM algorithm utilized for this task is based on the minimization of the objective function (eq. 1), which represents the distance from any given data point to a cluster center, weighted by the membership grade of that data point. By iteration, the cluster centers and the membership grade are updated, and the objective function is minimized to find the best location of the clusters.

$$J_m = \sum_{j=1}^{C} \sum_{i=1}^{N} u_{ij}^{m} \left\| x_i - c_j \right\|^2 ,$$ (1)

where

$d_{ij} = | x_i - c_j |^2$, is the distances of the pattern x_i to the cluster centroid c_j,
$| |$ is any norm expressing the similarity between any measured data and the center,
u_{ij} is the degree of membership of x_i in the cluster j,
x_i is the i-th of d-dimensional measured data, c_j is the centroid of the cluster,
N is the number of data points,
C is the number of clusters, the parameter m is the weighted exponent for u_{ij} and controls the "fuzziness" of the resulting cluster,
m is any real number greater than 1 and is called the fuzzifier parameter, for which 2 is usually chosen.

Fuzzy partitioning is carried out through an iterative optimization of the objective function shown above, with the updating of membership u_{ij} and the cluster centers c_j by:

$$u_{ij} = \frac{1}{\sum_{u=1}^{C} \left(\left\| x_i - c_j \right\| / \left\| x_i - c_u \right\| \right)^{2/m-1}}$$ (2)

$$\text{where } c_j = \frac{\sum_{i=1}^{N} u_{ij}^{m} \cdot x_i}{\sum_{i=1}^{N} u_{ij}^{m}}$$

The algorithm is comprised of the following steps:

a. Initialize U (membership matrix), called the fuzzy partition matrix, where u_{ij} denotes the membership degree of a datum x_i to cluster i,

$$U = \left[u_{ij} \right] matrix, U^{(0)} ;$$

b. Compute the vectors of the center prototypes

$$C^{(k)} = \left[c_j \right] \text{ with } U^{(k)} ;$$

c. Compute the distances: D_{ijA}^2

$$D_{ijA}^2 = \left(x_i - c_j\right)^T A\left(x_i - c_j\right), \text{ a squared inner-product norm.}$$

Depending on the data and the application, different types of similarity measures may be used to identify classes, where the similarity measure controls how the clusters are formed. Some examples of values that can be used as similarity measures include distance, connectivity, and intensity;

d.   Update the partition matrix $U^{(k)}$, $U^{(k+1)}$;

e.   Iteration stop

$$\text{if } \left\| U^{(k+1)} - U^{(k)} \right\| < \varepsilon \text{ then STOP, otherwise return to step b.}$$

This will stop when $\max_{ij}\left\{\left\| u_{ij}^{(k+1)} - u_{ij}^{(k)} \right\|\right\} < \varepsilon$, where ε is a criterion between 0 and 1 (fuzzy membership), whereas k are the iteration steps.

Cluster validity refers to the algorithm problem that attempts to find the best fit for the fixed number of clusters and the parameterized cluster shapes. To perform validity measures, different indexes are calculated that indicate the level of partition (Xie et al. 1991). The indexes calculated are: Partition Coefficient (measures the amount of "overlapping" between clusters), Partition Index (the ratio of the sum of compactness and separation of the clusters), Classification entropy (basically a measurement of the fuzziness of the cluster partition only), Separation Index (the inverse of the partition index measurement), Xie and Beni's Index (aims to quantify the ratio of the total variation within clusters and the separation of clusters) and Dunn's Index (identifies compact and well-separated clusters)(Abonyi et al. 2003 & Balasto B et al. 2003). Table 1 shows the formulas for calculating each index.

The cluster algorithm also attempts to find the best fit for a fixed cluster number and initial conditions; nevertheless, this does not mean that the best fit is significant, since the cluster number could be incorrect. In the case of our data, Figure 1 shows the validation indexes for different fits for the cluster number. The strategy to follow to determine the appropriate cluster number is to calculate a large cluster number and reduce the number based on the data obtained from the validation indexes. It is worth mentioning that each index alone would not be very representative, therfore a set of validations indexes is considered. We take into account that the partitions with fewer groups are better, when the differences between validation values are less. The cluster partition properties are evaluated using PC, CE, SC and the Xie-Beni Index. Cluster properties such as compactness (or variation) and separation are evaluated using the Dunn Index.

Using the data for vehicle crime from 2005-2006 for 437 cases, the PC has a decreasing monotonic trend for C=4, 5 and CE has a monotonically increasing trend. For C=22, the S, SC and XB indexes arrive at their minimum values of de 0.0001, 0.0203 and 0.0025, respectively. The Dunn Index was 2.1038, the determination of the optimal number cluster was primarily based on the SC, DI, S and XB indexes, which affirms that the interpretation using different methods makes it possible to assign an optimal number to clusters.

Partition Coefficient (PC). The optimal number for the cluster corresponds to the maximum PC value. This index tends to decrease, losing a direct connection with the data.

$$PC(c) = \frac{1}{N} \sum_{i=1}^{C} \sum_{j=1}^{N} \left(u_{ij}\right)^2$$ where u_{ij} is the membership of data point j in the cluster, c is the cluster partitions.

Classification Entropy (CE). This index tends to increase until it remains at similar values.

$$CE(c) = -\frac{1}{N} \sum_{i=1}^{c} \sum_{j=1}^{N} u_{ij} \log\left(u_{ij}\right)$$

Partition Index (SC). A lower SC value indicates a better partition.

$$SC(c) = \sum_{i=1}^{C} \frac{\sum_{j=1}^{N} u_{ij}^m \left\|x_j - v_i\right\|^2}{N_i \sum_{k=1}^{C} \left\|x_k - v_i\right\|^2}$$ where v_i is the cluster center of the j-th cluster

Separation Index (S). The more the clusters are separated, the smaller is S, indicating an optimal value for the partition.

$$S(c) = \sum_{i=1}^{C} \frac{\sum_{j=1}^{N} (u_{ij})^2 \left\|x_j - v_i\right\|^2}{N \min_{i,k} \left\|x_k - v_i\right\|^2}$$

Xie and Beni's Index (XB). The optimal number of clusters should minimize the value of the index.

$$XB(c) = \sum_{i=1}^{C} \frac{\sum_{j=1}^{N} (u_{ij})^m \left\|x_j - v_i\right\|^2}{N \min_{i,j} \left\|x_k - v_i\right\|^2}$$

Dunn's Index. To define the optimal number for the cluster, the maximum value for the DI must be obtained.

$$DI(c) = \min_{j \in c} \left\{ \min_{j \in c, i \neq j} \left\{ \frac{\min_{x \in C_i} d(x,y)}{\max_{k \in c} \left\{ \max_{x,y \in} c^d(x,y) \right\}} \right\} \right\}$$

where d is a distance function

Table 1. Different validation measurements proposed in the literature.

Figure 2 (left image) shows a vehicle crime data set for the city of Hermosillo, with the result shown on the city-block network. The right image shows the optimal partition solution, as well as the membership gradient for each cluster. A close-up is represented in Figure 2, where we can see the zones with more crime — streets and areas that need more public safety measures.

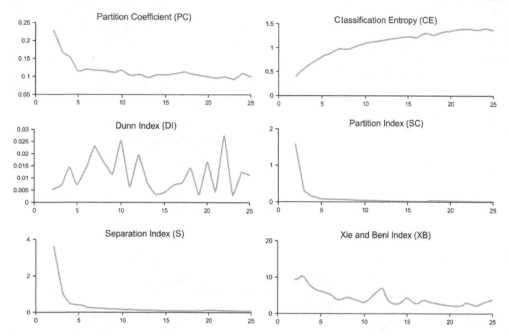

Fig. 1. These graphs show the PC, CE, SC, DI, S and XB indexes. The analysis of all of these makes it possible to determine how many clusters are to be represented.

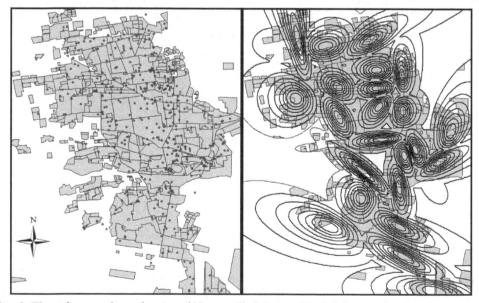

Fig. 2. These figures show the city of Hermosillo Mexico. The left image shows a data set related to vehicle crime; the right image shows the result obtained, of 22 clusters. Data are displayed over the city-block network.

The crime event is dynamic, thus a more detailed study is needed to consider the temporal portion of the data (months, weeks and days). The membership geovisualization method used was a Sammon mapping (Sammon, 1969), which preserves inter-pattern distances using the Euclidian interpoint distance norm.

$$S_{sammon} = \frac{1}{\sum_{i<j} d_{ij}} \sum_{i<j} \frac{\left(d_{ij} - D_{ij}\right)^2}{d_{ij}}$$

where d_{ij} represents the proximity of point data i and j in the original data space and D_{ij} represents the Euclidian distance between mapped points i and j in the projected space. The project is nonlinear and the stress function is defined as:

$$\sum_{i<j} \frac{\left(d_{ij} - D_{ij}\right)^2}{d_{ij}}$$

Figure 3 shows the geovisualization of the data, where the map's contours are drawn using the selection of membership groups with similar partition values. The areas with greater

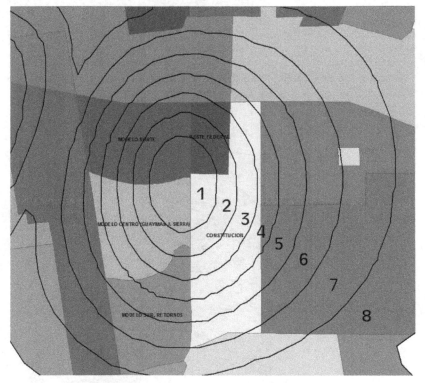

Fig. 3. Geo-projection result of Sammon's mapping. Close-up of hot-spots generated for vehicle crime during 2005-2006. The hot-spot map identifies places and neighborhoods needing measures to resolve public safety concerns, with different degrees of urgency.

membership are assigned a value of 1. As the values move away from the ideal value or the center of the set, decreasing values are assigned on a continuous scale from 1 to 0. The values found in the transition zone are shown as intermediate contours. It can be seen that there are up to four blocks in one cluster (representation of the urban region of the city of Hermosillo). Considering the transition contours and regional representations related to stolen vehicles enables defining better strategies to address the problem. The figure numerically shows the monitoring zones according to different degrees of urgency.

In practice, data for different criminal acts can occur at any time; the data are dynamic and changing. Working with fuzzy hot-spot information makes it possible to consider a spatial distribution with grades of membership, enabling administrators and professionals in crime prevention to use the data as a detection strategy as well as to spatially identify different priority zones, taking into greater account urban geographic spaces.

3.2 School infrastructure analysis

One factor in the level of development of a society is the degree of education. The topic of education has two spatial aspects: first, the identification of zones covered by elementary schools (primary and secondary school categories) and second, the identification of the deficit, based on the comparison of the number of allotments offered versus the population density throughout the zone.

Figure 4 shows the areas in terms of the presence of private and public elementary schools in the Alvaro Obregon district of Mexico City. In fuzzy clustering, the data points for the primary location may belong to more than one cluster, and associated with each of the points are membership grades indicating the degree to which the data points belong to the different clusters.

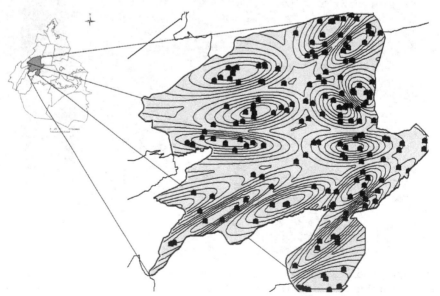

Fig. 4. The Alvaro Obregon district in Mexico City. Zones with elementary school coverage.

The membership zones obtained with fuzzy clusters indicate that 13 areas are benefited by schools. The validation of the optimal clusters is shown in Figure 5. PC has a decreasing monotonic trend and CE has an increasing monotonic trend, representing the increase in the cluster number. In both cases, the connection with the data structure is not direct. SC, S and XB have values of 0.0003, 0.0341 and 1.8785, respectively, and arrive at a local minimum. The DI has a maximum value of 0.524 and affirms the number C=13. With the different methods of analysis, 13 is chosen as the optimal cluster number.

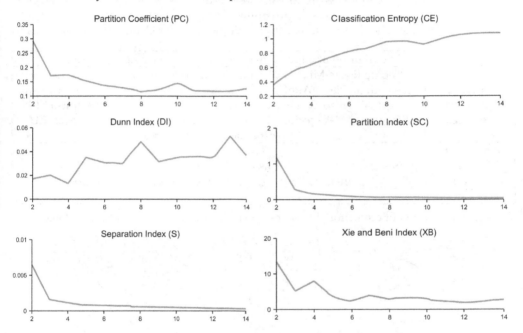

Fig. 5. Graphic representation of the validation index values used to find the optimal cluster number.

To identify service offerings and demand, and whether they are sufficient, the spatial distribution of the population density was analyzed. The 3 highest membership levels next to 1 were determined for the number of children between 6 and 12 years of age located in this zone. The results show the fact that the educational establishments are not spatially distributed according to the population density of these children, and that the potential population of children between 1 and 4 years of age calls for increasing these services in the future. Zones with low membership are sectors where measures could be taken to avoid this school deficit (Table 2). The results shown in Table 2 indicate that this type of analysis enables defining the geospatial problematic at the neighborhood as well as the street level.

The FL tool is fundamental to strategies for locating elementary schools to improve services. A study of this type must take into account the number allotments offered by the educational institution.

The area of influence of an educational establishment does not necessarily have a circumferential shape. But the existence of topographic and geographic borders must also be considered because they sometimes constitute significant limitations in identifying a student's route to his or her school. A diagnostic for the student's travel distance network is shown by Reyes-Guerrero (1986), who defines the degree of membership in a class for each one of the nodes on the graph (nodes represent the elements that belongs to each region), making it possible to define neighborhood relationships.

Figure 6 represents the analysis of distance from cluster centers, considering which of the clusters with greater school density are in closer proximity to each other. This analysis makes it possible to prevent excessive proximity in order to avoid, as much as possible, a spatially inadequate school distribution. In fact, the demand for elementary schools was so

	Distribution of educational services. (Alvaro Obregon, Mexico City)
Areas with current educational services	Molino de Rosas-Mixcoac; Molino de Santo Domingo-Acueducto; Olivar de los Padres; Piloto Adolfo López Mateos; Pueblo Santa Fe-Gamitos; San Angel –Pogreso; San Bartolo Ameyalco; Torres de Potrero; Alfonso XIII; Bosques 1A-2A seccion; Ceguayo-Cuevitas; Jardines del Pedregal- CU; Jardines del Pedregal-Loreto
Areas with deficit of educational services	Presidentes - Golondrinas – Lomas de Capula; Colinas de Tarango – Lomas de Tarango; San Clemente norte y sur; Cedros

Table 2. Distribution of educational services for children between 6 and 12 years of age.

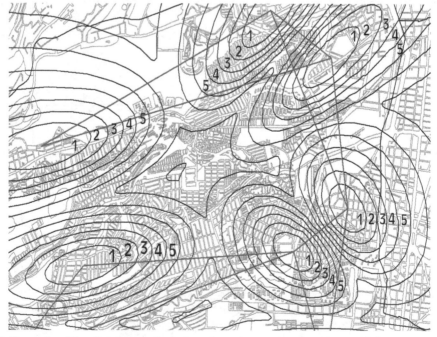

Fig. 6. Example of the distance analysis based on cluster centers; zones with less membership represent those with low elementary school coverage for the population.

great that establishing one was considered beneficial to the local community. Identifying the precise location of the school is now important. Educational planning requires a geographic distribution study of the current density of schools.

4. Fuzzy-based data fusion model

Though the concept of data fusion is easy to understand, it varies from study to another. Data fusion has also been referred to as merging, combination, synergy and integration. In terms of formal data fusion tasks, it is desirable to design an architecture that combines information from different sources, thus obtaining high-quality information. Current fusion methods utilize tools such as weighted average, neural networks (multi-sensory fusion), rules-based knowledge, wavelets (multiresolution fusion), graph pyramids, and more recently, fuzzy logic. Data fusion is frequently described in literature as occurring on three levels: pixel, attribute and decision (Pohl et al. 1998, Wald 2002, López-Caloca 2006). A general idea about how different authors handle these fusion levels is described below.

a.   Pixel level. Images come from different sources, which are combined from pixel to pixel. The fusion process should preserve the relevant information from the entered images on the synthetic image (pattern preservation). Although the word "pixel" is not really adequate, the pixel is the basis for the information and does not have semantic meaning.
b.   Attribute level. The figures (geometric, structural or spectral) are drawn from crude images and fused afterwards. Fusion at the figure level requires recognizable objects extracted from diverse data sources using a segmentation process. The figures correspond to characteristics extracted from the initial images, such that they provide form; selection is based on the practical use of the application. The classified maps are combined and the spacial information related to each pixel's neighbor is taken into account in order to improve the fit.
c.   Decision level. Decision fusion can be defined as the process of fusing information from several individual data sources after each data source has undergone a preliminary classification. The results of classification are combined by using their weighted significance.

For hard classifiers, image pixels are assigned to a given category, although errors in pixel classifications exist (pixels that may belong to a different category). When assigning a pixel to a class, there is a risk of it being assigned to a class to which it does not belong (misclassified) or pixels may be over-classified. Fuzzy classification considers that one category admits a property between 0 and 1. The idea is to permit simultaneous assignment to various categories with different degrees of property, and later reclassify the fuzzy boundaries.

The fuzzy classification problem has been extensively studied in remote sensing (Lizarazo & Elsner, 2011, Amici et al. ,2004). A fuzzy classifier is mainly applied when the data have a high degree of spectral mixture. Shackelford and Davis (2003) present a fuzzy logic classifier and object-based approach. The individual pixels in the image are first classified with a fuzzy classifier, making use of both spectral and spatial information. The segmented image is then used with additional object feature information to classify the image objects. Huntsherger (1985) described the application of the technique, called iterative fuzzy clustering, with the aim that the segmentation process not be affected by noise and degradation from image acquisition. Likewise, combinations such as fuzzy-support vector machine (F2-SVM) (Borasca, 2006) enable demodulating the relations between one pattern and the proposed classes in the F2-SVM framework. Other classification approaches attempt to take advantage of the strengths of each algorithm. For example, in the combination of two techniques—fuzzy topology and the Maximum Likelihood Classifier (MLC) (Liu et al., 2011), known as FTMLC—one membership function is created for each pixel using FTMLC and the pixels with greater membership are assigned a certain class, while those with less membership are left at the boundaries for a later process. Connectivity is sought for pixels at the boundaries with respect to their 8 neighbors, in such a manner that the one with the higher number of connected pixels belongs to that class. As a result, pixels on fuzzy borders are re-classified and, therefore, are given a higher assignment.

In the search for better solutions to problems of imprecise information, data fusion emerges as an alternate tool which, for example, can use the strengths of different classifiers in order to obtain a better approximation, with the resulting classification proportions resulting in less redundancy and complementary information.

The aggregation of information from multiple sources using a fuzzy system requires specifying the value of the input variable, membership functions and production rules (Klein, 2004, Raol, 2011). Each data source furnishes one or various admissions. An expert develops the standards specifying the outlet actions in terms of fuzzy sets, combinations of fuzzy input, and the definition of property functions that define the property of the fuzzy sets for output.

Fusion tasks at the pixel level have applied FL and neural fuzzy algorithms (Zhao et al., 2005, Meitzler, 2002, Singh, 2004). Their implementation considers two or more admission images for the fuzzy method. The implementation is carried out by assigning the admission variables with the same image size, deciding the number and type of functions for membership to the admission images, applying the fuzzy action using the rules developed in the pixel values of each admission image—which provides a fuzzy set represented by a membership function—and, lastly, applying the defuzzification of the outlet image.

In the fusion framework at the decision level, fuzzy algorithms have also been successfully used in various applications. Chanussot et al. (1999) propose a variety of strategies to combine images based on fuzzy fusion techniques with the aim of drawing roads. As in the case of fuzzy modeling, they combine the results from various detectors of boundaries. The neural-fuzzy-fusion method (NFF) combines a set of fuzzy classifiers in a system called a multiple classifier system (MCS). The application of this method to remote sensing images has demonstrated that the NFF-MCS produces good results (Shankar et al., 2006).

Support vector machines (SVM) have been applied to different classification problems (Mounrakis et al., 2010). The precision of these generally surpasses conventional algorithms. Fauvel et al. (2006, 2007) conducted fusion processes by combining spectral and spatial information. While the SVM enables working with the spectral information of an image, the spatial information is defined by means of morphological profiles, with the fusion process performed using different voting schemes (for example, absolute maximum and majority voting). Mathieu Fauvel et al. (2007) discuss the optimization of classifications of urban zones with high-resolution images, considering the use of various classifiers (conjugate gradient neural network and a fuzzy classifier). The inputs for the fusion process were the posterior probabilities from the outputs of the neural network and the membership degrees for the fuzzy classifier; i.e., the methodology consists of processing the data with each classifier alone and assigning to the algorithms each pixel's grade of membership for the classes considered. Then, the combination rule from the fuzzy decision is utilized to combine the results furnished by the algorithms, in accordance with the capabilities of the classifiers used. When modeling the output classifier, such as a fuzzy set, certainty is measured by the grade of uncertainty and the estimates of the global exactness of each classifier. The results can integrate a good deal of complementary information for the final classification process.

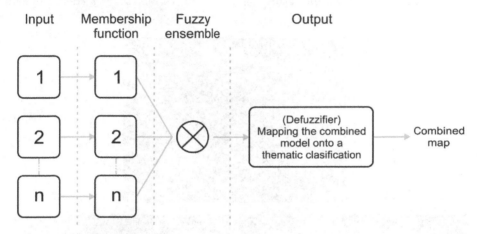

Fig. 7. Experimental fuzzy fusion scheme

Figure 7 shows a proposed fuzzy fusion technique. Images were classified with the Support Vector Machine (SVM) algorithm. In SVM, a function set is analyzed with this classifier, in such a manner that the function is approximated with less discrepancy between the a priori knowledge and the training data. Classes are divided in feature space; SVM separates two class sets by means of a hyper-plane (H) of linear or nonlinear functions. Available kernels include linear, polynomial, radial basis function and sigmoid. The kernel transformation allows for finding a new feature space in which linear hyper-planes are appropriate for class separation. In order to avoid or minimize the former errors, at the moment of adjusting the data it searches for the Structural Risk Minimization (SRM). In this work, two kernels were utilized — sigmoid and polynomial. The literature reports that both segmentation results present high precision. For the purposes of this task, the fusion of both segmentation results and the application of our proposed fuzzy fusion techniques are proposed. The resulting SVM classifications furnish redundant and complementary results. The methodology consists of data processing with each classifier and assigning each pixel's membership grade to the algorithms for the classes being considered; these are the inputs in the fusion process. The classified images were re-mapped into membership values ranging from 0 to 1, using a specified fuzzy function; in this case, a linear transformation.

The fuzzy fusion technique is used to combine two or more fuzzy membership results using fuzzy as a simple operator to create, in the case of suitability, the most suitable model. The fuzzy sets A and B will return the minimum value of the sets of cells located at the standard intersection $(A \cap B)(x) = \min [A(x), B(x)]$. Finally, the defuzzification action is conducted by assigning the segmented regions to each class. Defuzzification is a process that converts a fuzzy set or fuzzy number into a crisp value or number.

The proposed method represented in Figure 7 is applied using images in Figure 8. For the purpose of evaluating the combination of elements extracted during the segmentation process, segmentation with SVM (sigmoid) was applied to images 8B and 8C. These images consist of information with little definition, but include complementary information. Fuzzy fusion was applied later, and the result was evaluated with the segmentation of reference image 8A.

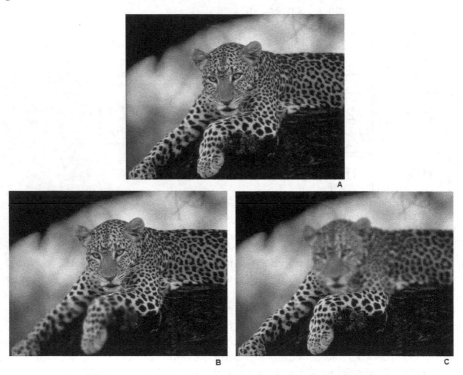

Fig. 8. Original images. A) reference, B) Image degraded in the leopard's extremities and C) image degraded in the face of the leopard. (Image example, Barnea & Hassner, 2006).

All images were segmented into 6 classes (Figure 9) that define the background of the image and the leopard shape (spots, face, skin), where image C is a classified reference image, A and B are classified results of the images with lack of sharpness and information, image D is a result of applying the fusion images from A and B using the fuzzy methodology. The segmentation accuracy (SA) was calculated, which is defined as the percentage of the number of correctly classified pixels to the total number of pixels. The well-classified pixels were considered using reference image C. The SA for image A was 89.60%; the SA for image B, 83.12%, and finally, the SA for the fusion image D was 87.14%.

This approach enables combining objects extracted after the segmentation process, improving the class boundaries and thereby having better knowledge of the objects observed when all the information is not originally available. The method was also applied with SPOT-5 satellite images.

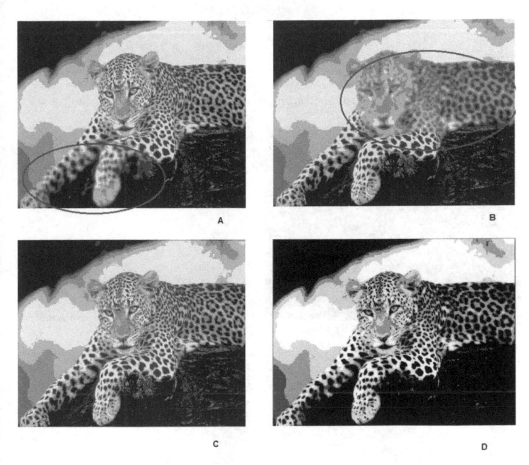

Fig. 9. A) and B): Images with less information are shown inside circular areas with less information, C) reference image and D) image fusion result.

We mentioned previously the interest in the fusion of images using fuzzy tools and applying them to remote sensing images. Fuzzy fusion techniques enable alleviating the problem of improving real and complex classifications as well as improving and complementing information. This approach shows the fusion of two SVM classifications by applying the sigmoid and polynomial kernels to a SPOT image with a landscape representative of an agricultural area. These results are shown in Figure 9B and 9C, with the fusion shown in 9D.

In order to conduct quantitative comparisons of the two algorithms, the concept of uniformity (Levine & Nazif, 1985, Cheng-Chia et al. 1997) was applied. This method is applied when a reference image or real data do not exist. Let I be the segmented image and S_I the area of the entire image. R_i denotes the set of pixels in region i. The uniformity of a segmentation result is defined by:

$$U = 1 - \frac{\sum_{i=1}^{S} \sigma_i}{K} \tag{3}$$

where S is the number of classes, σ^2 denotes i within-class variance of the i-th class, K is a normalization factor that limits the maximum value of the measurement to 1. We find that the proposed fuzzy fusion method obtains a similar uniformity value (0.889) with respect to

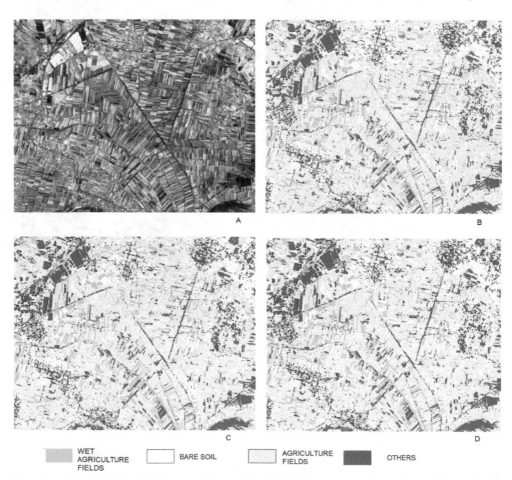

Fig. 10. A) Original, B) SVM (sigmoid kernel), C) SVM (polynomial kernel) and D) fuzzy fusion result

the other SVM classifiers (sigmoid and polynomial kernel), which obtain uniformity values of (0.840). One last measurement that can be performed with the error of the results is the verification process, by calculating overall reliability. Photo interpretation was used, such as real land — as well as the verification of maps classified based on the definition of proposed thematic categories (agriculture fields, bare land, among others). The overall reliability was 84.8% for SVM (sigmoid), 83.9% for SVM (polynomial), and lastly, 84.4% for the fuzzy technique. The results indicate that fuzzy fusion has an acceptable thematic quality and may be an alternative to integrate information, in this example, and to obtain well-defined images.

This section illustrates a simple fusion model with the application of fuzzy concepts, shows its function in providing complementary information (Figure 9) and presents another example applied to geospatial data (Figure 10), such as thematic classification maps obtained from a single satellite image, which can be combined to reduce uncertainty. With this example, we demonstrate that fusion along with fuzzy techniques make it possible to model spatial properties.

5. Conclusion

This work demonstrated the advantages of utilizing fuzzy methods for spatial analysis and image processing applications. For crime analysis, we were able to identify patterns by looking at the geography of the incidents and identifying hot-spots. Zones with a high spatial concentration of schools were also identified, as well as the existence of geographic areas needing this service. Finally, the application of fuzzy fusion enabled combining information within the framework of fuzzy modeling in order to improve and complete information, as is the case when using different classifiers.

It is therefore possible to conclude from these examples that the models designed and applied in this work allowed us to identify different aspects of spatial patterns, where the main elements of the study were part of the geographical landscape.

For geospatial analysis, the challenge to explore more applications with fuzzy methodologies continues to evolve. In the next phase, other elements of geospatial structures could naturally be explored, such as the causes of certain phenomena in the regions where crime occurs, in educational planning or in the functioning of social urban processes. The generation of robust scientific knowledge is needed in order to address problems that in the past have not been possible to study with non-fuzzy computational algorithms.

Although several mathematical models have been designed for geospatial applications, topological concepts and geographic neighborhood models using fuzzy set tools have received little attention in the area of modeling. Future work will integrate the idea of fuzzy topology proposed by Reyes-Guerrero (1986) to include the topological space as a new mathematical structure, applying the design of fusion and classification algorithms to topology, contiguity and the degree of membership to a border or interior region.

6. Acknowledgment

The authors thank to Dr. Elvia Martínez, José Manuel Madrigal, Camilo Caudillo and José Luis López, Rafael García for their contributions to this work.

7. References

Abonyi J & Szeifert F.,(2003), Supervised fuzzy clustering for the identification of fuzzy classifiers, *Pattern Recognition Letters*, Vol. 24, No.14, pp. 2195-2207.

Altman D.(1994), Fuzzy set theoretic approches for handling imprecision in spatial analysis, *Int. J. Geographical Information systems*, Vol.8, No.3, pp.271-289.

Amici G., Dell'Acqua F., Gamba P., and Pulina G., (2004), A comparison of fuzzy and neuro-fuzzy data fusion for flooded area mapping using SAR images, *International Journal of Remote Sensing*, vol. 25, no. 20, pp. 4425–4430.

Barnea A. and Hassner T. (2004-2006) Image example Available from: http://www.wisdom.weizmann.ac.il/~vision/alumni/hassner/Fusion/#examples

Balasto B., Abonyi J., and Feil B., (2003), Fuzzy Clustering and Data Analysis toolbox, for use with matlab, Veszprem University, Hungary , Available from: http://www.mathworks.com/matlabcentral/fileexchange/7473.

Bezdek J.C., (1973), Fuzzy mathematics in pattern classification, Ph.D. dissertation, Cornell Univ., Itheca, NY.

Borasca, B.; Bruzzone, L.; Carlin, L.; Zusi, M. (2006), A fuzzy-input fuzzy-output SVM technique for classification of hyperspectral remote sensing images, In *Signal Processing Symposium*, NORSIG 2006. Proceedings of the 7th Nordic, pp. 2-5,ISBN:1-4244-0412-6.

Burrough P.A. (1996), Natural Object with indeterminate Boundaries, *In Geographic objects with indeterminate boundaries*. GISDATA2, Edited Burrough P.A. & Frank A.U., Series Editors Masser I. and Salgé F. Taylor & Francis. Printed in Great Britain. ISBN 0-7484-0386-8, p. 3,71.

Chanussot J, Mauris G, Lambert P., (1999), Fuzzy fusion techniques for linear features detection in multitemporal SAR images, *IEEE Trans Geosci Remote Sens*. Vol.37, No.3, pp. 2287–2297.

Cheng T., (2002), Fuzzy Objects: Their Changes and Uncertainties, *Photogrammetric Engineering & Remote Sensing,*. Vol. 68, No. 1, pp. 41-49.

Cheng T., Fisher P & Zhilin L.,(2004) Double vagueness: uncertainty in multi-scale fuzzy assignment of duneness , *Geo-Spatial Information Science* ,volume 7, Number 1, 58-66, DOI: 10.1007/BF02826677.

Cheng-Chia Chang, Ling-Ling Wang, (1997), A fast multilevel thresholding method based on lowpass and highpass filtering, *Pattern Recognition Letters* , Vol. 18, pp. 1469–1478

Couclelis H., (1996), Toward an operational typology of geographic entities with ill-defined boundaries. In:. *Geographic objects with indeterminate boundaries*, Burrough P.A. & Frank A.U. , (Eds), pp. 71–85, (London: Taylor & Francis). Cross V., Firat A., (2000), Fuzzy objects for geographical information systems, *Fuzzy Sets and Systems* , Vol. 113,pp 19-36.

Erwig M., & Schneider M, (1997), Vague Regions, In: *5th Int. Symp. on Advances in Spatial Databases (SSD'97)*, LNCS 1262, 298-320

Fauvel, M. Chanussot, J. Benediktsson, J.A. , (2006), Decision Fusion for the Classification of Urban Remote Sensing Images, *IEEE Transactions on Geoscience and Remote Sensing*, Vol. 44 , No.10, pp. 2828 – 2838,

Fauvel, M. Chanussot, J. Benediktsson, J.A. ,(2007), Decision fusion for hyperspectral classification, In *Hyperspectral data exploitation, theory and application*, edited by Chang C.I., , pp.315-351. John wiley & Sons,Inc, ISBN:978-0-471-74697-3

Galton A., (2000), In Qualitative Spatial Change pp.121,129. Oxford University press. ISBN 0-19-823397-3. New York.

Grubesic T.H.,(2006),On the Aplication of Fuzzy Clustering for Crime Hot Spot Detection, *Journal of Quantitave Criminology*, Vol. 22, No 1.,pp. 77-105.

Guesgen H.W., Fuzzy Reasoning about Geographic Regions, (2005),*In Fuzzy Modeling with Spatial Informationfor Geographic Problems* , Editors: Petry F.E., Robinson V.B., Cobb M.A., pp.1-14, Springer Berlin Heidelberg, ISBN 3-540-23713-5 , New York.

Huntsherger T.L., Jacobs C.L., Cannon R.L.,(1985), Iterative fuzzy image segmentation *Pattern Recognition*, Vol. 18, No. 2, pp. 131-138 .

Jacquez G.M., Maruca S.,Fortin M.J.,(2000), From fields to objects: A review of geographic boundary analysis. *J. Geograph Syst*, Vol.2, pp.221-241.

Kavoras M.,(1996), Geoscience modeling: from Continuous fields to entities, *In Geographic objects with indeterminate boundaries*. GISDATA2, Series Editors Ian Masser and Francois Salgé. Taylor & Francis. V, ISBN 0-7484-0386-8, Great Britain.

Klein L.A.(2004), In Sensor and Data Fusion. A tool for information assessment and decision Making. *SPIE* Press, Bellingham, pp. 258-259, 296. ISBN 0-8194-5435-4, Washington USA.

Levine, M.D., Nazif, A.M., 1985. Dynamic measurement of computer generated image segmentation, *IEEE Trans. Pattern Anal. Machine Intell*. Vol. 7, No.2,pp.155–164.

Liu K., Shi W., Zhang H.,(2011), A fuzzy topology-based maximum likelihood classification, *ISPRS Journal of Photogrammetry and Remote Sensing*, Vol.66, pp. 103–114.

Lizarazo I. & Elsner P., (2011), Segmentation of Remotely Sensed Imagery: Moving from Sharp Objects to Fuzzy Regions, *In Image Segmentation*, Edited by: Pei-Gee Ho, Publisher: InTech, ISBN 978-953-307-228-9.

López-Caloca A. A., Martínez-Vivero & Chapela-Castañares J.I. (2009), "Application of a clustering-remote sensing method in analyzing security patterns", *Proc. SPIE 7344*, 734407; doi:10.1117/12.818911.

López-Caloca A.A. (2006), Advanced Image Fusion Techniques for Remote sensing. Thesis doctor of engineering, UNAM, Mexico.

Meitzler T., Bednarz D., Sohn E.J., Lane K., Bryk D., Kaur G., Singh H., Ebenstein S., Smith G.H., Rodin Y., Rankin J.S., (2002), "Fuzzy Logic based Image Fusion." *Aerosense,* Orlando April 2-5.

Molenaar M. & Cheng T., (2000), Fuzzy spatial objects and their dynamics, *ISPRS Journal of Photogrammetry & Remote Sensing,* Vol. 55, pp. 164–175.

Mountrakis G., Im J., Ogole C. (2011), Support vector machines in remote sensing: A review, *ISPRS Journal of Photorammetry and Remote Sensing* , Vol.66,pp. 247-259

Raol J. R. , (2011), In Multi-Sensor Data Fusion with MATLAB, CRC Press Taylor & Francis Group, pp. 215-351.

Reyes-Guerrero M. del C., (1986), Neighborhood models: an alternative for the modeling of spatial structures, *Thesis doctor of philosophy, Simon Fraser University*. pp. 65,109,123,156, Canada.

Pohl, C. and van Genderen, J.L. (1998), Multisensor image fusion in remote sensing : concepts, methods and applications, *International journal of remote sensing*, Vol.19, No. 5, pp. 823-854.

Sammon J.W Jr., (1969), A nonlinear mapping for data structure analysis, *IEEE Transactions on Computers*, Vol. C-18, No.5, pp.401-409.

Shackelford A.K., & Davis C.H., (2003), A Hierarchical Fuzzy Classification Approach for High-Resolution Multispectral Data Over Urban Areas, *IEEE Transactions on Geoscience and remote sensing*, Vol. 41, No.9, pp.1920- 1932.

Shankar B. U, S.K., A. and Bruzzone L.,(2006), Remote Sensing Image Classification: A Neurofuzzy MCS Approach, *Computer Vision, Graphics and Image Processing In Lecture Notes in Computer Science*, Vol.4338, pp. 128-139, DOI: 10.1007/11949619_12 .

Silván-Cárdenas J.L., Wang L., Zhan F.B.,(2008), Representing geographical objects with scale-induced indeterminate boundaries: A neural network-based data model, *International Journal of Geographical Information Science*,vol.1,p p. 1–24, ISSN 1365-8816.

Singh, H.; Raj, J.; Kaur, G.; Meitzler, T.; (2004), Image Fusion using Fuzzy Logic and applications , Fuzzy Systems, *On Proceedings. 2004 IEEE International Conference*, Vol. 1, pp. 337 – 340, ISSN: 1098-7584.

Usery E.L., (1996), A conceptual framework and fuzzy set implementation for geographic features. In: P.A. Burrough and A.U. Frank (Eds). *In Geographic objects with indeterminate boundaries* (London: Taylor & Francis), pp. 71–85.

Wald L., 2002. Data Fusion. Definitions and Architectures - Fusion of Images of Different Spatial Resolutions. Presses de l'Ecole, Ecole des Mines de Paris, Paris, France, ISBN 2-911762-38-X, 200 p.

Xie X.L., and G. A. Beni G.A., (1991), Validity measure for fuzzy clustering, *IEEE Trans. PAMI*, Vol. 3, No. 8, pp. 841-846.

Zadeh, L.A., (1975), Fuzzy logic and approximate reasoning, *Synthese*, Vol. 30, pp. 407–428.

Zadeh, L.A., (1976), A fuzzy-algorithmic approach to the definition of complex or imprecise concepts, *International Journal of Man-Machine Studies* , Vol.8, pp. 249–291.

Zadeh L. A.(1994), Fuzzy logic, neural network and soft computing. *Fuzzy systems, communications of the ACM*, Vol. 37, No. 2.

Zadeh L.A., (2010), Toward a Logic of Everyday Reasoning, *Logic Colloquium, UC Berkeley*, Available from http://www.cs.berkeley.edu/~zadeh/presentations.html

Zhao L., Xu B., Tang W. and Chen Z,(2005), A Pixel-Level Multisensor Image Fusion Algorithm Based on Fuzzy Logic, *Fuzzy Systems and Knowledge Discovery , Lecture Notes in Computer Science*, Vol. 3613, pp.476, DOI: 10.1007/11539506_89.

Generation Reliability Evaluation in Deregulated Power Systems Using Monte Carlo Simulation and Fuzzy Systems

H. Haroonabadi
Islamic Azad University (IAU)-Dezful Branch,
Iran

1. Introduction

The power systems main emphasis is to provide a reliable and economic supply of electrical energy to the customers (Billinton & Allan, 1996). A real power system is complex, highly integrated and almost very large. It can be divided into appropriate subsystems in order to be analyzed separately (Billinton & Allan, 1996). This research deals with generation reliability assessment in power pool markets. Therefore transmission and distribution systems are considered reliable (Hierarchical Levels-I, HL-I) as shown in Fig. 1.

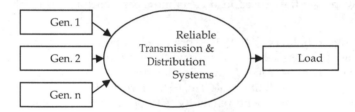

Fig. 1. Power pool market schematic for generation reliability assessment

Most of the methods used for generation reliability evaluation are based on the "loss of load or energy" approach. One of the suitable indices that describes generation reliability level is "Loss of Load Expectation" (*LOLE*), that is the time in which load is more than the available generation capacity.

Generally, the reliability indices of a system can be evaluated using one of the following two basic approaches (Billinton & Allan, 1992):

- Analytical techniques
- Stochastic simulation

Simulation techniques estimate the reliability indices by simulating the actual process and random behavior of the system. Since power markets and generators' forced outages have stochastic behavior, Monte Carlo Simulation (MCS), as one of the most powerful methods for statistical analysis of stochastic problems, is used for reliability assessment in this research.

Generation reliability depends absolutely on the generating units specifications. The main function in traditional structure for Unit Commitment (UC) of the generators is to minimize generation costs. Since the beginning of the 21st century, many countries have been trying to deregulate their power systems and create power markets (Salvaderi, 2000), (Mountford & Austria, 1999), (Draper, 1998), (Puttgen et al, 2001), (Mc Clanahan,2002). In the power markets, the main function of players is their own profit maximization, which severely depends on the type of the market. As a result, generation reliability assessment depends on market type and its characteristics.

Generally, economists divide the markets into four groups, varying between perfect competition market and monopoly market (Pindyck & Rubinfeld, 1995). This study deals with the evaluation of generation reliability in different kinds of power pool markets based on the market concentration. Let's review some of the papers proposed till now.

An optimization technique is proposed in (Wang et al, 2009) to determine load shedding and generation re-dispatch for each contingency state in the reliability evaluation of restructured power systems with the Poolco market structure. The problem is formulated using the optimal power flow (OPF) technique. The objective of the problem is to minimize the total system cost, which includes generation, reserve and interruption costs, subject to market and network constraints.

In reference (Azami, R. et al, 2009) the effect of emergency demand response program on composite system reliability of a deregulated power system is evaluated using an economic load model, AC power-flow-based load curtailment cost function and reliability evaluation techniques.

Reference (Wang & Billinton, 2001) has presented some reliability models for different players in a power system, where generation system is represented by an equivalent multi-state generation provider (EMGP). The reliability parameters of each EMGP are shown by an available capacity probability table (ACPT), which is determined using conventional techniques. Then, the equivalent reliability parameters for each state (including state probability, frequency of encountering the state and the equivalent available generation capacity) are determined.

Reference (Haroonabadi & Haghifam, 2009) compares generation reliability in various economic markets: Perfect Competition, Oligopoly and Monopoly power pool markets. Also, due to the stochastic behavior of power market and generators' forced outages, Monte Carlo Simulation is used for reliability evaluation.

In researches dealing with power marketing and restructuring, market behavior and its economic effects on the power system should be considered. Therefore, this research considers power pool market fundamentals and deals with generation reliability assessment in power pool market using MCS and an intelligent system. Also, sensitivity of reliability index to different reserve margins and times will be evaluated. In Section-2, the fundamentals of power pool market will be discussed. In Section-3, the algorithm for generation reliability assessment in power pool market will be proposed, and finally in Section-4, the case study results will be presented and discussed.

2. Power pool markets fundamentals

Market demand curve has negative gradient, and the amount of demand decrease is explained by "price elasticity of demand". This index is small for short terms, and big for long terms; because in longer terms, customers can better adjust their load relative to price (IEA, 2003). Demand function, generally, is described as $P=a-b.Q$. Therefore, price elasticity of demand is explained as:

$$E_d = \left| \frac{dQ}{dP} \right| = \frac{1}{b} \tag{1}$$

Let's suppose forecasted load by dispatching center is an independent power from price that equals to Q_n. Therefore, demand function can be obtained as:

$$P = a - b.Q = b.Q_n - b.Q = \frac{Q_n}{E_d} - \frac{Q}{E_d} \tag{2}$$

Typically, as shown in Fig. 2, price elasticity in power markets is 0.1-0.2 for the next 2-3 years and 0.3-0.7 for the next 10-20 years (IEA, 2003).

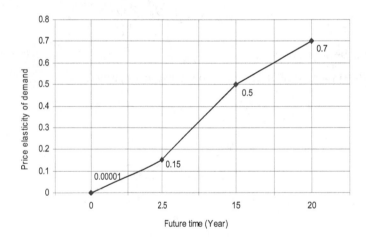

Fig. 2. Price elasticity of demand for various times

Offer curve of a company, which participates in a market without any market power is part of the marginal cost curve that is more than minimum average variable cost (Pindyck & Rubinfeld, 1995). Also, total offer curve of all companies is obtained from horizontal sum of each company's offer curve. This curve is a merit order function. In economics, if sale price in a market becomes less than minimum average variable cost, the company will stop production; because the company will not be able to cover not only the fix cost but even the variable cost (Pindyck & Rubinfeld, 1995). Due to the changing efficiency and heat rate of power plants, marginal cost is less than average variable cost. Therefore, in power plants, average variable cost replaces marginal cost in economic studies (Borenstein, 1999).

In a perfect competition market, equilibrium price and equilibrium amount are obtained from the intersection of total offer curve and demand curve. On the other hand, in a monopoly market, the monopolist considers the production level, which maximizes his profit. It is proved that the monopolist considers the level of production in which marginal cost of each firm (and total marginal cost of all firms) equals to the marginal revenue of the monopolist (Pindyck & Rubinfeld, 1995):

$$MC_1 = MC_2 = ... = MC = MR \tag{3}$$

Where:

$$MR = a - 2.b.Q = b.Q_n - 2.b.Q = \frac{Q_n}{E_d} - \frac{2.Q}{E_d} \tag{4}$$

Comparison of (2) and (4) shows that if there is no market power, offer curve of industry for each market (from perfect competition market to monopoly market) will equal marginal cost; but negative gradient of demand exponent curve (*DE*) varies between *b* (for demand function in perfect competition market) and *2b* (for marginal revenue in monopoly market). Therefore, generally, demand exponent curve can be expressed as:

$$DE = a - K.b.Q = \frac{Q_n}{E_d} - \frac{K.Q}{E_d} \tag{5}$$

Where, *K* varies between 1 and 2.

Fig. 3 shows the typical total offer and demand exponent curves.

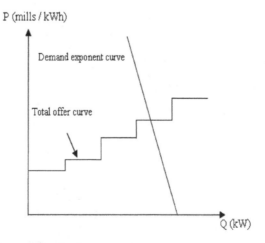

Fig. 3. Typical total offer and demand exponent curves

3. Proposed method for generation evaluation in power markets

In power markets, Hirschman-Herfindahl Index (*HHI*), which is obtained from (6), is used for market concentration measurement (IEA, 2003):

$$HHI = \sum_M q_i{}^2 \qquad (6)$$

If market shares are measured in percentages, HHI will vary between 0 (an atomistic market) and 10000 (monopoly market). According to a usual grouping, the US merger guidelines stipulate an assumption that markets with a HHI below 1000 is unconcentrated, a HHI between 1000 and 1800 is moderately concentrated, and a HHI above 1800 is highly concentrated (FTC, 1992).

As mentioned before, according to the type of market and HHI values, negative gradient of demand exponent curve varies between b and 2b. Therefore, for modeling the market, a fuzzy number is proposed in this study to estimate the gradient coefficient of demand exponent curve (K) based on the HHI values. Membership functions of unconcentrated, moderately concentrated and highly concentrated markets' fuzzy sets and the equation to estimate gradient coefficient are shown in Fig. 4 and (7), respectively.

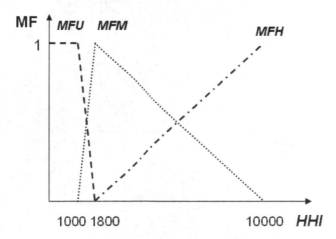

Fig. 4. Membership functions of unconcentrated, moderately concentrated and highly concentrated markets' fuzzy sets

$$K = (MFU + 1.5 \times MFM + 2 \times MFH) \qquad (7)$$

As Fig. 4 and (7) show, while the proposed coefficient (K) covers all kinds of markets with different concentration degrees, the changes of these degrees are not sudden, rather they are gradual and continuous. Also, the proposed method and fuzzy logic are valid for all power pool markets.

Generation reliability of a power system depends on many parameters, especially on reserve margin, which is defined as (IEA, 2002):

$$RM\% = \frac{Installed \quad Capacity - Peak \quad Demand}{Peak \quad Demand} \times 100 \qquad (8)$$

The algorithm of generation reliability assessment in power pool markets using Monte Carlo simulation and proposed fuzzy logic is as follows (Fig. 5):

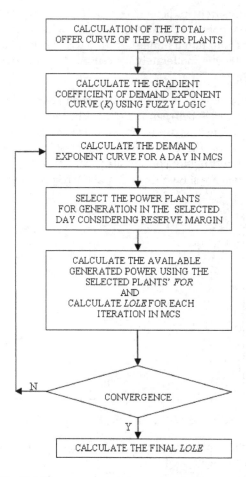

Fig. 5. Flow chart of HLI reliability assessment in power markets using MCS

1. *HHI* is obtained based on characteristic of the market. The gradient coefficient of demand exponent curve (*K*) is calculated using Fig. 4 and (7).
2. Calculation of the total offer curve of power plants.
3. Select a random day and its load (Q_n), and calculate demand exponent curve using (5).
4. The power plants, selected for generation in the selected day, are determined from the intersection of the power plants' total offer curve and demand exponent curve with regards to the reserve margin.
5. For each selected power plant in the previous step, a random number between 0-1 is generated. If the generated number is more than the power plant's Forced Outage Rate (*FOR*), the power plant is considered as available in the mentioned iteration; otherwise it encounters forced outage and thus can not generate power. This process is performed

for all power plants using an independent random number generated for each plant. Finally, sum of the available power plants' generation capacities is calculated. If the sum becomes less than the intersection of power plants' total offer curve and demand exponent curve, we will have interruption in the iteration, and therefore, *LOLE* will increase one unit; otherwise, we will go to the next iteration. The algorithm of available generated power and *LOLE* calculations for each iteration in MCS is shown in Fig. 6.

6.   The steps 3 to 5 are repeated for calculation of final *LOLE*.

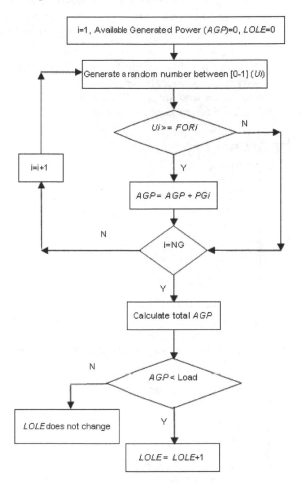

Fig. 6. Algorithm of available generated power and *LOLE* calculations for each iteration using MCS

4. Numerical studies

IEEE - Reliability Test System (IEEE-RTS) is used for case studies. The required data for IEEE-RTS can be found in (Reliability Test System..., 1979). The following assumptions are used in various case studies:

1. All case studies are simulated for the second half of the year, based on the daily peak load of the mentioned test system.
2. All simulations are done with 5000 iterations.
3. Each case study is simulated for two different times (present time and the 2nd next year) and two different reserve margins (0%, 9%).
4. Annual growth rates of the power plants' generation capacity and consumed load are considered as 3.4% and 3.34%, respectively.
5. Annual growth rates of oil and coal costs are considered as 4% and 1%, respectively. Nuclear fuel cost (including uranium, enrichment and fabrication) is considered as a fixed rate. Also, annual growth rate of variable Operating and Maintenance (O&M) cost is considered as 1%.

In the first case study, each power plant is assumed as an independent company. Therefore, HHI equals 634, and the market is unconcentrated. Using Fig. 4 and (7), K is calculated as 1 (Fig. 7). Based on this assumption and using MCS algorithm, $LOLE$ values are obtained versus different times and reserve margins as shown in Fig. 8.

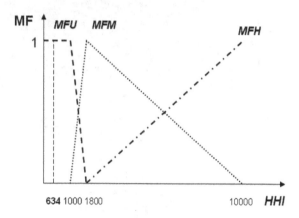

Fig. 7. The gradient calculation of demand exponent curve using membership functions for the first study

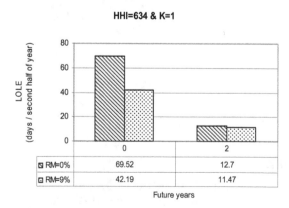

Fig. 8. $LOLE$ values for the first study

In the second study, all the power plants based on their types (including oil, coal, nuclear and water plants) are classified. Therefore, *HHI* equals 2984, and *K* is calculated as 1.5722 (Fig. 9). Based on this assumption and using MCS algorithm, *LOLE* values are obtained versus different times and reserve margins as shown in Fig. 10.

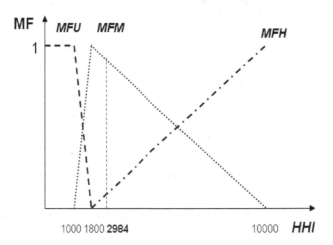

Fig. 9. The gradient calculation of demand exponent curve using membership functions for the second study

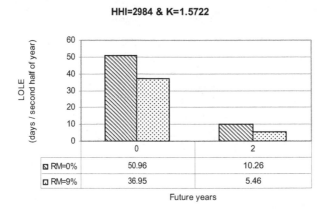

Fig. 10. *LOLE* values for the second study

In the third study, all fossil power plants (including oil and coal power plants) are classified in one company, and other power plants are as in the second case study. Therefore, the types of power plants are fossil, nuclear and water. As a result, *HHI* equals 5290, and *K* is calculated as 1.7128 (Fig. 11). Based on this assumption and using MCS algorithm, *LOLE* values are obtained versus different times and reserve margins as shown in Fig. 12.

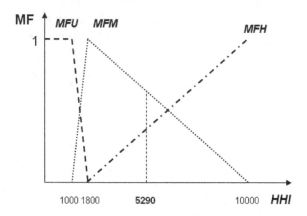

Fig. 11. The gradient calculation of demand exponent curve using membership functions for the third study

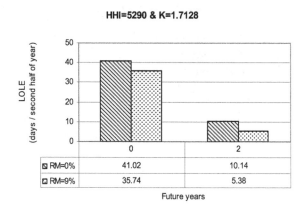

Fig. 12. *LOLE* values for the third study

In the fourth study, it is assumed that all power plants belong to a monopolist, and the market is fully concentrated and monopoly. Therefore, *HHI* equals 10000, and *K* is calculated as 2 (Fig. 13). Based on this assumption and using MCS algorithm, *LOLE* values are obtained versus different times and reserve margins as shown in Fig. 14.

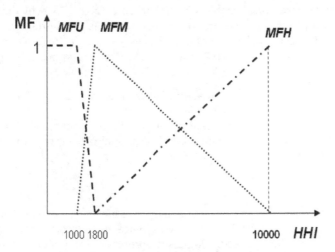

Fig. 13. The gradient calculation of demand exponent curve using membership functions for the fourth study

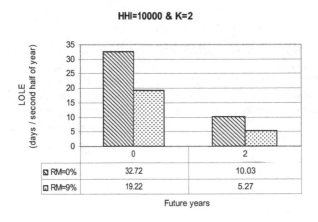

Fig. 14. *LOLE* values for the fourth study

In all case studies, if reserve margin increases, *LOLE* will decrease and reliability will improve.

As mentioned before, in longer terms, customers can better adjust their load relative to the price. Therefore, price elasticity increases in longer terms, and according to (5), demand exponent curve reaches less gradient. As a result, intersection of the power plants' total offer curve and demand exponent curve will occur at less demand. This matter leads to operate from fewer power plants. Therefore, in each case study, if time increases, *LOLE* will decrease.

If market becomes more concentrated or *HHI* becomes bigger, *K* will find bigger value. Therefore, according to (5), intersection of the power plants' total offer curve and demand exponent curve will occur at less demand. Therefore, *LOLE* will decrease. So that in the fourth study (monopoly market), *LOLEs* are the least values comparing to the other case studies.

It is to be noted that since available capacity of hydro plants in IEEE-RTS are different in the first and the second halves of the year, therefore, simulations were done for the second half of the year. Evidently, the proposed method can be utilized for every simulation time. Also, in this study, it was supposed that the annual additional generation capacity is uniformly distributed between all the present generators.

5. Conclusion

This research deals with generation reliability assessment in power pool market using Monte Carlo simulation and intelligent systems. Since changes of market concentration in power markets are gradual, a fuzzy logic was proposed for calculation of the gradient coefficient of demand exponent curve. Due to the stochastic behavior of market and generators' *FOR*, MCS was used for the simulations. In this research, *LOLE* was used as reliability index and it was shown that if market becomes more concentrated, *LOLE* will decrease and reliability will improve. Also, if price elasticity of demand increases, *LOLE* will decrease.

Follows can be considered for future researches:

1. Reliability indices evaluate in HL-II zone in which both generation and transmission systems are considered.
2. Bilateral contracts consider in the power market as well as pool market.
3. If the generation planning scenarios in a power system are specified, then they can be used instead of uniformly distribution of annual additional generation capacity.
4. Reserve market can be considered as an independent market of the main energy market.

6. Symbol List

MC: Marginal cost (mills/kWh)
MR: Marginal revenue (mills/kWh)
$5Q$: Quantity of power (kW)
P: Electrical energy price (mills/kWh)
RM: Reserve margin (%)
E_d : Price elasticity of demand (kW²h/mills)
Q_n: Forecasted load (kW)
$LOLE$: Loss of load expectation (days/second half year)
FOR: Forced outage rate of power plants
q_i: Share of ith company in the pool market (%)
M: Number of independent companies in the market
a: Demand exponent curve cross of basis (mills/kWh)
b: Demand exponent curve gradient (mills /kW²h)

HHI: Hirschman - Herfindahl index
DE: Demand exponent curve
K: Gradient coefficient of demand exponent curve
MFU: Membership function of unconcentrated market
MFM: Membership function of moderately concentrated market
MFH: Membership function of highly concentrated market
NG: Number of selected plants for generation in the market
AGP: Available generated power

7. References

Azami R., Abbasi A.H., Shakeri J., Fard A.F. (2009), Impact of EDRP on Composite Reliability of Restructured Power Systems, *Proceedings of PowerTech IEEE Bucharest Conference*, pp. 1-8.

Billinton R., Allan R. (1992). *Reliability Evaluation of Engineering Systems*, Second edition, Plenum press, ISBN: 0-306-44063-6, New York.

Billinton R., Allan R. (1996). *Reliability Evaluation of Power Systems*, Second edition, Plenum press, ISBN: 0-306-45259-6, New York.

Borenstein Serverin (1999). Understanding competitive pricing and market power in wholesale electricity market, *University of California energy institute*.

Draper E. L. (1998). Assessment of Deregulation and Competition, *IEEE Power Engineering Review*, Vol. 18, No. 7 (Jul 1998), pp. 17-18, ISSN: 0272-1724.

Haroonabadi H. & Haghifam M.-R. (2009). Generation Reliability Evaluation in Power Markets Using Monte Carlo Simulation and Neural Networks. *Proceedings of 15th International Conference on Intelligent System Applications to Power Systems (ISAP)*, pp. 1-6, Print ISBN: 978-1-4244-5097-8, Curitiba, Nov 2009.

International Energy Agency (IEA) (2002). *Security of Supply in Electricity Markets - Evidence and Policy Issues*, IEA, ISBN: 92-64-19805-9, France.

International Energy Agency (IEA) (2003). *The Power to Choose- Demand Response in Liberalized Electricity Markets*, IEA, ISBN: 92-64-10503-4, France.

Jaeseok Choi; Hongsik Kim; Junmin Cha & Roy Billinton (2001). Nodal probabilistic congestion and reliability evaluations of a transmission system under the deregulated electricity market, *Proceedings of IEEE Power engineering society summer meeting,*, pp. 497-502, Print ISBN: 0-7803-7173-9, Vancouver, 15 Jul 2001-19 Jul 2001.

Mc Clanahan R. H. (2002). Electric Deregulation, *IEEE Industry Application Magazine*, Vol. 8, No. 2 (Mar/Apr 2002), pp. 11-18, ISSN: 1077-2618 .

Mountford J. D., Austria R. R. (1999). Keeping The Lights On, *IEEE Spectrum*, Vol. 36 (Jun 1999), pp. 34-39, ISSN: 0018-9235.

Pindyck Robert S. & Rubinfeld D. L. (1995). *Microeconomics*, Third edition, Prentice Hall, ISBN: 7-302-02494-4, USA.

Puttgen H. B.; Volzka D. R. & Olken M. I. (2001). Restructuring and Reregulation of The US Electric Utility Industry, *IEEE Power Engineering Review*, Vol. 21, No. 2 (Feb 2001), pp. 8-10, ISSN: 0272-1724.

Reliability Test System Task Force of The IEEE Subcommittee on the application of probability Methods, IEEE Reliability Test System, *IEEE Transactions*, Pas-98, No.6, Nov/Dec 1979, pp. 2047-2054.

Salvaderi L. (2000). Electric Sector Restructuring in Italy, *IEEE Power Engineering Review*, Vol. 20, No. 4 (Apr 2000), pp. 12-16, ISSN: 0272-1724.

The U.S. Department of Justice and Federal Trade Commission (FTC) (1992). http://www.ftc.gov/bc/docs/horizmer.htm.

Wang P. & Billinton R. (2001). Implementation of non-uniform reliability in a deregulated power market, *Proceedings of Canadian Conference on Electrical and Computer Engineerin*,. pp. 857- 861, Print ISBN: 0-7803-6715-4, Toronto, May 2001.

Wang P.; Ding, Y. & Goel, L. (2009). Reliability assessment of restructured power systems using optimal load shedding technique, *Generation, Transmission & Distribution, IET*, Vol. 3, Issue: 7 (July 2009), pp. 628 – 640, ISSN: 1751-8687.

Greenhouse Fuzzy and Neuro-Fuzzy Modeling Techniques

Gorrostieta-Hurtado Efren[1], Pedraza-Ortega Jesus Carlos[1],
Aceves-Fernández Marco Antonio, Ramos-Arreguín Juan Manuel[1],
Tovar-Arriaga Saúl[1] and Sotomayor-Olmedo Artemio[2]
[1]Facultad de Informática, Universidad Autónoma de Querétaro,
[2]Facultad de Ingeniería, Universidad Autónoma de Querétaro,
Querétaro,
México

1. Introduction

During the last decades, a considerable effort was devoted to develop adequate greenhouse climate and crop models, for driving simulation, control and managing (Guzmán-Cruz, *et. Al*, Rico-Garcia, *et al*). The study and design of greenhouse environmental models implies having a clear understanding of the greenhouse climate processes. These models must be related with the external influences of the outside weather conditions (such as solar radiation, outside air temperature, wind velocity, etc.), and with the control actions performed (such as ventilation, cooling, heating, among others). The practical goal of this work is to model the greenhouse air temperature and humidity using clustering techniques and made an automatically generator of fuzzy rules relations from real data in order to predict the behavior inside the greenhouse.

The soft computing techniques, such as neural networks, clustering algorithms and fuzzy logic, have been successfully applied to classification and pattern recognition. Besides, fuzzy logic is highly used when the system modeling implies information is scarce, imprecise or when the system is described by complex mathematical model. An example of this kind of structure is a greenhouse and it's inherit variables such as: indoor and outdoor temperature and humidity, wind direction and speed, etc. These variables present a dynamic and non-linear behavior; being the in-house temperature and internal humidity the key variables for the greenhouse control and modeling. In this chapter, the construction of fuzzy systems by fuzzy c-means and fuzzy subtractive clustering are described. Finally a comparison with adaptive neuro-fuzzy inference system (anfis) and neural networks will be presented.

2. Greenhouse model

The non-linear behavior of the greenhouse-climate is a combination of complex physical interactions between energy transfer such as radiation and temperature and mass transfer like humidity and wind (indoor and outdoor the greenhouse).

In this work the humidity and temperature are considered as the greenhouse key parameters, based on (Guzmán-Cruz, *et. Al*, Rico-Garcia, *et al*) observations.

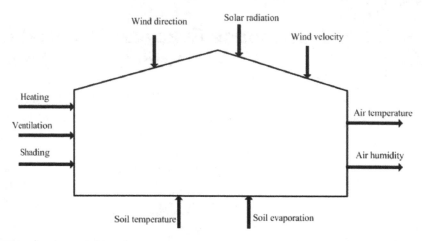

Fig. 1. Greenhouse variable scheme.

3. Fuzzy systems

Fuzzy inference systems (FIS) are also known as fuzzy rule-based systems. This is a major unit of a fuzzy logic system. The decision-making is an important part in the entire system. The FIS formulates suitable rules and based upon the rules the decision is made. This is mainly based on the concepts of the fuzzy set theory, fuzzy IF–THEN rules, and fuzzy reasoning. FIS uses "IF - THEN" statements, and the connectors present in the rule statement are "OR" or "AND" to make the necessary decision rules.

Fuzzy inference system consists of a fuzzification interface, a rule base, a database, a decision-making unit, and finally a defuzzification interface as described in Chang(et al 2006). A FIS with five functional block described in Fig.2.

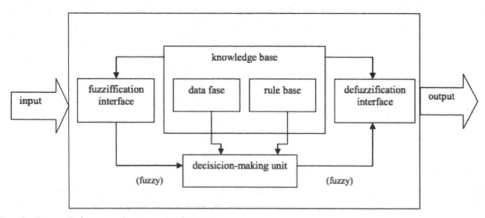

Fig. 2. Fuzzy Inference System Architecture

The function of each block is as follows:

- A rule base containing a set of fuzzy IF–THEN rules;
- A database which defines the membership functions of the fuzzy sets used in the fuzzy rules;
- A decision-making unit which performs the inference operations on the rules;
- A fuzzification interface which transforms the crisp inputs into degrees of match with linguistic values; and
- A defuzzification interface which transforms the fuzzy results of the inference into a crisp output.

The working of FIS is as follows. The inputs are converted in to fuzzy by using fuzzification method. After fuzzification the rule base is formed. The rule base and the database are jointly referred to as the knowledge base.

Defuzzification is used to convert fuzzy value to the real world value which is the output.

The steps of fuzzy reasoning (inference operations upon fuzzy IF–THEN rules) performed by FISs are:

- Compare the input variables with the membership functions on the antecedent part to obtain the membership values of each linguistic label. (this step is often called fuzzification.)
- Combine (through a specific t-norm operator, usually multiplication or min) the membership values on the premise part to get firing strength (weight) of each rule.
- Generate the qualified consequents (either fuzzy or crisp) or each rule depending on the firing strength.
- Aggregate the qualified consequents to produce a crisp output. (This step is called defuzzification.)

4. Fuzzy clustering techniques

There are a number of fuzzy clustering techniques available. In this work, two fuzzy clustering methods have been chosen: fuzzy c-means clustering and fuzzy clustering subtractive algorithms. These methods are proven to be the most reliable fuzzy clustering methods as well as better forecasters in terms of absolute error according to some authors[Sin, Gomez, Chiu].

Since 1985 when the fuzzy model methodology suggested by Takagi-Sugeno [Takagi *et al* 1985, Sugeno *et al* 1988], as well known as the TSK model, has been widely applied on theoretical analysis, control applications and fuzzy modeling.

Fuzzy system needs the precedent and consequence to express the logical connection between the input output datasets that are used as a basis to produce the desired system behavior [Sin *et al* 1993].

4.1 Fuzzy Clustering Means (FCM)

Fuzzy C-Means clustering (FCM) is an iterative optimization algorithm that minimizes the cost function given by:

$$J = \sum_{k=1}^{n} \sum_{i=1}^{c} \mu_{ik}^{m} \|x_k - v_i\|^2 \tag{3}$$

Where n is the number of data points, c is the number of clusters, xk is the kth data point, vi is the ith cluster center μik is the degree of membership of the kth data in the ith cluster, and m is a constant greater than 1 (typically m=2)[Aceves *et al* 2011]. The degree of membership μik is defined by:

$$\mu_{ik} = \cfrac{1}{\sum_{j=1}^{c} \left(\cfrac{\|x_k - v_i\|}{\|x_k - v_j\|} \right)^{2/(m-1)}} \tag{4}$$

Starting with a desired number of clusters c and an initial guess for each cluster center vi, i = 1,2,3... c, FCM will converge to a solution for vi that represents either a local minimum or a saddle point cost function [Bezdek *et al* 1985]. The FCM method utilizes fuzzy partitioning such that each point can belong to several clusters with membership values between 0 and 1. FCM include predefined parameters such as the weighting exponent m and the number of clusters c.

4.2 Fuzzy clustering subtractive

The subtractive clustering method assumes each data point is a potential cluster center and calculates a measure of the likelihood that each data point would define the cluster center, based on the density of surrounding data points. Consider m dimensions of n data point $(x_1, x_2, ..., x_n)$ and each data point is potential cluster center, the density function Di of data point at xi is given by:

$$D_i = \sum_{i=1}^{n} e^{\left(\frac{\|x_i - x_j\|^2}{\left(\frac{r_a}{2}\right)^2} \right)} \tag{5}$$

where r_a is a positive number. The data point with the highest potential is surrounded by more data points. A radius defines a neighbour area, then the data points, which exceed r_a, have no influence on the density of data point.

After calculating the density function of each data point is possible to select the data point with the highest potential and find the first cluster center. Assuming that X_{c1} is selected and D_{c1} is its density, the density of each data point can be amended by:

$$D_i = D_i - D_{c1} e \left(-\frac{\|x_i - x_{c1}\|^2}{\left(\frac{r_b}{2}\right)^2} \right) \tag{6}$$

The density function of data point which is close to the first cluster center is reduced. Therefore, these data points cannot become the next cluster center. r_b defines an neighbour area where the density function of data point is reduced. Usually constant $r_b > r_a$. In order to avoid the overlapping of cluster centers near to other(s) is given by [Yager *et al* 1994]:

$$r_b = \eta \cdot r_a \tag{7}$$

4.3 Fuzzy model contruction

When cluster estimation method is applied to a collection of input/output data, each cluster center illustrates a characteristic behavior of the system. Hence, each cluster center can be used as the basis of a rule that describes the system behavior. Consider a set of c cluster centers $\{x_1^*, x_2^*, x_3^*, \dots x_c^*\}$ in an M-dimensional space. Let the first N dimensions correspond to the input variables and the last M–N dimensional corresponds to output variables. Each vector x_i^* could be decomposed into two component vectors y_i^* and z_i^* where y_i^* contains the first N elements of x_i^* and z_i^* contains the last M–N elements

Then consider each cluster center x_i^* is represents a fuzzy rule that describes the system behavior. Given an input vector y, the degree to which rule i is fulfilled is defined by:

$$\mu_i = e^{-\alpha \|yy_i^*\|^2} \tag{6}$$

where α is the constant defined by [15].

$$\alpha = \frac{4}{r_a^2} \tag{7}$$

The output vector z is computed by:

$$z = \frac{\sum_{i-1}^{c} \mu_i z_i^*}{\sum_{i-1}^{c} \mu_i} \tag{8}$$

then this computational model is in terms of a fuzzy inference system employing *if-then* rules following the form:

$$\textbf{IF } x_1 \text{ is } A_1 \text{ and } x_2 \text{ is } A_2 \text{ and } \dots \textbf{ THEN } Z_1 \text{ is } B_1 \text{ and } Z_2 \text{ is } B_2 \dots \tag{9}$$

where Y_1 is the jth input variable and Z_1 is the jth output variable. A_1 is an exponential membership function and B_1 is a singleton for the ith rule that is represented by cluster center x_i^*, A_j and B_j are given by:

$$A_j(Q) = e^{-\alpha(q-x_{ij}^*)^2} \tag{10}$$

$$B_j = Z_{ij}^* \tag{11}$$

where y_{ij}^* is the jth element of y_i^* and z_{ij}^* is the jth element of z_i^*. This computational scheme is equivalent to an inference method that uses multiplication as the *AND* operator, weights the output of each rule by the firing strength, and computes the output as a weighted average of the output of each rule [7] [10] [14][19].

Equation 12 represents a dynamic system where the function is expressed by the current input variables and the previous output.

$$y(k) = f(y(k-n), u(k)) \tag{12}$$

Where the state-transition function in this particular case is the ARX (Auto Regressive eXogenous) function (equation 12). The output variables are represented by y(k) and the input variables by u(k). the variable e(k) represents white noise, whereas the system order is represented by the n variable.

$$y(k) = \sum_{j=1}^{n} a_j y(k-j) + \sum_{j=0}^{n} b_j u(k-j) + e(k) \tag{13}$$

Te fuzzy system in this case is the proposed by Takagi-Sugeno [8] in which the following equation is presented:

$$\textbf{\textit{IF }} x_1 \textbf{\textit{ is }} A_1 \textbf{\textit{ and }} x_2 \textbf{\textit{ is }} A_2 \textbf{\textit{ and }} ... \textbf{\textit{ THEN }} \zeta(x) \tag{14}$$

The function $\zeta(x)$ of the consequence corresponds to a part of a data-cluster as shown on equation 15

$$\zeta(x) = a^T x + b \tag{15}$$

5. Neural networks

Artificial neural networks (ANN's) can be used to solve complex problems where noise immunity is important. [12].These feature is why we choose ANN's to model a dynamic system and create a fuzzy inference system. There are two ways to train an ANN: supervised training and un-supervised training. Supervised training requires training set where the input and the desired output of the network are provided for several training cases, whilst un- supervised training requires only the input of the network, and the ANN is supposed to classify (separate) the data appropriately [10]. In this paper we decide to use a supervised ANN because our data source become from experimental measurements.

6. The perceptron

The neuron or node or unit, as it is called, is a processing element that takes a number of inputs, weights them, sums them up, and uses the result as the argument for a singular valued function, the activation function. (Figure 3) [12], [13].

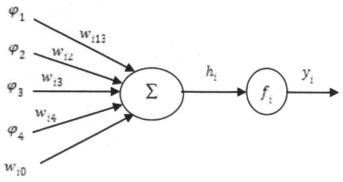

Fig. 3. Topology of perceptron.

To determine the weight value it is crucial to have a set of samples that correlates the output y_i, with the, inputs φ_i. The task of determining the weights from this example is called training or learning, and is basically a conventional estimation problem.[10]

7. The multilayer perceptron

Neurons can combine into a network in numerous fashions. Beyond any doubt the most common of these is the Multilayer Perceptron (MLP) network. The basic MLP-network is constructed by ordering the units in layers, letting each neuron in a layer take as an input only the outputs of neurons in the previous layer or external inputs. Due to the structure, this type of network is often referred to as a feedforward network. [10], [12], [13]. The MLP-network is straightforward to employ for discrete-time modelling of dynamic systems.[10]

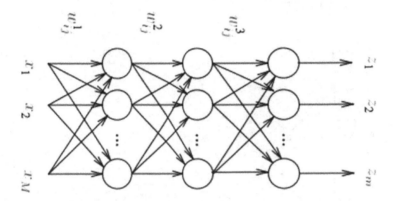

Fig. 4. Multilayer perceptron architecture.

8. The Adaptive Neuro-Fuzzy Inference System(ANFIS)

In a conventional fuzzy inference system, the number of rules is decided by an expert who is familiar with the system to be modelled. In this particular case study no expert was available and the number of membership functions assigned to each input is chosen empirically. This is carried out by examining the desired input-output data and/or by trial and error. This situation is much the same as ANN's. In this section ANFIS topology and the learning method used for this neuro-fuzzy network are presented. Both neural network and fuzzy logic are model-free estimators and share the common ability to deal with the uncertainties and noise. It is possible to convert fuzzy logic architecture to a neural network and vice versa.[15] This makes it possible to combine the advantages of neural network and fuzzy logic[7][8]. (see figure).

Layer 1: Every node in i in this layer is a square node with a node function

$$0_i^1 = \mu A_i(x) \tag{16}$$

Where x is the input node i, and A_i is the linguistic label(small, large, etc.) associated with this node function. In other words, 0_i^1 is the membership function of and it specifies the degree to which the A_i given x satisfies the quantifier A_i . Usually we choose $\mu A_i(x)$ to be bell shaped with maximum equal to 1 and minimum equal to 0, such as

$$\mu A_i(x) = \frac{1}{1 + \left[(\frac{x - c_i}{a_i})^2 \right]^{bi}} \tag{17}$$

where $\{ a_i, b_i, c_i \}$ is the parameter set. As the values of these parameters change, the best bell-shaped functions vary accordingly, thus exhibiting various forms of membership functions on linguistic label A_i. In fact, any continuous and piecewise differentiable functions, such as commonly used trapezoidal or triangular-shaped membership functions are also qualified candidates for node functions in this layer. Parameters in this layer are referred to as premise parameters.

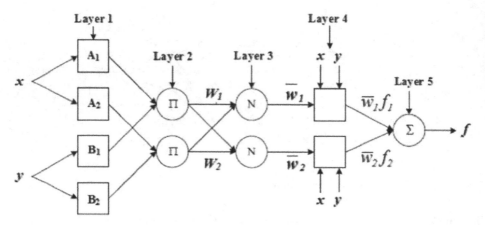

Fig. 5. ANFIS Architecture proposed by (Jang 1993).

Layer 2: Every node in this layer is a circle node labelled $\prod$ which multiplies the incoming signals and sends the product out. For instance,

$$w_i = \mu A_i(x) * \mu A_i(y), i = 1, 2 \tag{18}$$

Each node output represents the firing strength of a rule (In fact, other *T-norm* operators that perform generalized AND can be used as the node function in this layer).

Layer 3: Every node in this layer is a circle node labelled N. The ith node calculates the ratio of the ith rule's firing strength to the sum of all rules firing strengths:

$$\overline{w}_i = \frac{w_i}{w_1 + w_2}, i = 1, 2. \tag{19}$$

For convenience, outputs of this layer are called *normalized firing strengths*.

Layer 4: Every node in this layer is a square node with a node function

$$O_i^4 = \overline{w}_i f = \overline{w}(p_i x + q_i y + r_i) \tag{20}$$

Where $\bar{w}_i$ is the output of layer 3, and $\{\, p_i, q_i, r_i \,\}$ is the parameter set. Parameters in this layer will be referred to as consequent parameters.

Layer 5: The single node in this layer is a circle node labelled $\sum$ that computes the overall output as the summation of all incoming signals, ie.

$$O_1^5 = overall\,output = \sum_i \bar{w}_i f = \frac{\sum_i w_i f}{\sum_i w_i} \tag{21}$$

Thus we have constructed an adaptive network which is functionally equivalent to a fuzzy inference system [8],[9]. The hybrid algorithm is applied to this architecture. This means that, in the forward pass of the hybrid learning algorithm, functional signals go forward up to fourth layer and the consequent parameters are identified by the least and consequent parameters are identified by the least squares estimation. In the last backward and the premise parameters are updated by the gradient descent [8].

9. Experimental results

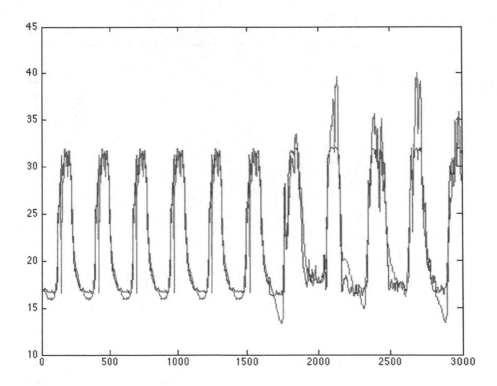

Fig. 6. Neural-Netorks Temperature Estimated.

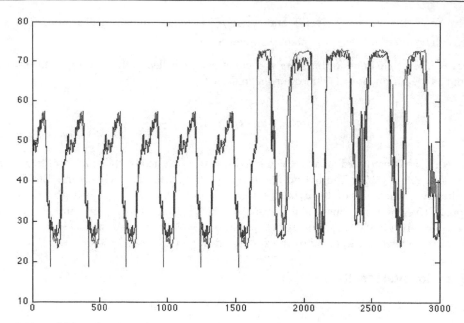

Fig. 7. Neural-Netorks Humidity Estimated

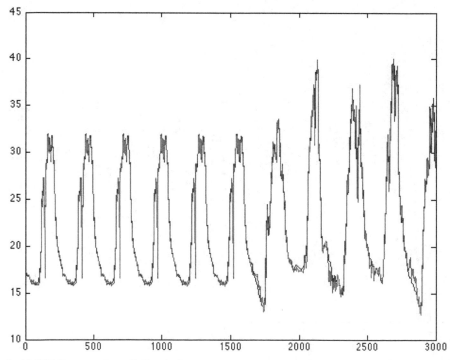

Fig. 8. ANFIS Temperature Estimated.

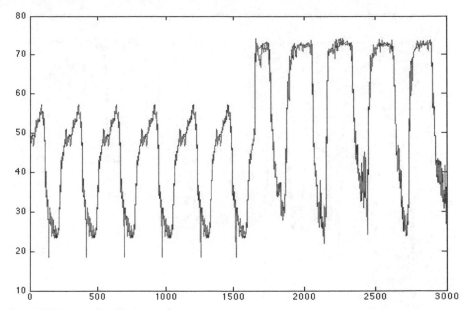

Fig. 9. ANFIS Humidity Estimated

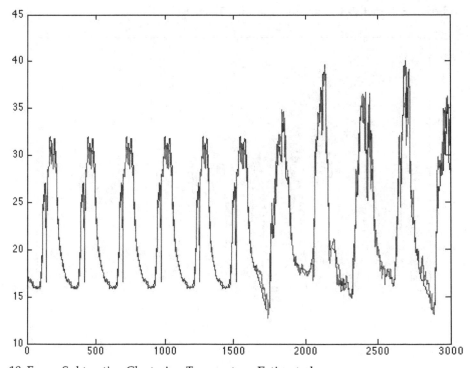

Fig. 10. Fuzzy Subtractive Clustering Temperature Estimated.

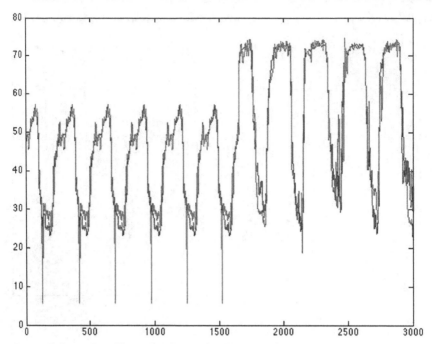

Fig. 11. Fuzzy Subtractive Clustering Humidity Estimated.

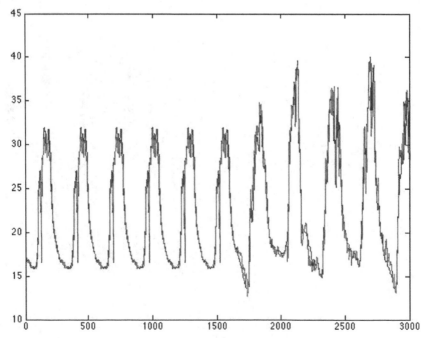

Fig. 12. Fuzzy C-Means Clustering Temperature Estimated.

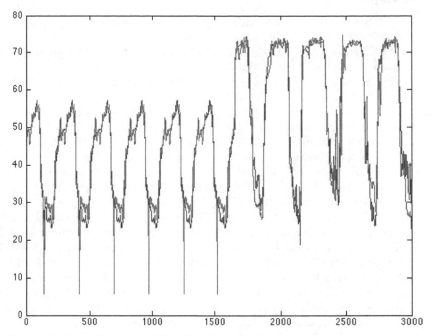

Fig. 13. Fuzzy C-Means Clustering Humidity Estimated.

Algorithm	Mean Average Error		Mean Square Error	
	Temperature	Humidity	Temperature	Humidity
ANN	1.3467	2.8587	4.3418	1.1590
ANFIS	0.3826	1.0634	0.3220	1.0634
Fuzzy Subtractive Clustering	2.2329	1.7653	12.4100	2.3595
Fuzzy C-Means	1.2329	0.7544	10.4050	1.5533

Table 1. Summary of Results

10. Conclusions and further work

In this chapter, we have introduced some clustering algorithms for fuzzy model identification, whose main purpose is modeling a system from experimental measured data.

Fuzzy model construction by clustering algorithms, however, will need further enhancement. For instance, mechanisms to find values for optimal cluster indexes still need further investigation because, determines the model structure. Here clustering evaluation functions and validation indexes could be of value when combined with genetic algorithms and support vector machines. The effectiveness of this approach will, however, depend on the accuracy of clustering techniques, and the issue still open. These are the questions to be addressed in future research.

11. References

Bezdek, J. C., "Pattern Recognition with Fuzzy Objective Function Algorithms", *Plenum Press, NY*, 1981.

Chang Wook A., "Advances in Evolutionary Algorithms: Theory, Design and Practice", Springer, ISSN: 1860-949X, 2006.

Chiu S, "Fuzzy model identification based on cluster estimation", *Journal of Intelligent and Fuzzy Systems*; September 1994, 2, pp. 267–78.

Ferreira, P.M., E.A. Faria and A.E. Ruano, 2002. Neural network models in greenhouse air temperature prediction. *Neurocomputing*, 2002 43: 51-75

Gomez, A. F., M. Delgado, and M. A. Vila, "About the Use of Fuzzy Clustering Techniques for Fuzzy Model Identification", *Fuzzy Set and System*,. 1999, pp. 179-188.

Guzman-Cruz, R., R. Castaneda-Miranda, J.J. Garia-Escalante, I.L. Lopez-Cruz, A. Lara-Herrera and J.I. de la Rosa, 2009. *Calibration of a greenhouse climate model using evolutionary algorithms*. Biosyst. Eng., 104: 135-142

Rico-Garcia, E., I.L. Lopez-Cruz, G. Herrera-Ruiz, G.M. Soto-Zarazua and R. Castaneda-Miranda, 2008. *Effect of temperature on greenhouse natural ventilation under hot conditions: Computational fluid dynamics simulations*. J. Applied Sci., 8: 4543-4551.

Rodrigo Castañeda-Miranda; Eusebio Jr. Ventura-Ramos; Rebeca del Rocío Peniche-Vera; Gilberto Herrera-Ruiz, *Fuzzy Greenhouse Climate Control System based on a Field Programmable Gate Array*, Biosystems Engineering. 2006 Vol. 94/2, pp 165–177

Sin, S. K., and De Figueiredo, "Fuzzy System Designing Through Fuzzy Clustering and Optimal preDefuzzification", *Proc. IEEE International Conference on Fuzzy Systems*. 1993 2, 190-195.

Sugeno, M., and G. T. Kang. "Structure Identification of Fuzzy Model", *Fuzzy Sets and Systems*. 1988, *28*, pp. 15-33.

Takagi, T., and M. Sugeno, "Fuzzy Identification of Systems and its Application to Modeling and Control", *IEEE Trans. Systems Man and Cybernetics*. 1985 *-15*, pp. 116-132.

Rico-Garcia, E., I.L. Lopez-Cruz, G. Herrera-Ruiz, G.M. Soto-Zarazua and R. Castaneda-Miranda, 2008. *Effect of temperature on greenhouse natural ventilation under hot conditions: Computational fluid dynamics simulations*. J. Applied Sci., 8: 4543-4551.

Yager, R. and D. Filev, "Generation of Fuzzy Rules by Mountain Clustering", *Journal of Intelligent & Fuzzy Systems*, 1994, 2, pp. 209- 219.

Permissions

The contributors of this book come from diverse backgrounds, making this book a truly international effort. This book will bring forth new frontiers with its revolutionizing research information and detailed analysis of the nascent developments around the world.

We would like to thank Elmer P. Dadios, for lending his expertise to make the book truly unique. He has played a crucial role in the development of this book. Without his invaluable contribution this book wouldn't have been possible. He has made vital efforts to compile up to date information on the varied aspects of this subject to make this book a valuable addition to the collection of many professionals and students.

This book was conceptualized with the vision of imparting up-to-date information and advanced data in this field. To ensure the same, a matchless editorial board was set up. Every individual on the board went through rigorous rounds of assessment to prove their worth. After which they invested a large part of their time researching and compiling the most relevant data for our readers. Conferences and sessions were held from time to time between the editorial board and the contributing authors to present the data in the most comprehensible form. The editorial team has worked tirelessly to provide valuable and valid information to help people across the globe.

Every chapter published in this book has been scrutinized by our experts. Their significance has been extensively debated. The topics covered herein carry significant findings which will fuel the growth of the discipline. They may even be implemented as practical applications or may be referred to as a beginning point for another development. Chapters in this book were first published by InTech; hereby published with permission under the Creative Commons Attribution License or equivalent.

The editorial board has been involved in producing this book since its inception. They have spent rigorous hours researching and exploring the diverse topics which have resulted in the successful publishing of this book. They have passed on their knowledge of decades through this book. To expedite this challenging task, the publisher supported the team at every step. A small team of assistant editors was also appointed to further simplify the editing procedure and attain best results for the readers.

Our editorial team has been hand-picked from every corner of the world. Their multi-ethnicity adds dynamic inputs to the discussions which result in innovative outcomes. These outcomes are then further discussed with the researchers and contributors who give their valuable feedback and opinion regarding the same. The feedback is then collaborated with the researches and they are edited in a comprehensive manner to aid the understanding of the subject.

Apart from the editorial board, the designing team has also invested a significant amount of their time in understanding the subject and creating the most relevant covers. They scrutinized every image to scout for the most suitable representation of the subject and create an appropriate cover for the book.

The publishing team has been involved in this book since its early stages. They were actively engaged in every process, be it collecting the data, connecting with the contributors or procuring relevant information. The team has been an ardent support to the editorial, designing and production team. Their endless efforts to recruit the best for this project, has resulted in the accomplishment of this book. They are a veteran in the field of academics and their pool of knowledge is as vast as their experience in printing. Their expertise and guidance has proved useful at every step. Their uncompromising quality standards have made this book an exceptional effort. Their encouragement from time to time has been an inspiration for everyone.

The publisher and the editorial board hope that this book will prove to be a valuable piece of knowledge for researchers, students, practitioners and scholars across the globe.

List of Contributors

Ahmad Esmaili Torshabi, Ali Negarestani and Mohamad Rahnema
Department of Electrical & Computer, Kerman Graduate University of Technology, Kerman, Iran

Marco Riboldi, Andera Pella and Guido Baroni
Bioengineering Unit, Centro Nazionale di Adroterapia Oncologica, Pavia, Italy

Jasenka Gajdoš Kljusurić, Ivana Rumora and Želimir Kurtanjek
University of Zagreb, Faculty of Food Technology and Biotechnology, Croatia

Hamid Medjahed, Dan Istrate, Lamine Bougueroua and Mohamed Achraf Dhouib
ESIGETEL-LRIT, Avon, France

Jérôme Boudy, Jean Louis Baldinger and Bernadette Dorizzi
Telecom SudParis, Evry, France

Ignazio M. Mancini, Salvatore Masi, Donatella Caniani and Donata S. Lioi
Department of Engineering and Physics of the Environment, University of Basilicata, Italy

Ines Brosso
Faculty of Computing and Informatics, Mackenzie Presbyterian University, Sao Paulo, Brazil

Alessandro La Neve
Department of Electrical Engineering, Centro Universitário da FEI, SP, Brazil

Yetis Sazi Murat
Pamukkale University, Faculty of Engineering, Civil Engineering Department, Transportation Division, Denizli, Turkey

Laiq Khan, Rabiah Badar and Shahid Qamar
Department of Electrical Engineering, COMSATS Institute of Information Technology, Abbottabad, Pakistan

C. Edward Lan
Department of Aerospace Engineering, University of Kansas, KS, USA

Ray C. Chang
Department of Aviation Mechanical Engineering, China University of Science and Technology, Taiwan (R.O.C.)

Celimuge Wu, Satoshi Ohzahata and Toshihiko Kato
University of Electro-Communications, Japan

Saptarshi Sasmal, K. Ramanjaneyulu and Nagesh R. Iyer
CSIR-Structural Engineering Research Centre, CSIR Complex, TTTI Post, Taramani, India

Antonio M. Ortiz and Teresa Olivares
Albacete Research Institute of Informatics, Spain

Samuel Azevedo, Rummenigge Rudson and Luiz Gonçalves
Universidade Federal do Rio Grande do Norte, DCA-CT-UFRN, Campus Universit[ario, Lagoa Nova, Natal, RN, Brazil

Tomasz Korol
Gdansk University of Technology, Poland

Alejandra A. López-Caloca and Carmen Reyes
Centro de Investigación en Geografía y Geomática, "Jorge L. Tamayo" A.C., CentroGeo, México

H. Haroonabadi
Islamic Azad University (IAU)-Dezful Branch, Iran

Gorrostieta-Hurtado Efren, Pedraza-Ortega Jesus Carlos, Aceves-Fernández Marco Antonio, Ramos-Arreguín Juan Manuel and Tovar-Arriaga Saúl
Facultad de Informática, Universidad Autónoma de Querétaro, México

Sotomayor-Olmedo Artemio
Facultad de Ingeniería, Universidad Autónoma de Querétaro, Querétaro, México

Printed in the USA
CPSIA information can be obtained
at www.ICGtesting.com
JSHW011505221024
72173JS00005B/1206

9 781632 383426